IN THE AGE OF GIORGIONE

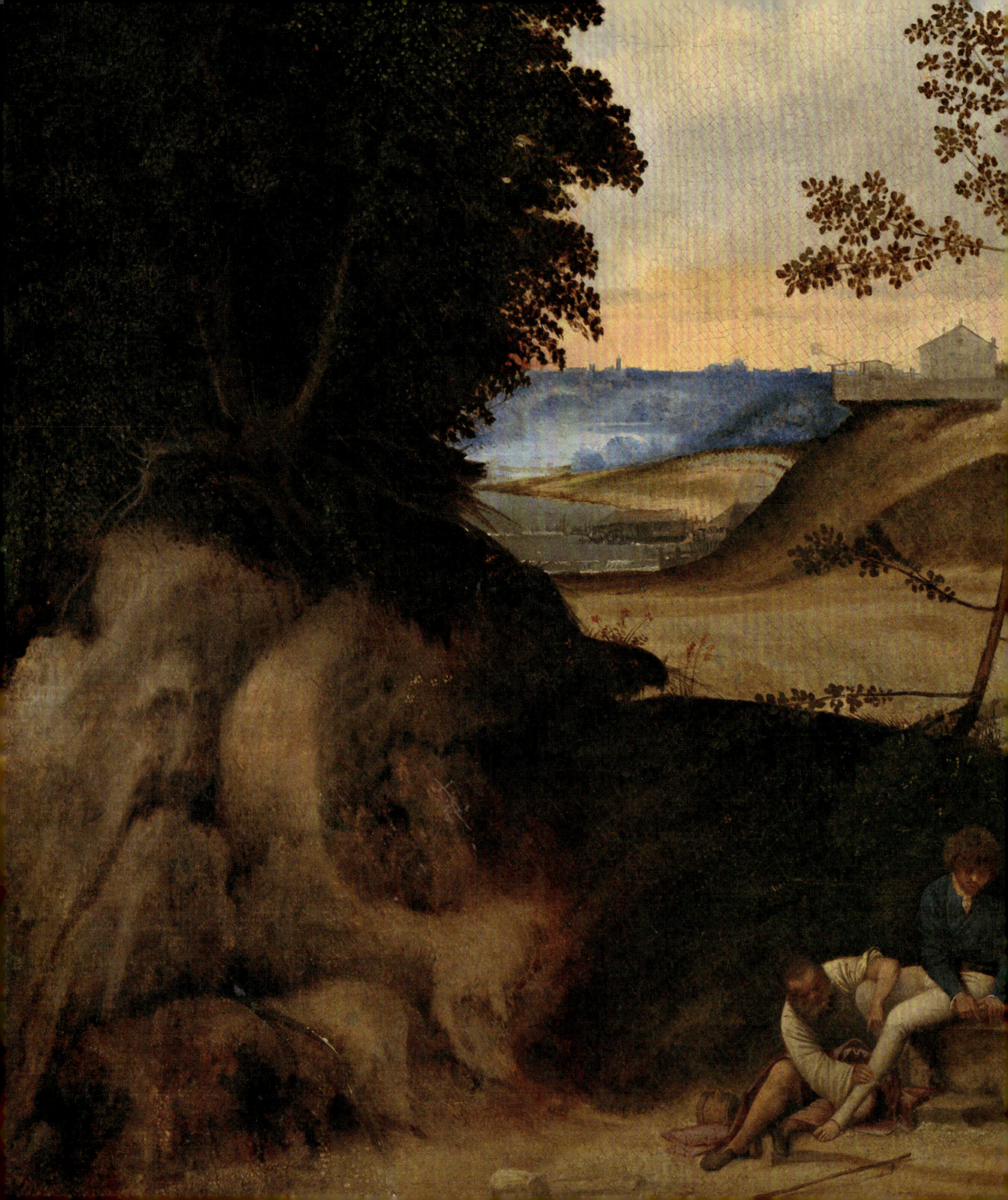

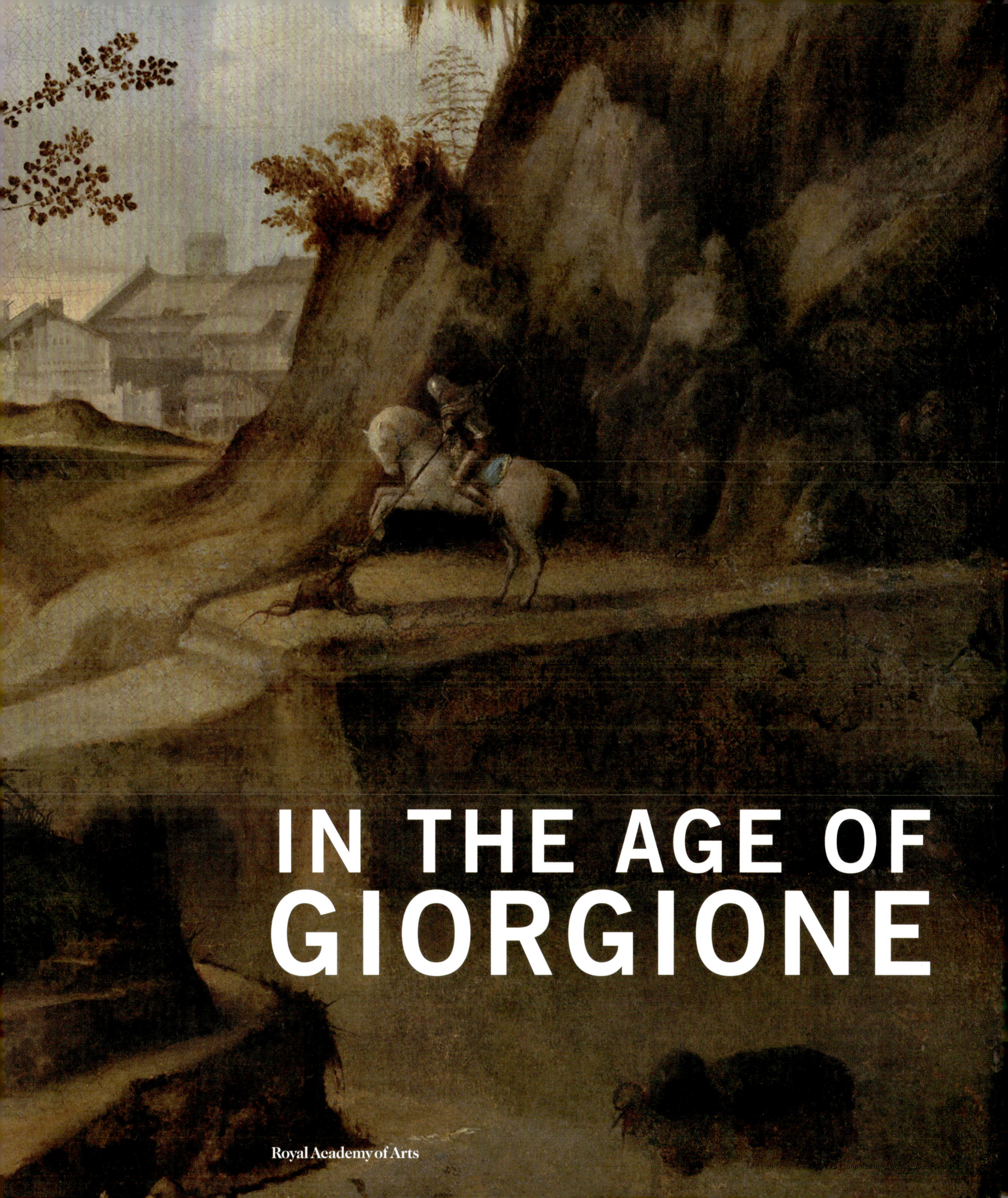

IN THE AGE OF GIORGIONE

Royal Academy of Arts

First published on the occasion
of the exhibition
'In the Age of Giorgione'
Royal Academy of Arts, London,
12 March – 5 June 2016

Exhibition Curators
Simone Facchinetti
Museo Adriano Bernareggi, Bergamo

Arturo Galansino
Palazzo Strozzi, Florence

Per Rumberg
Royal Academy of Arts, London

2009–2016 Season supported by

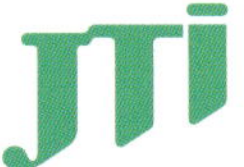

Supported by

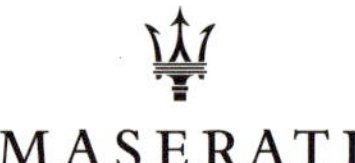

Royal Academy International Patrons

This exhibition has been made possible by the provision of insurance through the Government Indemnity Scheme. The Royal Academy of Arts would like to thank HM Government for providing Government Indemnity and the Department for Culture, Media and Sport and Arts Council England for arranging the indemnity.

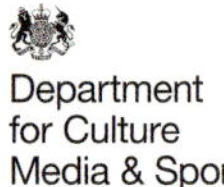

Artistic Director
Tim Marlow

Exhibition Organisation
Giulia Ariete
Idoya Beitia
Lucy Chiswell
Christopher Eperjesi
Belén Lasheras Díaz
Andrea Tarsia
Elana Woodgate

Royal Academy Publications
Beatrice Gullström
Alison Hissey
Carola Krueger
Simon Murphy
Peter Sawbridge
Nick Tite

Translation from the Italian
Caroline Beamish

Picture Research
Sara Ayad

Design
Isambard Thomas, London

Colour Separation and Printing
Conti Tipocolor, Italy

British Library Cataloguing-in-Publication Data
A catalogue record for this book is available from the British Library

ISBN 978-1-910350-27-0 (paperback)
ISBN 978-1-910350-26-3 (hardback)

Distributed outside the United States and Canada by Thames & Hudson Ltd, London

Distributed in the United States and Canada by Harry N. Abrams, Inc., New York

Editor's Note
Dimensions of all works of art are given in centimetres, height before width.

Illustrations
pages 2–3: detail of cat. 19
pages 6–7: detail of cat. 38
page 9: detail of cat. 28
pages 10–11: detail of cat. 41
page 12: detail of cat. 13
page 15: detail of cat. 5
pages 16–17: detail of cat. 34
pages 34–35: detail of cat. 2
pages 70–71: detail of cat. 26
pages 96–97: detail of cat. 31
pages 126–27: detail of cat. 42

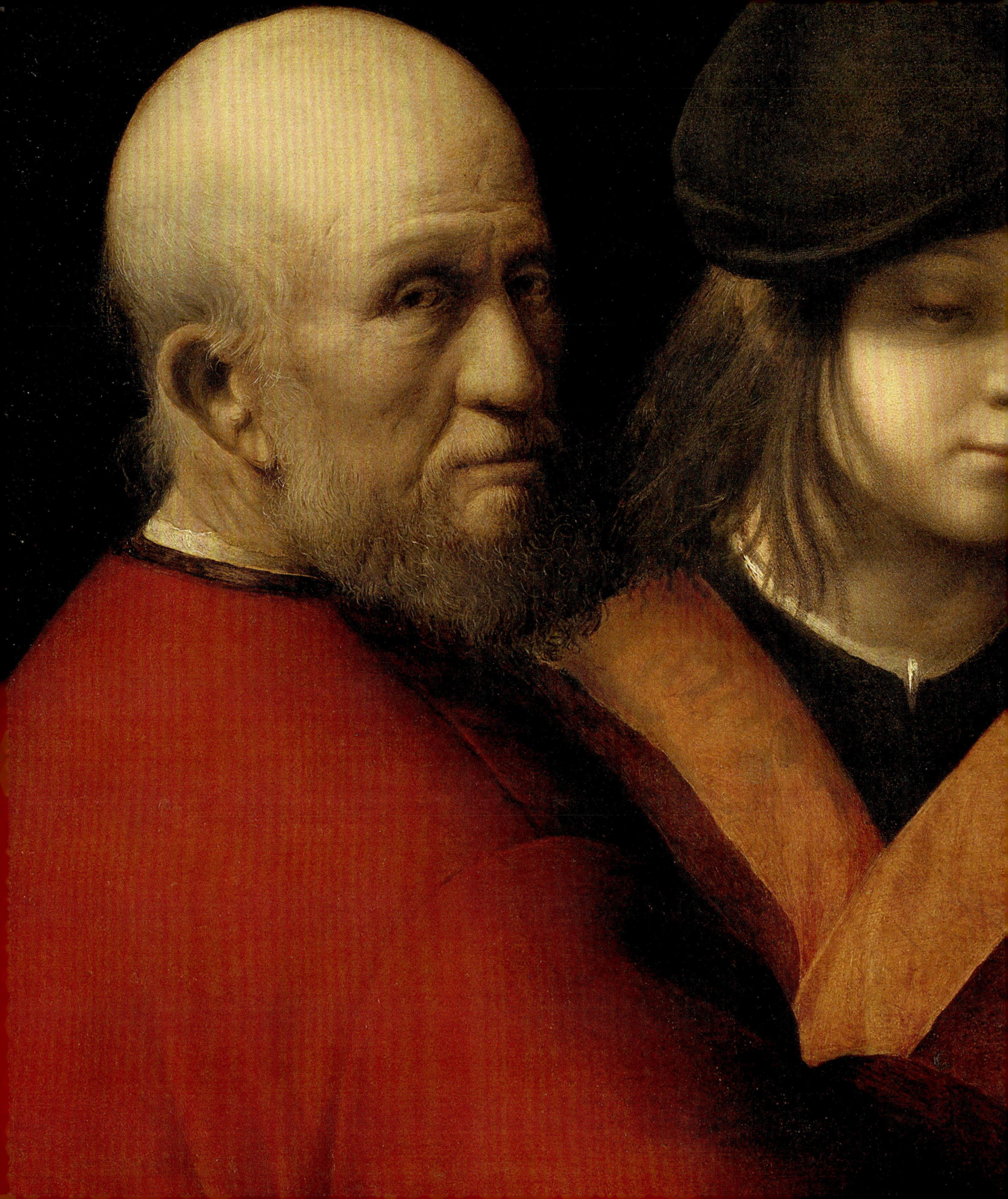

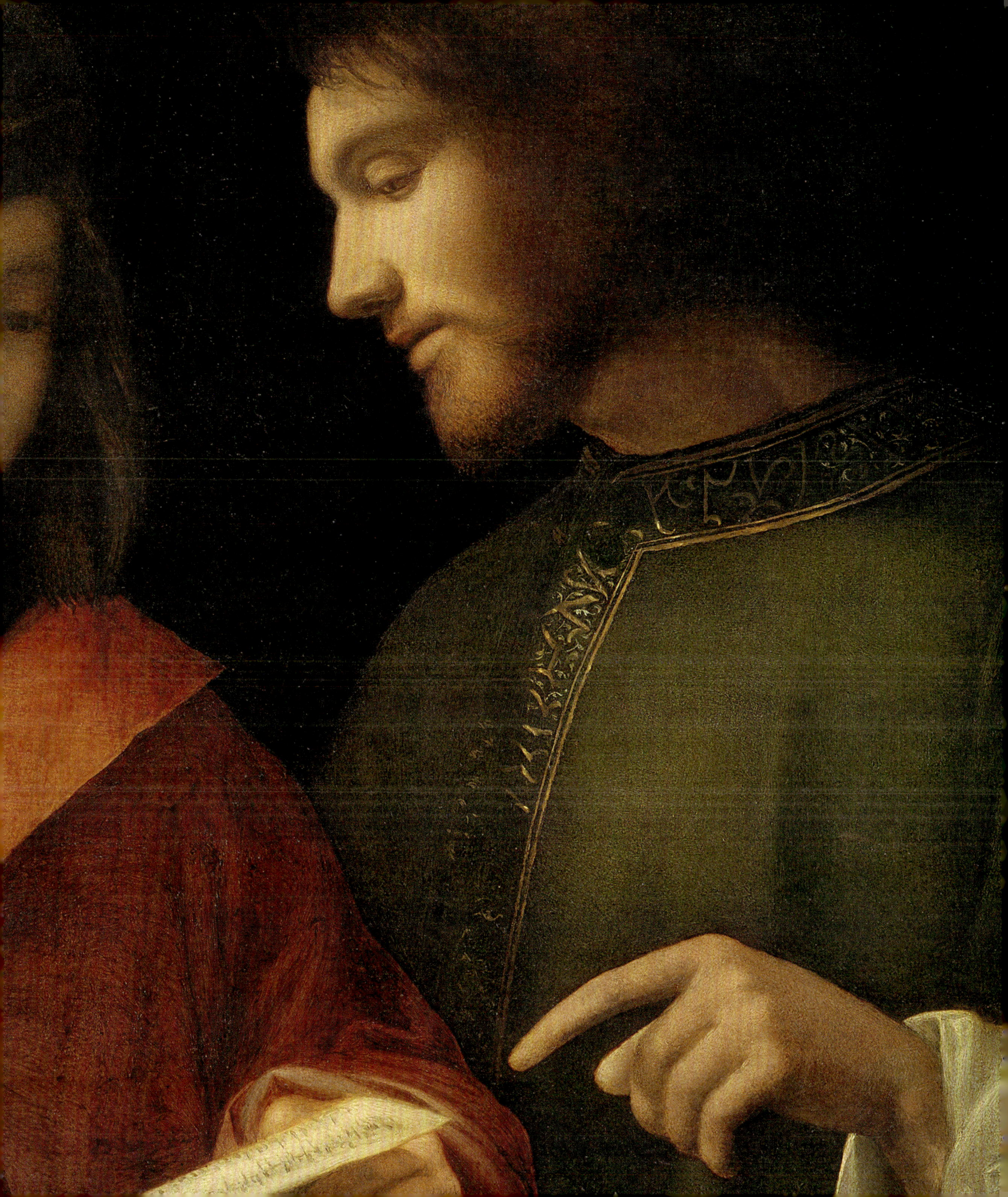

PRESIDENT'S FOREWORD

'All art constantly aspires towards the condition of music.'

'Something fabulous and illusive has always mingled itself in the brilliancy of Giorgione's fame.'

Giorgione established a form of pictorial poetry with such feeling for light and atmosphere that it has haunted Western painting ever since. I find it natural therefore to introduce this profoundly enigmatic artist with quotations from the famous essay 'The School of Giorgione' (1877) by the great aesthete Walter Pater.

The sense of enigma surrounding Giorgione's work does not arise merely because so little is known of his life, nor because so few paintings are firmly attributed to him, but rather I would say from the mystery woven into many of the paintings themselves. This comes from the apparent reserve he maintained concerning his intentions, along with the exquisite tact with which he combined subject, colour and design to touch the music of painting gently into existence. What the artist thought is what he painted; there is no record elsewhere.

Despite his early death in 1510, his legacy was felt powerfully in Venice and beyond. Giorgione worked largely for a new type of patron, the cultured and sophisticated connoisseur. He proposed a more lyrical type of portraiture and created a bucolic world as a serene backdrop to subjects both sacred and profane. Today, only a few paintings can be attributed to him with certainty yet they are 'among the most precious things in the world of art'.

Addressing in detail this complex question of attribution, 'In the Age of Giorgione' brings together many of the finest works of the Venetian Renaissance in the first decade of the sixteenth century. The exhibition sheds new light on a pivotal period during which the foundations for the Golden Age of Venetian painting were laid, assembling works from across Europe and the United States by such artists as Giorgione, Titian, Giovanni Bellini, Sebastiano del Piombo and Lorenzo Lotto, and also offering visitors the opportunity to discover works by lesser-known artists such as Giovanni Cariani.

The exhibition was made possible by JTI, our generous benefactor and long-term partner of exhibitions in the Sackler Wing of Galleries. Thanks are also due to Maserati, whom we warmly welcome as our sponsor, and to the Royal Academy's International Patrons for their generous donation. We are indebted to our lenders – institutions as well as private collectors – for making this exhibition possible. At the Royal Academy the project was supported by Tim Marlow, Artistic Director, and organised by Dr Arturo Galansino, formerly Curator at the Royal Academy and newly appointed Director General of the Palazzo Strozzi in Florence, and Dr Simone Facchinetti, Curator at the Museo Adriano Bernareggi in Bergamo, with Per Rumberg, Curator at the Royal Academy. Within the Academy's Exhibitions Department, Idoya Beitia, Lucy Chiswell, Belén Lasheras Díaz, Christopher Eperjesi, Giulia Ariete, and Katherine Oakes have all provided invaluable assistance. Last but not least, this beautiful catalogue is the result of the expertise and dedication of our Publications Department.

Christopher Le Brun PRA
President, Royal Academy of Arts

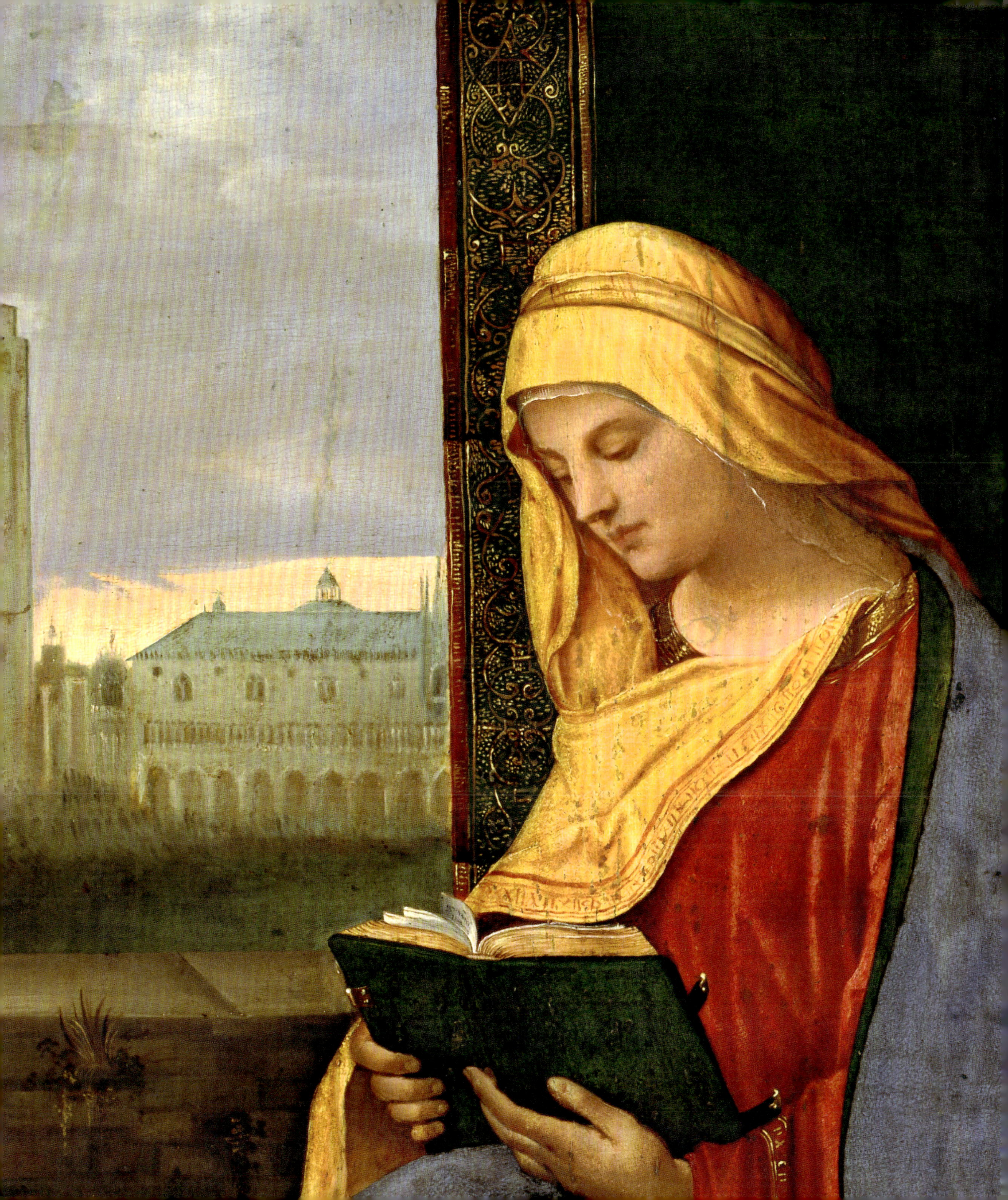

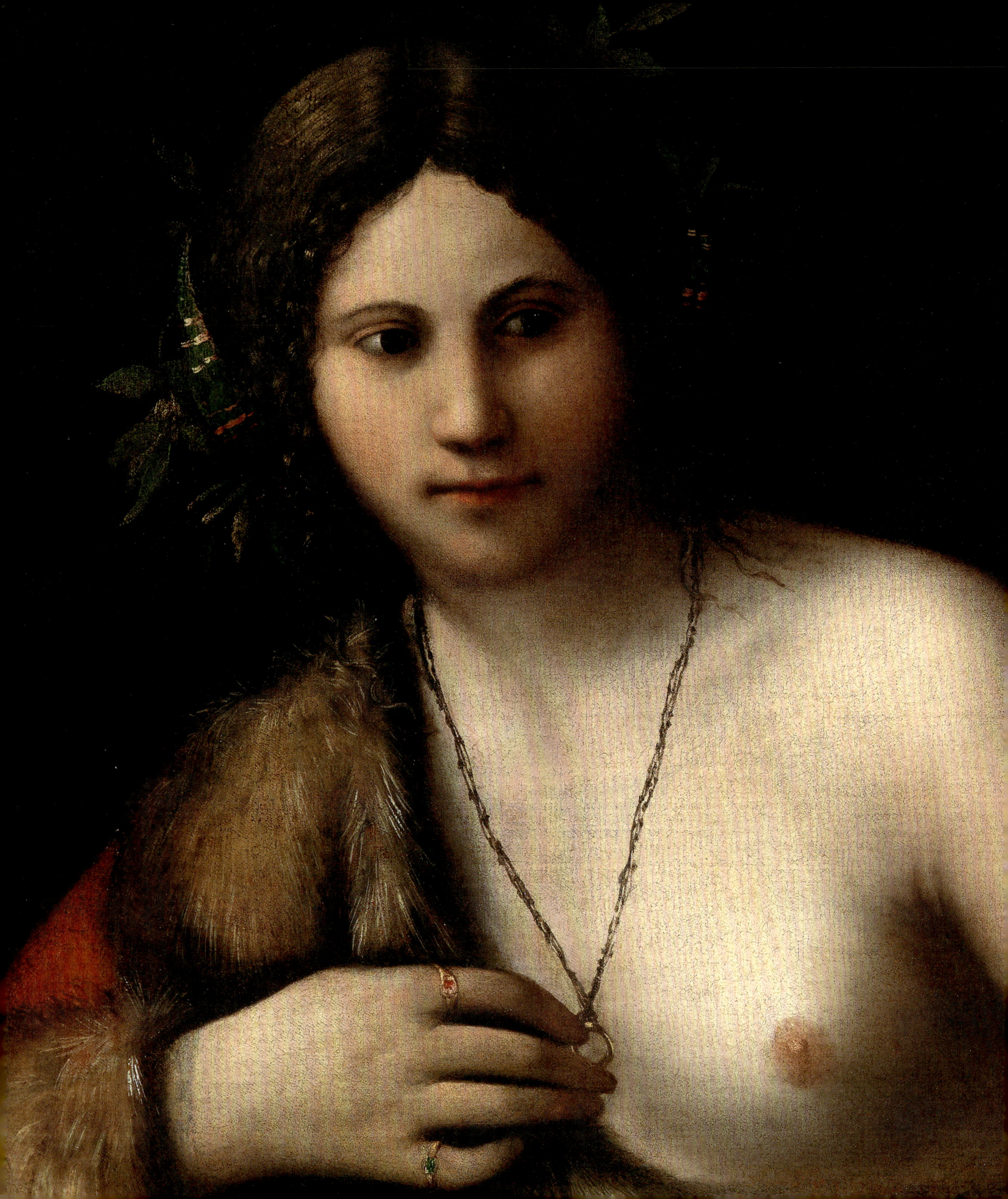

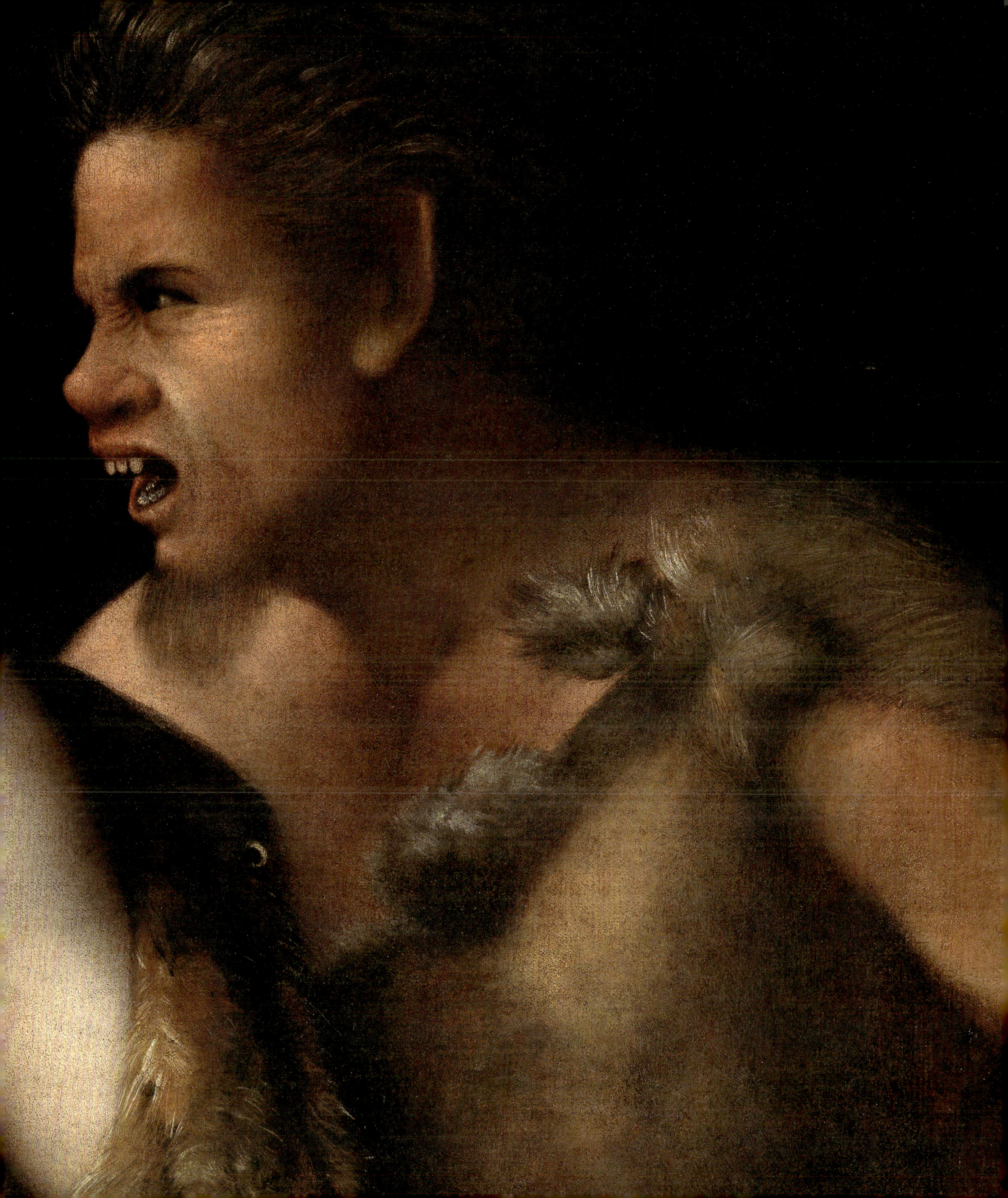

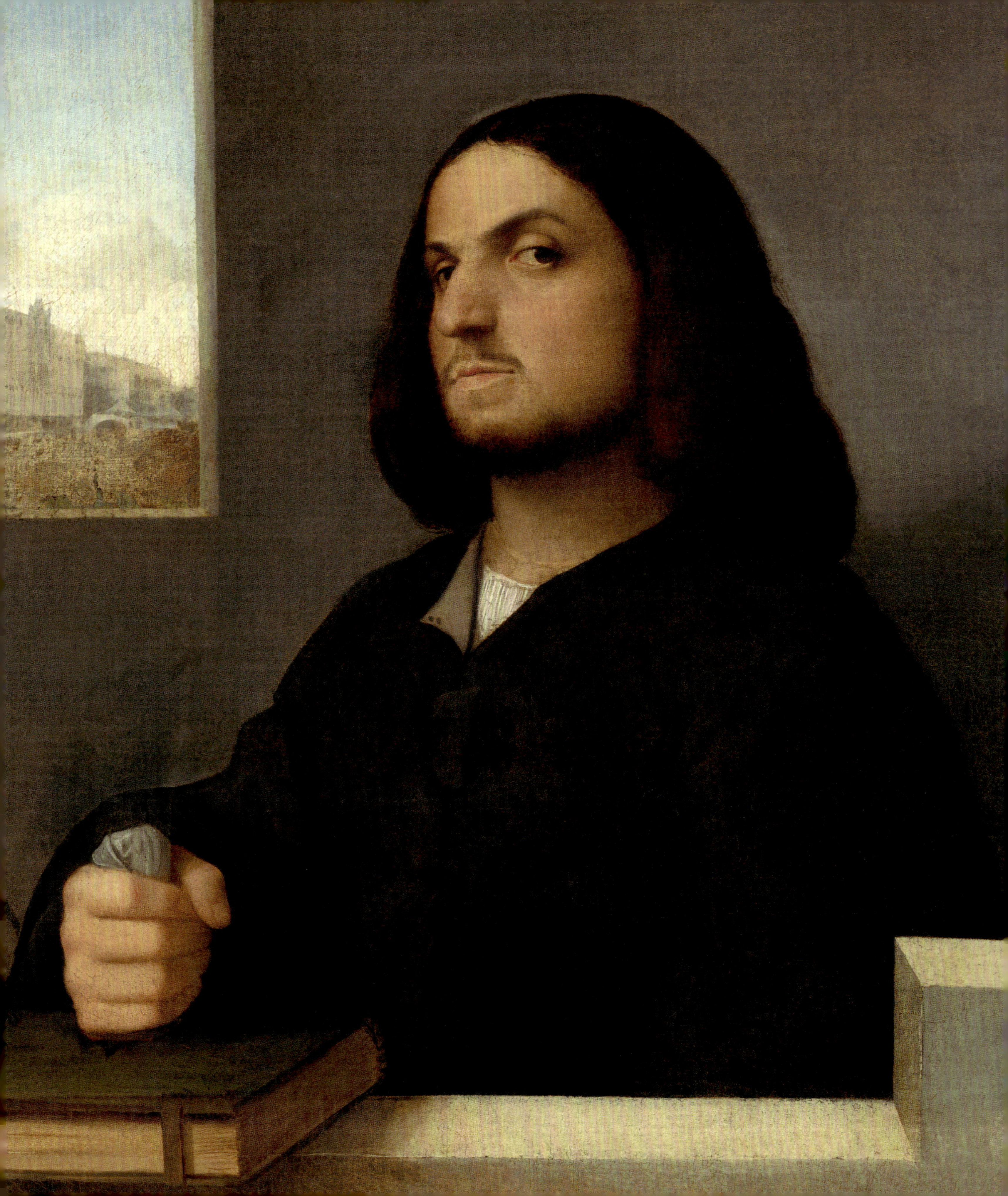

SUPPORTER'S STATEMENT

As a long-term Season Supporter of the Sackler Wing of Galleries, JTI is delighted to help bring this highly original exploration of the Venetian Renaissance to the Royal Academy of Arts.

'In the Age of Giorgione' showcases paintings from the first decade of the sixteenth century – foreshadowing the Golden Age of Venetian painting. This marks a unique opportunity for visitors to discover seminal works by Giorgione and the young Titian, as well as by Sebastiano del Piombo, Lorenzo Lotto and artists less familiar to a modern audience, such as Giovanni Cariani.

We do hope you enjoy this exhibition.

Daniel Sciamma
Managing Director UK, JTI

ACKNOWLEDGEMENTS

The Royal Academy of Arts would like to thank the following individuals for their invaluable assistance during the making of this exhibition and its catalogue:

Sébastien Allard, Irina Artemieva, László Baán, Colin B. Bailey, Alessandro Ballarin, Roberta Battaglia, Andrea Bayer, Anna Bisceglia, Julia Bischoff, Piero Boccardo, Irene Brooke, Christophe Brouard, Christopher Brown, David Alan Brown, Stephanie Buck, Gabriele Caioni, Caroline Campbell, Matteo Ceriana, Hugo Chapman, Maria Agnese Chiari, Keith Christiansen, Michael Clarke, Anna Coliva, Roberto Contini, Emanuela Daffra, Vincent Delieuvin, Francesca Del Torre Scheuch, Vittorio De Stefani, Duncan Dornan, Andreina Draghi, Jill Dunkerton, David Ekserdjian, Gimmo Etro, Marzia Faietti, Miguel Falomir, Sylvia Ferino-Pagden, Gabriele Finaldi, Hartwig Fischer, Claudio Giusti, Sabine Haag, Paul Hills, Peter Humfrey, Dominique Jacquot, Paul Joannides, David Kovitz, Bernd Lindemann, Eckart Lingenauber, Jacopo Lorenzelli, Andrea Lullo, Ellen McAdam, Neil MacGregor, Giulio Manieri Elia, Paola Marini, Andrea Marmori, Jonathan Marsden, Jean-Luc Martinez, Laura Mattioli, Antonio Mazzotta, Sara Menato, Fabrizio Moretti, Antonio Natali, Scott Nethersole, Lidia Patelli, Nicholas Penny, Silvana Pini, Mikhail Piotrovsky, Katia Pisvin, Franco Posocco, Earl A. Powell III, Guido Rebecchini, Maria Cristina Rodeschini, Sara Pietra Rossi, Francis Russell, Dóra Sallay, Xavier F. Salomon, Eike Schmidt, Klaus Schrenk, Heinrich Schulze Altcappenberg, Andreas Schumacher, Manfred Sellink, Desmond Shawe-Taylor, Rachel Sloan, Pippa Stephenson, Alexander Sturgis, Luke Syson, Stefania Tullio Cataldo, Massimo Valsecchi, Nico Van Hout, Ernst Vegelin, Roxana Velásquez, Marco Voena, Stefan Weppelmann, Aidan Weston-Lewis, Catherine Whistler, Matthias Wivel and Miguel Zugaza.

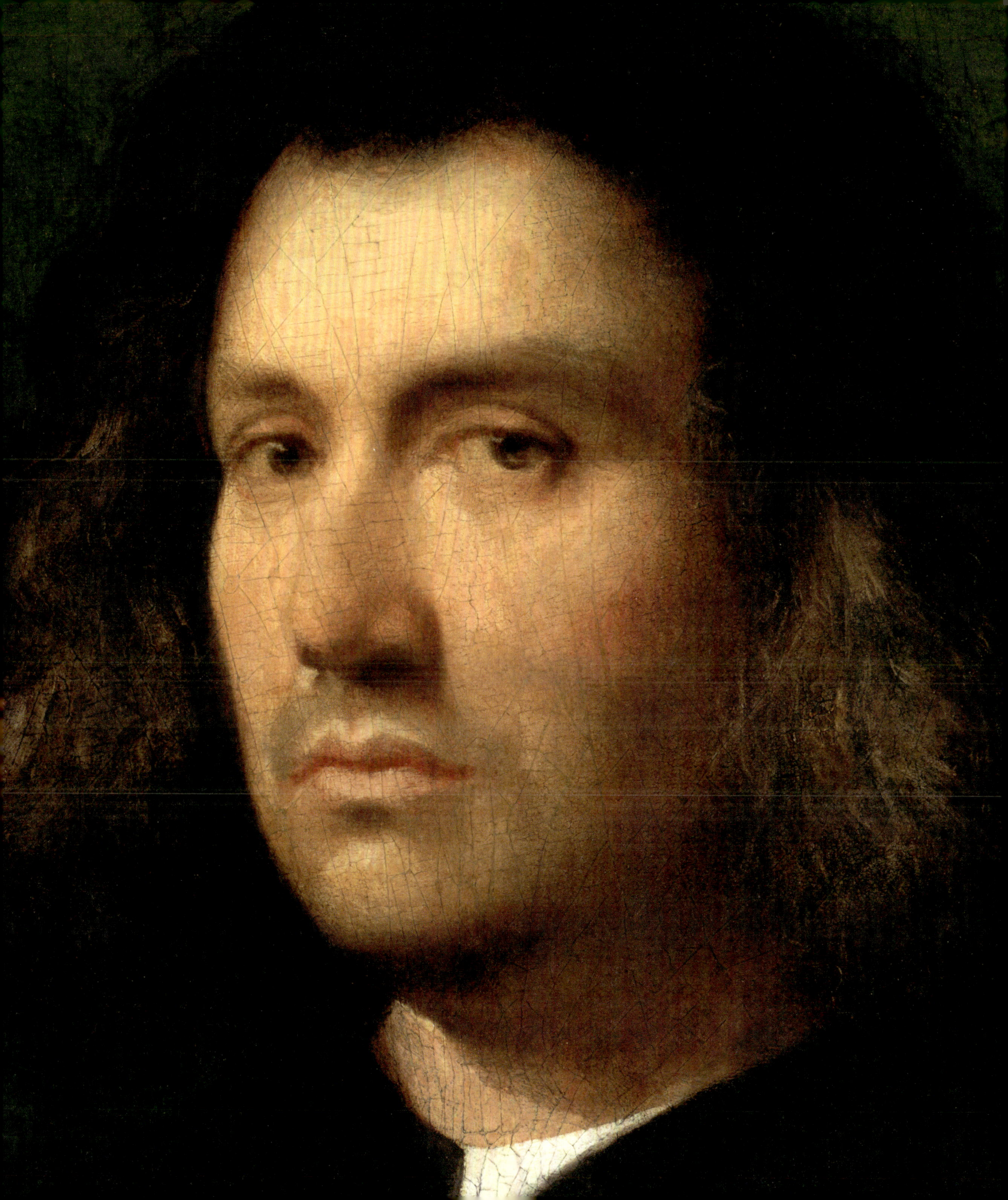

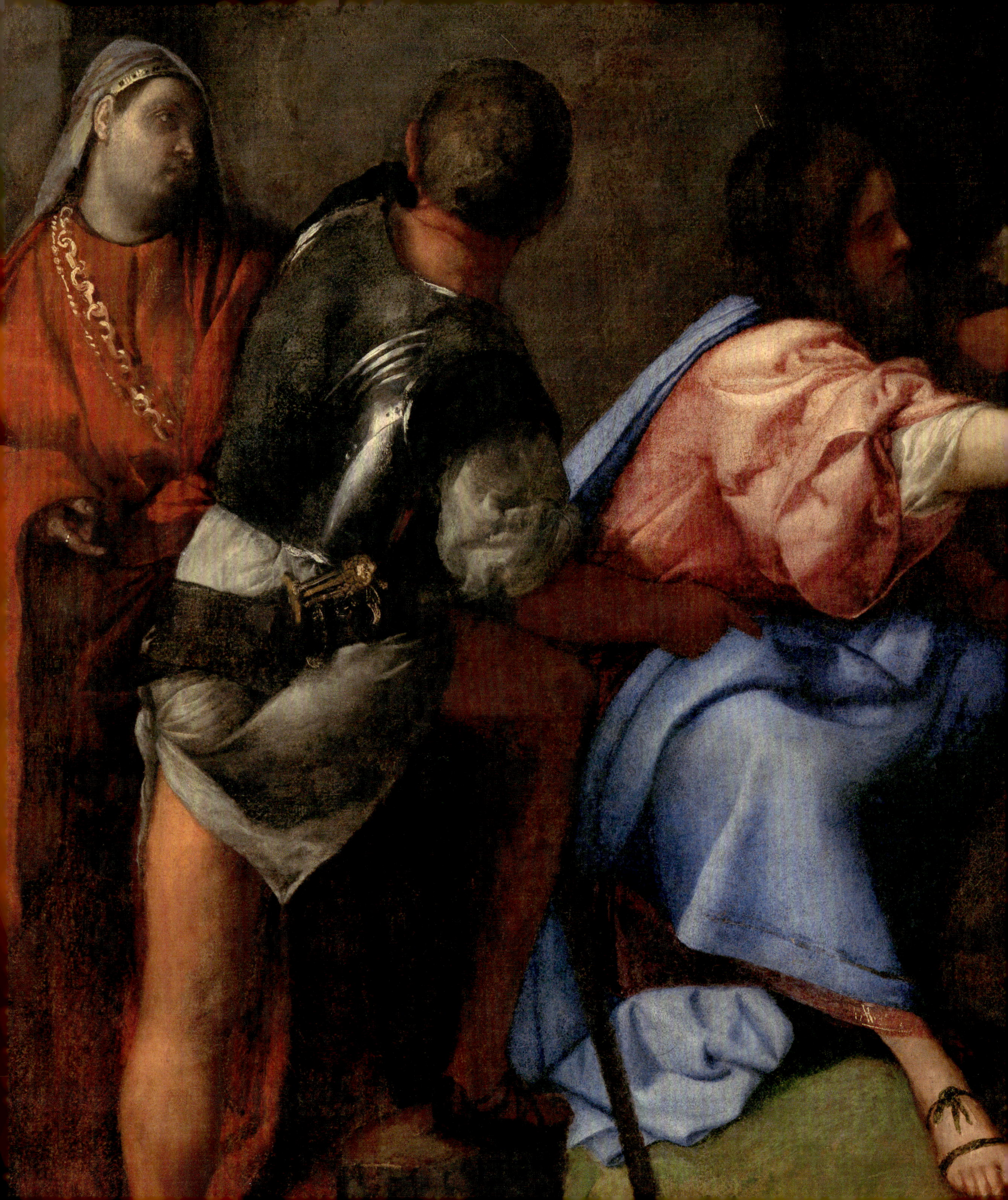

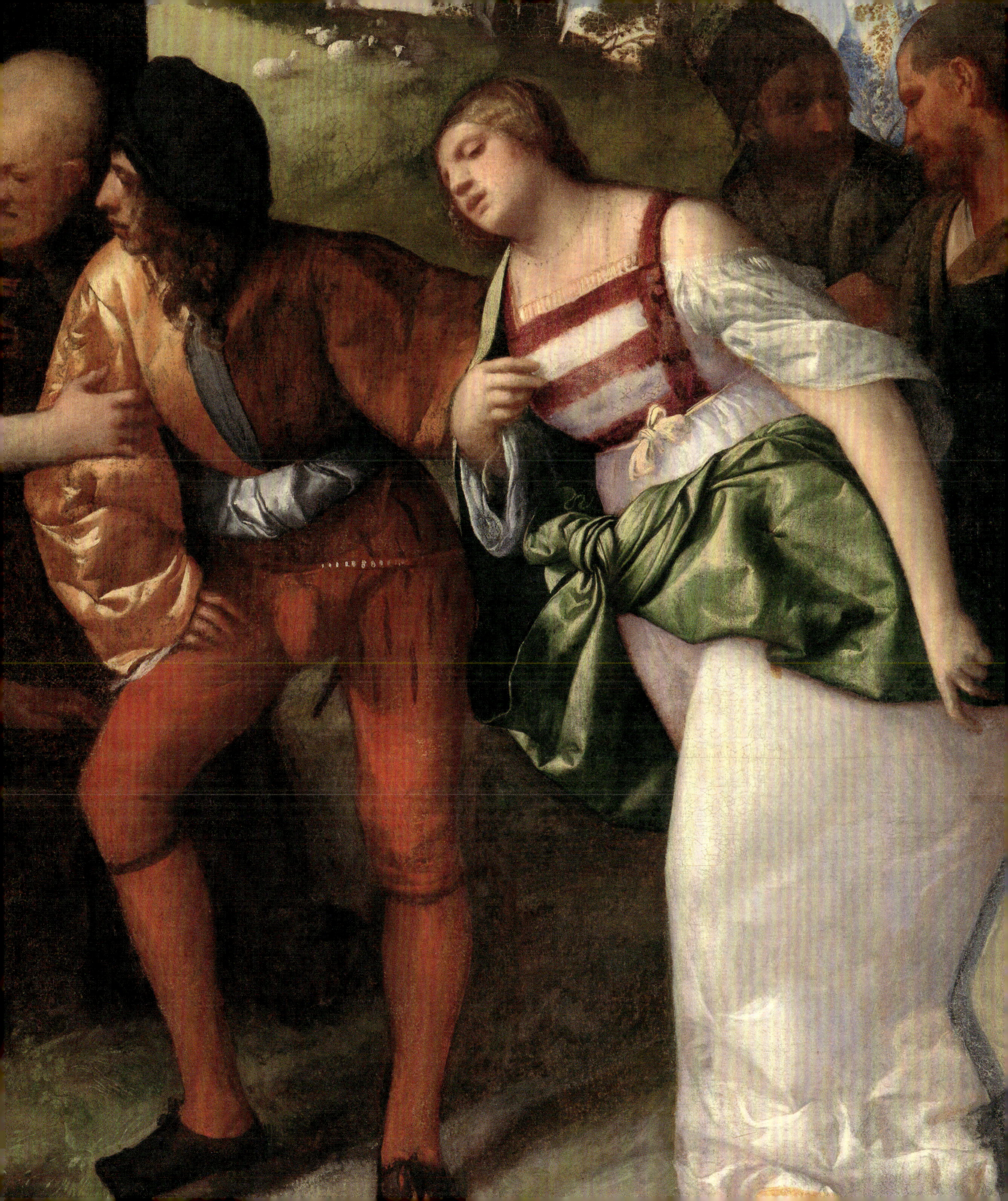

THE BIOGRAPHY OF A MYTH

Simone Facchinetti and Arturo Galansino

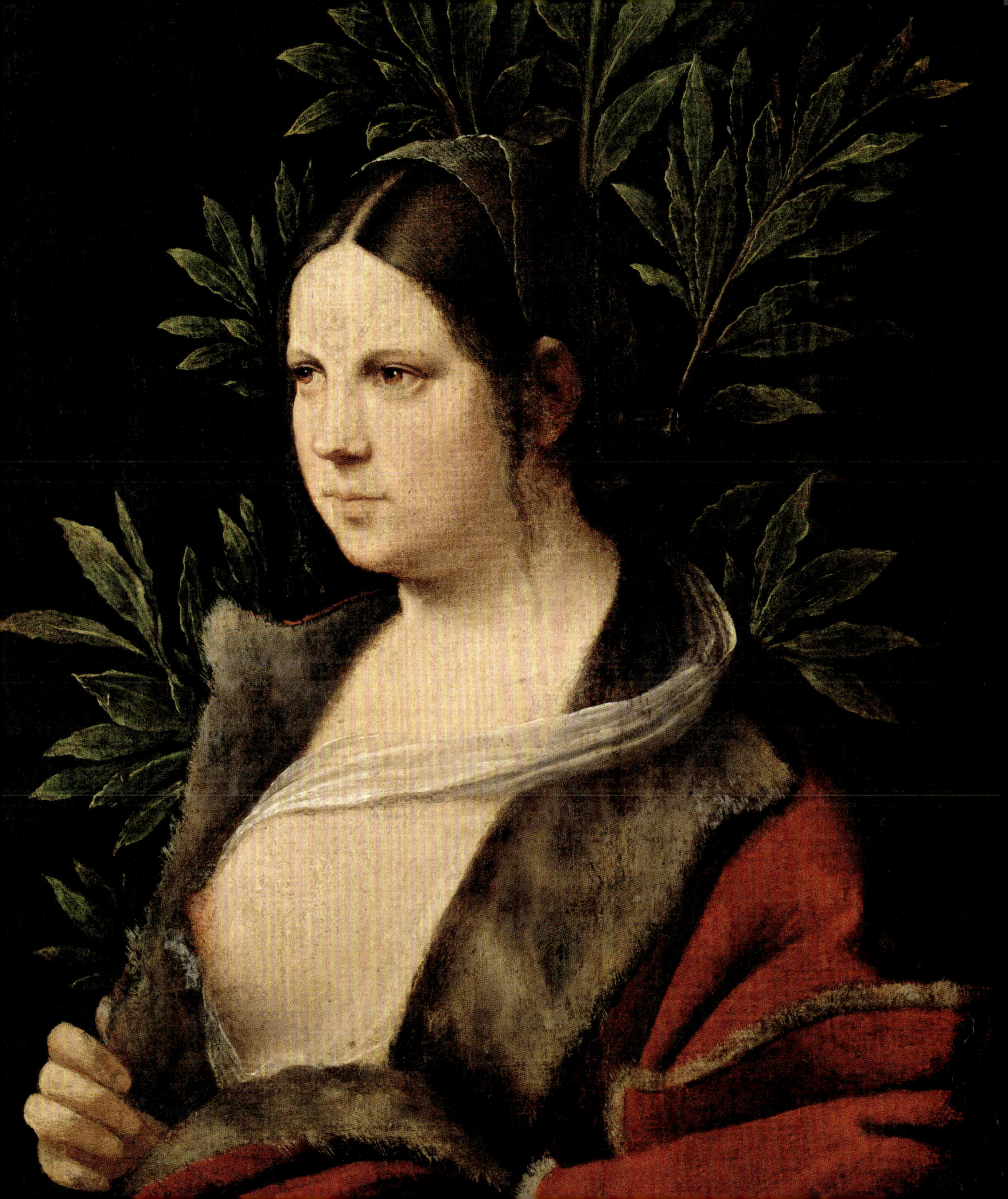

Fig. 1
GIORGIONE
Portrait of a Young Woman ('Laura'), 1506
Oil on canvas, 41 × 33.5 cm
Kunsthistorisches Museum, Vienna

The birth of a myth requires a set of very particular circumstances, and nowhere is this clearer than in the case of Giorgio da Castelfranco, called Giorgione. Documentary information about his life is so scarce as to be almost non-existent in respect of his verified work. Despite this – and perhaps because of it – his legend has taken shape. Each passing century has contributed to the flowering of the artist's myth; each age invents its own Giorgione.

In much the same way, each critic holds in his or her head a personal vision of the artist, as Bernard Berenson noted in 1895: 'Coming at last to the centre point of Venetian art, to the shadowy fluctuating, half-mythical figure of Giorgione, concerning whom there seems to be so little certainty that it may well be said: Every critic has his own private Giorgione.'[1] Berenson's frankness contrasts with the more visionary version of the myth expressed by Gabriele d'Annunzio:

> I see Giorgione poised overhead in the marvellous firmament, although without being able to perceive his mortal frame; I seek him in the mystery of the flaming cloud that envelops him. He seems more like a myth than a man. No poet on earth has a destiny to compare with his. Almost nothing is known of him, some people even conspire to deny his very existence. His name is written in no book and some would also deny him any verifiable output. Yet all the art of Venice seems inflamed by his revelation; the great Titian seems to have garnered from him the secret of infusing his creations with luminous blood. In truth, Giorgione represents the Epiphany of Fire in art. He deserves to be called 'bringer of fire', like Prometheus.[2]

The duality evoked by this juxtaposition of Berenson and D'Annunzio has repeated itself in cycles over the centuries.

Giorgione is dead

Giorgione's death is recorded entirely dispassionately in a letter of 25 October 1510 written by Isabella d'Este, Marchesa of Mantua, to one Taddeo Albano, who she hopes will procure one of his paintings for her:

> We believe that in the effects and the estate of Zorzo da Castelfrancho, the painter, there exists a painting of a night scene, very beautiful and unusual; if this were to be the case, we are extremely desirous of owning it. For this reason, we beg you to act with Lorenzo da Pavia and others who possess judgement in matters of art, and to see if this thing is truly excellent. If you find that it is, negotiate as best you can with the magnificent Messer Carlo Valerio, our cherished comrade, and with anyone else you deem useful, to obtain this picture for us, agreeing the price and giving him prior notice of it. When you judge that the deal is done, if it is advantageous, in case the item should be removed by others, do then as you think fit.[3]

Giorgione, written 'Zorzi' in local dialect, died in a Venetian plague hospital at the age of about thirty-three.[4] Among his possessions were garments and a few objects of modest value.[5] Albano's response must have come as a disappointment to his patroness:

> Zorzo died a few days ago of plague, and desiring to be of use to my lady I spoke with some of my friends who had had a lot of dealings with him, and they told me that there was no such picture in his estate. It is true that the said Zorzo executed one for Messer Thadeo Contarini, but according to my information it is not as perfect as the one sought by my lady. The same Zorzo also executed a nocturnal scene for one Victorio Becharo, which as far as I understand is a better composition, better finished than Contarini's painting. But this Becharo is not around these parts at the moment. And it has been given to me to understand that neither one nor the other is willing to sell at any price, for the reason that they wish to keep them for their own enjoyment.[6]

From documentation pertaining to Giorgione's poverty-stricken death we learn the names of his father (Giovanni Gasparini) and his stepmother (Alessandra), both of whom predeceased him. Giorgione's mother had died some time earlier than Giovanni and Alessandra, and thus Alessandra's heir, one Francesco Fisoli, laid claim to the artist's effects.[7]

More information has been recovered about Giorgione's death than about his entire life. Documentation relating to his work is limited to the inscriptions affixed to the back of two paintings: 'On 1 June 1506 this was made by the hand of master Giorgio from Castelfranco, the colleague of master Vincenzo Catena, at the instigation of misser Giacomo',[8] inscribed on the so-called *Laura* (fig. 1); and '15[06] / by the hand of Maestro Zorzi da Castelfranco',[9] inscribed on the *Terris Portrait* (cat. 5). There are only two other documents: official Venetian commissions dated to 1507 and 1508. The first concerns a large painting for the Sala del Maggior Consiglio at the Palazzo Ducale, and the second the decoration of the façade of the

Fig. 2
GIORGIONE
Nude, *c.* 1508
Fresco, 250 × 140 cm
Gallerie dell'Accademia, Venice

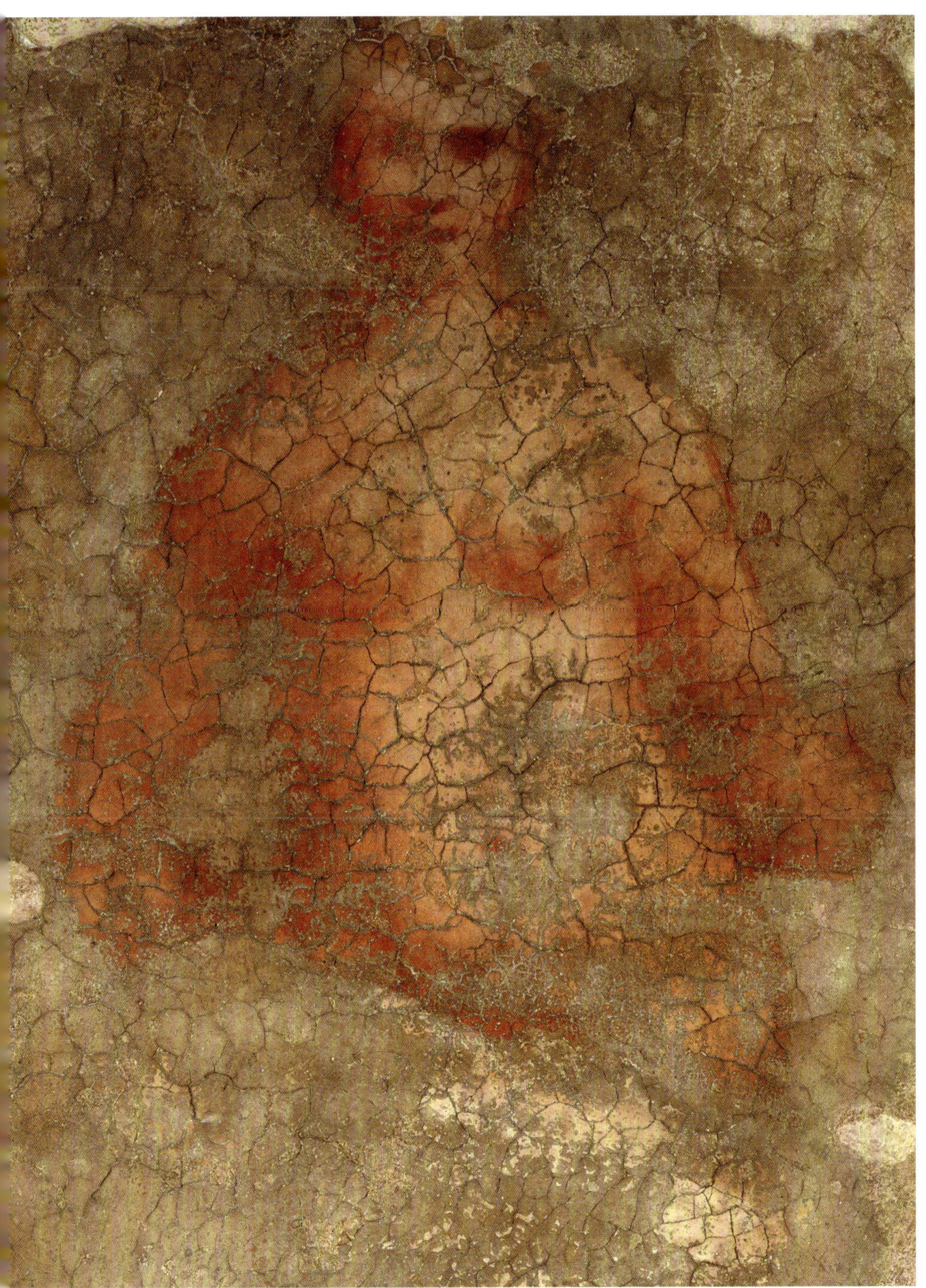

Fondaco dei Tedeschi. In both cases the works commissioned have disappeared, apart from a fragment of the Fondaco project now in the Gallerie dell'Accademia (fig. 2).

The two Lives of Giorgione

Giorgio Vasari, the Aretine artist and historian, gave shape to the myth of Giorgione in a biography published in his *Lives of the Artists*. In the first edition, published in Florence in 1550, he combined the small amount of pre-existing printed evidence about Giorgione's life with oral evidence gathered during his travels in and around Venice in 1541–42.

Vasari places Giorgione at the heart of the most important developments in Venetian painting, connecting him with the inexorable advance of the so-called *maniera moderna* (modern style). This judgement was based on claims made by Baldassare Castiglione in *The Book of the Courtier*, published in Florence and Venice in 1528: 'The following are most excellent in painting: Leonardo da Vinci, Mantegna, Raphael, Michelangelo and Giorgio da Castelfranco: nevertheless all work in different manners [...] each knows how to produce perfect work in his own style.'[10]

Castiglione sets his book's dialogues in the Palazzo Ducale at Urbino, and imagines them taking place in 1507, when he was a favourite at the court of Elisabetta Gonzaga. In that year Giovanni Bellini was the undisputed master painter of Venice, yet Castiglione makes no mention of him, and nor does he mention Titian; instead he identifies Giorgione as worthy of representing the past and future of the region's painting.[11]

In the second, enlarged, edition of his *Lives*, published in 1568, Vasari made a radical reassessment of Giorgione, based partly on fresh information from Cosimo Bartoli, the Florentine ambassador in Venice.[12] Although it is not possible to detail here all the points that were changed or modified, a few general trends can be noted. One surrounded the education of Giorgione, who was described in the first edition as a pupil of Bellini who 'endeavoured to be with the Bellinis in Venice' before emerging in the second edition as a master 'who surpassed the Bellinis by a long way'.[13] Vasari also

Fig. 3
PALMA VECCHIO
and PARIS BORDONE
Sea Storm, c. 1527–28 and c. 1534–36
Oil on canvas, 360 × 406 cm
Gallerie dell'Accademia, Venice

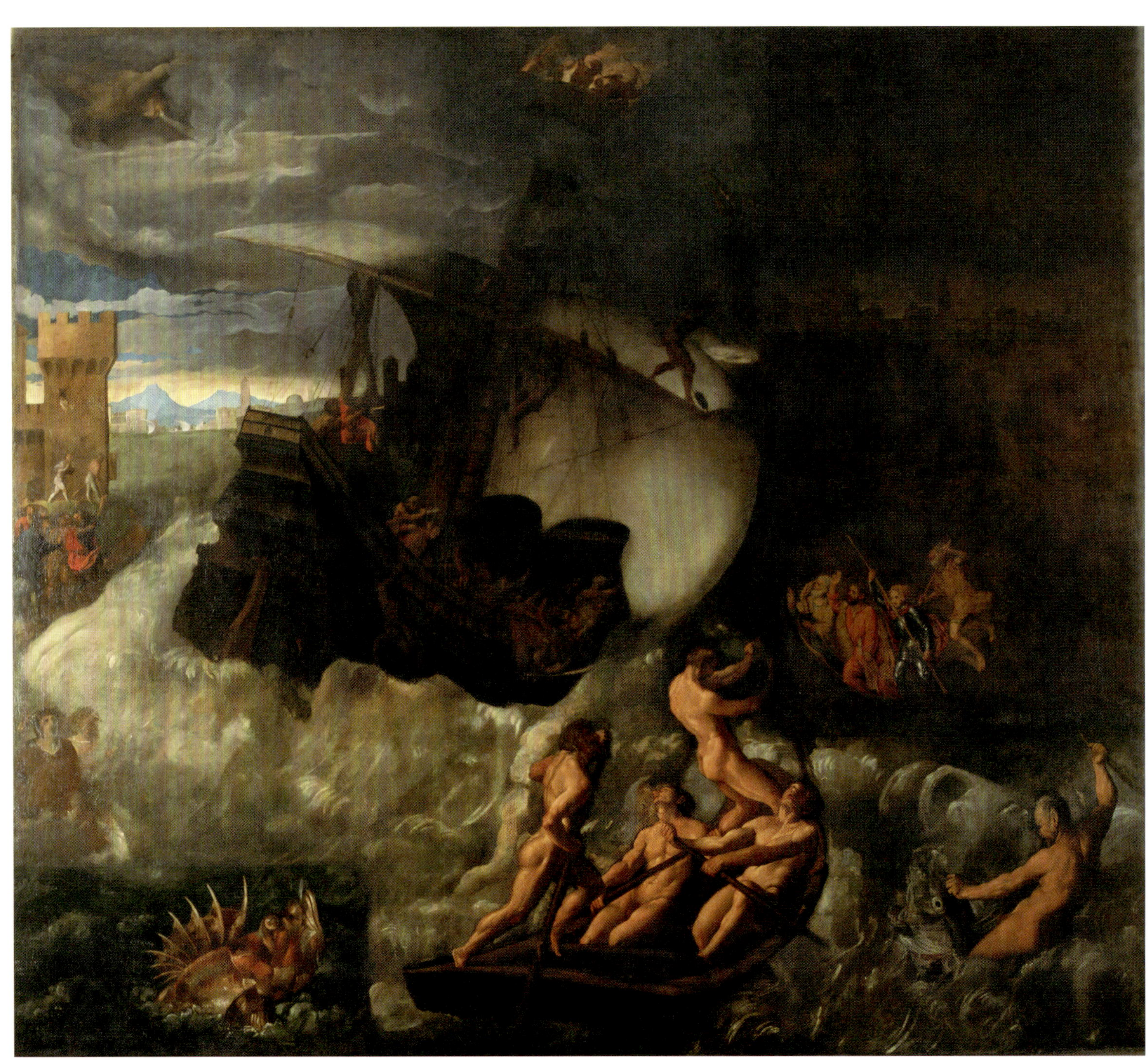

Fig. 4
Attributed to TITIAN
Christ Carrying the Cross, c. 1508–10
Oil on canvas, 68.2 × 88.3 cm
Scuola Grande di San Rocco, Venice

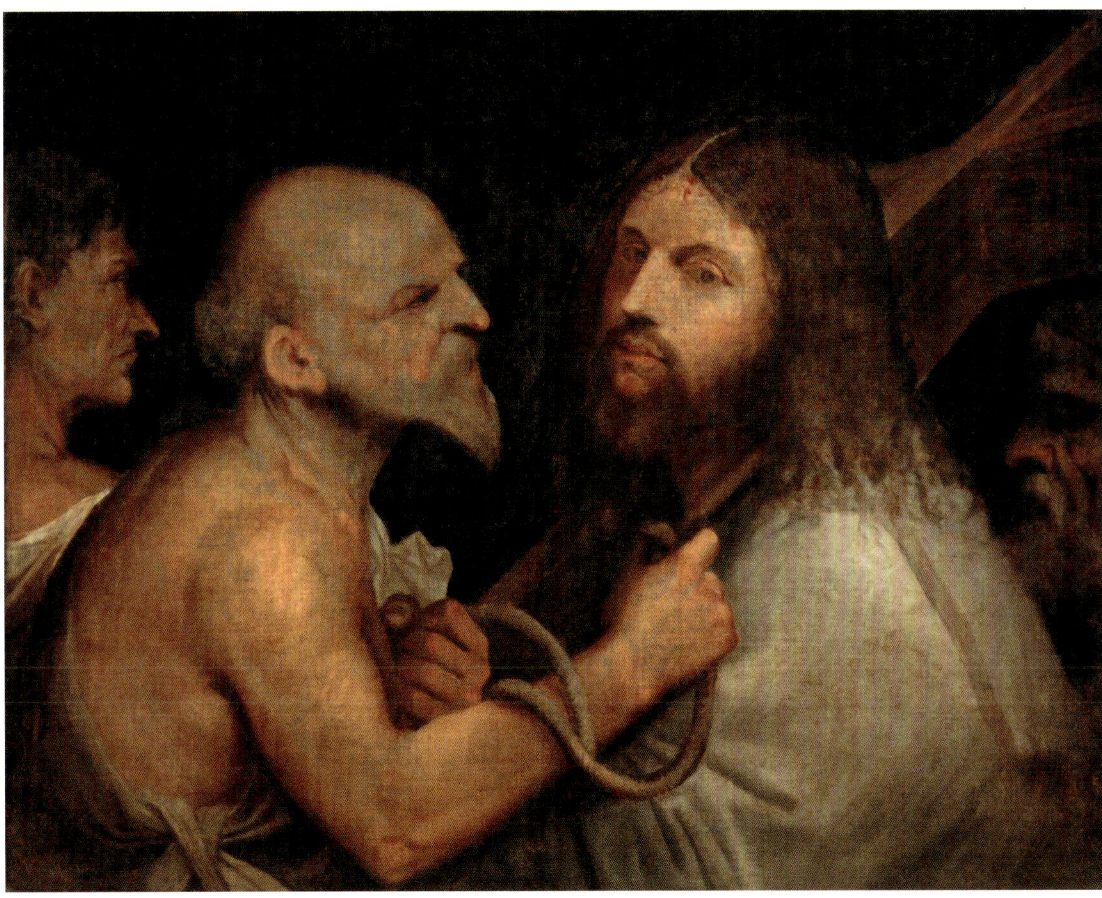

mentioned in the first edition his competition 'with those working in Tuscany', who had been noted in the first edition as the originators of the *maniera moderna*. According to the second edition, this competition had been dispatched as a result of Giorgione's encounter with the work of Leonardo da Vinci:

> Giorgione had seen some pieces by the hand of Lionardo with a beautiful gradation of colours, and with extraordinary relief effected, as has been related, by means of dark shadows, and this manner pleased him so much that he was for ever studying it as long as he lived, and in oil painting he imitated it greatly.[14]

Another discrepancy between the views expressed by Vasari in the two editions is the increasing emphasis on artists who developed their styles through contact with Giorgione, such as Sebastiano del Piombo and above all Titian, whom Vasari met. A number of paintings previously given to Giorgione are transferred to his pupils or his followers. The *Sea Storm* (fig. 3), considered in the first edition to be a fundamental work embodying the genius and expressive fervour of Giorgione, becomes in the second edition the key to Palma Vecchio's celebrity.[15]

The artist who benefits most from these reattributions is undoubtedly Titian. In some cases, such as his *San Marco Altarpiece*, Vasari records that Titian's stylistic similarity to Giorgione has caused confusion: 'On a small panel he painted Saint Mark seated amongst various Saints, whose faces are portrayed from nature, painted in oils with the greatest diligence: many people thought the painting was by the hand of Giorgione.'[16] The most notable example of reattribution across the two editions is *Christ Carrying the Cross* in the Scuola Grande di San Rocco, Venice (fig. 4), which is described in the first edition as follows: 'He worked on a painting of Christ carrying the cross, and a Jew pulls him along; the painting was placed in the church of Santo Rocco and today, because of the devotion many people feel for it, it performs miracles as can be witnessed.'[17] Vasari clearly continues to include the information in the second edition's account of Giorgione only out of forgetfulness, because by now he is convinced the painting is by Titian: 'for the church of Santo Rocho he painted […] a painting, Christ with the cross on his shoulder and a rope round his neck, pulled along by a Jew. This figure was thought by many to be by the hand of Giorgione, and is now the major devotional image in Venice.'[18]

The two editions of Vasari's *Lives* contain the roots of interpretation of Giorgione's work for centuries to come. The myth gained strength, with the result that it became increasingly difficult to identify Giorgione's works with any certainty.

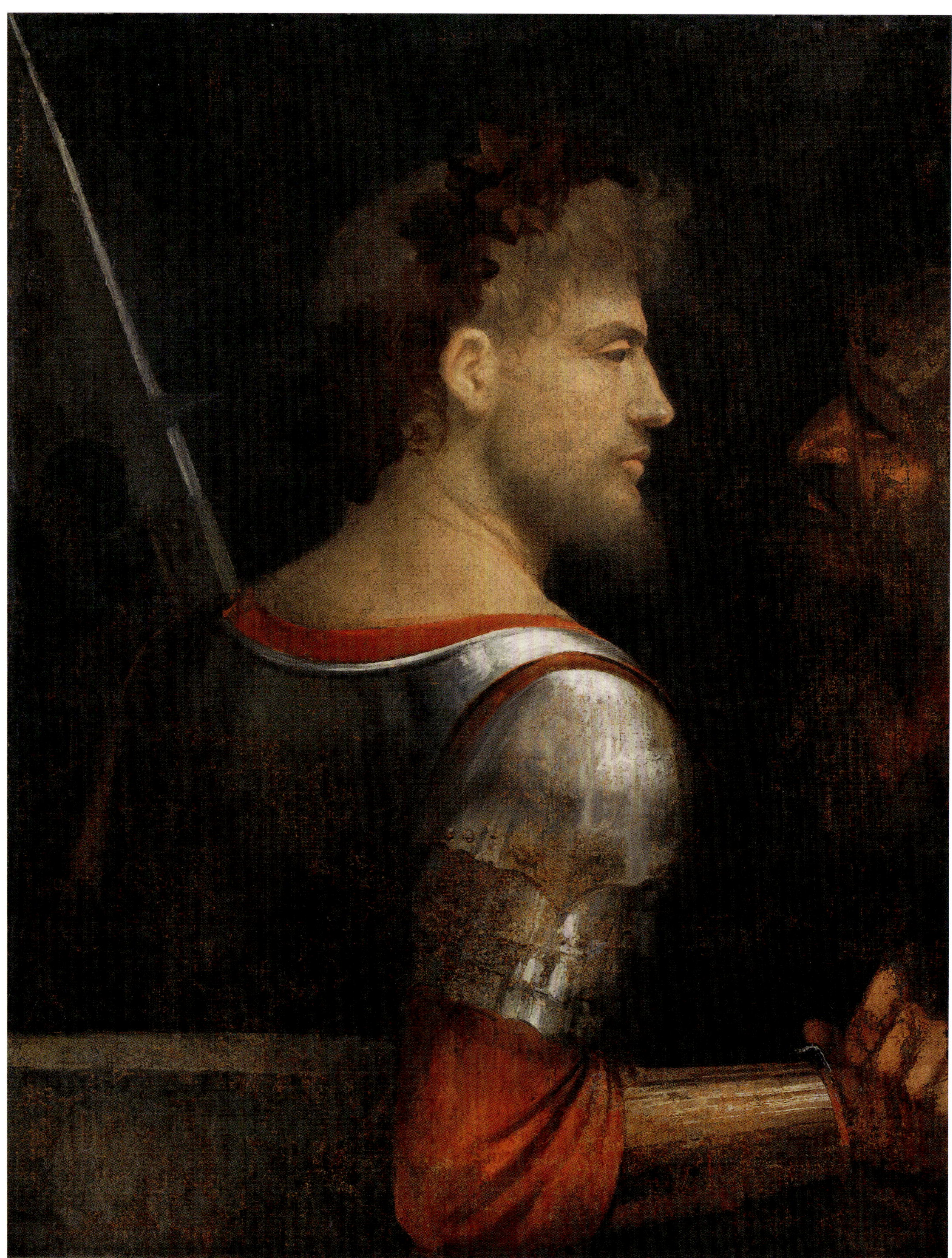

Fig. 5
GIORGIONE
Warrior, c. 1506–08
Oil on canvas, 72 × 56.5 cm
Kunsthistorisches Museum, Vienna

Marcantonio Michiel and the search for the 'real' Giorgione

The early sixteenth-century manuscript *Notizia d'opere di disegno* was edited in the late eighteenth century by Jacopo Morelli, librarian of the Biblioteca Marciana in Venice, and first published in 1800. The text's importance was immediately apparent, and indeed it became the main source of the artistic history of the Renaissance in northern Italy. The author was described as 'Anonimo Morelliano', until in 1864 evidence traced it to Marcantonio Michiel (1484–1552), a Venetian nobleman, humanist and collector and a near-contemporary of Giorgione.[19]

Between 1525 and 1543 Michiel visited eleven Venetian collections, noting work by Giorgione in many. Michiel knew some of those who had commissioned paintings from the artist, and gives their names, the titles of their paintings and a concise description of each.[20]

The discovery of the *Notizia* could not have come at a more opportune moment. It gave those taking part in the developing practice of connoisseurship an extraordinary opportunity: to identify the paintings Michiel had recorded as by Giorgione, many of which were hanging with incorrect attributions in collections and museums across Europe.

We should first examine the Venetian itinerary of Michiel, considered to be a 'major professional of art history in its real sense' operating at the time.[21] In 1525 he visited the residence of Girolamo Marcello, where he notes:

> The portrait of himself, Messer Jieronimo, armed and showing his back down to the waist, and with his head turned, by the hand of Zorzo de Castelfranco [fig. 5]. The canvas of the nude Venus sleeping in a landscape with cherubs, by the hand of Zorzo da Castelfranco; but the landscape and the cherubs were finished by the hand of Titian [fig. 6]. [...] And Saint Jerome as far as the waist, reading, was the work of Zorzo de Castelfranco.[22]

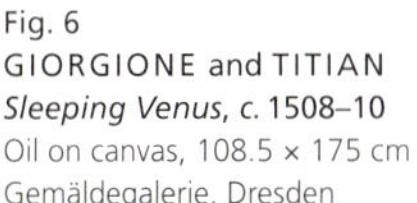

Fig. 6
GIORGIONE and TITIAN
Sleeping Venus, c. 1508–10
Oil on canvas, 108.5 × 175 cm
Gemäldegalerie, Dresden

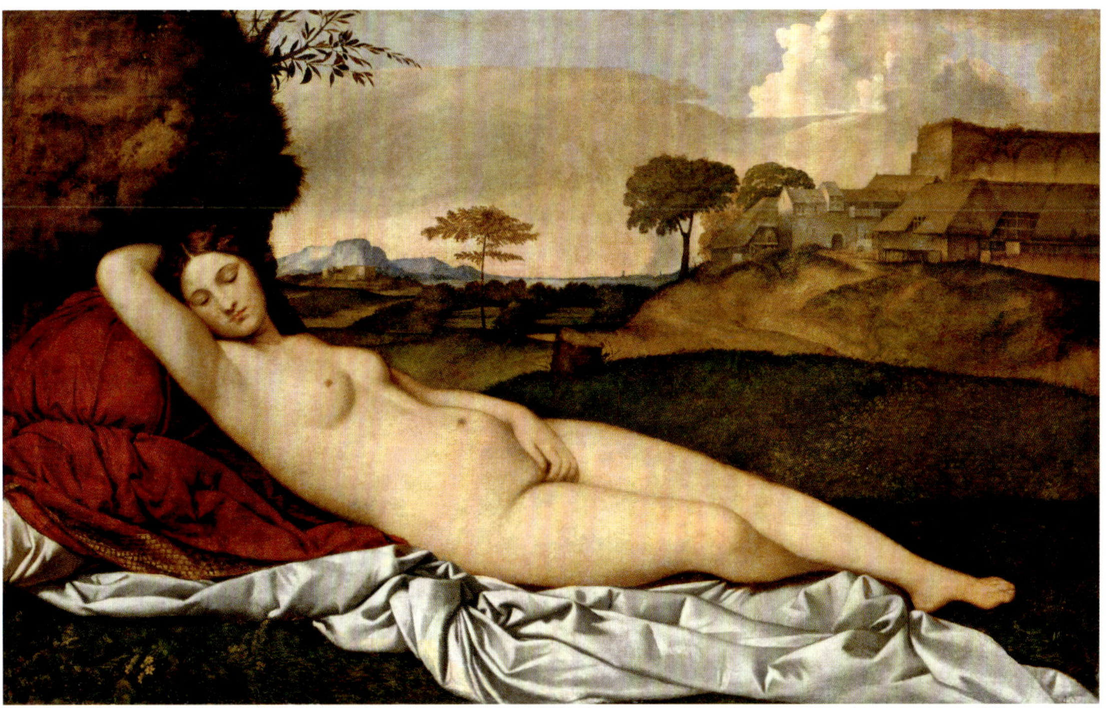

Fig. 7
GIORGIONE
Three Philosophers, c. 1504–08
Oil on canvas, 123 × 144 cm
Kunsthistorisches Museum, Vienna

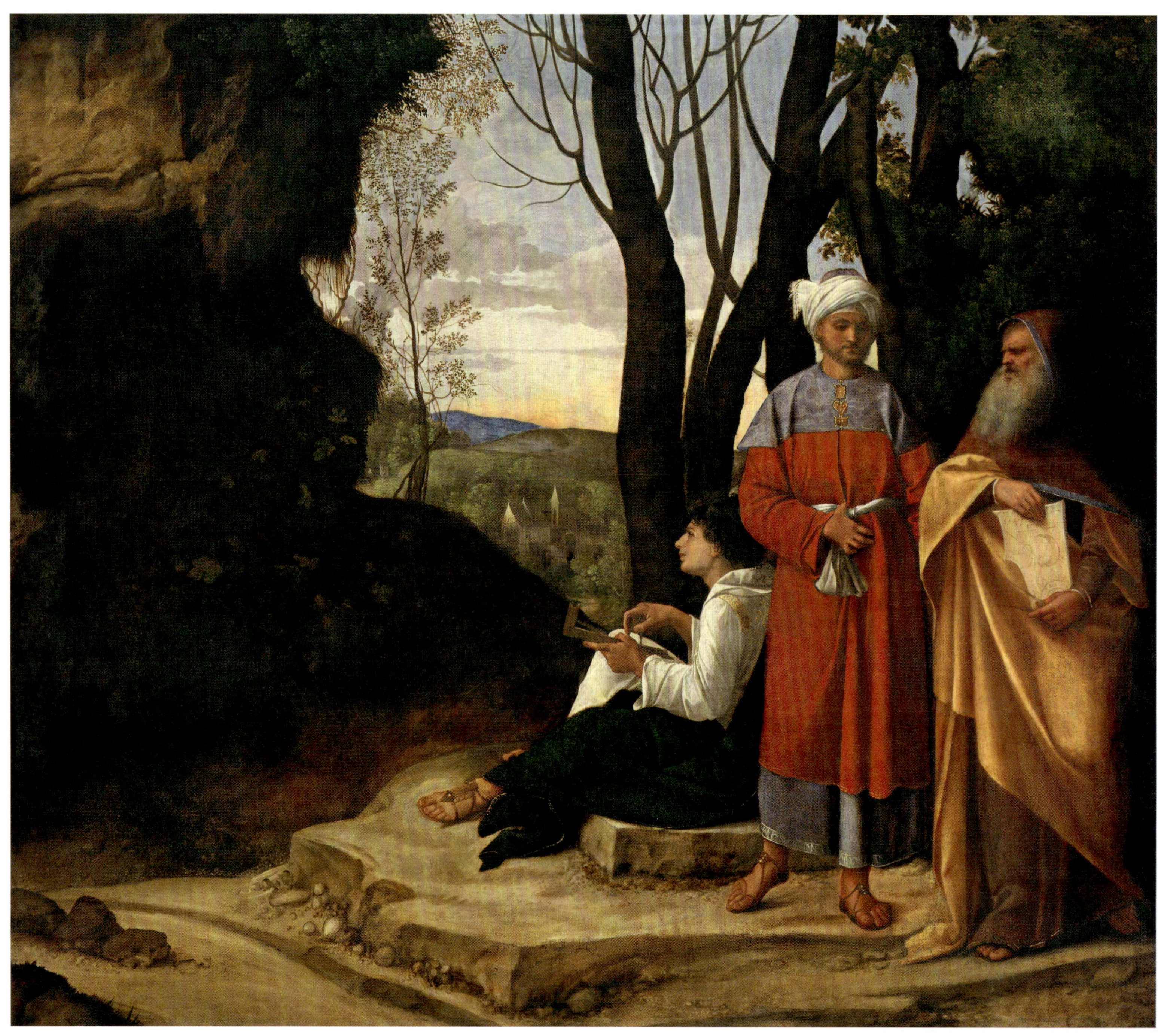

Fig. 8
GIORGIONE
La Tempesta, c. 1504–08
Oil on canvas, 83 × 73 cm
Gallerie dell'Accademia, Venice

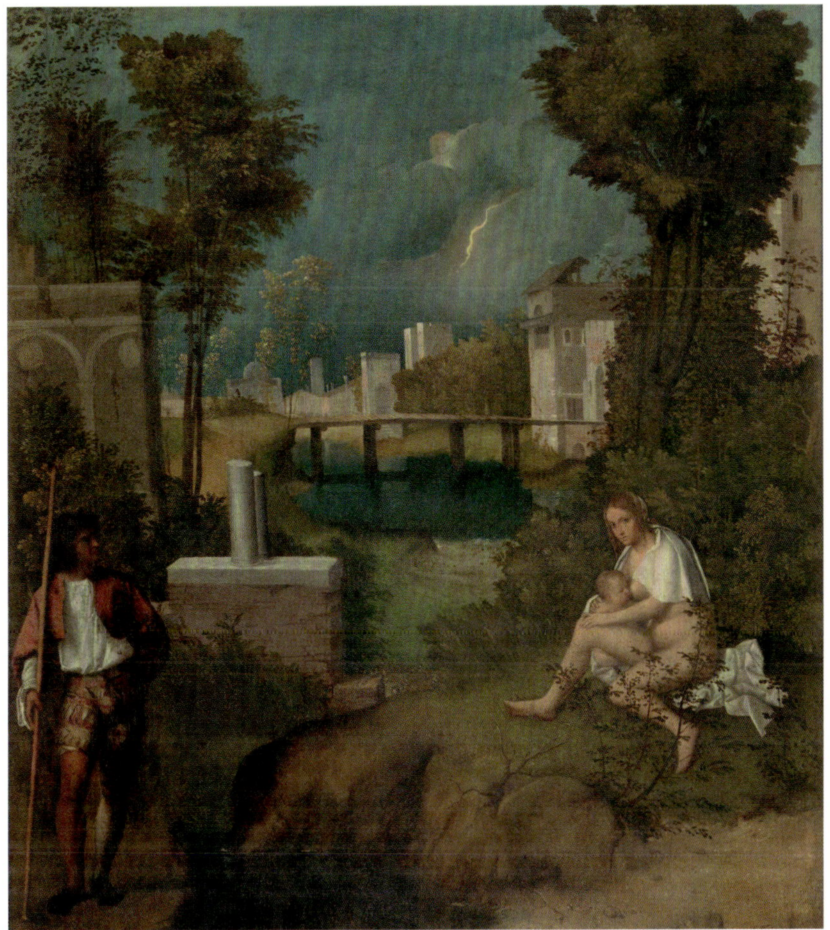

During the same year Michiel described the collection of Taddeo Contarini:

> The oil painting of the three Philosophers in a landscape, two standing and one seated looking at the sun's rays, with that rock so admirably faked, was begun by Zorzi of Castelfranco and finished by Sebastiano Veneziano [Sebastiano del Piombo; fig. 7]. […] The large oil painting of hell with Aeneas and Anchises was by the hand of Zorzi de Castelfranco. […] The landscape painting of the birth of Paris, with two standing shepherds, was by the hand of Zorzo da Castelfranco, and it was one of his earliest works.[23]

In 1528, in the home of Giovanni Antonio, he observed, 'The soldier armed to the waist but without a helmet, by the hand of Zorzi de Castelfranco.'[24]

In 1530 Michiel visited the residence of Gabriele Vendramin, and mentions 'The small landscape on canvas with the storm, with the gypsy and the soldier, was by the hand of Zorzi de Castelfranco [fig. 8]. […] The dead Christ on the tomb with the angel supporting him, was by the hand of Zorzi da Castelfranco, completed by Titian.'[25]

In 1531, in the collection of Giovanni Ram, he noted that 'The painting of the head of the young shepherd holding a fruit in his hand was by the hand of Zorzi da Castelfranco. The painting of the head of the boy holding an arrow was by the hand of Zorzo da Castelfranco [fig. 9].'[26]

Finally, in 1532 in the home of Andrea Odoni, he states that 'Saint Jerome, naked, sitting in the desert by moonlight was by the hand of —— taken from a painting by Zorzi de Castelfranco.'[27] Although this last was not an autograph work by Giorgione, Michiel had clearly recognised the composition of Saint Jerome as his.

Not only was Michiel an observer of the work of Giorgione, he was also a passionate collector. His connoisseurship emerges in the flash of recognition he experienced before a drawing he saw in 1543 in the collection of Michele Contarini in Venice: 'The pen and ink nude in a landscape was by the hand of Zorzi, and it is the same nude as I possess in paint by the same Zorzi.'[28] Michiel was also thought to possess *Il Tramonto* (cat. 19).

Even in Michiel's day, it was not always possible to attribute works to Giorgione with conviction. Uncertainties appear within his manuscript, for example in the description of a work seen in the house of Antonio Pasqualini: 'The head of Saint James, with the staff, was by the hand of Zorzi da Castelfrancho, or by one of his disciples, taken from the Christ in San Rocco.'[29]

Deconstruction of the myth: the role of connoisseurship

In 1978, on the occasion of the fifth centenary of what is thought to be the artist's birth, Francis Haskell gave a celebrated lecture at Venice's Gallerie dell'Accademia, entitled 'La sfortuna critica di Giorgione' ('The Critical

Fig. 9
GIORGIONE
Boy with an Arrow, c. 1500
Oil on panel, 48 × 42 cm
Kunsthistorisches Museum, Vienna

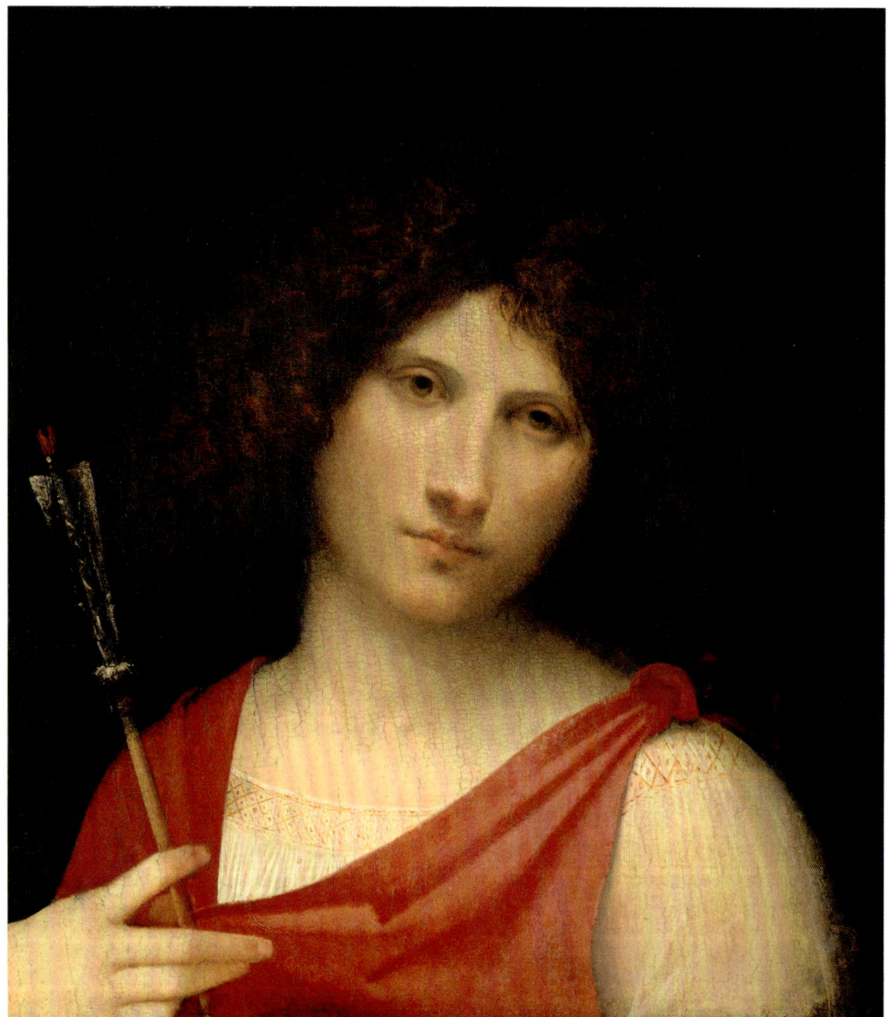

Misfortune of Giorgione').[30] Haskell drew attention to the important collection of Philippe d'Orléans (1674–1723), which contained undoubted masterpieces by Raphael, Titian, Veronese and Rubens. According to a sumptuous catalogue published in 1786,[31] that collection also included seven paintings by Giorgione, almost the same number that Michiel had listed in the early sixteenth-century Venetian collections he visited. Over time, Haskell explained, it had become clear that not one of the paintings owned by the Duc d'Orléans was a verifiable Giorgione. Haskell's point was that genuine works by Giorgione are rare indeed, and if even one or two cases of mistaken identity were to be included in his *œuvre*, our understanding of the artist would be fundamentally affected.

It has been estimated that about forty paintings were attributed to Giorgione during the sixteenth century, more than two hundred and fifty in the seventeenth, and yet still more during the eighteenth and the beginning of the nineteenth. The total began to diminish during the nineteenth century, and today the number has returned to the forty estimated in the sixteenth century. One cause of this is the rise of connoisseurship among art historians, who have played a vital role in debating and drawing up a convincing *œuvre* for the artist.

Some sense of the impact of their reappraisal can be gained from Walter Pater's response to it, which appears in the chapter dedicated to the school of Giorgione in his *The Renaissance* (1877). Pater could not countenance the idea that the book he labelled the 'new Vasari' – Joseph Archer Crowe and Giovanni Battista Cavalcaselle's *A History of Painting in North Italy* (1871) – should presume to establish so swiftly which paintings were, or were not, genuinely painted by Giorgione:

> And, as we might expect, something fabulous and illusive has always mingled itself in the brilliancy of Giorgione's fame. The exact relationship to him of many works – drawings, portraits, painted idylls – often fascinating enough, which in various collections went by his name, was from the first uncertain. Still, six or eight famous pictures at Dresden, Florence and the Louvre, were with no doubt attributed to him, and in these, if anywhere, something of the splendour of the old Venetian humanity seemed to have been preserved.
>
> But of those six or eight famous pictures it is now known that only one is certainly from Giorgione's hand. [...]
>
> It became fashionable for wealthy lovers of art, with no critical standard of authenticity, to collect so-called works of Giorgione, and a multitude of imitations came into circulation. And now, in the 'new Vasari', the great traditional reputation, woven with so profuse demand on men's admiration, has been scrutinised thread by thread; and what remains of the most vivid and stimulating of Venetian masters, a live flame, as it seemed, in those old shadowy times, has been reduced almost to a name by his most recent critics.[32]

Fig. 10
ANONYMOUS VENETIAN PAINTER
Portrait of a Woman, c. 1510–20
Oil on canvas, 97 × 75 cm
Galleria Borghese, Rome

A collection of connoisseurs

The series of excerpts that follows introduces some of the significant individuals who have played their part in attempts to 'reconstruct' Giorgione, and illustrates their thoughts about the artist's work. It should be borne in mind that the selection is drawn from a restricted group of students of Giovanni Morelli (1816–1891), founder of the 'experimental method'. Morelli was convinced that painters left incontrovertible evidence of their own style in tiny details within their compositions, such as earlobes or the shape of hands. He was sure that examination of such details in a painting would establish the name of its author. Morelli's art-historical revolution had a European resonance. One needs only to look at the long line of his major publications from 1874 to 1880 to see how far-reaching the effects of the phenomenon were, from Germany to England and Italy. In 1891, the year of Morelli's death, Wilhelm von Bode spoke of it in terms of the spread of an epidemic, which he named 'Lermolieffmania'; an allusion to Ivan Lermolieff, the pseudonym that Morelli used to conceal his name. And Lermolieffmania's victims in the last quarter of the nineteenth century ranged from Jacob Burckhardt to Sigmund Freud, and from Arthur Conan Doyle to Bernard Berenson. If with the first and the last of these we remain within the strict confines of art history, the other two are witness to the broader appeal of the theory. Indeed, Freud was to compare Morelli's experimental method with psychoanalytic techniques. Thus, although Morelli had no direct pupils (if one excludes Gustavo Frizzoni), he had a host of adherents.

Our anthology begins with Morelli himself, and concludes in 1954, the year before 'Giorgione e i Giorgioneschi', the exhibition at the Palazzo Ducale in Venice, and reportedly the 'most difficult exhibition in the world'.[33]

Although Morelli himself was responsible for some substantial errors, he deserves praise for his redefinition of Giorgione's *œuvre*. In the opinion of Berenson, his discovery of the Dresden *Venus* (fig. 6) was 'one of the most memorable deeds of modern criticism',[34] and few would dispute the claim. At the time, the Dresden painting was believed to be by the seventeenth-century painter Giovanni Battista Salvi, known as Sassoferrato.

Here is Morelli's description of the process of discovery:

> We come back to the picture described hastily but accurately by the Anonymous, as he saw it in the year 1525 at the house of Jeronimo Marcello at Venice: a 'Sleeping Venus with Cupid in an open landscape'. This wonderful painting is generally thought to be lost; whether correctly, is another question. I believe that I can point it out, and this time I need not take my readers far. The glorious picture, hitherto veiled from the eyes of art critics, is to be found at the Dresden Gallery. To my own satisfaction I can testify that I recognised the hand and genius of Giorgione in this enchanting picture before I knew of its having been mentioned as such in the list of [Jacopo] Morelli's Anonymous.[35]

Morelli, however, was not infallible and his experimental method was anything but scientific. This is demonstrated by the case of the extremely modest portrait found in the Galleria Borghese in Rome (fig. 10), attributed by Morelli to Giorgione after an 'encounter' with the spirit of the painter:

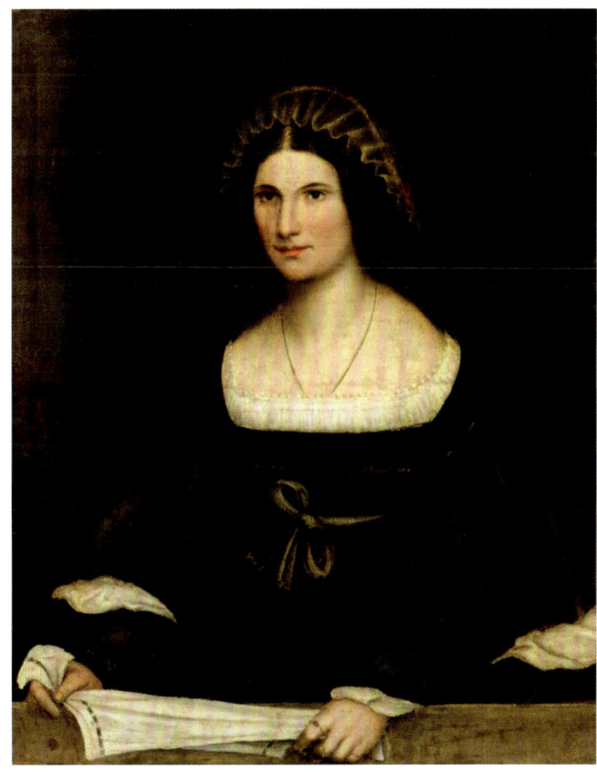

We will omit some more or less unimportant pictures, and, in conclusion, devote a little more time to a wonderful portrait which long attracted a large share of my attention, and is catalogued as the work of an 'unknown master'. It represents a woman of about twenty-eight; her dark eyes, full of fire and passion, are overshadowed by a low and intelligent forehead [...] The simple treatment of this mysterious figure reveals a great artist – but whom? Before examining this attractive portrait critically, I thought of Dosso [....] Then it occurred to me that it might be of Sebastiano del Piombo's early period; but for him also the conception appeared too profound, and the form of hand too nearly akin to the *quattrocento*. One day, as I stood before this mysterious portrait, entranced, and questioning, the spirit of the master met mine, and the truth flashed upon me. 'Giorgione, thou alone', I cried in my excitement; and the picture answered, 'Even so.'[36]

As part of an obituary of his teacher Enrico Costa (1867–1911), Carlo Gamba (1870–1963) published a letter sent from Dresden in 1891. Costa had evidently been inspired by Giorgione's *Venus* in that city's collection and talked at length about the painter from Castelfranco. Indeed, Costa is himself a kind of Giorgione of art history: a celebrated figure despite the few works to his name.

Those who knew Enrico Costa at that time know how much light he could have thrown on the most intricate problems of art history [...] since in his criticism as much as in his letters he appeared to be the cool analyst of details observed in works of secondary importance; observing the works of the great masters he would abandon himself to flights of true ecstasy, sometimes expressing his feelings with admirable lyricism. 'Giorgione', he wrote from Dresden in the spring of 1891, 'all the richest art, full of *joie de vivre*, full of that pleasure in objects and, so to speak, through all his pores, light, the beauty of nature and of mankind, all the peace and tranquillity of real life, enjoying everything the earth has to offer to make man happy, all this is evoked by the name of this enchanting artist. How many hours have I spent in the Louvre in front of his *Concert*. We seem to blend into the scene, our eyes dazzled by the distant sea igniting the setting sun; we hear the wind rustling the leaves of the trees as it passes, we hear the harmonies of the *Concert* [...].

'Yes, indeed, the *Concert* is truly a symphony of art. The delightful landscape which, from the grassy meadow in which the party is grouped, slopes gently down to the sea, interrupted here and there by bushes and by a stream already clothed in damp shade, the diaphanous blue shade of evening; a gleam of the sun's rays still lights up a group of houses, the thick, green, shady trees nearby and the mountains of the most beautiful indigo on the horizon; if this landscape is the work of a great artist it is something more as well [...]. Only one other stupendous creation is worthy of comparison: the landscape containing the three ages of man in the Bridgewater Gallery. In this, it is true, Titian was only following in the footsteps of the Master of Castelfranco. [...] And one might ask: what is the meaning of this painting? For shame! What does Beethoven's seventh symphony mean? Both imply nothing more than that you are feeling and responding.'[37]

Gamba claimed to have heard the art historian Adolfo Venturi repeating the claim of Bernard Berenson (1865–1959) that 'Every critic has his own private Giorgione.'

One of the first times I had the honour of talking to Adolfo Venturi, in the house of mutual friends, I heard him say (as a kind of joke) that since so very few documents relating to Giorgione had survived, each person could create their own personal version of the artist, according to their point of view. And he was perfectly right; at the time, every art critic fashioned his own Giorgione according to his way of seeing.[38]

Berenson himself was a follower of Morelli, and considered to be one of the most influential art historians of the twentieth century. In his later years he began to question the validity of the discipline on which he had spent his whole career, commenting, on the subject of Giorgione:

I had spent the great part of a year playing patience with ordinary and X-ray photos of every painting attributed to Giorgione in the last 60 years. I did the same with all known pictures that can be classified as Giorgionesque. I had meant to write a book, a comprehensive book on the subject. At the end I realised that it would take me another year to do the kind of book I had in mind and that I had no time to spare for it. Besides, I ended by doubting whether I had much to publish that others would not do as well. I would leave many problems not only unsettled but not more advanced towards a satisfactory solution.

At the same time a glancing suspicion of the uselessness of arguing about attributions and dating overcame me. I have waded through such swamps of argument to reach with my own eye conclusions opposite to those so minutely laboured by the writer. My present conviction is that what counts in the art of attribution is not this or that minute comparison but a sense of the painter's artistic personality. That sense comes only after a long and loving intimacy and by no short cuts. And least of all by comparing minutiae of questionable significance.

So I have abandoned the idea of composing a ponderous work on Giorgione.[39]

The philological reconstruction of Giorgione's *œuvre* poses such exceptionally complicated problems that the

Fig. 11 (overleaf)
JACOPO DE' BARBARI
View of Venice, 1500
Woodcut in six blocks,
139 × 282 cm
British Museum, London

limitations of connoisseurship become evident. In the early twentieth century, one of the cornerstones of Giorgione's *œuvre*, the *Concert champêtre* in the Musée du Louvre (fig. 15), was reassigned to Titian's early career.[40] This created a dangerous precedent that had the potential to affect a number of works whose attribution was poised precariously between the two artists. Such changes had been prefigured in the shifts in attribution between the two editions of Vasari's *Lives*.

Re-presenting Giorgione: recent exhibitions

The 1955 exhibition in Venice was the largest ever devoted to Giorgione and the Giorgioneschi; the first 62 items in the catalogue were referred to as 'works by Giorgione, works ascribed to him by only some of the critics, and paintings by anonymous artists in his circle'.[41] The body of work displayed was so mixed that it was almost impossible to discern the artist's essence.

A key moment in the study of Giorgione was – for some, at least – reached with the legendary exhibition 'Le Siècle de Titien' at the Musée du Louvre in 1993. The room devoted to Giorgione was crowded with masterpieces; however, the visitor was requested to adopt a position 'between faith and reason'.[42]

The contribution made by the two related exhibitions held in Venice and Vienna during 2003 and 2004 is unassailable.[43] Giorgione was the sole subject of both, considered in the light of myth and enigma, words that formed the subtitle to the pair of exhibitions. The collaborative exhibition held in 2006 at Washington DC and Vienna embraced an artistic landscape that encompassed Bellini, Giorgione, Titian and some of their leading followers.[44] Finally, we should recall the monographic exhibition held in 2009 in Castelfranco Veneto, the artist's birthplace.[45] All these exhibitions took a different approach to confronting the myth of Giorgione, demonstrating that complexities remain prevalent.

* * *

This brief introduction sums up the confusion that has reigned in the perception of Giorgione ever since his own day. The aim of the exhibition is to shed a little light on the problem and, at the same time, to introduce it to the wider public without wishing to provide definitive answers to the questions of attribution, dating and interpretation.

Exhibitions often change the perception of an artist and it is because of this that curators like to say that catalogues ought to be written not before but after shows. This paradox is more valid than ever in the case of 'In the Age of Giorgione'.

This is a highly experimental exhibition, in which doubts are declared and certainties are few. The 'case of Giorgione' is presented to the visitor in the jumbled state in which we see it, without our concealing any of its complexities. For these reasons, in captions, the attribution 'Giorgione' is used only where we are reasonably sure, and dates are provided wherever we feel it is possible to do so. We hope the journey in search of Giorgione, and the quality of the masterpieces exhibited, notwithstanding the problems of attribution, will inspire our visitors. In addition, we hope the exhibition will help art historians discuss this much-shared enigma anew, and perhaps advance its resolution.

The difficulties of the undertaking are evident at both a practical and theoretical level. Despite its impressive quality, the selection of works is not, and could never have been, exhaustive. Many of the 'certain' works, those precious fixed stars in Giorgione's unstable *œuvre* – paintings signed or documented, or cited by Michiel – could not come to London, either for reasons of conservation or because they are too important to leave the museums that own them.

Nevertheless, to take a purely monographic approach with Giorgione would be, even if it were possible, too limiting. By opening up the exhibition to examine the Venetian context at the beginning of the cinquecento we present more clearly the artistic identity of the master, and show how he shaped a generation of artists. That said, many of the pictures exhibited here are – or have at one time been, according to various critics – considered works by the Master of Castelfranco.

From this critically confused past, within the galleries of the Royal Academy, we hope to start building the Giorgione of the future.

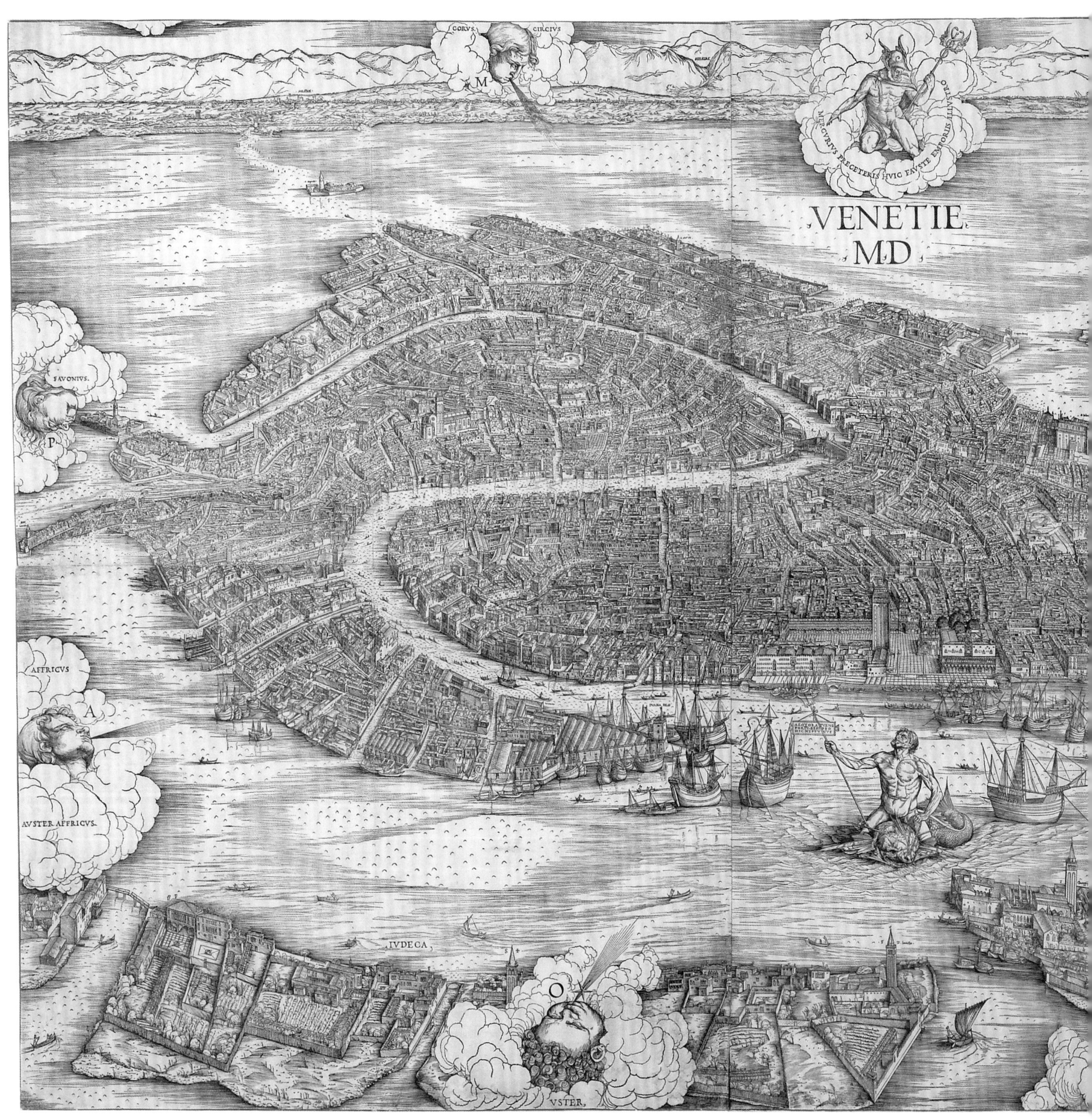
CORVS
CIRCIVS
M
MERCVRIVS PRECETERIS HVIC FAVSTE EMPORIIS ILLVSTRO
VENETIE
MD
FAVONIVS
P
AFFRICVS
A
AVSTER AFFRICVS
IVDECA
O
VSTER

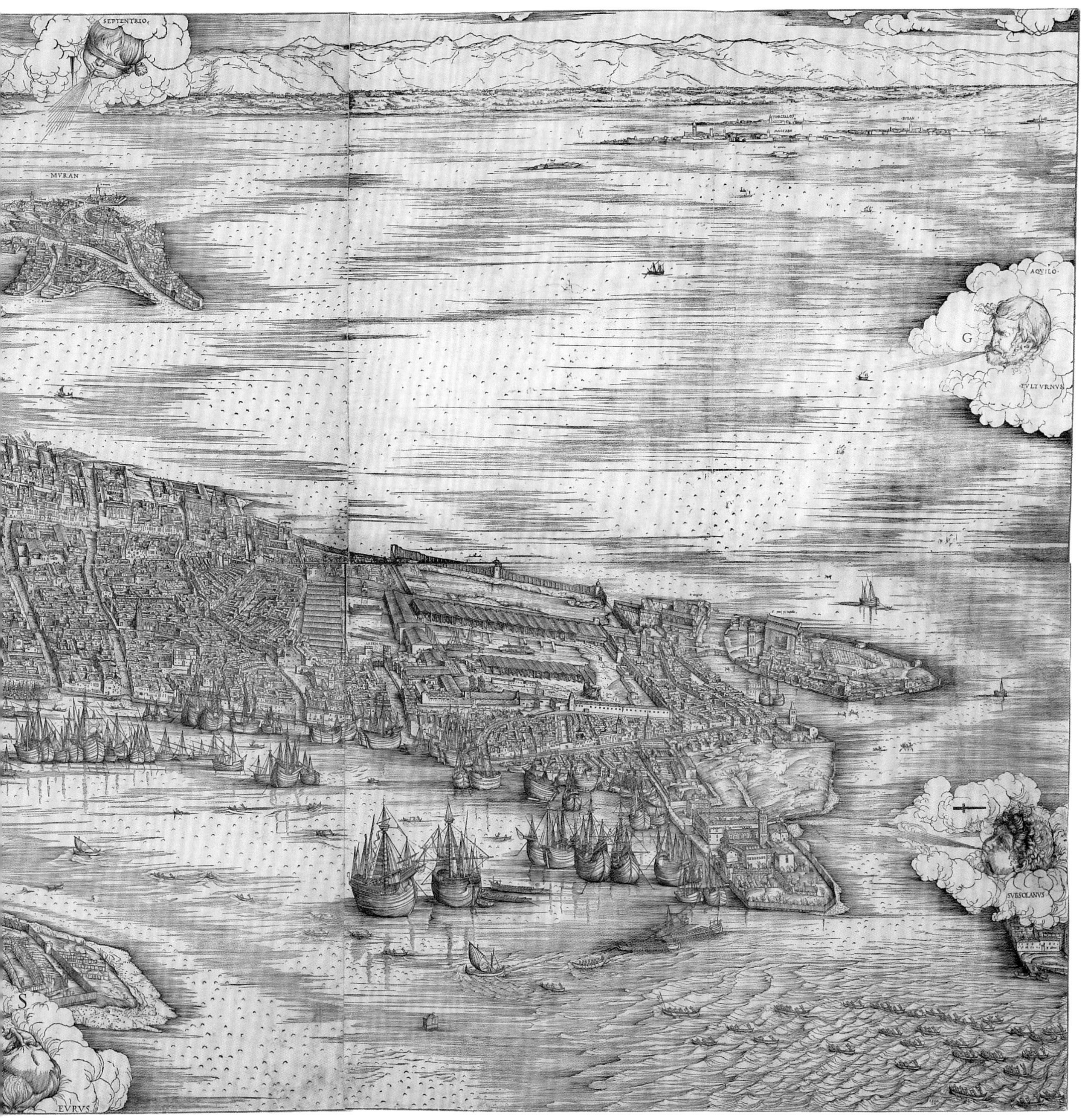
SEPTENTRIO
TORCELLO
BVRAN
MVRAN
AQVILO
G
VVLTVRNVS
SVBSOLANVS
S
EVRVS

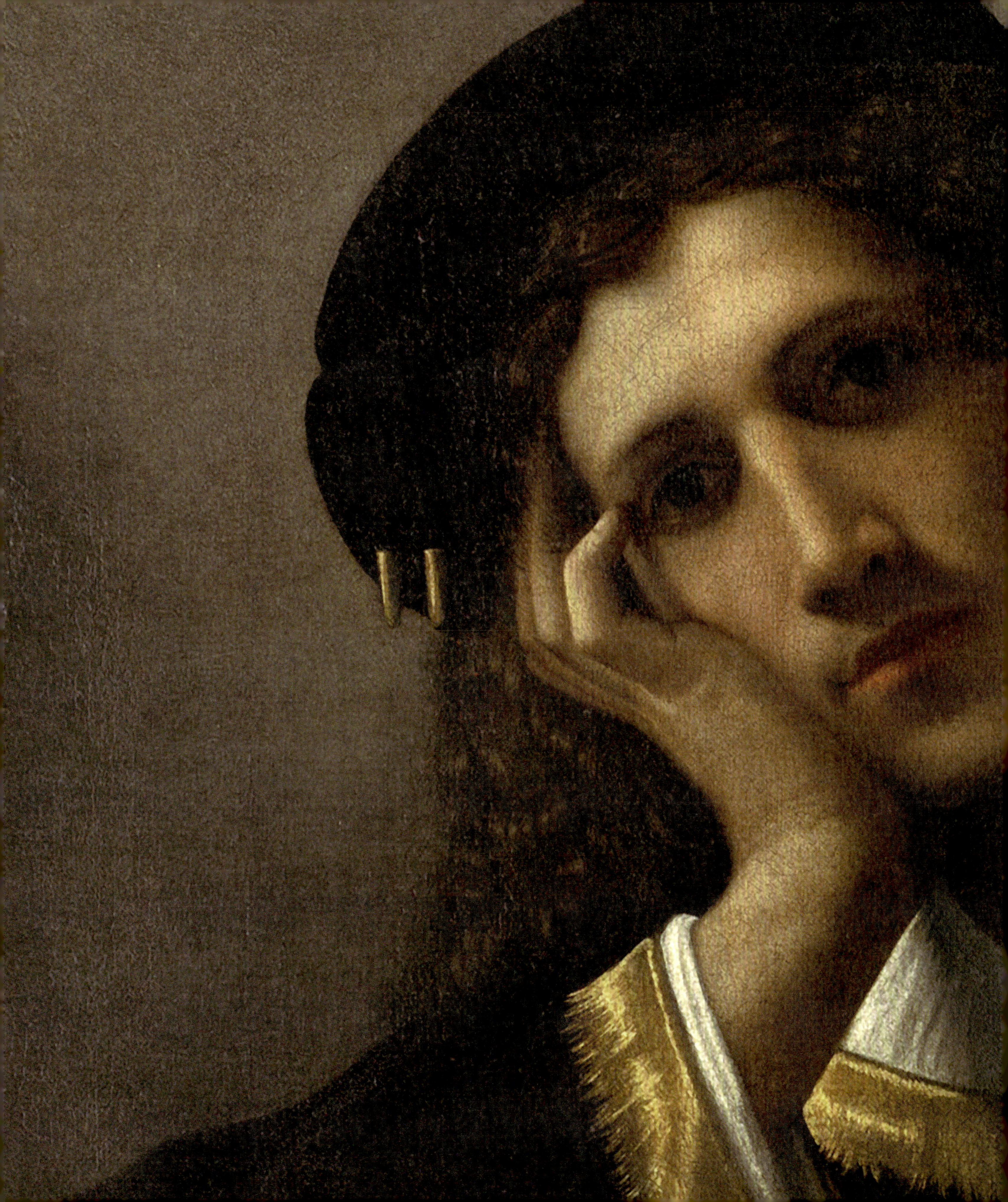

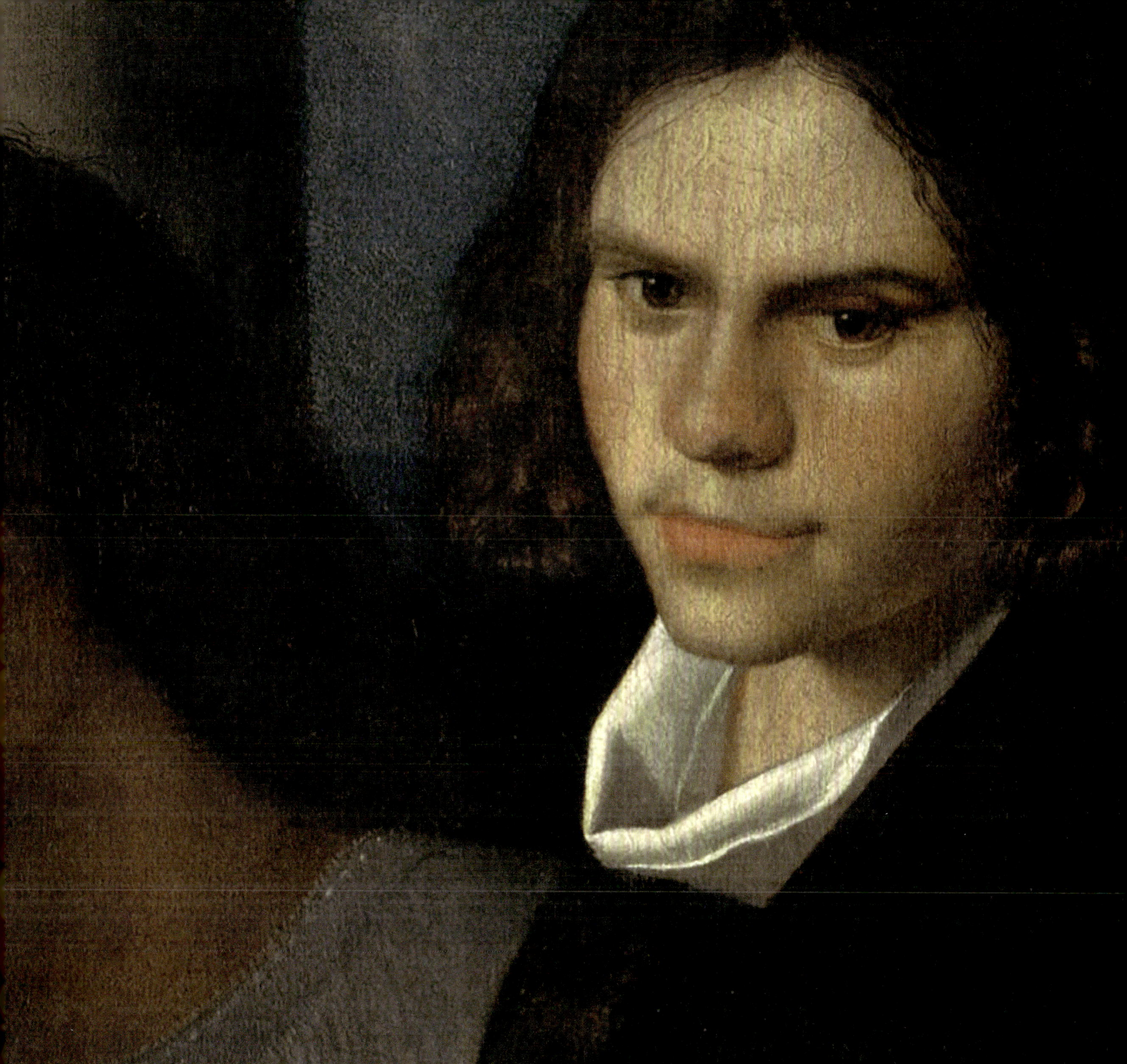

PORTRAITS

Fig. 12
GIOVANNI BELLINI
Doge Leonardo Loredan, c. 1501
Oil on panel, 61.6 × 45.1 cm
The National Gallery, London

In the earliest years of the sixteenth century almost no city in Italy, or even in Europe, could compare with Venice as an artistic centre. The most prominent painter in Venice at the time was the ageing Giovanni Bellini, who died in his eighties in 1516. Albrecht Dürer, who arrived in the city in 1506, considered him to be the greatest of all artists: 'He is very old and he is still the best of all the painters.'[1]

The new generation of painters, pioneers in the development of the so-called *maniera moderna* (Vasari's celebrated definition of the 'modern style') was identified with Giorgione. Its 'founders', Sebastiano del Piombo and above all Titian, were to become the uncontested leaders of the artistic movement that followed him. In this milieu, marked by a state of continuous flux, the artistic genres were also undergoing a series of rapid changes.

Developments in the visual arts were accompanied by developments in the field of letters; Venice was establishing itself as a literary hub thanks to the presence of the publisher Aldo Manuzio and the humanist Pietro Bembo.

The new interpretation of portraiture emerged into this unique environment, and the genre grew further and further away from the formula established by Bellini during his long career. It could be claimed that the change involved the inclusion of the viewer in the mechanics of constructing the image (the viewer's presence formerly having been held at a distance, if not completely excluded, from any possible relationship with the subject of the portrait). Giorgione was able to capture his direct relationship with the sitter, and arouse an appreciation of his or her state of mind. This distinction makes it possible to separate 'modern' portraits, executed in compliance with these new codes, from the portraits of the past. The new codes predicate an anatomy of the emotions as well as an anatomy of the physiognomy.

Giorgio Vasari's biography of Bellini is eloquent on the subject of the portrait, particularly as regards the development of the genre in Venice in that period. Vasari claims that Bellini's achievement depended on the execution of one portrait, the picture of Doge Leonardo Loredan (fig. 12), who occupied the most important position in the Republic of Venice: 'The earliest works of Giovanni were a number of portraits from life, particularly the portrait of Doge Loredano.'[2] There is no doubt that the portrait, now in the National Gallery, London, represents a consummate expression of a genre, perhaps its highest point. In any case, this was an official commission and the viewer's function is solely to admire the authority of the sitter. The painting dates from about 1501, the year of Loredan's election as Doge.

Vasari writes at length about the extraordinary popularity of Bellini's portraits:

> And having devoted himself to making portraits from the life, he introduced into Venice the fashion that everyone of a certain rank should have his portrait painted either by him or by some other master; wherefore in all the houses of Venice there are many portraits, and in many gentlemen's houses one may see their fathers and grandfathers, up to the fourth generation, and in some of the more noble they still go back to a fashion which has ever been truly of the greatest praise and existed even among the ancients. Who does not feel infinite pleasure and contentment, to say nothing of the honour and adornment that they confer, at seeing the images of his ancestors, particularly if they have been famous and illustrious for their part in governing their republics, for noble deeds performed in peace or in war, or for learning or any other notable and distinguished talent? And to what other end [...] did the ancients set up images of their great men in public places, with honourable inscriptions, than to kindle in the minds of their successors a love of excellence and of glory?
>
> For Messer Pietro Bembo, then, before he went to live with Pope Leo X, Giovanni made a portrait of the lady that he loved, so lifelike that, even as Simone Sanese had been celebrated in the past by the Florentine Petrarca, so was Giovanni deservedly celebrated in his verses by this Venetian.[3]

Bembo's sonnet 'O imagine mia celeste et pura',[4] inspired by Petrarch, addresses the portrait of his beloved – who has, in the world of the poem, had her portrait painted by Bellini:

> Oh image of mine, celestial and pure,
> who to my eyes shines brighter than Sun,
> your countenance mirrors the face of the one
> engraved in my heart with such painstaking care,
> I think my Bellini has given, with the face,
> her costume as well; when she I admire
> it sets me on fire. And you – cold as stone
> Misfortune has struck.
> Like the sweet, modest woman I bear in my mind,
> you show your compassion for my lasting pain;
> when I then beg for mercy you do not reply.
> Your demeanour in this is less cruel than hers,
> all my hopes are not scattered by you to the winds,
> at least when I seek you, you do not hide away.

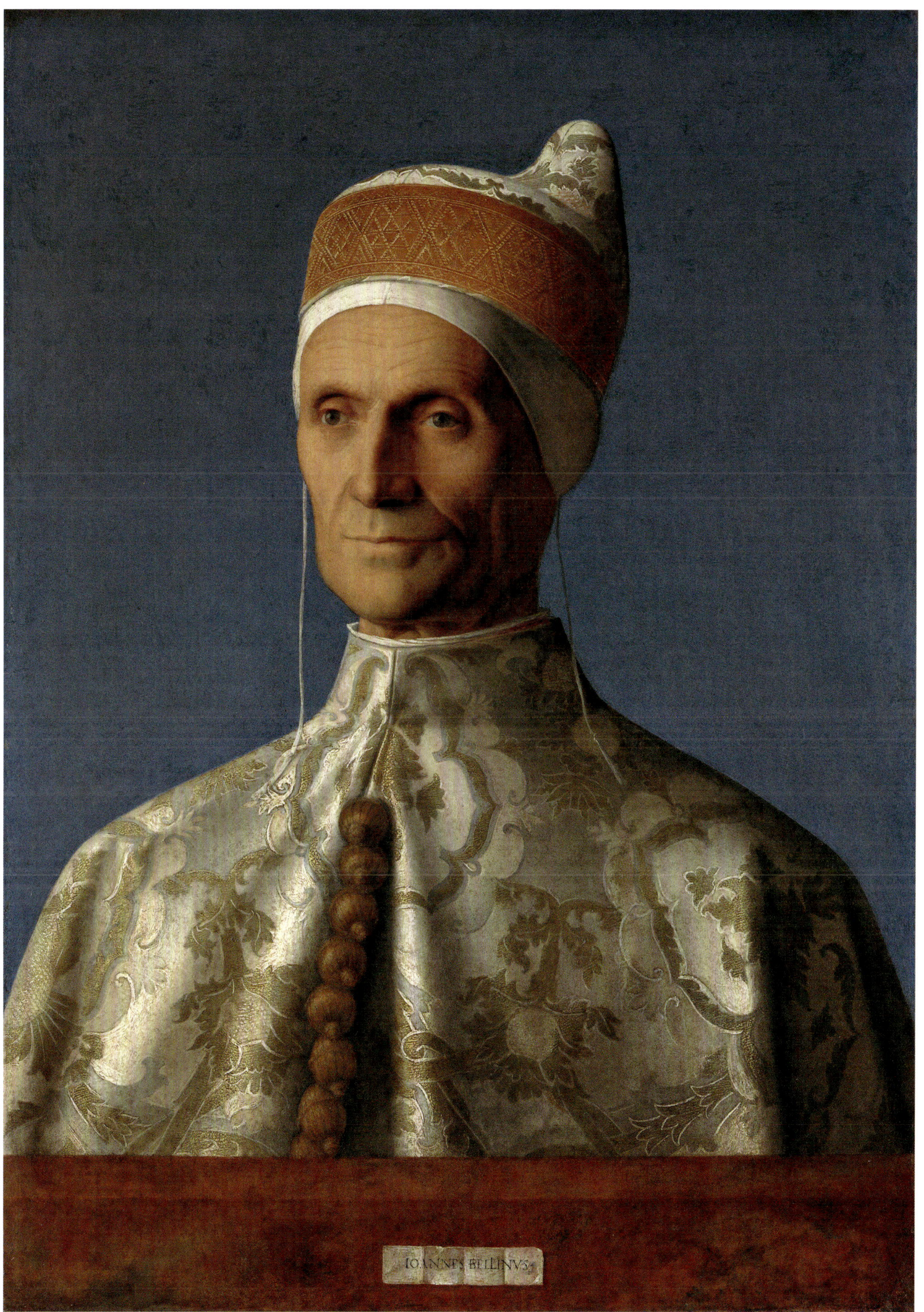
IOANNES BELLINVS

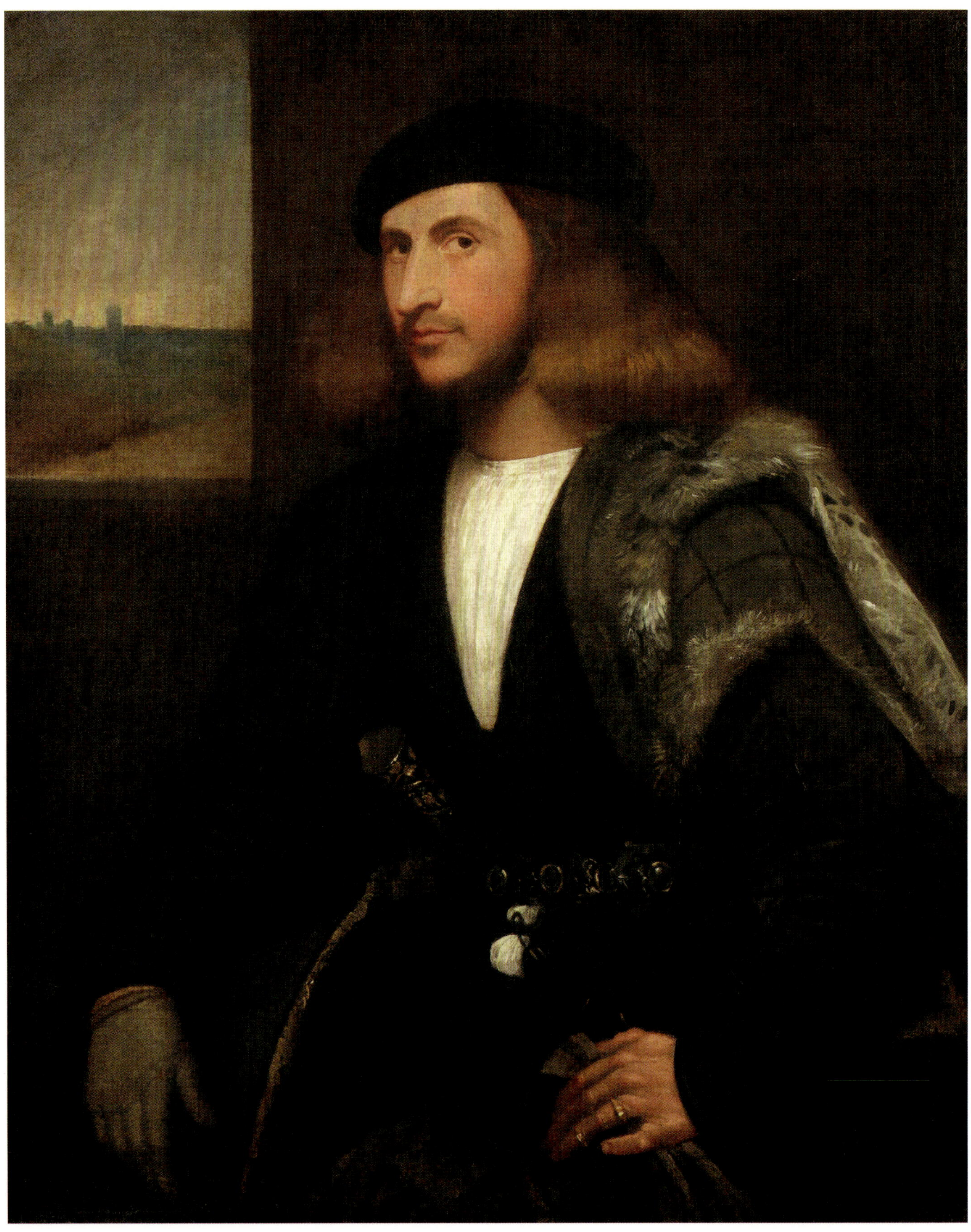

Fig. 13
GIOVANNI CARIANI
Portrait of a Man, c. 1510–15
Oil on canvas, 81.5 × 68.5 cm
Chatsworth House, Derbyshire

Bellini's painting from the Royal Collection (cat. 3), is a work of great importance. It stands at the midpoint of the history of portraiture, in perfect balance between the *manieras* of the past and the future. Whether it represents the features of Bembo is still debated; Bembo was an author closely involved with the examination of amorous emotions, notably in his most celebrated dialogue, *Gli Asolani* – a *prosimetrum*, interspersing poetry with prose – printed in Venice in 1505.

If we compare this painting with Giorgione's earliest portrait (cat. 1) it is clear that the sitter in the work from the Royal Collection, although not separated from us by the traditional parapet, is somehow inaccessible, whereas the subject of the Berlin portrait approaches in friendly fashion, putting his hand on the division. The gesture and attitude of this sitter invites us to relate to him as a character, rather than a representation. The same cannot be said of the remote Royal Collection portrait. The comparison is not as simple as it appears. In order to interpret a portrait one needs to know for whom and in what circumstances it was painted, and who enjoyed it at the time – information we lack.

To explain the impression given by a painting such as Giorgione's *Terris Portrait* (cat. 5), it is helpful to quote from Vasari's description of Giorgione's method of painting:

> He began to give more softness and greater relief to his paintings, with beautiful *maniera*; he still was in the habit of looking for subjects that were alive and natural, and of representing them as he knew best, with colours, alternating raw and tender colours as the live subject showed him, without drawing. He was very sure that painting directly with colours, without preparatory study or drawing on paper, was the truest and best way of proceeding, and the only genuine method.[5]

The advantage of painting directly would seem to be that the method allows the composition to be adapted to the sitter's state of mind, to the extent that it absorbs the psychological nuances of a given moment. Comparison of Giorgione's portrait with portraits by Dürer from the same period (such as cats 4 and 6) is instructive in this respect: Dürer freezes and defines his forms by means of a number of tiny details, whereas Giorgione gives vibrancy by pursuing the impression of a moment, even as it changes. Although we shall never know anything about the early history of the *Terris Portrait*, it leaves us with the feeling we have confronted an individual willing to communicate with us. One has the distinct impression of being able to grasp the subject's emotional identity. The Giorgionesque portrait defies simple classification; it offers a viewer the opportunity to invest the sitter directly with sentiments according to his or her own perceptions, thereby turning a representation into a character.

Some of Giorgione's portraits (or those attributed to him) have been connected with Bembo's *Gli Asolani*. The Venetian author was the veteran of a number of passionate love affairs: first with an unknown woman, then with Maria Savorgnan and finally with Lucrezia Borgia, Duchess of Ferrara, to whom the text was dedicated. It has been suggested that Giorgione painted some of the characters in Bembo's narrative, or, more convincingly, that the subjects of Giorgione's portraits were informed readers of the famous amorous work. In *Portrait of a Young Man and His Servant* (cat. 2), the single central figure seems to exude a need to share his disappointment in love directly with the viewer. We gather this from his gesture, and also from the Seville orange he holds in his hand. The fruit is symbolic of the nature of love, at once bitter and sweet.

The new directions introduced to the art of portraiture by Giorgione spread among a restricted circle of friends and collectors. In addition to Sebastiano and Titian, the position of contemporary witness to this novel style seems to have been reserved for Giovanni Cariani, a painter who may have met Giorgione through the latter's keenest collector and patron, Gabriele Vendramin (1484–1552). We should not forget that Vendramin is supposed to have had his portrait, now lost, painted by Cariani,[6] instigating the contact that was quite probably the source of the artist's development along Giorgionesque lines (see, for example, fig. 13).

1

Portrait of a Young Man ('Giustiniani Portrait'), c. 1497–99

GIORGIONE (GIORGIO DA CASTELFRANCO) CASTELFRANCO VENETO, 1478 – VENICE, 1510

Oil on canvas, 57.5 × 45.5 cm

Gemäldegalerie, Staatliche Museen zu Berlin, inv. 12A

NOTES

1 Perhaps that carried out by Luigi Cavenaghi in 1887.

2 Thomson de Grummond 1975, p. 352.

3 Richter 1960, p. 517.

4 Anderson 1981, ill. 166.

5 Morelli 1892, p. 219.

6 Wickhoff 1909, p. 37; Rosand 1978, p. 66; Joannides 2001, p. 206; and Joannides 2010B, p. 55.

7 Justi 1908, vol. 1, pp. 133–37.

8 Richter 1937, p. 209, no. 7.

9 Cortesi Bosco 2005, pp. 54–57; Cortesi Bosco 2009, p. 113–22.

10 Pope-Hennessy 1966, p. 132.

11 Ballarin 1979, p. 229; Paris 1993 (Alessandro Ballarin), pp. 297–99, no. 16.

The identity of this young man, seen behind a parapet on which he rests his right hand, is unknown. His upper body is set at a slight angle, with his head a little turned and his gaze directed straight at the viewer. His doublet of mauve satin is fastened by ribbons tied in bows; the top one is undone, revealing a white undershirt. The initials 'V V' on the parapet were added during a nineteenth-century restoration.[1] Similar initials appear on the so-called *Goldman Portrait* (cat. 13); they are generally taken to stand for V[ivus] V[ivo] ('The living [made it] for the living), or 'V[irtus] V[incit]' ('Virtue conquers').[2]

The painting's name (*Giustiniani Portrait*) is derived from the earliest documented owners: the Giustiniani family of Padua. In 1884 the German art historian and dealer Jean Paul Richter (1847–1937) acquired the canvas from the family as the work of Sebastiano del Piombo. Correspondence between Richter and his mentor, the connoisseur Giovanni Morelli, reveals that it was in fact the latter who first attributed the painting to Giorgione. In a letter of 25 November 1887, Morelli mentions the name of Giorgione, adding the following rhetorical question: 'To which other master would you attribute it? It appears to me almost too vivid and ingenious for Sebastiano.'[3] A photograph taken in 1887 shows the painting hanging in Richter's house in Florence.[4] It is described by Morelli in this location: 'In it we have one of those rare portraits such as only Giorgione, and occasionally Titian, were capable of producing, highly suggestive, and exercising over the spectator an irresistible fascination.'[5] In 1891 Wilhelm von Bode acquired the painting for the Gemäldegalerie in Berlin.

If we put aside the traditional reference to Sebastiano, adopted by Wickhoff, or the attribution to the young Titian by Rosand and Joannides,[6] the *Giustiniani Portrait* is one of the few paintings modern scholars attribute almost unanimously to Giorgione.

Debate around the presumed date of the portrait has gradually converged towards Giorgione's early career. According to Carl Justi it is Giorgione's earliest portrait,[7] painted in about 1500, still linked in part to the examples of Giovanni Bellini and Antonello da Messina. In Justi's view, the novel element is Giorgione's ability to translate the sitter's thoughts and feelings into painting. Georg Gronau also deemed the painting to be very early, on the basis of the sitter's resemblance to the two male figures portrayed at the centre of the *Trial of Moses* (cat. 16). In 1937 Richter established points of comparison between the present work and the *Judith* in St Petersburg (c. 1500–04) and the *Castelfranco Altarpiece* (fig. 17), which he believed to date from 1504,[8] although we now know that the latter dates from 1500.[9] One point on which scholars appear to agree is the introspective expression of the sitter. In 1966 John Pope-Hennessy saw the *Giustiniani Portrait* as the earliest example of a painting in which the 'motions of the mind' of an individual are laid bare.[10]

More recently, Alessandro Ballarin insisted on a very early date of about 1497.[11] The fact that the painting does not appear to reflect the influence of Leonardo da Vinci suggests a date before 1499, when Leonardo briefly visited Venice. The position of the sitter and the intrusion of his hand into the viewer's space are also to be found in the so-called *Paris* (or *Boy with an Apple*), formerly Knoedler, New York, sometimes attributed to Giorgione.

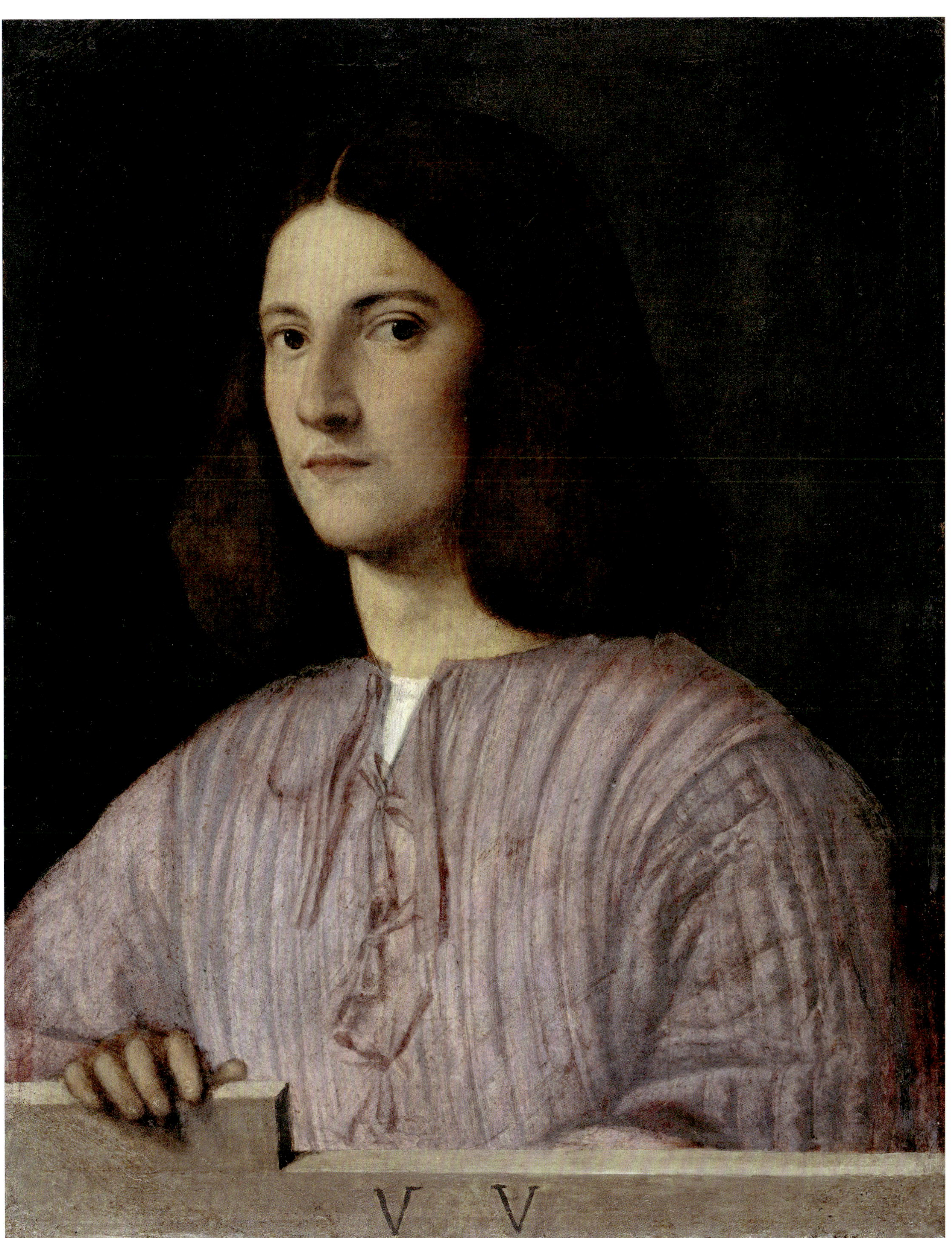
V V

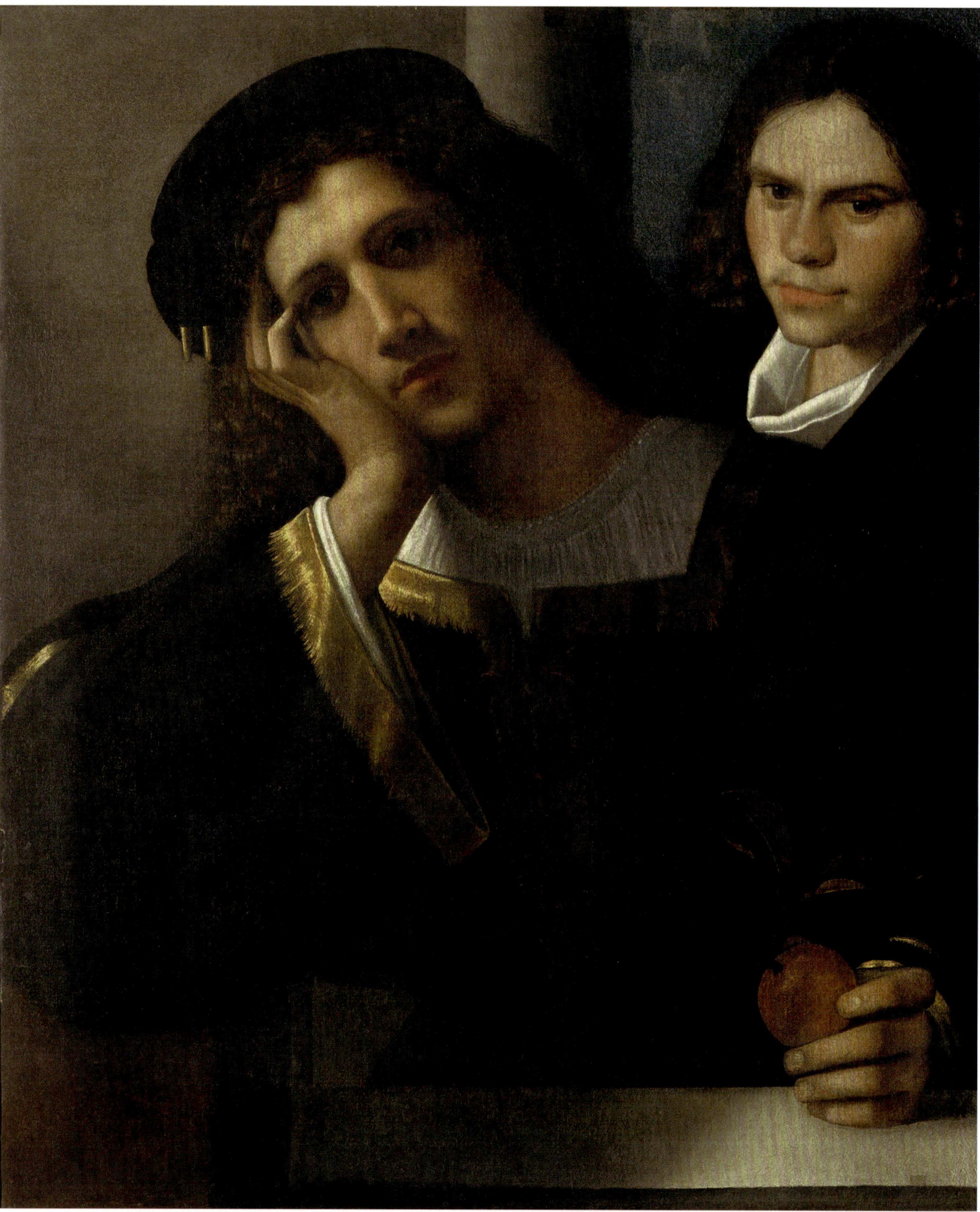

2 Portrait of a Young Man and His Servant

ATTRIBUTED TO GIORGIONE (GIORGIO DA CASTELFRANCO) CASTELFRANCO VENETO, 1478 – VENICE, 1510

Oil on canvas, 80 × 67.5 cm

Museo Nazionale del Palazzo di Venezia, Rome, inv. PV. 902

The bold arrangement of this double portrait has no precedents in Venetian painting of the period. The composition emphasises the main figure, who appears half length, elegantly dressed at a window. His head rests lightly on his hand; one side of his face is bathed in light, while the other remains in the shade.

It has been suggested that the man may be lovelorn. This interpretation, implied by the sitter's melancholy demeanour and his distant expression, is supported by the fruit in his left hand: a Seville orange. In some sixteenth-century sources this type of bitter-tasting orange was associated with the bittersweet nature of love. Just behind the sitter a young man, his face fully illuminated, attempts to meet the viewer's gaze full on. His different attitude serves to emphasise the absorption and inner concentration of the painting's protagonist, who is evidently lost in painful contemplation of the trials of love.

The earliest description of the painting can be found in 1624, in the inventory of the property of Cardinal Carlo Emanuele Pio of Savoy (1585–1641): 'Two Portraits in one frame by Giorgione medium size, one of them holds his hand to his temple and holds a Seville Orange in his other hand black frame touches of gold.'[1] By 1734, when the painting was in the collection of Tommaso Ruffo (1663–1753) at Ferrara, it was described as the work of 'Dosso Dossi of Ferrara'. It entered the Palazzo Venezia with the same attribution in 1919, from the collection of Fabrizio Ruffo of Motta Bagnara (1845–1917).

Emilio Ravaglia's attribution to the Venetian period of Sebastiano del Piombo[2] had the advantage of shifting the painting into the close circle around Giorgione. Only a few years after Ravaglia, Roberto Longhi made direct reference to Giorgione, considering the painting to be a late work, along with the Munich *Daphnis* (cat. 23) and the Budapest *Portrait of a Young Man* (cat. 10).[3] At the time the attribution to Giorgione in the 1624 inventory was not known, and Longhi's suggestion (although reiterated several times) received little attention.[4] The name of Domenico Mancini was preferred,[5] or that of Francesco Torbido,[6] on the grounds of a comparison with the double portrait in the Uffizi (cat. 9) and of the theory put forward by Giovanni Battista Cavalcaselle.[7]

Although the attribution of the painting to Giorgione has not been universally endorsed, it won increasing approval during the second half of the twentieth century. Alternative proposals have not moved far beyond the circle of Giorgione, and no other convincing hypothesis has been proposed.

A fresh outlook was offered by Alessandro Ballarin who interpreted the double portrait as an early work by Giorgione painted in about 1502,[8] and crucial to the explanation of the birth of a 'courtly, neo-Platonist and new style of portraiture'. The painting was thus analysed in the light of the culture promulgated in Pietro Bembo's *Gli Asolani*, written in 1502 but not published until 1505.[9] This line of reasoning has attracted many supporters,[10] but it also has its detractors.[11]

The difficulty of establishing this attribution cannot be denied, even though there seem to be links with the Berlin portrait (cat. 1), generally ascribed to Giorgione's early years. On the other hand, it has no obvious connection with the so-called *Laura* (fig. 1) or the *Terris Portrait* in San Diego (cat. 5).

NOTES

1 Testa 1994, pp. 95, 97–98, no. 37.

2 Ravaglia 1922, p. 475.

3 Longhi 1927C, vol. 1, p. 244, note 15.

4 Longhi 1946, p. 57.

5 Fiocco 1929, pp. 133–34; Berenson 1932, p. 325; Gamba 1949, p. 217.

6 Wilde 1933, p. 97; Robertson 1955, p. 276.

7 Crowe and Cavalcaselle 1871, vol. 1, p. 511; vol. 2, p. 163.

8 Ballarin 1979, pp. 234–35.

9 Ballarin 1983, pp. 498–530; Paris 1993 (Alessandro Ballarin), pp. 316–70, no. 23.

10 Lucco 1995, p. 96; Dal Pozzolo 2009B, pp. 314–19; Padua 2013 (Sarah Ferrari), pp. 153–54. no. 2.12.

11 Perissa Torrini 1993, p. 126, no. 8A; Anderson 1996, pp. 340–41; Washington DC 2006 (David Alan Brown), pp. 255–57, no. 50.

3 Portrait of a Man (Pietro Bembo?), *c.* 1505

GIOVANNI BELLINI VENICE, c. 1430 – 1516

Oil on panel,
43.8 × 35.2 cm

The Royal Collection,
RCIN 405761

NOTES

1 Mazza 2004, pp. 70–71, 260, doc. 20.

2 Vivian 1971, p. 76, no. 285.

3 Shearman 1983, p. 42.

4 Crowe and Cavalcaselle 1871, vol. 1, p. 182.

5 Shearman 1983, p. 42.

6 Logan 1894, p. 8; Berenson 1894, p. 88.

7 Morelli 1890, pp. 264, 269.

8 Law 1898, no. 117.

9 Gronau 1922, pp. 154–55.

10 Gronau 1928, p. 20.

11 Cust 1928, p. 247; Collins Baker 1929, p. 8; Berenson 1932, p. 100.

12 Hendy and Goldscheider 1945, pp. 27, 34.

13 Ridolfi 1648, vol. 1, p. 73.

14 Pincus 2008, pp. 89–119.

15 Brown 2013, pp. 317–25.

16 Padua 2013 (David Alan Brown), p. 325, no. 5.4.

17 Padua 2013 (Davide Gasparotto), pp. 208–09, no. 3.19.

The head and shoulders of this fair-haired and strong-featured man stand out against a landscape. The man is dressed in a black jacket with a white shirt collar showing around his neck. His black cap is pulled over a dense mass of hair. The red marble parapet bears a label with the painter's signature written in elegant cursive script: 'joannes bellinus'. In the background one can make out a fortified tower and a crenellated bridge leading to the city beyond. The mountain range on the horizon is almost as pale as the sky and the clouds above. The sitter looks into the distance.

The earliest reference to the painting was made while it was in the collection of Zaccaria Sagredo (1653–1729), which was then considered one of the most remarkable in Venice.[1] Joseph Smith (*c.* 1682–1770), the city's British Consul, bought the painting – inventoried as 'Portrait by Gio Bellino' – from the Sagredo heirs in 1752.[2] Ten years later it was acquired, together with Smith's entire collection, by King George III of England (1738–1820), listed as 'J Bellino: The Portrait of himself with his name on board'.[3] The panel underwent a process of restoration, probably in the nineteenth century, and the repainting seems to have been so extensive that it became difficult to appreciate the quality of the painting beneath. In 1871 Joseph Archer Crowe and Giovanni Battista Cavalcaselle discounted the suggestion that the portrait is by Bellini, partly because of its state of conservation.[4] Their handwritten notes described it as 'all repainted'.[5]

In 1894 Mary Logan and Bernard Berenson ascribed the painting to Francesco Bissolo, a pupil of Giovanni Bellini.[6] They adhered loyally to the theory propounded by Giovanni Morelli, who maintained that genuine work by Bellini is signed only in Roman capitals, whereas the paintings signed in cursive script are to be ascribed to Bissolo.[7] Herbert Cook believed that the quality of this portrait was too high for it to be by Bissolo and proposed an attribution to Vincenzo Catena (his opinion was reported by Ernest Law in 1898).[8] In 1922 Georg Gronau demonstrated the unreliability of Morelli's theory about Bellini's signatures, providing various indisputable examples.[9] Thus he managed to reinstate the original attribution of the present portrait, which, in his opinion, was painted by Bellini in about 1505.[10] The panel underwent further restoration in 1928 and the repainting was removed. Following the restoration campaign, the attribution to Bellini was confirmed by Lionel Cust, Roberto Longhi, Charles Henry Collins Baker and Bernard Berenson.[11]

Once the portrait's attribution had been settled, the question of the identification of its sitter received further attention. In 1945 Philip Hendy and Ludwig Goldscheider were the first to suggest the name of the Venetian writer and humanist Pietro Bembo (1470–1547).[12] Their suggestion was based on a portrait by Giovanni Bellini depicting 'Pietro Bembo before he became a Cardinal', mentioned by Carlo Ridolfi.[13]

The problem is difficult to resolve, however plausible and attractive these suggestions may be. The sitter's apparent age in the portrait is indeed compatible with that of Pietro Bembo. The idea that the signature might allude to the new typographical characters introduced in Bembo's publications by Aldus Manutius is also very attractive.[14] Finally, it is tempting to imagine that Bellini's portrait might depict Bembo at the time of the publication of *Gli Asolani* (1505, Venice), his most celebrated work; however, there is no positive proof that could allay doubts about the identification of the sitter. David Alan Brown has recently reviewed this complex question in a balanced manner.[15] The undisputed portraits of Bembo are all much later than this one by Bellini. The earliest is to be found on a medallion struck by Valerio Belli in about 1532. A portrait of Bembo painted by Lucas Cranach the Younger has recently come to light in a private collection.[16] Finally, a portrait by Titian has been tentatively identified as a portrait of Bembo.[17] It has to be admitted, however, that none of these portraits resembles the sitter in Bellini's portrait.

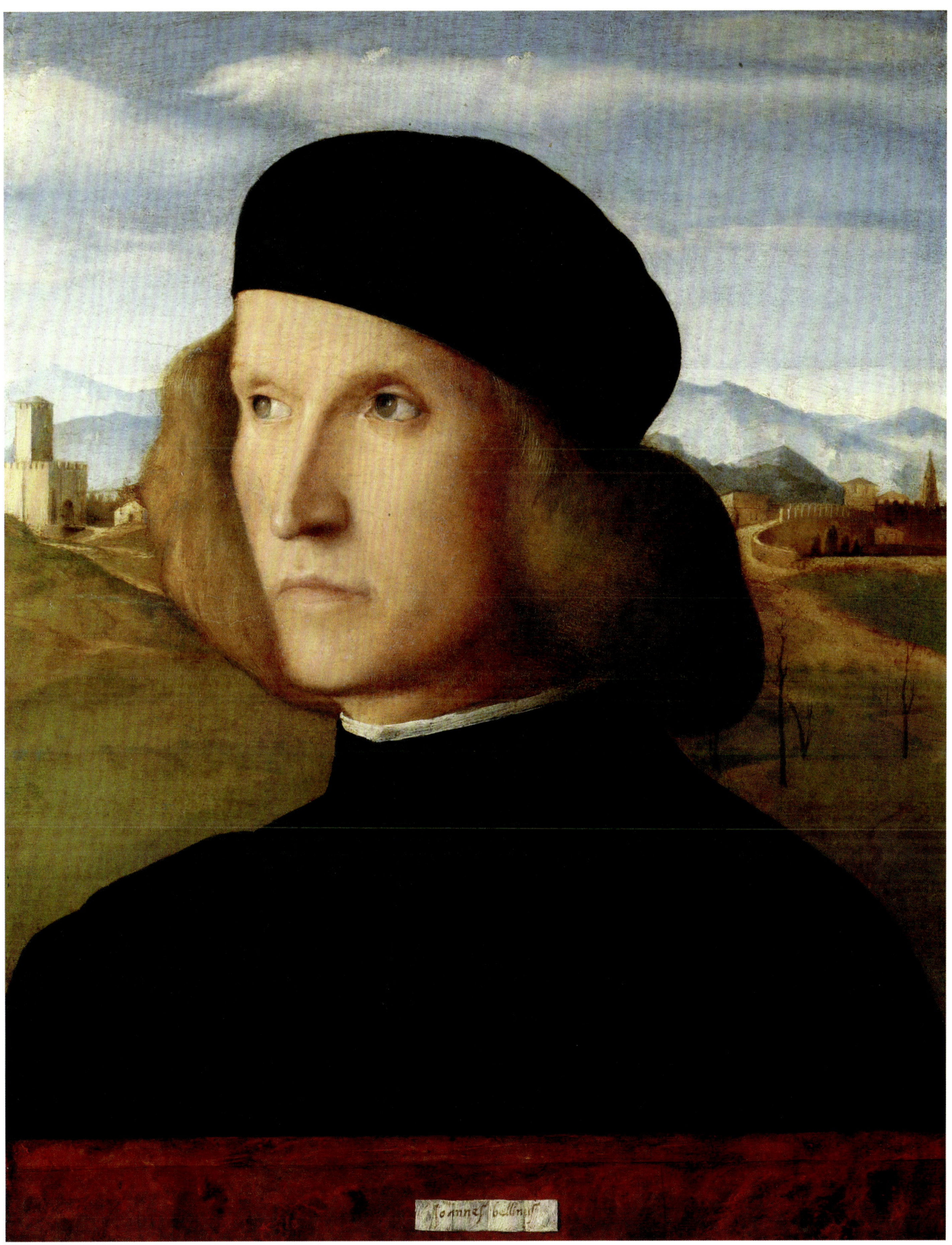
Joannes bellinus

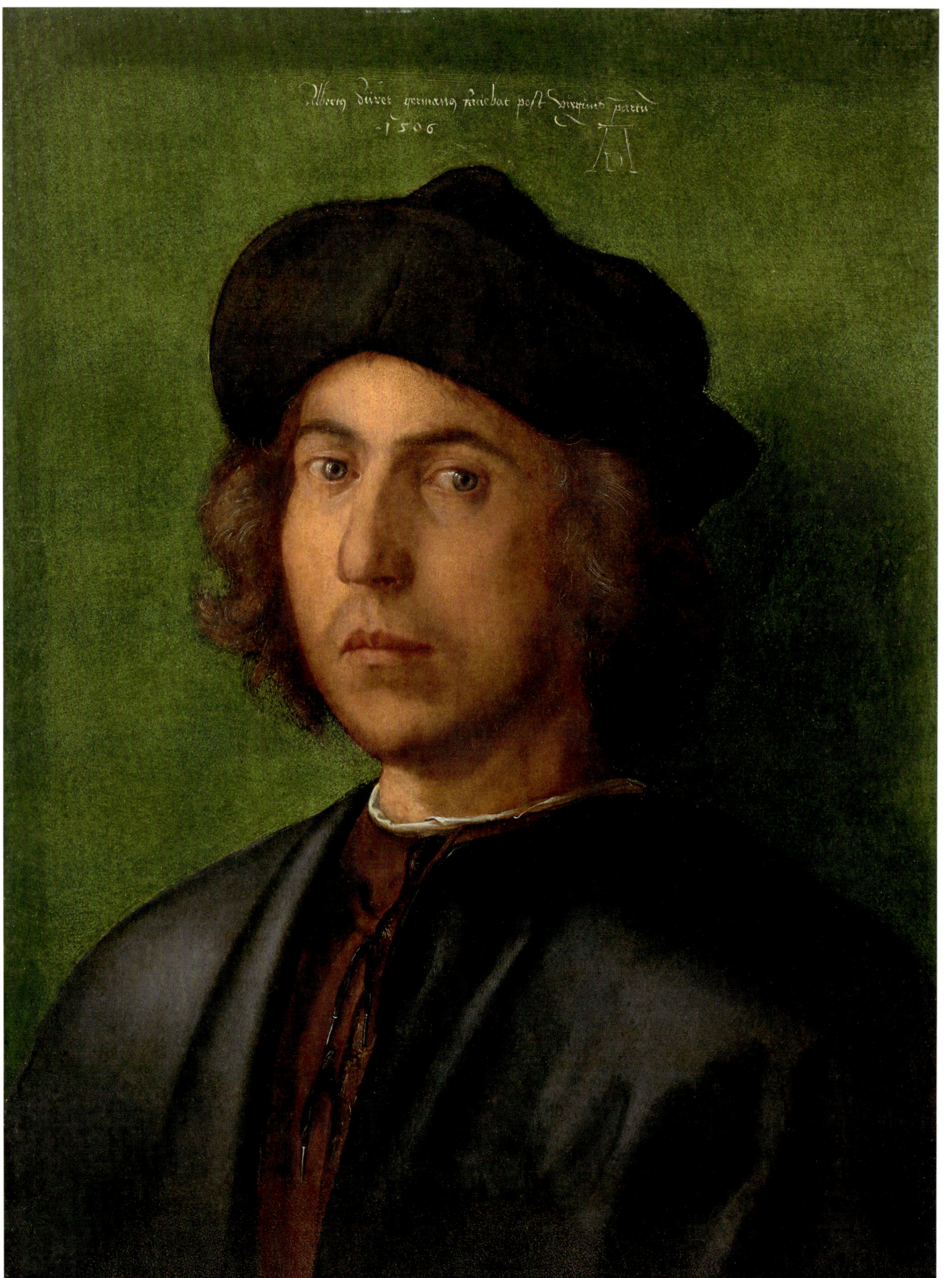

4 Portrait of a Man, 1506

ALBRECHT DÜRER NUREMBERG, 1471–1528

Oil on panel, 46 × 35 cm

Palazzo Rosso, Musei di Strada Nuova, Genoa, inv. PR 47

NOTES

1 Fara 2007, p. 53.

2 Ravà 1920, p. 177.

3 Gronau 1936, p. 292.

4 Ordeni 1666, no. G. 40.

5 Mündler 1855–58, p. 134.

6 Anderson 2000, p. 89.

7 Panofsky 1943, vol. 2, p. 17, no. 78.

8 Garas 1972, pp. 125–33.

9 It is not, for example, given any credence by Anzelewsky (1991, vol. 1, pp. 204–05, no. 96).

10 Bologna 2008 (Piero Boccardo), p. 142, no. 30; Dal Pozzolo 2009B, p. 332.

11 Paris 1993 (Alessandro Ballarin), p. 339.

The sitter's identity is unknown, although various suggestions have been made. The half figure stands out clearly against the green background. Above his head an elegant inscription in cursive script bears the artist's signature and the painting's date: 'albertus dürer germanus faciebat post virginis partum / 1506'. The painter's distinctive monogram appears at the end of the inscription.

The clothing suggests that the painting was made during cold weather, in winter. Despite a drastic nineteenth-century cleaning the remaining touches of pale colour allow us to guess that the sitter's dark-brown leather cloak is lined with fur. Similar white brush strokes are scattered through his brown hair, beneath his heavy black hat. Other details, including the window's reflection in the sitter's right eye, demonstrate Dürer's indisputable skill.

The painting's inscribed date places it during Dürer's second stay in Venice, between the end of 1505 and January 1507. On 23 September 1506 Dürer announced in a letter to his friend Willibald Pirckheimer that he had at last finished his largest public commission in Venice, the altarpiece of the *Feast of the Rose Garlands* (National Gallery, Prague) for San Bartolomeo, the church used by the German community, near the Fondaco dei Tedeschi. In the letter Dürer declares: 'You should know also that I shall be ready to leave in four weeks at the latest, because before I go I have to paint a number of people to whom I have promised a portrait.'[1] A number of the influential Germans who posed for the altarpiece also commissioned portraits, for instance Burkhard of Speyer (cat. 6).

The portrait used to be part of the collection of Gabriele Vendramin (1484–1552), as we learn from the inventory of his property drawn up between 1567 and 1569: 'A small portrait by Alberto Duro his own self-portrait.'[2] It should be borne in mind that the Vendramin collection contained at least two important paintings by Giorgione, *La Tempesta* (fig. 8) and *La Vecchia* (cat. 39). Georg Gronau first suggested the attribution of the present portrait to Dürer in 1936, on the grounds that the Vendramin collection included other works by the artist.[3]

The painting ended up in the hands of the painter and dealer Nicolas Régnier (1591–1667). The catalogue of his sale held in Venice in 1666 included the following item: 'A painting by Alberto Duro, the portrait of a man dressed in black on a green ground, [...] an extremely rare piece, and it is signed with his characteristic AD, about two and a half *quarte* high and one and two-thirds wide.'[4] The painting was acquired by Giuseppe Maria Durazzo (1624–1701) in 1670 and, through his heirs, remained in the Palazzo Rosso until it was presented to the Comune di Genova in 1874.

In the opinion of the German scholar Otto Mündler, who visited the Palazzo Rosso in 1856, the painting had unfortunately lost a great deal of its charm thanks to repeated cleaning and restoration.[5] Equally it is difficult to appreciate Giovanni Morelli's doubts regarding the attribution of the painting, despite the fact that it is signed and dated. Morelli wrote the following comment in a notebook in 1861: 'Portrait of a man, panel, pinkish complexion, attributed to Dürer (?). It bears an inscription and the date.'[6] In 1943 Erwin Panofsky also commented on the painting's state of conservation, considering it 'entirely ruined, but probably genuine'.[7] Klára Garas proffered a new interpretation in 1972, comparing the Genoa painting with Giorgione's *Terris Portrait* (cat. 5) and suggesting that the two depict the same person: Christoph Fugger, a scion of the powerful German family that had commissioned the *Feast of the Rose Garlands*.[8] To endorse this identification, Garas highlighted Fugger's critical role in the commission of the façade of the Fondaco dei Tedeschi from Giorgione and Titian. This hypothesis, appealing as it may be, must remain a matter of speculation.[9]

The present painting has been repeatedly used to illustrate Giorgione's influence on Dürer,[10] and vice versa.[11]

5 Portrait of a Man ('Terris Portrait'), 15[06?]

GIORGIONE (GIORGIO DA CASTELFRANCO) CASTELFRANCO VENETO, 1478 – VENICE, 1510

Oil on panel, 30.2 × 25.7 cm

The San Diego Museum of Art, gift of Anne R. and Amy Putnam, inv. 1941.100

NOTES

1 Vienna 2004 (Jaynie Anderson), pp. 202–05, no. 9.

2 Richter 1937, pp. 95, 124, 226, no. 48, 253–54.

3 Richter 1937, p. 226.

4 Fiocco 1941, pp. 14, 30; 1948, p. 33.

5 Andrews 1947, pp. 50–53.

6 Garas 1972, pp. 125–35.

7 Rome 2007 (Piero Boccardo), p. 124, no. 1.13.

8 Schupbach 1978, pp. 164–65.

9 Della Pergola 1955B, vol. 1, p. 114, no. 203; De Marchi 2004, pp. 95–99.

10 Originally Charles Hope, quoted in Hornig 1987, p. 231; Paris 1993 (Alessandro Ballarin), pp. 337–41, no. 28; Dal Pozzolo 2009B, pp. 333–34.

11 Pignatti 1969, pp. 67–68, 109–10, no. 26; Pallucchini 1978, p. 15; Volpe 1981B, p. 402, no. 9; Pignatti 1990, pp. 69, 71; Perissa Torrini 2004, p. 26.

12 Garas 1972, pp. 125–35; Paris 1993 (Alessandro Ballarin), pp. 337–41, no. 28; Vienna 2004 (Jaynie Anderson), pp. 202–05, no. 9; Dal Pozzolo 2009B, pp. 333–34; Castelfranco Veneto 2009 (Giorgio Fossaluzza), p. 443.

13 Marciari 2015, p. 125.

The painter has chosen to depict the sitter in close proximity. The man's focused expression generates the inescapable sensation that the viewer is being scrutinised; it is difficult to avoid a gaze of a character who examines us so closely.

The head, turned very slightly, is set against a green background. A diagonal shaft of light falls and illuminates the hair spread over the sitter's shoulders. The greying hair suggests that this man, of unknown identity, is about forty years old. No contemporary Venetian portrait carries such emotional intensity. To find anything comparable we need to go back to the last Venetian portrait by Antonello da Messina, dated 1478, now in the Staatliche Museen, Berlin. The San Diego painting belongs to a much later date, as we are informed by the inscription on the back of the panel: '15[06?] / Di man de m° zorzi da castel franco.' The two final digits of the date are illegible, and as we shall see, have been the subject of various interpretations. We do not know if the writing is that of Giorgione himself or – perhaps more likely – of the man who commissioned the portrait, wishing to record its date and author. Investigations reveal that a previous drawing on the panel depicted a pastoral scene with three figures, one of them seen from behind.[1]

Our knowledge of the critical and collecting history of the painting begins at the end of the nineteenth century, when the work was recorded in the collection of David Curror. From there it moved to the collection of Alexander Terris, and it was at this time that it made its first appearance in scholarly texts.[2] Before its publication, the San Diego work was examined by numerous connoisseurs (among them Tancred Borenius, Georg Gronau, Detlev von Hadeln, Wilhelm Suida, Adolfo and Lionello Venturi), all of whom were in agreement over its authenticity.[3] Since that time no one has questioned the attribution of the painting to Giorgione, with the exception of Giuseppe Fiocco who, in the 1940s, queried the authenticity of the inscription, maintaining that the panel could 'at best be attributed to Palma Vecchio'.[4]

The main questions regarding the painting concern its date and the sitter's identity. None of the various proposals for the subject is totally convincing, and it is unlikely that this is the artist's self-portrait, as was supposed when it was given to the San Diego Museum of Art in 1941.[5]

Any resemblance to Albrecht Dürer's *Portrait of a Man* (cat. 4) is too vague for Klara Garas's suggestion, that this is the same sitter, to be convincing.[6] The proposition is even more unlikely since the identification of Christoph Fugger as the sitter for Dürer's portrait has been so decisively challenged (see Piero Boccardo's recapitulation).[7] On the basis of the fairly dubious facial resemblance, the name of Gian Giacomo Bartolotti, known as Il Parma, has been proposed; we know this doctor through Titian's c. 1515 portrait now in the Kunsthistorisches Museum, Vienna.[8] For the time being we cannot be sure of the sitter's identity – as is the case with all Giorgione's portraits. An early copy of the San Diego painting in the Borghese Collection in Rome, identified by Federico Zeri, offers no further insight.[9]

The final two digits of the inscribed date on the back of the panel have been interpreted in the most varied fashion. It has become widely accepted that the third number could not be a '1' because the first '1' has a serif.[10] However, in the script of the time no rules were fixed, and numbers could be given serifs in different ways (or not at all). Some critics read the date as '1510', basing this on their conviction that the San Diego portrait represents the artist's style at its most extreme.[11]

Despite this, the remains of the final numbers appear to have a distinctly rounded shape, which would rule out 1, 2, 4 and 7. Some suggest the date reads '1506', in light of the influence Dürer had on Giorgione during his stay in Venice.[12]

The hypothesis of 1506 seems most likely, in view of the similarities between this portrait and Giorgione's only other dated work, the so-called *Laura* (fig. 1) in the Kunsthistorisches Museum in Vienna (inscribed 1506). Recent technical analysis also suggests the date should be read as 1506.[13]

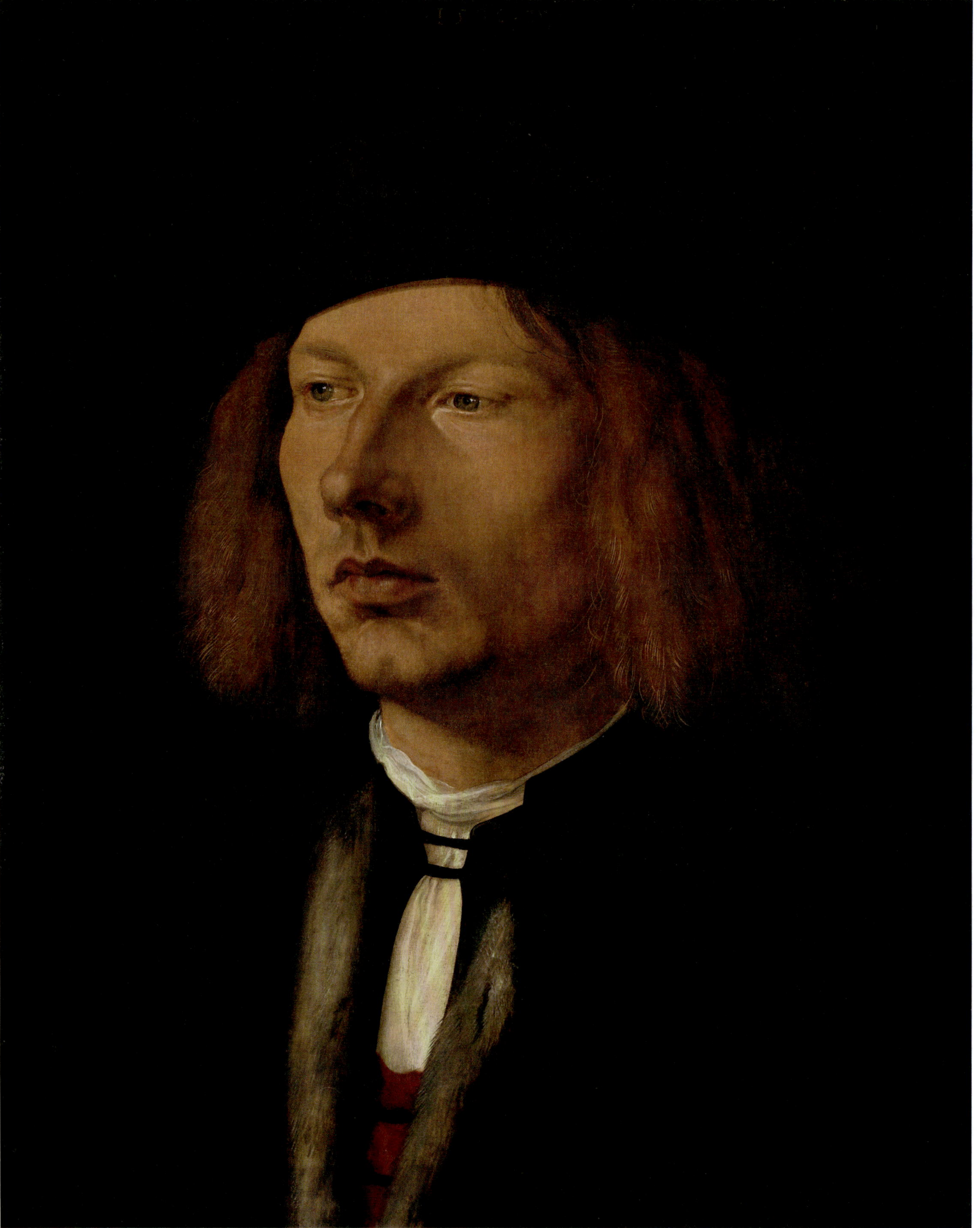

6 Portrait of Burkhard of Speyer, *c.* 1506

ALBRECHT DÜRER NUREMBERG, 1471–1528

Oil on panel,
31.7 × 26 cm

The Royal Collection,
RCIN 404418

NOTES

1 Saffrey 1990, p. 281.

2 Anzelewsky 1991, vol. 1, p. 205.

3 Fara 2007, p. 53.

4 Millar 1960, p. 68.

5 London 2011 (Lucy Whitaker), pp. 74–76, no. 23.

The sitter, dressed entirely in black, is seen in front of a black background. His head is turned slightly, and his bright gaze is directed into the distance. Great attention is given to the man's prominent nose and fleshy mouth as well as his thick reddish hair. Some of the strands are lighter in colour and are rendered, one at a time, with incredible detail. Albrecht Dürer clearly wanted to show off his skill and signed and dated the small panel with great pride in the centre of the upper edge. The sitter can be identified thanks to an anonymous watercolour now in the Schlossmuseum, Weimar, that bears the name 'Burcardus de Burcardis Spirensis 1506'.

Burkhard of Speyer appears in another painting by Dürer, the *Feast of the Rose Garlands* (National Gallery, Prague), the celebrated altarpiece painted for the church of San Bartolomeo in Venice in 1506. Burkhard can be seen kneeling on the left, behind Cardinal Domenico Grimani. The garlands of roses are received in order of precedence: Pope Julius II and the Emperor Maximilian receive theirs, respectively, from the Christ Child and the Virgin, the Cardinal from the hands of Saint Dominic, and Burkhard of Speyer from one of the angels. Not everyone in the painting is honoured with a garland, an indication that Burkhard occupied a particularly prominent position within the German community in Venice. He was in fact the almoner of the church of San Bartolomeo.[1] Nothing further is known about him. It has been suggested that he may have been related to Johannes Burkhard, Master of Ceremonies to Pope Sixtus IV and Bishop of Orte and of Civita Castellana,[2] but there is no evidence to prove this.

The painting dates from Dürer's second stay in Venice, between the end of 1505 and January 1507. On 23 September 1506 Dürer informed his friend Willibald Pirckheimer that he had finished the *Feast of the Rose Garlands*. In the same letter, the artist declared to Pirckheimer: 'You should know also that I shall be ready to leave in four weeks at the latest, because before I go I have to paint a number of people to whom I have promised a portrait.'[3] The present painting must be one of these.

The panel appears in the inventory of the collection of King Charles I of England (1600–1649). Abraham van der Doort (c. 1575/80–1640) describes it in the Chair Room at Whitehall Palace: 'Done by Alberdure. Item a red faced mans picture wth out a – beard in long reddish haire in a black Capp wth a black habbitt lined wth white furr a little of his white shirt and redd wascott seene. in a smale waved ebbone frame painted upon Board.'[4]

While in the collection of Charles I this painting was hung alongside other works by Dürer, including his *Self-portrait* (1498; Museo Nacional del Prado, Madrid) and the *Painter's Father*, now believed to be after Dürer (1497; National Gallery, London).[5]

7 Portrait of an Archer

ATTRIBUTED TO GIORGIONE (GIORGIO DA CASTELFRANCO) CASTELFRANCO VENETO, 1478 – VENICE, 1510

Oil on panel,
53.5 × 41.5 cm

Scottish National Gallery, Edinburgh, bequest of Mary Hamilton Campbell, Baroness Ruthven, 1885, inv. NG690

The artist has here used a device designed to involve the viewer: the young archer looks as if he has been taken by surprise, as though someone behind him has called his name. He appears to have turned rapidly, bringing his hand to his chest to gesture at himself, his half-open mouth suggesting he has said something. The virtuosity of the painter is clear, and is made even more so by the astonishing effect of the reflection of the hand on the breastplate. The leather glove protects the index finger but leaves the others bare. This and the metallic breastplate confirm his identity as an archer, the title under which the painting was sold at Christie's in London on 30 June 1827: 'Giorgione Himself as an Officer of the Archers'.[1] It is presumed that Lord and Lady Ruthven acquired the painting, as their daughter Mary (1789–1885) bequeathed it to the National Galleries of Scotland.[2]

Although it is difficult to reconstruct the painting's early provenance, it was proposed that it belonged to the collection of Jacob van Veerle in Antwerp. Carlo Ridolfi described it as follows in 1648: 'youth with soft hair and armour, in which is reflected his hand of exquisite beauty.'[3] The painting mentioned by Ridolfi was subsequently acquired by the Portuguese jeweller Diego Duarte (1612–1691), and is recognisable as the work ascribed to Giorgione in the inventory of his collection in 1682: 'The likeness of a man half-length wearing a cuirass with a gloved hand on the cuirass.'[4]

The painting's attribution has been controversial. In 1913 Lionello Venturi referred only to a 'Giorgionesque intention',[5] which he considered was not matched by the quality of the work; he therefore proposed the name of Giovanni Cariani. Superficial similarities with *Knight and Groom* (cat. 9) in the Uffizi were sufficient to reassign the Edinburgh painting to the artist Francesco Torbido.[6] Bernard Berenson's tentative attribution in 1936 to the Lombard painter Calisto Piazza is incomprehensible,[7] while a more convincing suggestion was made by George Martin Richter in 1937, who thought the work might be a copy of a lost original by Giorgione.[8]

In 1964 Klara Garas introduced a new approach by investigating the historical references to the panel's early provenance.[9] Garas did not, however, commit herself on the question of authorship. In 1979 Alessandro Ballarin attributed the work with certainty to Giorgione, and dated it to about 1501, placing it within his reconstruction of the artist's *œuvre* of portraits;[10] included in this were *Portrait of Francesco Maria della Rovere* in Vienna (cat. 8), *Portrait of a Young Man and His Servant* at the Palazzo di Venezia (cat. 2), the Uffizi *Knight and Groom* (cat. 9), *Portrait of a Young Man with a Green Book* in San Francisco (cat. 14) and *Portrait of a Young Man* in Budapest (cat. 10), all dated to within the years 1502 and 1503 (Ballarin published the same sequence, with one or two minor chronological differences, again in 1993).[11] The attribution to Giorgione was accepted by Mauro Lucco in 1995 and by Enrico Maria dal Pozzolo in 2009;[12] Peter Humfrey and Sylvia Ferino-Pagden were much more uncertain.[13]

The condition of the painting makes it necessary to consider the question of attribution with caution. As Richter surmised in 1937, this could indeed be an early copy of a lost original.[14] That it has Giorgionesque elements is beyond doubt. One need only compare *Portrait of an Archer* with *Christ Carrying the Cross* in Vienna (cat. 47), Titian's *Il Bravo* (c. 1515; Kunsthistorisches Museum, Vienna) or Palma Vecchio's *Portrait of a Man* (c. 1515–20; Alte Pinakothek, Munich) to feel sure that a prototype by Giorgione must have existed to inspire these works. *Portrait of a Man* was described by Giorgio Vasari in words that could apply to the Edinburgh painting. He draws attention to its innovative qualities: 'in it we see eyes turned in such a way that Lionardo da Vinci or Michelagnolo Buonarroti would not have painted them otherwise. But it is better to keep silent about the grace and gravitas and other attributes to be seen in this portrait, because it is not possible to say as much of its perfection as would exhaust its merits.'[15]

NOTES

1 Edinburgh 2004 (Peter Humfrey), p. 78, no. 12.

2 Brigstocke 1993, p. 194.

3 Ridolfi 1648, vol. 1, p. 106; Garas 1964, pp. 57–58.

4 Garas 1964, p. 57. 'Een Mans konterfeytsel half lijf in't harnas met de hant gehantschoent op't harnas.'

5 Venturi 1913, p. 235.

6 Arslan 1932, p. 6; Viana 1933, p. 33; Morassi 1942, p. 217.

7 Berenson 1936, p. 383.

8 Richter 1937, p. 216, no. 19.

9 Garas 1964, pp. 57–58.

10 Ballarin 1979, p. 235.

11 Ballarin 1993A, pp. 281–94.

12 Lucco 1995, p. 146; Dal Pozzolo 2009B, pp. 311–12.

13 Edinburgh 2004 (Peter Humfrey), p. 78, no. 12; Vienna 2004 (Sylvia Ferino-Pagden), p. 206, no. 10.

14 Richter 1937, p. 216, no. 19.

15 Vasari 1568, vol. 4, pp. 551–52.

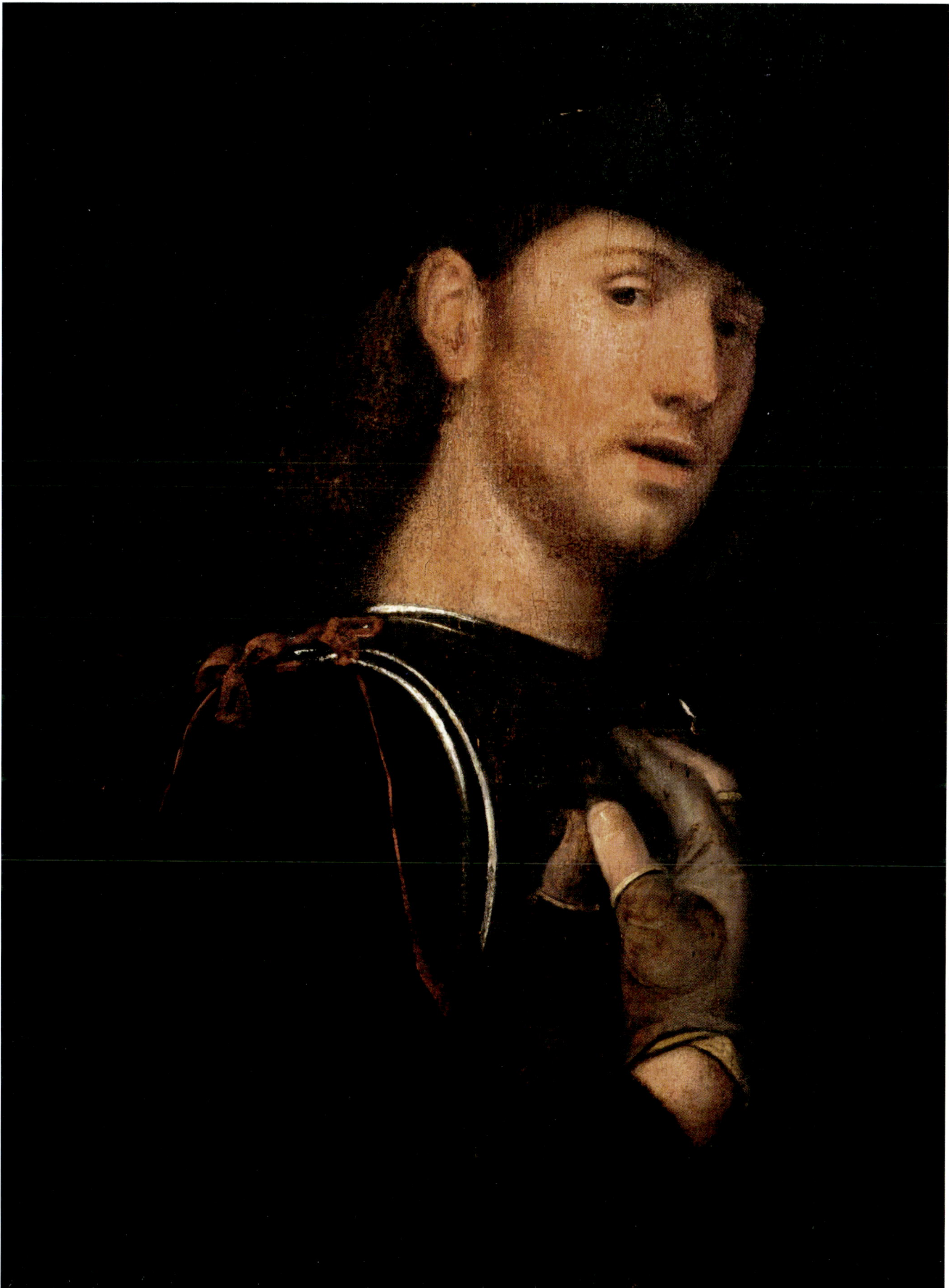

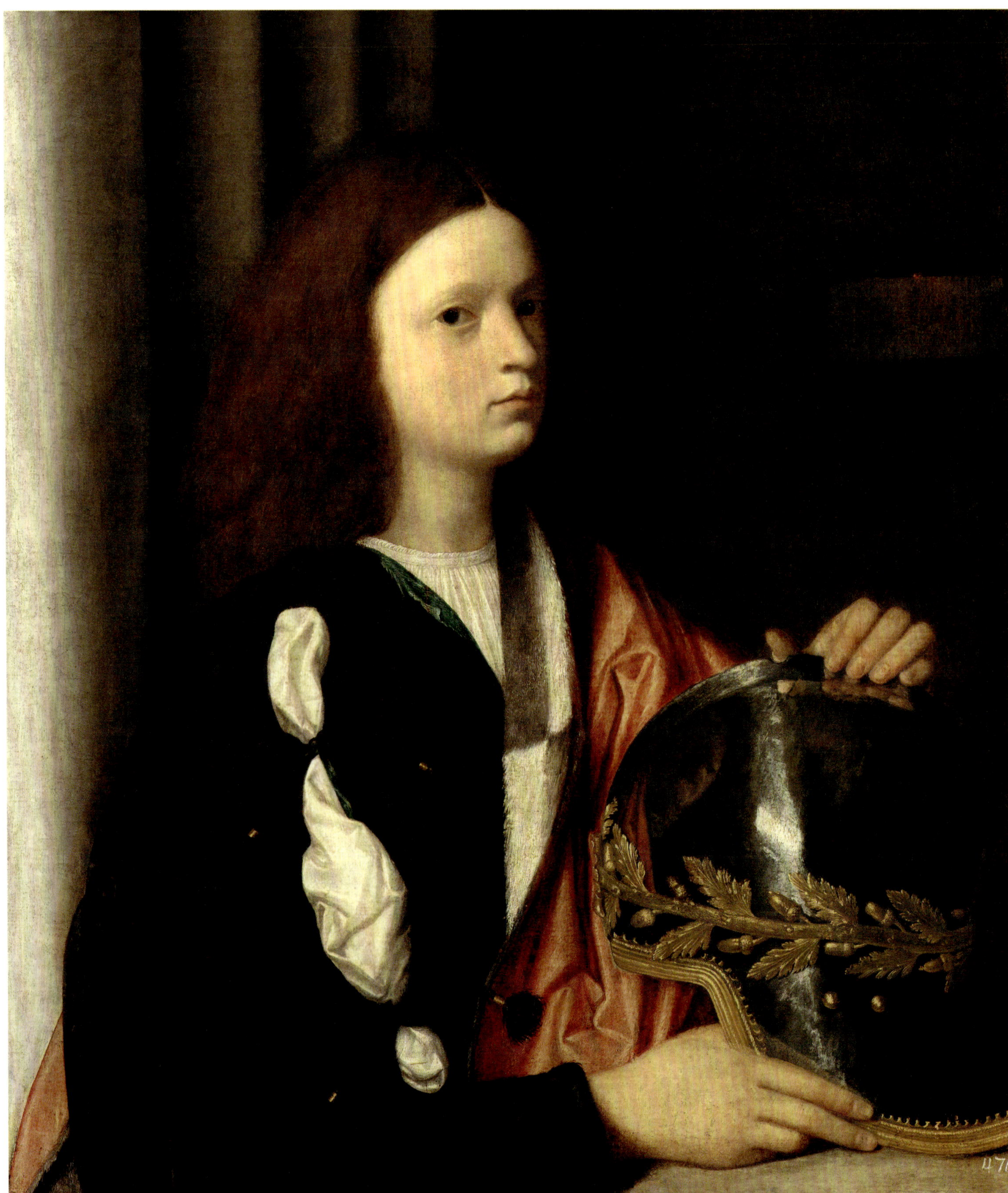

8

Portrait of Francesco Maria della Rovere, *c.* 1505

ATTRIBUTED TO SEBASTIANO DEL PIOMBO (SEBASTIANO LUCIANI) VENICE, *c.* 1485 – ROME, 1547

Oil on panel (transferred to canvas), 73 × 64 cm

Kunsthistorisches Museum, Vienna, Gemäldegalerie, inv. 10

NOTES

1 A branch of oak leaves suggests the connection to the prestigious Della Rovere family (literally, 'of the oak tree').

2 Waterhouse 1952, p. 14, no. 1.

3 Shakeshaft 1986, p. 114.

4 *Theatrum Pictorium* 1660, no. 191.

5 Crowe and Cavalcaselle 1871, vol. 2, p. 488.

6 Morelli 1893, p. 36.

7 Berenson 1932, p. 364.

8 Suida 1935, pp. 83–86.

9 Sangiorgi 1976, p. 356.

10 Longhi 1946, p. 59.

11 Berenson 1957, vol. 1, p. 85.

12 Pallucchini 1944A, p. 153.

13 Baldass and Heinz 1964, p. 53; Pignatti 1969, pp. 38–39, A 63; Freedberg 1971, p. 78, note 44.

14 Dal Pozzolo 2009B, p. 327.

15 Ballarin 1979, pp. 234–35; 1983, ill. 355; Paris 1993 (Alessandro Ballarin), pp. 302–06, no. 18.

16 Padua 2013 (Sarah Ferrari), p. 193.

17 Pallucchini 1981, p. 527.

18 Ferino-Pagden 2008, pp. 3–5; San Francisco 2011 (Francesca Del Torre), pp. 60–69.

19 Anderson 1996, p. 314.

The young sitter is portrayed with a dark wall behind him and, to one side, a receding colonnade. There is a timidity about the boy, who may be finding it difficult to maintain a pose that requires him to hold a ceremonial helmet far larger than his head. Not only is the helmet an expedient means of demonstrating the artist's technical skill in depicting the bright reflections on its metal surface; it also conveys precise information about the young man's lineage.[1]

The painting was mentioned in the collection of Bartolomeo della Nave (*fl.* early seventeenth century) of Venice; from which it was acquired in 1638 by James, Marquess of Hamilton (1606–1649), initially on behalf of King Charles I of England (1600–1649): 'A picture of Guido Ubaldi [d]ella Rovere Duke of Urbino 3 *palmes* square of every side made by Raffael.'[2] There must have been some uncertainty about this attribution, as in Hamilton's next inventory of paintings, compiled before 1643, it was listed as: 'A young man holding a helmet Coregio.'[3] The name of Antonio Allegri, known as Correggio, was repeated even after Leopold Wilhelm of Habsburg (1614–1662) had acquired the Hamilton collection, following the marquess's execution in 1649. The painting was subsequently transferred to Brussels and an engraving of it was included in the *Theatrum Pictorium* (1660), the catalogue illustrating the archduke's collection, this time under the name of 'I. Palma Senior' (Palma Vecchio).[4]

In 1871 Joseph Archer Crowe and Giovanni Battista Cavalcaselle challenged the traditional attribution, remarking that it seemed: 'more like a portrait by Bernardino Licinio than one by Palma'.[5] Giovanni Morelli joined the debate in 1893 proposing the name of Pellegrino da San Daniele.[6] Bernard Berenson wondered in 1932 whether it might be by Michele da Verona.[7] As can be gathered from the sheer variety of names put forward, even the most eminent scholars seem to have been groping in the dark.

Wilhelm Suida, in 1935, was first to suggest the name of Giorgione.[8] Basing this on an observation made by Georg Gronau, Suida identified the painting as that recorded at the Palazzo Ducale in Urbino, listed among the property of the Della Rovere dukes in an inventory of their possessions dating from 1623–24: 'a medium-sized portrait of a member of the noble House of Urbino as a boy with a helmet in his hand and dressed in old-fashioned attire in a walnut frame: around the helmet branches of oak, emblem of Duke Guidobaldo [Della Rovere].'[9]

The Della Rovere family coat of arms consists of a golden oak tree on an azure field. According to Suida the portrait cannot be of Guidobaldo della Rovere (b. 1514) but instead depicts Francesco Maria (b. 1490). Setting aside the identity of the sitter, Suida's attribution to Giorgione has proved controversial.

In 1946 Roberto Longhi ascribed the portrait to an unknown 'painter from mainland Veneto',[10] while Berenson, writing in 1957, believed it to be a copy of a lost original by Giorgione, possibly executed by Michele da Verona.[11] Rodolfo Pallucchini made a more likely proposal in 1944, suggesting the name of Sebastiano del Piombo and a date of about 1506–07. Pallucchini's attribution was based on a comparison with the *sacra conversazione* in the Gallerie dell'Accademia, Venice (cat. 30),[12] and has gained a number of supporters, past[13] and present.[14]

Alessandro Ballarin has defended the attribution of the painting to Giorgione on a number of occasions.[15] He was the first to connect the work's execution with the appointment of Francesco Maria della Rovere, the future Duke of Urbino, to the prefecture of Rome in 1502. Ballarin later altered the painting's presumed date to 1500, on stylistic grounds.

A weakness of this reconstruction is that this painting does not match the familiar effigy of Francesco Maria della Rovere, which appeared on a coin, a *ducato d'oro*.[16] In addition, it has been observed that Giorgione's *œuvre* as a portraitist lacks 'organic coherence' when this painting is included.[17] The attribution of this painting to Giorgione has been rejected because of these well-founded doubts[18] and inconsistencies.[19]

9

Knight and Groom

ATTRIBUTED TO GIORGIONE (GIORGIO DA CASTELFRANCO) CASTELFRANCO VENETO, 1478 – VENICE, 1510

Oil on canvas,
90 × 73 cm

Galleria degli Uffizi, Florence,
inv. 911

NOTES

1 Boccia 1980, pp. 106–07, nos 99–101.

2 Köpl 1889, p. CXXXVI, no. 281.

3 Mechel 1783, p. 5, no. 10.

4 Berti 1980 (Antonio Paolucci), p. 213, no. P396.

5 Crowe and Cavalcaselle 1871, vol. 1, p. 511; vol. 2, p. 163.

6 Morelli 1886, pp. 54–55.

7 Gamba 1905, pp. 39–40.

8 Berenson 1907, p. 192; Venturi 1913, pp. 323–24; Wilde 1933, p. 132; Robertson 1955, p. 276.

9 Wittkower 1927, pp. 191, 215; Venturi 1928, pp. 900–01; Berenson 1932, p. 141; Gamba 1954, pp. 176–77; Hornig 1976, pp. 75–79, 113–16, no. 35; Berenson 1968, vol. 1, p. 83; Berti 1980, p. 213, no. P.

10 Justi 1908, vol. 1, pp. 212–16.

11 Longhi 1946, pp. 57.

12 Ballarin 1979, pp. 232–36; 1983, pp. 503–09, 514–25; in Paris 1993, pp. 313–16, no. 22.

13 Lucco 1990, p. 89.

14 Lucco 1995, p. 95.

15 Dal Pozzolo 2009B, pp. 168, 174.

16 Anderson 1996, p. 326; Pedrocco 1999, p. 202, no. A8; Vienna 2004 (Sylvia Ferino-Pagden), pp. 208–10, no. 11; Tempestini 2010, p. 101.

17 Ballarin 1979, pp. 232–36.

This young knight has a pensive air. His body is set at an angle with his head tilted, his elbow rests on the parapet, and he holds his sword perfectly upright. The height of the large, two-handled sword suggests that he is seated. Behind the knight a groom is seen in profile, looking away from the viewer. He holds a jousting lance in his right hand, decorated with red stripes. Strangely the groom also wears the *barbotto* (bevor), a piece missing from his master's armour. More jousting and battle equipment is laid out on the parapet: spurs, a helmet and an iron mace.

This light armour, made for equestrian use, is Lombard in origin and can be dated to the second decade of the sixteenth century.[1] The same type of helmet appears in other paintings executed in that decade; it is identical to the helmet in Titian's *Jacopo Pesaro Being Presented by Pope Alexander VI to Saint Peter* (cat. 31), and similar designs are to be found in two paintings by Vittore Carpaccio: his *Young Knight in a Landscape* (1510; Museo Thyssen-Bornemisza, Madrid) and the *Martyrdom of the Ten Thousand Christians on Mount Ararat* (1515; Gallerie dell'Accademia, Venice).

The earliest reference to this painting occurs in 1718, when it was included in the inventory of the imperial collections at Prague Castle, as a work by the 'School of Titian': 'Two men in armour with a broadsword.'[2] In 1781 the art dealer and curator Christian von Mechel displayed it as part of the new arrangement at the imperial Gemäldegalerie in the Belvedere Palace in Vienna. Here it was attributed to Giorgione; however the sitter was erroneously identified as Erasmo da Narni (1370–1443) – known as Il Gattamelata – and his son Antonio.[3]

In 1821 the painting was moved to the Galleria degli Uffizi, where it appeared in an inventory of 1825 with a reference to Giorgione.[4] For almost a century after its arrival in Florence, no attention was paid to this illustrious attribution: on the contrary, most nineteenth- and early twentieth-century connoisseurs were convinced that it belonged to the Veronese School, while Joseph Archer Crowe and Giovanni Battista Cavalcaselle attributed it to Francesco Torbido.[5] Giovanni Morelli believed that the painting had nothing to do with either Giorgione or Torbido and instead declared it the work of Michele da Verona, an artist often mistaken for Paolo Morando, called Cavazzola.[6]

During the twentieth century Cavazzola's name became more closely associated with the painting; this followed a firm attribution by Carlo Gamba,[7] who compared the portrait to work by Cavazzola from the second half of the sixteenth century. Many scholars repeated the earlier attribution to Torbido;[8] however, over time, others found the proposal of Cavazzola convincing.[9]

Ludwig Justi believed that the portrait in the Uffizi is a faithful copy of a lost original by Giorgione.[10] Roberto Longhi went further, reclaiming for Giorgione both this painting and another double portrait, that of a young man and his servant in the Palazzo di Venezia (cat. 2).[11] Alessandro Ballarin followed Longhi,[12] as did Mauro Lucco.[13] The latter recognised the similarity of the helmet in Titian's *Jacopo Pesaro Being Presented by Pope Alexander VI to Saint Peter* to the helmet seen here, and surmised that the figure in armour might represent the same bishop, Jacopo Pesaro, portrayed on the eve of his departure for the 1502 naval battle against the Turks.[14] Enrico Maria Dal Pozzolo has also accepted the attribution to Giorgione.[15]

The attribution of the painting has proved particularly difficult given the lack of firm links with works by Giorgione.[16] A date of about 1502, as suggested by Ballarin,[17] should result in clear similarities between the portrait and the saint in armour in the *Castelfranco Altarpiece* (fig. 17), which dates from about 1500, but there are none. It is possible that the painter of the Uffizi portrait is an artist who had contact with Giorgione, yet worked in the decade following his death.

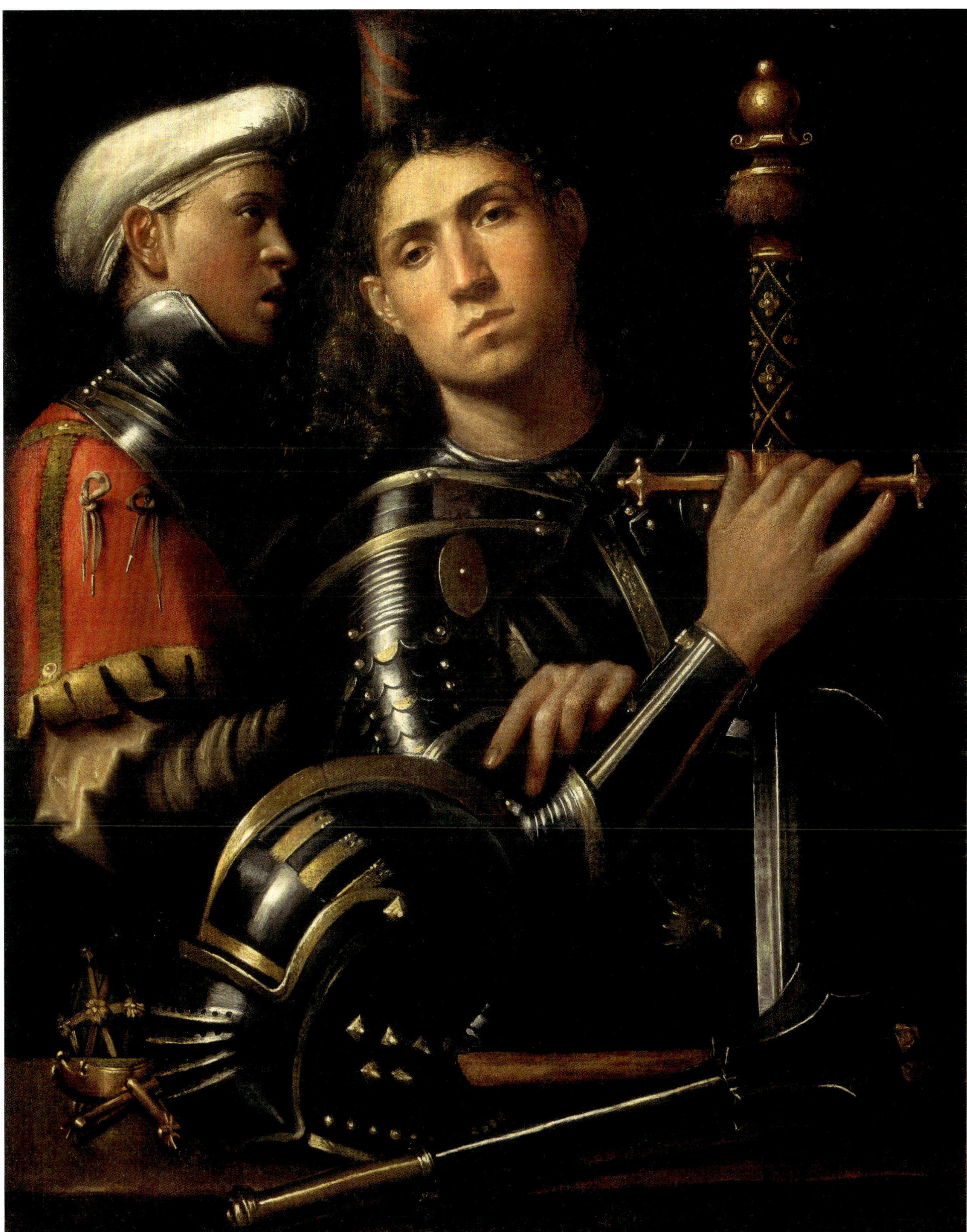

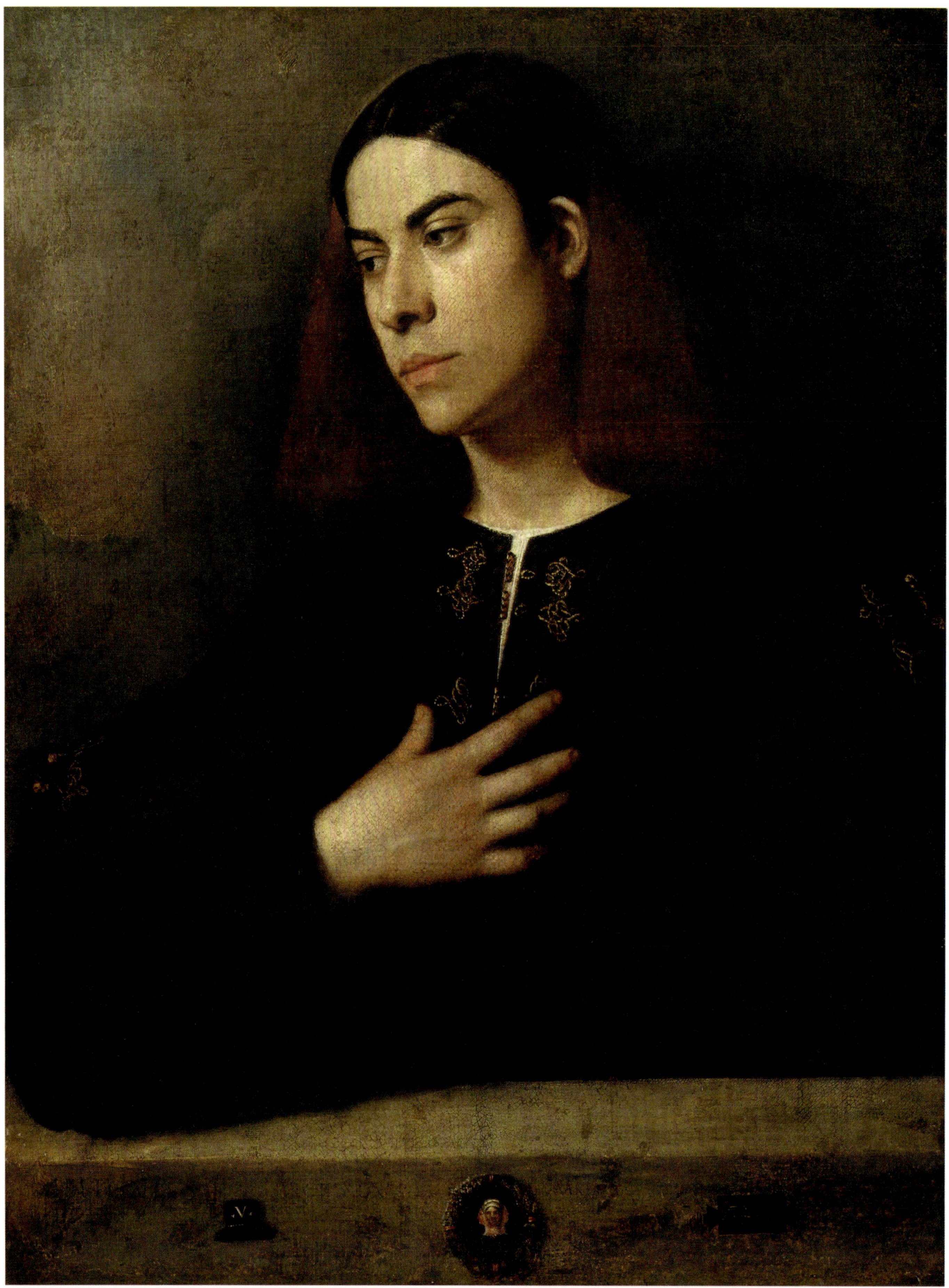

10

Portrait of a Young Man (Antonio Brocardo?)

GIORGIONE (GIORGIO DA CASTELFRANCO) CASTELFRANCO VENETO, 1478 – VENICE, 1510

Oil on canvas, 72.5 × 54 cm

Szépművészeti Múzeum, Budapest, gift of Archbishop János László Pyrker, 1836, inv. 94

The young man wears a black damask coat embellished with gold embroidery and metal fastenings. He is seen from the front, with his head to one side and a downward gaze. An air of concentration and deep thought is emphasised by the hand he holds to his chest. To the left, the background appears to be filled with clouds, and to the right is a wall.

The sitter's elbow rests on a sill, at the centre of which is a three-headed device representing the virtue of Prudence. These heads are surrounded by a garland, tied by a ribbon, whose contents allude to the four seasons: flowers for spring, corn for summer, grapes for autumn and walnuts for winter. At either end of the sill are plaques, one in the shape of a hat bearing the letter 'V', the other with two handles and an inscription, worn away in parts, that identifies the sitter as 'Antonius Bro[kar]dvs Mari[...]'. The final word could be a patronymic: the Venetian poet Antonio Brocardo was the son of Marino Brocardo, a well-known doctor of the time. The exact date of Antonio's birth is not known, but he died young in 1531. He is remembered for a literary controversy with Pietro Bembo (1470–1547).[1] Tradition has it that he died after a violent 'slander' was unleashed against him by the writers and poets who took Bembo's side. Pietro Aretino (1492–1556), in particular, boasted of having penned the sonnet that killed the young poet.[2]

The painting comes from the collection of Archbishop János László Pyrker (1772–1847), who donated some one hundred and fifty paintings to the nascent Magyar Nemzeti Múzeum.[3] From 1820 to 1827 Pyrker had been Patriarch of Venice and it was during this period that he acquired the portrait, then thought to be by Titian's son and collaborator Orazio Vecellio.[4]

Contrary to what is generally believed, Giovanni Morelli did not think that the Budapest portrait should be accredited to Giorgione. He doubted this attribution for a number of reasons, and drew attention to the painting's poor state of conservation: 'Unfortunately this portrait has been harmed by time and by restoration, and it is difficult to recognise within it the style of the master; I therefore prefer not to catalogue this enchanting portrait alongside Giorgione's authentic works of art.'[5] Numerous pentimenti were uncovered by X-ray analysis carried out on the painting in 1960. Some of these are visible to the naked eye, such as the portion of landscape that appears in the background, which, at an earlier stage, had been perfectly framed by a window.[6] A fundamental alteration was also made to the direction of the sitter's gaze; originally, this was directed upwards.

The crucial question is the authenticity – or lack of authenticity – of the inscription, which could provide evidence for the identity of the sitter. Investigation into this has been inconclusive. György Kákay-Szabó explained that restoration had caused 'paint to remain only in the tiniest cracks' in this area.[7] Giorgione could not have painted a portrait of Antonio Brocardo (the poet would have been too young at Giorgione's death in 1510), therefore the main supporters of this attribution consider the inscription to be apocryphal. No reason has yet been established as to why a later hand might have wished to ennoble a personality as controversial as Brocardo by falsifying the inscription.

The scholars favouring the attribution to Giorgione include Roberto Longhi, Giuseppe Fiocco, Rodolfo Pallucchini, Carlo Volpe, John Pope-Hennessy, Alessandro Ballarin, Mauro Lucco, Jaynie Anderson, Enrico Maria Dal Pozzolo and Sarah Ferrari.[8] Supporters of this attribution take widely differing positions on the painting's date, spanning the period between 1503 and 1510.

In 1908 Herbert Cook was the first to relate the Budapest work to the portrait now in San Francisco (cat. 14).[9] This juxtaposition encouraged Antonio Morassi to suggest an attribution to Giovanni Cariani for both portraits.[10] More recently this suggestion has won the approval of Marianne Koos and Sylvia Ferino-Pagden.[11]

Other hypothetical attributions, to Bernardino Licinio or to Vittor Belliniano,[12] are unconvincing.

NOTES

1 Mutini 1972, pp. 383–84.

2 Caterino 2012, p. 2.

3 Gnaccolini 1996, p. 116.

4 Garas 1973, p. 62.

5 Morelli 1886, p. 164.

6 Kákay-Szabó 1960, pp. 320–24.

7 Kákay-Szabó 1960, pp. 323–24.

8 Longhi 1927C, vol. 1, p. 244, note 15; Fiocco 1941, p. 29; Pallucchini 1944B, p. XII; Volpe 1963, unpaginated; Pope-Hennessy 1966; pp. 132, 135–36; Ballarin 1979, p. 237; Ballarin 1983, pp. 510–11; Paris 1993 (Alessandro Ballarin), pp. 324–29, no. 25; Lucco 1995; p. 94; Anderson 1996, p. 307; Dal Pozzolo 2009B, pp. 326–27; Padua 2013 (Sarah Ferrari), pp. 154–56, no. 2.13.

9 Cook 1908, p. 58.

10 Morassi 1942, pp. 102–03.

11 Vienna 2004 (Marianne Koos), pp. 228–31, no. 16; Ferino-Pagden 2008, pp. 2, 9–10.

12 Venturi 1900, pp. 221, 223–25; London 1983 (Francis Richardson), p. 171, no. 37.

11 Portrait of a Young Man, *c.* 1511

ATTRIBUTED TO LORENZO LOTTO VENICE, *c.* 1480 – LORETO, 1556/57

Black, red and white chalk and wash on prepared paper, 33.5 × 29.9 cm

The Samuel Courtauld Trust, The Courtauld Gallery, London, inv. D.1978.PG.90

NOTES

1 Berenson 1901, pp. 241–42.

2 Hadeln 1925, p. 32.

3 Popham 1931, p. 71, no. 257.

4 Tietze and Tietze-Conrat 1944, p. 185, no. 765.

5 Banti (Antonio Boschetto) 1953, p. 69, no. 23.

6 Berenson 1956, p. 102.

7 Seilern 1959, vol. 2, pp. 32–33, no. 90.

8 Pouncey 1965. This is the only study on the subject.

9 Ballarin 1970, p. 49.

10 Rearick 1981, pp. 28–29.

11 Volpe 1981A, pp. 138–39.

12 Farr 1987, p. 128.

13 London 1991 (Helen Braham), p. 104, no. 48.

14 Pordenone 2000 (Vittoria Romani), p. 86; Rearick 2001, p. 86; Agosti 2001, pp. 248–49.

15 Ballarin 2010, vol. 2, pp. 951–55.

No painting is known to correspond to this drawing. The head, tilted slightly forwards, is sketched in with black chalk on paper covered in a green wash. Black is also used for the shoulders, which are more lightly sketched. The rendering of the skin on the recently shaved cheeks is striking, as is the closed mouth touched with red chalk. The tangle of hair on the left is unfinished. Touches of white have been applied to the forehead, the cheekbones and the nose. The sitter's eyes are directed right at the viewer.

Bernard Berenson published the sheet for the first time in 1901, and lavished praise upon it: 'The toss of the head, the vivacity, and all the morphological peculiarities are characteristic of Lotto. The date can be no other than that of the Della Torre Portraits at the National Gallery. This is the one and only drawing by Lotto that merits consideration as draughtsmanship.'[1] The National Gallery's *Physician Giovanni Agostino della Torre and His Son, Niccolò* is signed and dated 1515.

The attribution to Lorenzo Lotto was accepted by Detlev von Hadeln in 1925,[2] by Arthur E. Popham in 1931,[3] and by Hans Tietze and Erica Tietze-Conrat in 1944.[4] Anna Banti's 1953 monograph on Lotto was influenced by the ideas of her husband, Roberto Longhi. That book's entry for the drawing, written by Antonio Boschetto, introduced the idea that it could be earlier than previously suggested, proposing a date towards the end of the first decade of the sixteenth century.[5] In 1956 Berenson considered it still to be 'perhaps Lotto's best drawing,'[6] dating it to between 1530 and 1535. In 1959 Antoine Seilern described the drawing as 'Attributed to Lorenzo Lotto'.[7] He argued that it related to none of the other drawings accepted to be by Lotto. His reaction was also based on the fact that Berenson's 1901 monograph featured a high number of questionable works, including numerous drawings. Seilern chose to date the sheet to about 1508–10, on the basis of comparison with the figures of Saint Sigismund and Saint Vitus in the *Recanati Polyptych* signed by Lotto (1508; Museo Civico, Recanati).

In his 1965 study of Lotto as a draughtsman, Philip Pouncey made no mention of the Courtauld drawing.[8] His omission was criticised in 1970 by Alessandro Ballarin who, like Berenson, considered the sheet to be 'Lotto's finest drawing', dating it to around 1515.[9] In 1981 William R. Rearick agreed with the attribution.[10] That same year Carlo Volpe, following his mentor Roberto Longhi, connected the drawing with Lotto's documented collaboration with Raphael on the *Stanze* at the Vatican Palace, Rome, in 1509.[11] According to Volpe, Raphael's influence would explain the possible stylistic incongruities of the drawing.

In 1987 Dennis Farr summarised the controversial history of the work's attribution, concluding that it was by Lotto, dating from about 1508–10.[12] Helen Braham exhibited the drawing in 1991, leaving the chronology very open (*c.* 1508–20), although she stresses – following a suggestion made by Aileen Ribeiro – that the dress worn by the sitter connects it to the fashion of about 1510.[13]

Vittoria Romani, Rearick and Giovanni Agosti view the work as belonging to the years Lotto spent in Bergamo, from 1513 to 1525.[14]

Recently Alessandro Ballarin completed an in-depth analysis of the drawing's technique, dating it to about 1511. He proposed a complex network of stylistic influences ranging from Raphael to Leonardo (in particular during the latter's second stay in Milan).[15]

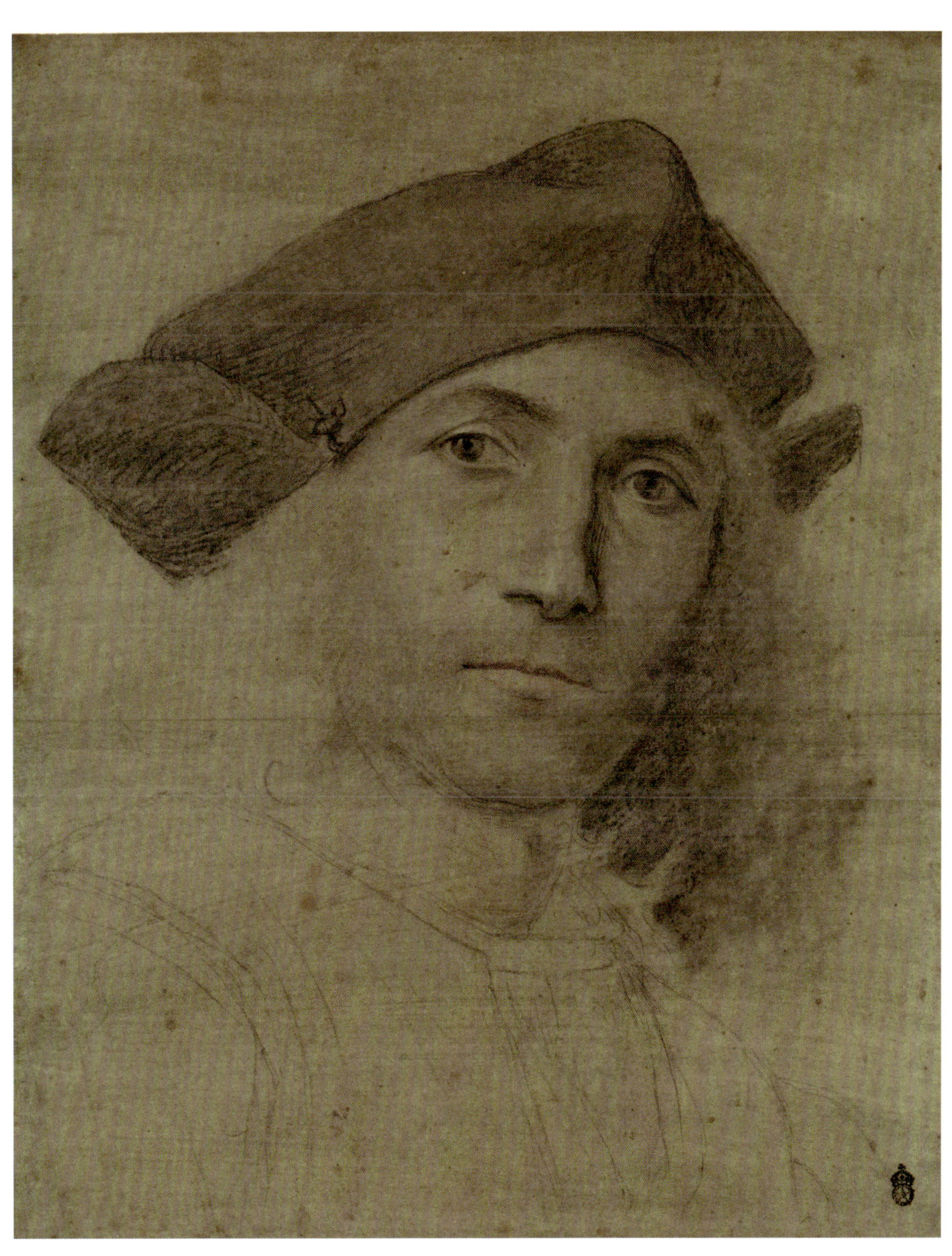

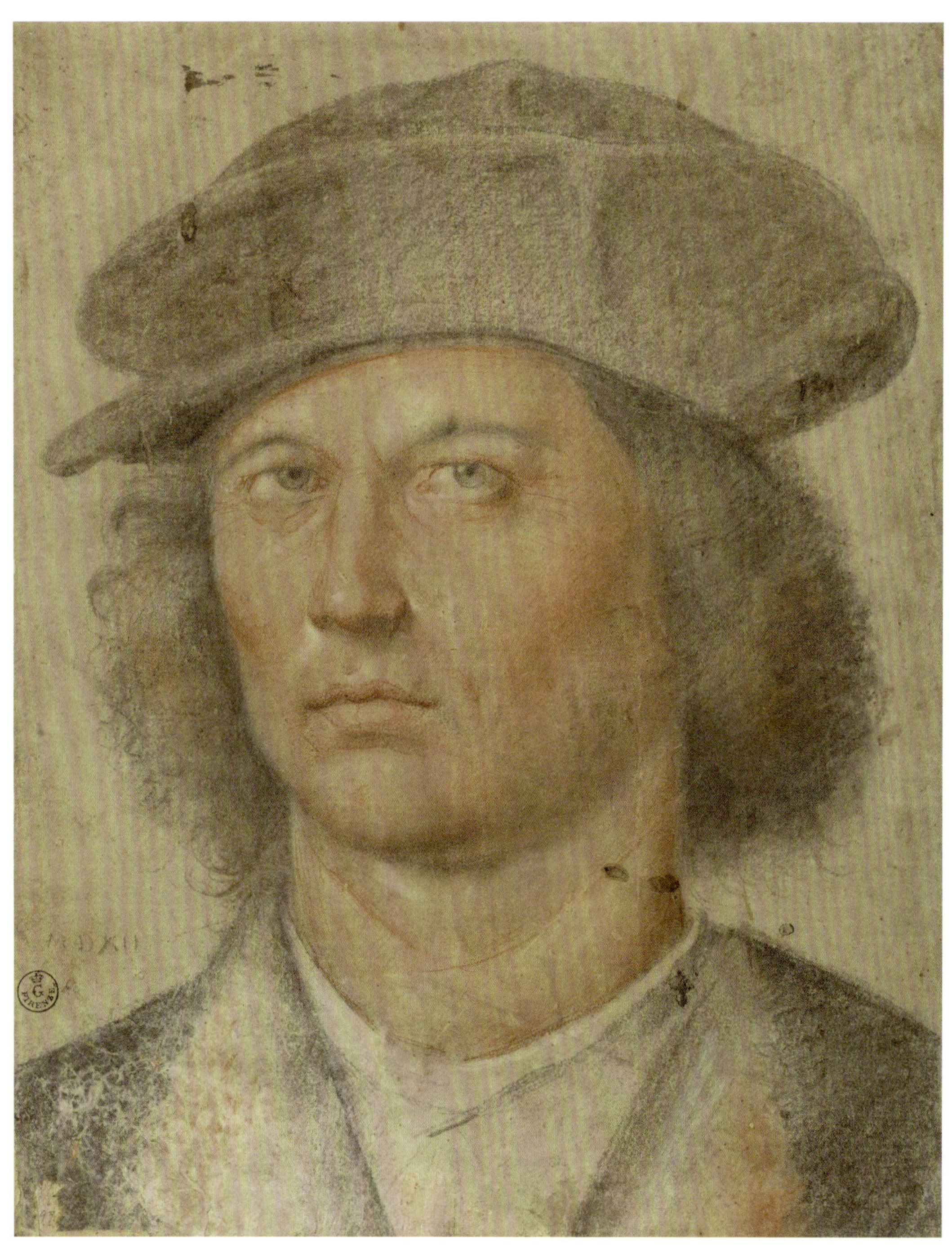

12

Portrait of a Young Man, 1512

ATTRIBUTED TO GIOVANNI CARIANI FUIPIANO AL BREMBO, BERGAMO, c.1485 – VENICE, AFTER 1547

Black, red and white chalk on paper, 36.4 × 28.6 cm

Galleria degli Uffizi, Florence, Gabinetto Disegni e Stampe, inv. 2081 F

NOTES

1 Agosti 2001, pp. 416–19, no. 97.

2 Pelli Bencivenni, before 1793, vol. 2, no. 3.

3 Ricci 1914, unnumbered, no. 7.

4 Paris 1935 (Charles Sterling), p. 228, no. 522; Parker 1956, p. 4; Puerari 1957, p. 193.

5 Agosti 2001, p. 419.

6 Ballarin 2010, vol. 2, pp. 956–58.

In this large study from life, the artist depicts the bust of a young man seen from the front, his head slightly turned but gazing straight at the viewer. His bull-like neck, prominent jaw and sulky, slightly threatening gaze are striking.

The drawing may be a preliminary study for a painting or an independent work in its own right. The head is skilfully depicted using coloured chalks on a yellow-grey ground. The red stands out on the cheeks, the nose and the mouth. This concentration of colour in the flesh tones emphasises the light touches of white chalk that mark the highlights of the face and accentuate the cool, grey-blue eyes.

The sheet is dated at lower left. The verso bears the inscription: 'Giorgione da Castelfranco / L. 3 de Bolognini'.

We owe the reconstruction of the history of this drawing to Giovanni Agosti.[1] It is first mentioned before 1793, in the inventory of Giuseppe Pelli Bencivenni, where it is catalogued as a work by Dosso Dossi;[2] this attribution to the Ferrarese painter persisted until the intervention of Adolfo Venturi (mentioned by Corrado Ricci in 1914) who preferred the Cremonese Boccaccio Boccaccino.[3] This attribution was soon taken up, and accepted by Charles Sterling in 1935, and Karl Parker in 1956; Puerari's 1957 monograph on Boccaccino suggested that the drawing might be a self-portrait of the artist.[4]

In 2001 Agosti attributed the drawing to an 'anonymous Paduan artist, early sixteenth century'. The unidentified artist in question must have hailed from the Venetian mainland, and been familiar with the works made in Venice from 1505 to 1507 by Albrecht Dürer. Agosti mentioned an attribution, proposed by Andrea De Marchi, to the young Giovan Gerolamo Savoldo.[5]

Alessandro Ballarin has subsequently proposed further details about the artist's cultural background. Having discounted the names of Girolamo Romanino, Altobello Melone and Amico Aspertini, he suggested that the author could be

> A Lombard, trained in Venice on the work of Dürer and Giorgione, and who notwithstanding carries an idea of form somewhat reminiscent of Bramante. [...] We do not possess any pastel drawings by Giorgione, but if we want to imagine how he would have used pastels at this crucial phase of his life, we need only look closely at this drawing in the Uffizi.[6]

There are few candidates who fit Ballarin's description. The first would be Sebastiano del Piombo; however, his studies, whether drawn or in paint, never convey such marked, unmediated realism. The second is Giovanni Cariani, who, at the beginning of the second decade of the sixteenth century, displayed familiarity with the work of Giorgione, Dürer and Sebastiano. His work of this period demonstrates an inability to idealise, to embellish the sitter – as can be seen in the *Saint Agatha* in Edinburgh (cat. 46).

If we accept that the date 1512 is in the artist's hand, we can compare the drawing with other works by Cariani from about the same time, such as the *Concert* (c. 1510–15; National Gallery of Art, Washington DC). The level of realism displayed in the three male portraits in that painting – in particular, the heads, the treatment of the flesh tones and the level of expressive intensity – is similar in style to the present drawing.

13

Portrait of a Young Man ('Goldman Portrait')

ATTRIBUTED TO TITIAN (TIZIANO VECELLIO) PIEVE DI CADORE, *c.*1488/90 – VENICE, 1576

Oil on canvas, 76.2 × 63.5 cm

National Gallery of Art, Washington DC, Samuel H. Kress Collection, inv. 1939.1.258

NOTES

1 Thomson de Grummond 1975, p. 352.
2 Paris 1993 (Alessandro Ballarin), p. 376.
3 Doetsch 1895, p. 13, no. 48.
4 Berenson 1897, p. 278.
5 Cook 1906, p. 338.
6 Gronau 1908, p. 505.
7 Venturi 1913, p. 306.
8 Valentiner 1922, no. 5.
9 Offner 1924, p. 264.
10 Paris 1993 (Alessandro Ballarin), pp. 375–79, no. 41.
11 Shapley 1979, p. 215.
12 Burroughs 1938, pp. 116–18.
13 Pignatti 1969, pp. 112–14, no. 31; Pignatti 1979, pp. 116–18, no. 31; Pignatti 1990, p. 73.
14 Morassi 1942, pp. 144, 184.
15 Brown 1990, p. 66, note 17.
16 Anderson 1996, p. 345.

The sitter is depicted in a room, posed behind a parapet. The window behind him looks out onto the Palazzo Ducale in Venice, seen over the Molo, from across the lagoon. The interior is bare, with nothing to distract the attention of the viewer, who can concentrate fully on the singular appearance of the man. The artist has studied the moment and mood with great care. The sitter seems to be looking down, producing a sense of superiority. His upper body is seen in a three-quarter profile with his head turned and his eyes looking in the opposite direction, conveying a sense of movement suddenly interrupted. His tight-lipped mouth, prominent jaw and closed fist resting on a book emphasise the strong-willed, determined nature of this unknown gentleman. In his hand he appears to be gripping a plain white handkerchief. The inscription on the parapet reads 'V V O' (which emerged only after Mario Modestini's restoration of the painting in 1962). The letters have been interpreted as 'V[ivus] V[iv]o', ('The living [made it] for the living'),[1] or as 'V[irtus] V[incit] O[mnia]', ('Virtue conquers all').[2]

The painting appeared for the first time in 1886, at a sale at Christie's in London; it was attributed to Giorgione and entitled *Portrait of a Lawyer*. In the 1895 catalogue of the sale of the collection of the German industrialist Henry Doetsch (1839–1894) the picture was downgraded to the hand of Bernardino Licinio.[3] The first photograph of the painting, reproduced by Bernard Berenson, accompanied an essay in which the scholar attempted to describe the appearance of some of Giorgione's lost works, deducing their appearance from presumed copies. The present portrait appeared in this latter category, and was assumed to be by Licinio or Francesco Beccaruzzi. Berenson suggested that the model for it was by Giorgione, basing his view on a comparison with the so-called *Giustiniani Portrait* (cat. 1): 'We again find the same head, the same brow, the same slightly raised left eyebrow, the same feeling about the mouth.'[4]

After the portrait had been exhibited at the Burlington Fine Arts Club in London in 1905, Herbert Cook supported the attribution to Giorgione,[5] but a few years later it was queried by Georg Gronau.[6] The German scholar compared the sitter to Shylock from Shakespeare's *The Merchant of Venice*; he maintained that it was difficult to associate Giorgione with such a vividly characterised temperament. Leaving aside the 1913 intervention of Lionello Venturi, who ascribed the portrait to Sebastiano del Piombo (along with the *Concert champêtre* in the Louvre, fig. 15, and *Christ and the Adulteress* in Glasgow, cat. 34),[7] the painting was exhibited at the Metropolitan Museum of Art in 1920 under the name of Titian. It then became part of the collection of the New York banker Henry Goldman (1857–1937). A new reading of the painting was offered in 1922 by Wilhelm R. Valentiner, who agreed with the attribution: 'At that moment Titian was just finishing himself as an artist who had taken Giorgione for his model, and having learned everything the other could teach him was asserting not only his independence, but equality.'[8] The attribution to the young Titian and a date of about 1507–10 received considerable support. Endorsed two years later by Richard Offner,[9] they became gradually accepted, including at the exhibition in Paris in 1993.[10] Many scholars agreed with the attribution to Titian;[11] others reintroduced the name of Giorgione, particularly following the X-ray examinations published by Alan Burroughs that revealed several alterations.[12] Some of these were quite significant examples of overpainting: in a first version of the composition, the protagonist's hand was gripping the hilt of a dagger, in the second a scroll and in the third the present handkerchief. This reworking of the canvas opened the way to speculation that the painting was begun by Giorgione and finished by Titian. According to Terisio Pignatti the canvas is a late work by Giorgione.[13] More recently, based on an idea by Antonio Morassi,[14] it has been suggested that the artist should be identified as Giovanni Cariani. David Alan Brown claimed in 1990 that the *Goldman Portrait* 'could be the work of Cariani because of the aggressive psychological demeanour of the man portrayed'.[15] Jaynie Anderson accepted his attribution in 1996.[16] The attribution to Cariani remains difficult to prove because of the absence of any obvious features in common with certified works by the artist. An attribution to Titian seems still to be the most plausible for the present painting, with a date close to that of *Christ and the Adulteress* (cat. 34), about 1511.

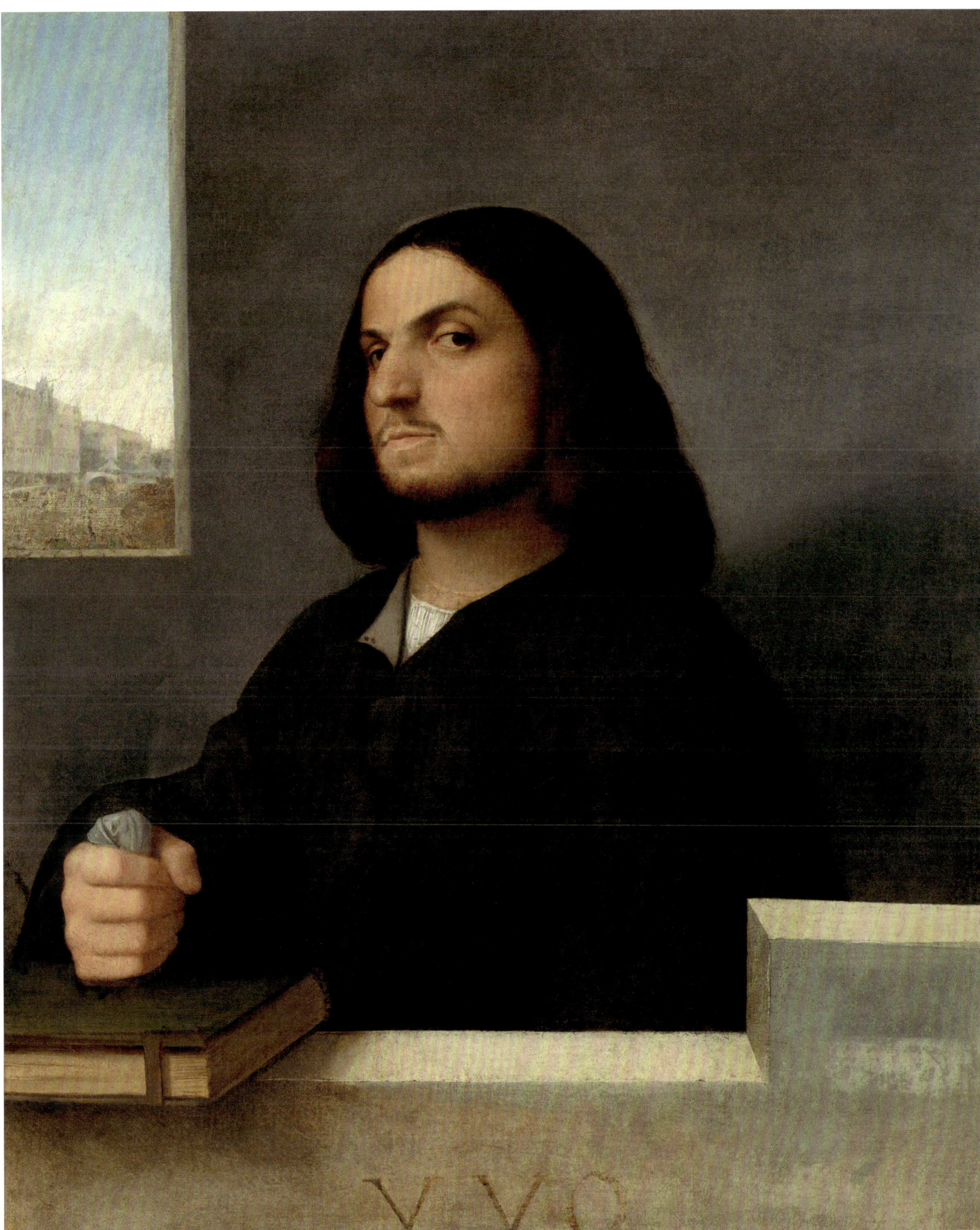
V V O

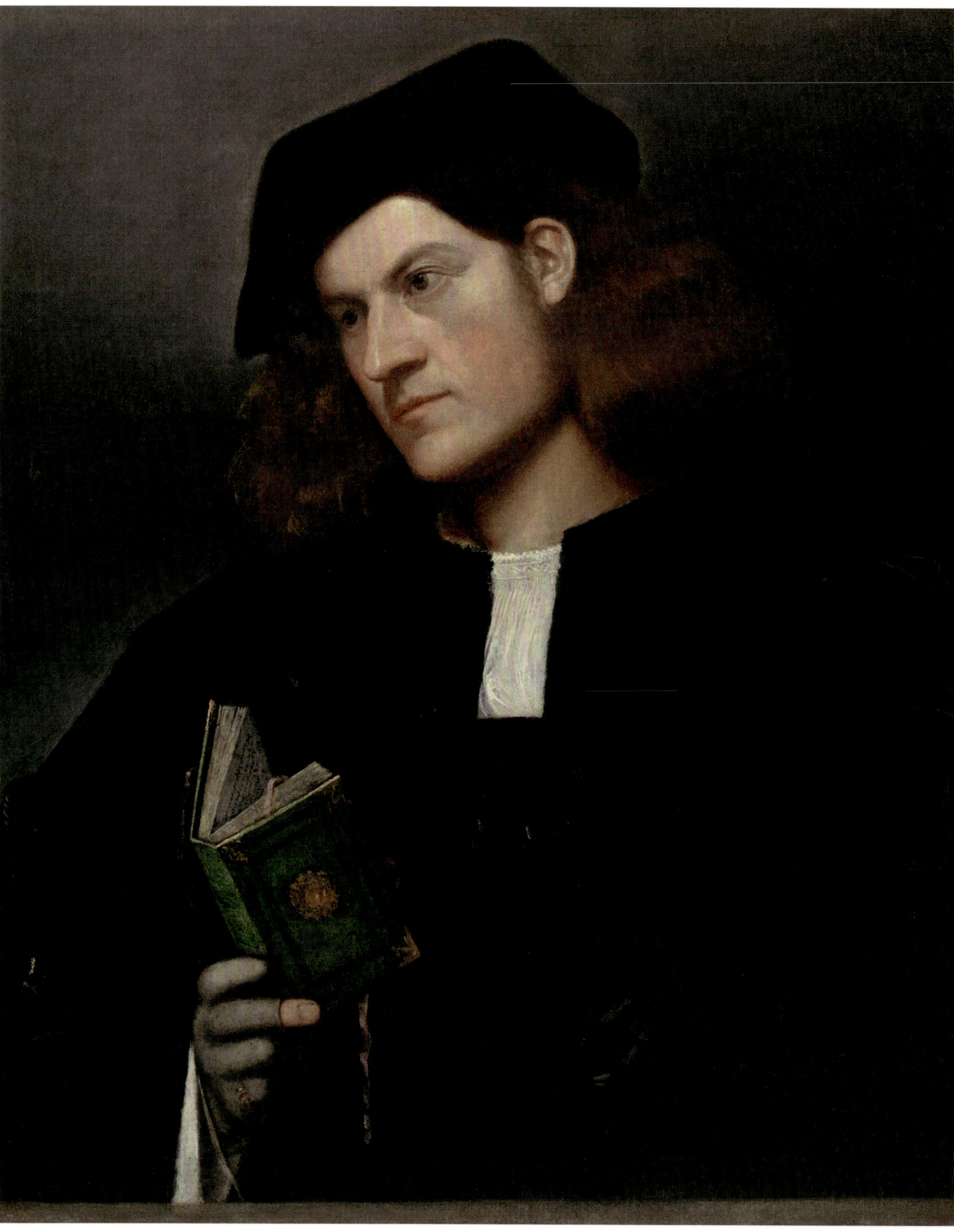

14 Portrait of a Young Man with a Green Book, c. 1510–15

ATTRIBUTED TO GIOVANNI CARIANI FUIPIANO AL BREMBO, BERGAMO, c. 1485 – VENICE, AFTER 1547

Oil on canvas,
68.6 × 55.9 cm

Legion of Honour,
Fine Arts Museums of San Francisco,
gift of the Samuel H.
Kress Foundation,
inv. 61.44.16

NOTES

1 Padua 2013, p. 147.

2 London 1907, p. 3, no. 4.

3 Venturi 1900, pp. 221, 223–25.

4 Holmes 1909, p. 73; Cook 1910, p. 328.

5 Borenius 1913, vol. 3, p. 163, no. 137.

6 Venturi 1928, p. 465.

7 Morassi 1942, pp. 103, 170–71.

8 Berenson 1932, p. 470.

9 Furlan 1988, p. 337, no. A27.

10 Venturi 1913, pp. 258–59; Suida 1955, p. 14.

11 Ballarin 1993A, pp. 293; Paris 1993 (Alessandro Ballarin), pp. 326–29. Macola 2007, pp. 90–96, 176–80, no. 8.

12 Padua 2013 (Alessandro Ballarin), pp. 147–50, no. 2.8.

13 Dal Pozzolo 2009B, p. 327

14 Vienna 2004, (Marianne Koos), pp. 228–31, no. 16; Ferino-Pagden 2008, pp. 2, 9–10.

The sitter, posed against a grey background, is seen half length and with the upper left of his body lit by a shaft of light. The small book he holds open is beautifully bound in green. A fingertip has been cut from his glove to enable him to turn the pages; however his gaze is directed away from the book and the viewer, and beyond the edge of the painting. His head is turned to one side, slightly inclined; he appears to be reflecting on a passage that has caught his imagination.

The earliest mention of this painting was made by Giovanni Battista Cavalcaselle, who saw it in the 'house of Count Rinaldi in Treviso' in the 1860s. Cavalcaselle suggested that the work most probably came from the Onigo family. His concise yet accurate handwritten notes have been reproduced in full by Alessandro Ballarin,[1] but do not appear in *A History of Painting in North Italy*, by Cavalcaselle and Joseph Archer Crowe, published in 1871.

In 1907 Herbert Cook acquired the painting through the good offices of the Florentine antique dealer Elia Volpi. It hung that year in the Winter Exhibition at the Burlington Fine Art Club in London, ascribed to Giorgione. Cook also published the first photograph of the painting, anticipating the complex attributional issues the picture would raise:

> Now we have a fine portrait of the young Giovanni Onigo, attributed to no lesser artist than Giorgione himself. This portrait has recently come into the possession of this writer, and it is published here for the first time. The authorship of Giorgione will certainly be debated: some people say that it is by Cariani, others by Pordenone, others by Licinio and so on. [...] The style bears a certain resemblance to the style of the so-called *Brocardo* in Budapest, considered by many critics to be a genuine work by Giorgione. For the time being, judgement is reserved. The right answer may elude us for a few more years, or might follow the lucky discovery of a relevant document.[2]

So far no such document has come to light and the problem of attribution remains the subject of debate among connoisseurs. As Cook observes, the San Francisco painting has often been discussed in parallel with the *Portrait of a Young Man* in Budapest (cat. 10). In 1900 Adolfo Venturi attributed the latter with certainty to Bernardino Licinio.[3] For this reason the painting in the Cook collection shared the same attribution for some years.[4] A suggestion made by Tancred Borenius in 1913 replaced the name Licinio with that of Giovanni Cariani;[5] this was subsequently supported by Adolfo Venturi in 1928[6] and, with impressive conviction, by Antonio Morassi in 1942.[7]

The name of Pordenone, alluded to by Cook, was proposed seriously for the first time by Bernard Berenson in 1932,[8] and welcomed by a group of disciples whose numbers grew (see the summary by Caterina Furlan, who herself supported this attribution).[9] Scholars proceeding with more caution continue to regard the painting as anonymous and 'from the circle of Giorgione'.[10]

Alessandro Ballarin's attribution to Giorgione and a date of around 1502 was supported by Novella Macola.[11] The picture was looked at alongside the Budapest portrait and *Portrait of a Young Man and His Servant* (cat. 2). Ballarin has recently confirmed his conviction regarding the attribution, backing it up with extraordinarily detailed formal analysis.[12] However, one of the foundations of his argument – the Budapest portrait – cannot be attributed to Giorgione with certainty.

Cariani seems to be the most likely author of the San Francisco painting, and Enrico Maria Dal Pozzolo has recently shown himself in favour of this attribution.[13] The ascription made by some scholars, giving the Budapest portrait to Cariani, should also be emphasised.[14]

The comparison most likely to support attribution of the San Francisco work to Cariani remains the extraordinary *Concert* in the National Gallery of Art, Washington DC (c. 1510–15). Numerous common elements link the two paintings: the monochrome background, the cool flesh tones, the weight and proportion of the heads, the strong naturalism of the sitters. With this in mind, the most realistic date for *Portrait of a Young Man with a Green Book* would be somewhere between 1510 and 1515.

15

Portrait of a Lute Player, *c.* 1515

GIOVANNI CARIANI FUIPIANO AL BREMBO, BERGAMO, *c.* 1485 – VENICE, AFTER 1547

Oil on canvas, 71 × 65 cm

Musée des Beaux-Arts, Strasbourg, inv. 236

A young lute player is shown in half length, seated in a partly wooded landscape. In the distance, a man has stopped abruptly on a path that leads to a farmhouse, perhaps attracted by the music. The lute player is placed very close, at a large scale, creating a sense of unmediated contact with the viewer. His tilted head indicates a state of lyrical abandon produced by the sound of his music. At the same time, his direct gaze implies he might be directing an amorous appeal to the viewer, probably the person for whom the picture had been created. This interpretation is bolstered by the existence of a woodcut created to accompany the *Opere* of Antonio Tebaldeo, which were published in Venice in 1507. The illustration depicts a landscape with a lute player, who is about to be struck by a dart aimed by Cupid.[1]

The sitter's high status is suggested by his rich, fur-lined cloak, and the fact that only the wealthy could afford to own and learn such an instrument.[2]

Wilhelm von Bode – at the time Director of the Berlin Museums – acquired the painting for Strasbourg from an unnamed collection in Venice in 1890. The original attribution to Giovanni Cariani was made by Bode himself and, despite some disagreements at the outset, has been widely accepted.[3] Carlo Loeser considered *Portrait of a Lute Player* the best painting in the Strasbourg collection.[4] Adolfo Venturi also held it in exceptional esteem, although he thought it beyond the abilities of Cariani.[5] György Gombosi also disagreed with the attribution – he ascribed the painting to Palma Vecchio, and dated it to around 1515.[6]

Nevertheless it seems that the Giorgionesque subject of the work might have influenced the way the painting was dated. Pietro Zampetti termed it 'one of the [...] psychologically most penetrating of works in which conformity with the Master of Castelfranco is almost total'.[7] Rodolfo Pallucchini, however, noted: 'its subject and psychology belong to Giorgione, but are expressed in Titianesque terms'.[8]

The diversity of opinions about the artist's identity is reflected in the broad range of dates suggested for the work. Ernst Günter Troche,[9] followed by Pierre Rosenberg,[10] considered the work to date from Cariani's Venetian period, placing it somewhere between 1510 and 1517. More recently Francesco Rossi felt it belonged to his youthful period because of its romantic characteristics.[11]

Alessandro Ballarin, who returned to the question of the painting's date on several occasions, has made the most convincing proposal. He first contrasted the present work with *Portrait of a Man* (fig. 13), which he regarded as 'perhaps after 1520'.[12] He later placed it between the *Concert* in Warsaw (*c.* 1515) and the group of *Albani Portraits* (1519; private collection).[13] Finally he demonstrated how the influence of Sebastiano del Piombo, noticeably present in Cariani's work around 1510, gradually diminishes. Comparison of the *Concert* (*c.* 1510–15; National Gallery of Art, Washington DC) and *Portrait of a Lute Player* in Strasbourg clearly illustrates this thesis, suggesting that the present work is later in date than the painting in Washington DC.[14]

NOTES

1 Gentili 1990, pp. 65–67; 2001, p. 69.

2 Bordeaux 2005 (Christophe Brouard), p. 110, no. 41.

3 Roy and Goldenberg 1996, p. 26, no. 9.

4 Loeser 1896, p. 282.

5 Venturi 1899.

6 Gombosi 1932, p. 174.

7 Zampetti 1968, p. 12.

8 Pallucchini 1983, p. 26.

9 Troche 1934, p. 120, no. 16.

10 Paris 1965 (Pierre Rosenberg), no. 62.

11 Bergamo 2001 (Francesco Rossi), p. 148.

12 Ballarin 1968, p. 244.

13 Ballarin 1970–71, p. 113, no. 87.

14 London 1988 (Alessandro Ballarin), p. 30.

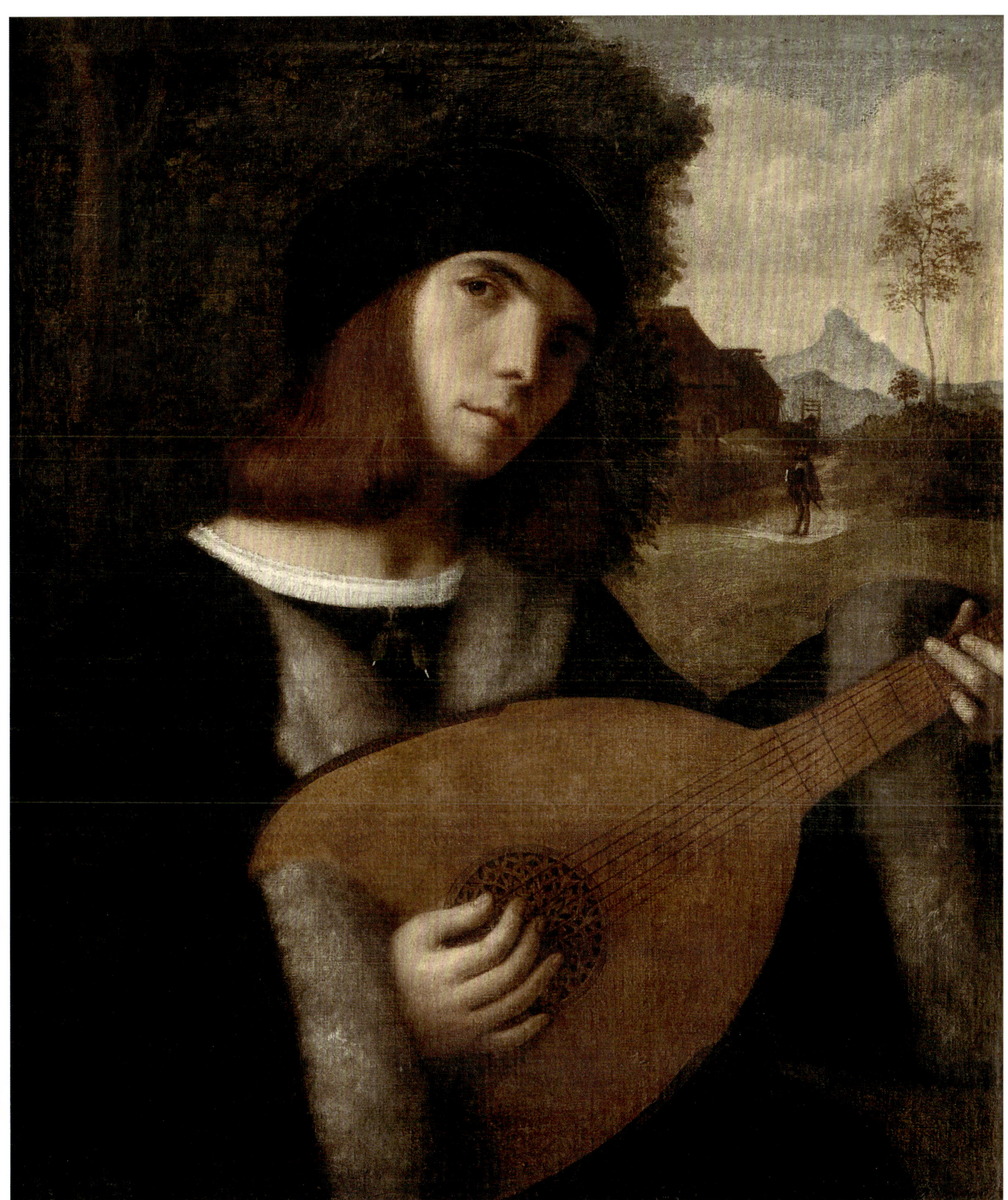

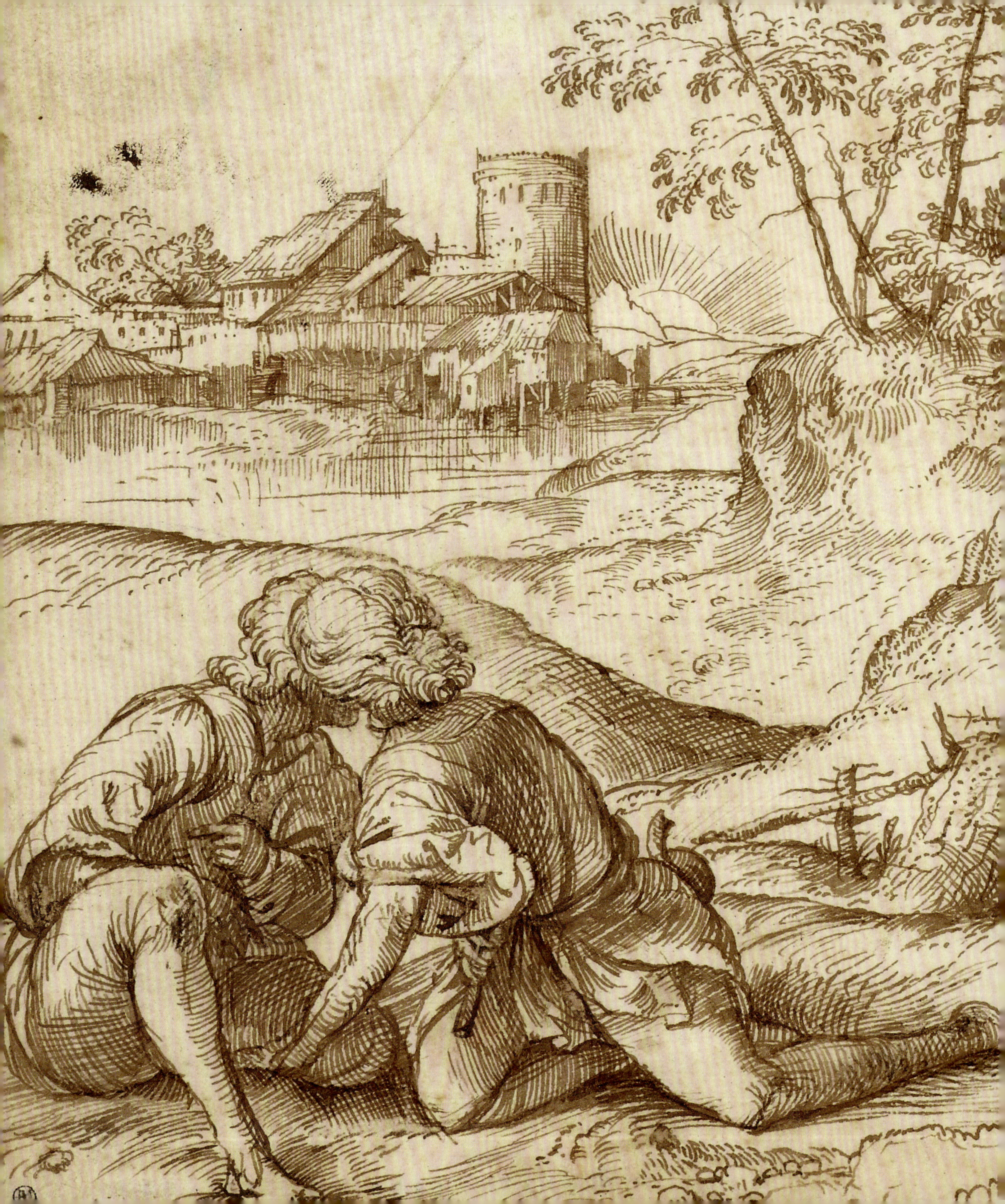

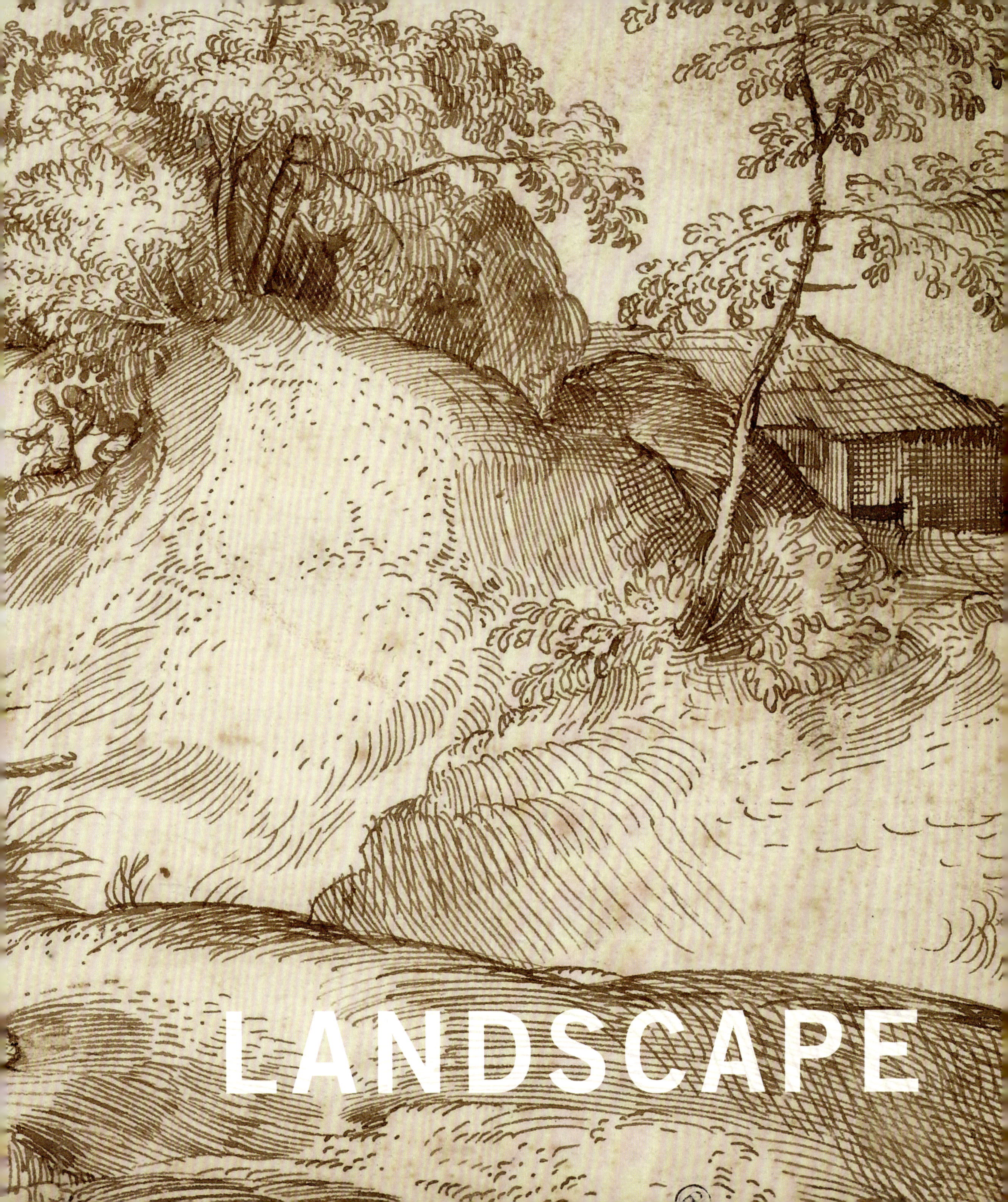
LANDSCAPE

The German artist Albrecht Dürer is considered to be one of the earliest practitioners of modern European landscape painting. The watercolours that document his first trip to Italy, made during the years 1494–95, are the outcome of investigative studies executed by an extraordinary intellect; they bear a resemblance to depictions made in the same sorts of location by Leonardo da Vinci. Dürer's landscapes – observed from a raised viewpoint, or looking up at a foreshortened view of a section of countryside (such as cat. 17) – reveal a process of close observation of the natural world that produces analytical depictions of rocks, trees, flowers and animals. His studies were unknown to contemporary painters. They were simply material for personal study, and were only occasionally intended for reuse in his celebrated engravings.

In the notes of Marcantonio Michiel (1484–1552) we possess valuable evidence of the birth and development of landscape painting as a subject in Venice. Michiel was a Venetian nobleman, humanist and collector, whose work (later published as *Notizia d'opere di disegno*) is considered to be the chief source of information on the art of northern Italy; on the art of Giorgione he is unrivalled.

Ernst Gombrich underlined the fact that Michiel was the first person to use the term 'landscape' advisedly, to describe a painting of such a subject.[1] This is of particular interest to us because he described a number of Giorgione's paintings, including the celebrated *La Tempesta* (fig. 8), bringing them together as 'landscape' paintings. It is also worth considering the possibility that Michiel's 'eye' and his spirit of observation may well have been close to those of Giorgione: there was only a small difference in their ages, and they belonged basically to the same generation.

Worth noting above all is Michiel's especial predilection for landscapes painted in analytical detail, such as those in the Flemish tradition. This can be inferred from his very precise description of such paintings, for example, his first encounter with Antonello da Messina's *Saint Jerome in His Study* (c. 1475; National Gallery, London): 'The buildings face westwards, the landscape is natural, detailed and finished; it is glimpsed through a window, and through the door of the study, fleetingly. The whole painting, its delicacy, colours, drawing, strength, relief, is perfect.'[2] Similar appreciation was shown when Michiel observed the remarkable landscape background to Giovanni Bellini's *Saint Francis in the Desert* (fig. 14): 'The Panel of S. Francis in the desert, in oils, was the work of Zuan Bellino [...] and it has an accompanying landscape which is wonderfully detailed and finished.'[3]

In reporting the presence of 'landscape' in the paintings of Giorgione, Michiel sees it either as one of the distinct but integral parts of a painting, or as the main subject. The *Sleeping Venus* in Dresden (fig. 6) illustrates the first case: 'The painting of the naked Venus sleeping in a landscape with cupids was by the hand of Zorzo da Castelfranco; but the landscape and the cupids were finished by Titian.' Writing along very similar lines, Michiel refers to an unidentified painting (a replica of which he himself owned): 'The nude in pen and ink in a landscape was by Zorzi, and the painted nude that I own is by the same Zorzi.'[4]

The *Birth of Paris*, known through a seventeenth-century copy by David Teniers the Younger (Private collection), belongs to the second type: 'The canvas with the birth of Paris, with the two standing shepherds, was painted by Zorzo da Castelfranco, and was one of his earliest works.' In addition there is *La Tempesta*: 'The small landscape on canvas with the storm, with the gypsy and the soldier, was by the hand of Zorzi da Castelfranco.'[5] Michiel notes the main subject of the Venetian painting as being a landscape – with the storm. The presence of a gypsy and a soldier are noted as afterthoughts. He is not clear as to what the meaning of the painting might be.

To this day, Giorgione's *La Tempesta* has no universally accepted interpretation. Quite the reverse: a seemingly infinite number of suggestions exist. Among the many hypotheses it seems useful to recall John Shearman's theory that the painting might conceal a challenge – across the centuries – to the ancient Greek artist Apelles. According to Pliny, Apelles is said to have given form to the image of a storm, a feat thought impossible to repeat.[6]

Obviously, in Giorgione's day, landscape did not exist as a discrete genre. Nevertheless it was increasingly beginning to be perceived as a presence in artworks.

Fig. 14
GIOVANNI BELLINI
Saint Francis in the Desert, c. 1476–78
Oil and tempera on poplar panel,
124.6 × 142 cm
The Frick Collection, New York,
Henry Clay Frick Bequest

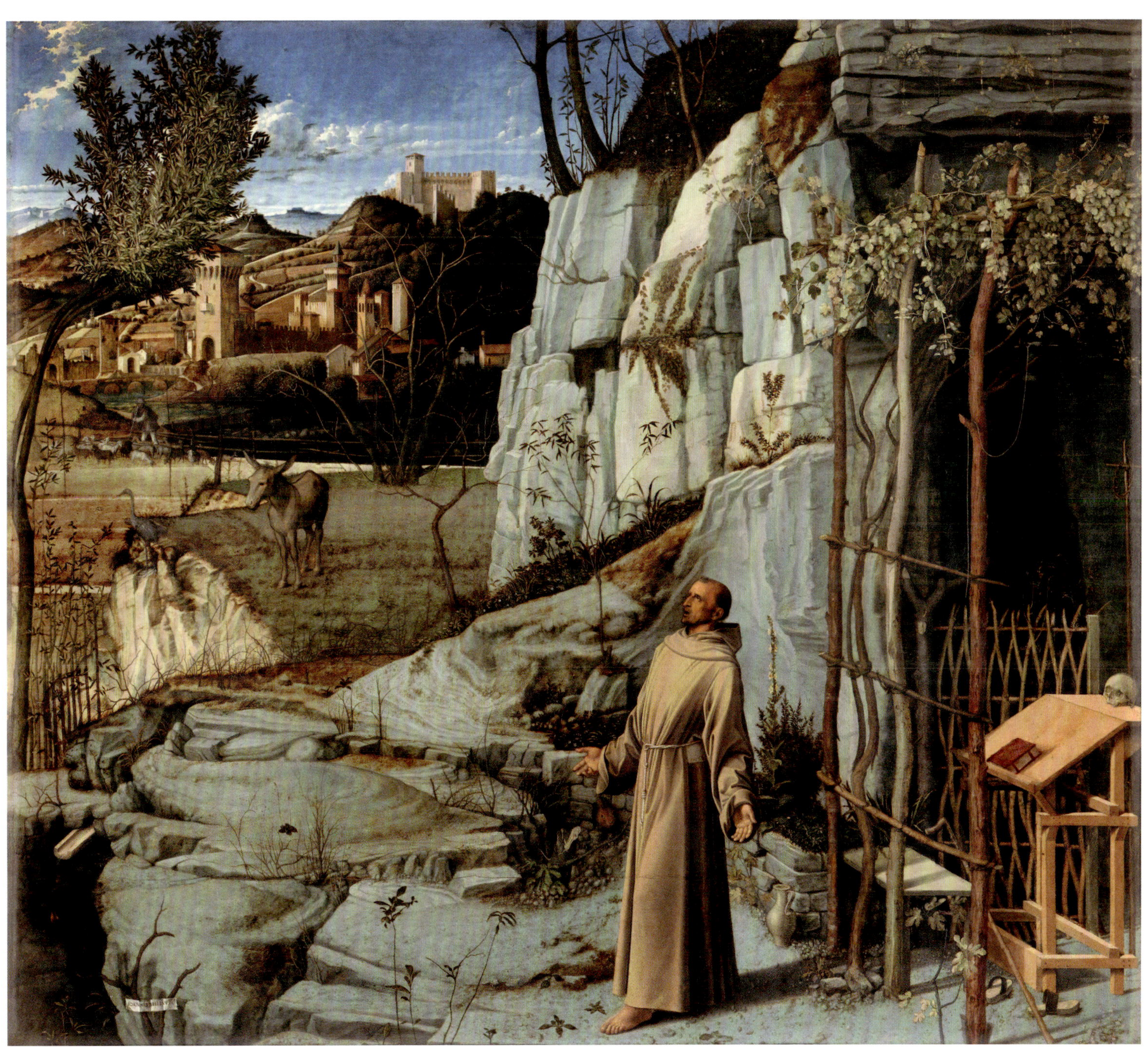

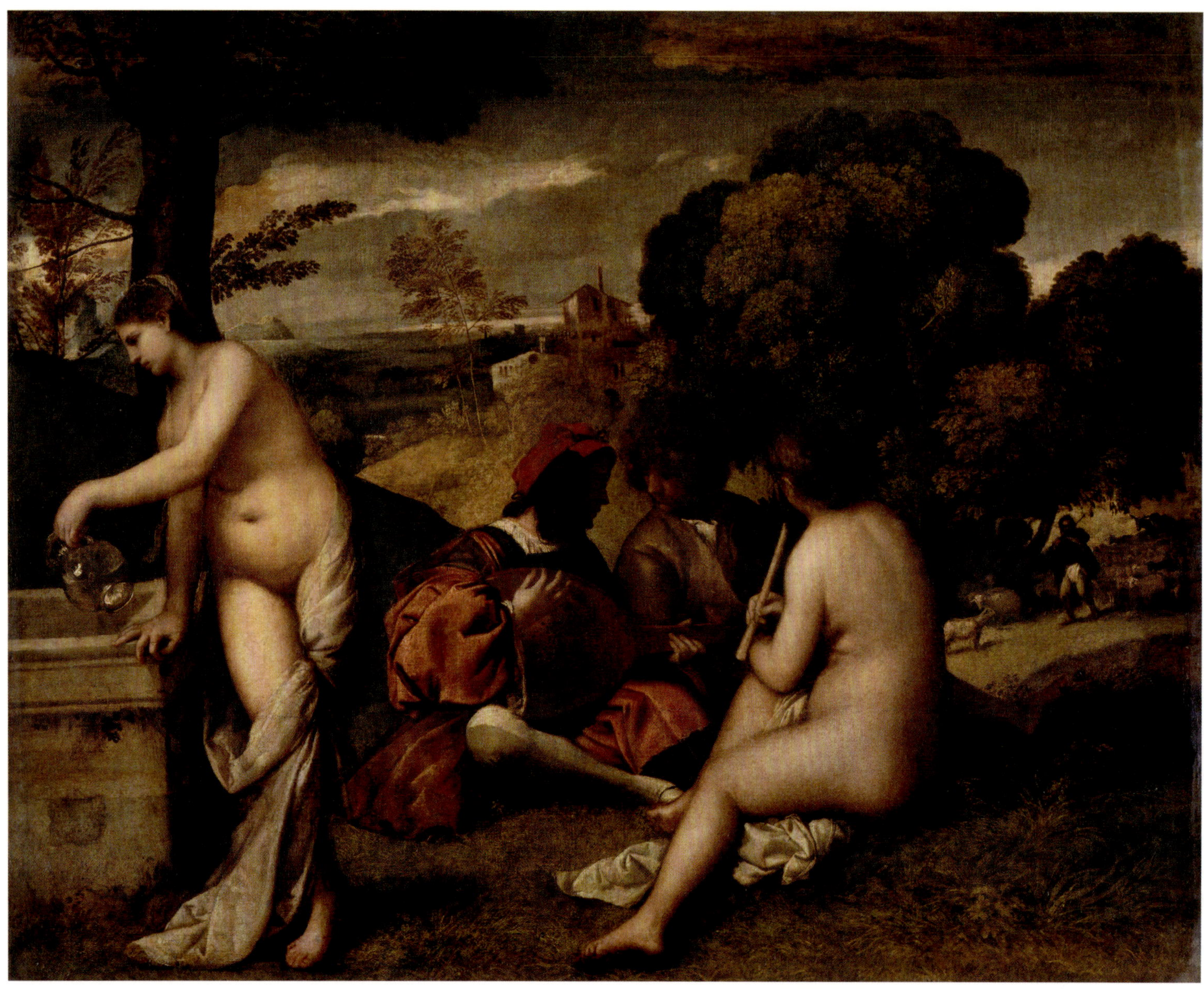

No longer simply the backdrop against which a scene with figures was arranged, it was progressively becoming an important component of the composition. Among the numerous paintings inspired by the models of Giorgione is the newly discovered *Venus and Cupid* by Giovanni Cariani (fig. 16).

This contemporary trend was evident in literature too, most notably in the acclaimed pastoral text *Arcadia* (Venice, 1502), by Jacopo Sannazaro, one of the most successful authors of the day. Virgil had already lauded the pastoral paradise of Arcadia as a place where tranquillity could be enjoyed. Now the topic was brought up to date by the modern sensibilities of a Neapolitan author.

The tragedies of Sophocles were published by Aldus Manutius in Venice in 1502. It has been suggested quite recently that the mysterious subject of Giorgione's *Il Tramonto* (cat. 19) could be found in Sophocles' tragedy of *Philoctetes*.[7] This is an interesting hypothesis. Whatever the truth of the matter, the close ties between the literary and the artistic worlds form a backdrop to works that mark the development of landscape in Venetian painting. The possibility has also been entertained that *Il Tramonto* belonged to Michiel himself.[8]

On the death of Giorgione in 1510, Isabella d'Este, Marchesa of Mantua, was eager to get hold of a painting by the artist that she said depicted a night scene. We have no idea what the painting – regarded as 'unusual', signifying rare and singular – looked like; we can however include it without hesitation in the category of 'landscape'. Perhaps it shared the same subject as a copy taken from an original by Giorgione and described briefly

Fig. 15
TITIAN
Concert champêtre, *c.* 1510
Oil on canvas, 118 × 138 cm
Musée du Louvre, Paris

by Michiel as being in the house of the collector Andrea Odoni: 'Saint Jerome naked sitting in a desert by moonlight.'[9]

The serene, bucolic world depicted by Giorgione was soon to become the essential background for both sacred and profane scenes. The generation born in Giorgione's shadow could not avoid following him – and this led to landscapes that became less subsumed within the narratives figuration entails and instead increasingly self-sufficient, independent subjects in their own right. This can be observed in the work of two of the artists closest to Giorgione, both of whom were intimately involved within his professional sphere: Sebastiano del Piombo and Giulio Campagnola. Sebastiano was engaged in a painting (fig. 7) in which landscape played a central role, as can be gathered (once again) from Michiel: 'The canvas in oils of the three philosophers in a landscape, two standing and one seated contemplating the sun's rays, with rock so admirably imitated, was begun by Zorzi da Castelfranco and finished by Sebastiano Veneziano [Sebastiano del Piombo].'[10]

In works such as cats 20, 21, 23 and 24, both Sebastiano and Campagnola grapple with mythological subjects, painting them in naturalistic landscape backgrounds and with contemporary sensibility. The innovations that entered the tight-knit band of Giorgione's followers spread rapidly, as the early works of Lorenzo Lotto and Girolamo Romanino reveal. Lotto in particular merges the style of Giorgione with that of Dürer (who was in Venice in 1506, the period to which Lotto's admirable painting in the Louvre, cat. 18, is dated).

The figurative legacy of Giulio Campagnola was inherited by his pupil Domenico Campagnola, who promulgated an increasingly schematic and standardised version of landscape. Giorgione's lead was followed by Titian, via the *Concert champêtre* (fig. 15), which may well be the work most emblematic of the future of landscape. It has been remarked that Giorgionesque landscape seems to find an echo in the words of Baldassare Castiglione who, in a passage in his 1528 *The Book of the Courtier*, compared the arts and proclaimed the superiority of the painter over the sculptor. In his opinion, the latter cannot:

> show the colour of auburn hair, nor the glow of armour, nor a dark night or a storm at sea – no thunder or lightning – nor the burning of a city, nor the pink glow of early dawn with those rays of gold and purple; in fact he cannot depict sky, sea, earth, crowds, woods, meadows, gardens, rivers, cities nor houses; all of which the painter can represent.[11]

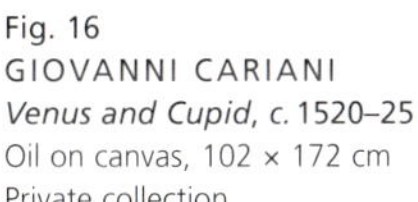

Fig. 16
GIOVANNI CARIANI
Venus and Cupid, *c.* 1520–25
Oil on canvas, 102 × 172 cm
Private collection

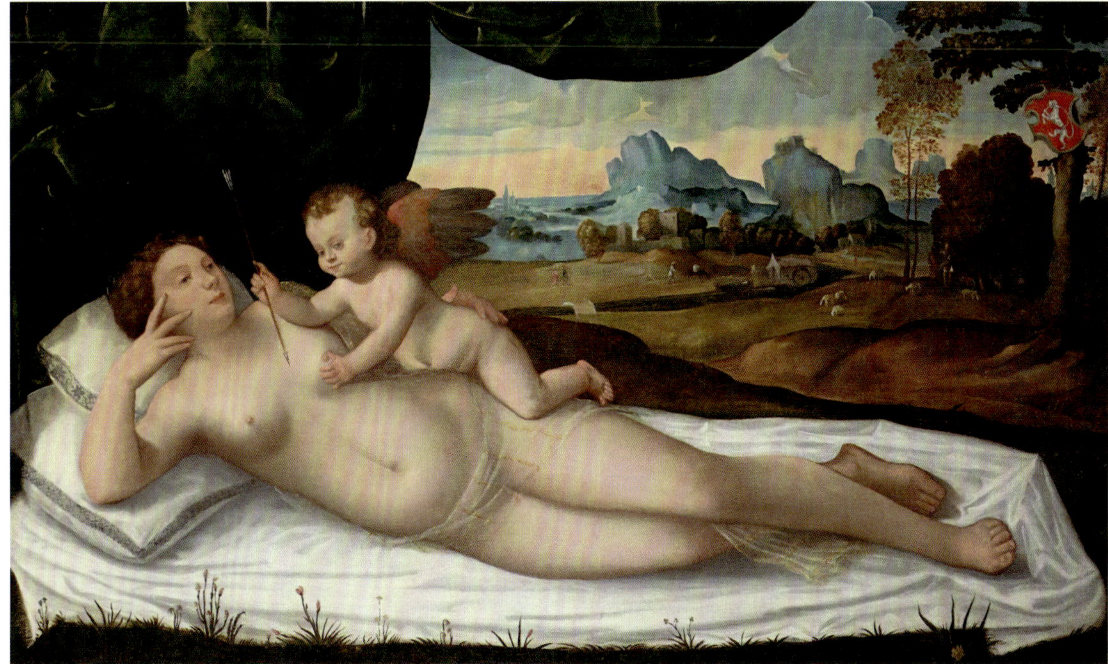

16 Trial of Moses, *c.* 1496–99

GIORGIONE (GIORGIO DA CASTELFRANCO) CASTELFRANCO VENETO, 1478 – VENICE, 1510

Oil on panel,
98 × 72 cm

Galleria degli Uffizi, Florence,
inv. 945

NOTES

1 Haitovsky 1990–91, pp. 28–29.

2 Lauber 2002B, p. 111, no. 54; Borean and Mason 2002, p. 156.

3 Berti 1980 (Antonio Paolucci), p. 295, no. P724.

4 Rosini 1843, p. 158; Crowe and Cavalcaselle 1871, vol. 2, pp. 123–27.

5 Fiocco 1915, pp. 152–55.

6 Fiocco's theory has supporters and detractors: Dal Pozzolo is in favour (2009B, p. 144), while Brown disagrees (2010, p. 96, no. 25).

7 Morassi 1941, p. 155; Venice (Pietro Zampetti) 1955, p. 10, no. 5.

8 Longhi 1946, pp. 17, 57.

9 Longhi 1946, p. 17.

10 Rearick 1979, pp. 189–91.

11 Ballarin 1979, pp. 228–29.

The Pharaoh is seated on a throne on a high plinth, which is covered by a long red carpet. He turns towards the old scribe who had suggested that the infant Moses should be killed for having thrown down the Pharaoh's crown when it was put on his tiny head; this had been interpreted as a sign that Moses would overthrow the ruler in later life. The female figure to the left may be the Pharaoh's daughter Termutis, who had found Moses in a basket in the rushes in the Nile and saved him. A woman dressed in black holds the baby while pages proffer a further test of two shallow bowls, one filled with burning coals, the other with gold coins. Moses is about to put a hot coal in his mouth, which was taken as a sign of his innocence by the Pharaoh, and is thought to have caused the 'slow speech' mentioned in Exodus (IV, 10). The relief on the side of the plinth has been identified as depicting Prometheus creating a human from clay.[1]

The *Trial of Moses* is inspired by the first-century manuscript the *Antiquities of the Jews* by Flavius Josephus. The artist has set the scene in a Veneto landscape, with a cluster of dwellings in the distance. The painting is a pendant to the *Judgement of Solomon*, also in the Uffizi. The antithetical versions of justice dispensed by the King of Egypt and the King of the Israelites are evident.

The earliest reference to this painting dates from 1680, when it was mentioned (with no attribution) in the collection of Salvatore Orsetti in Venice. The collection was inherited by Salvatore from his father Cristoforo, who died in 1664, and is recorded as: 'Small panel painting with a Turk on a throne, a woman is holding out to him a naked baby, and other figures.'[2] The next mention of the painting occurs in 1692, when it is listed among the possessions of the Grand Duchess of Tuscany at Poggio Imperiale (the inventory number 1,763 is inscribed, with a paintbrush, on the back of the panel). The painting was already attributed to Giorgione when it entered the Uffizi in 1795, a verdict confirmed by the inventory of 1825.[3] In 1828 the painting was reproduced in an etching by Carlo Lasinio, still accredited to Giorgione.

This attribution was endorsed by Giovanni Rosini in 1843, followed by Joseph Archer Crowe and Giovanni Battista Cavalcaselle in 1871,[4] who were the first to suggest that it was from his earlier years – an opinion that enjoyed wide critical support. However, it soon became apparent that the painting did not fit easily into Giorgione's catalogue, which was gradually being compiled. For this reason it was suggested that a collaborator might have been involved. The most ingenious name proffered by Giuseppe Fiocco in 1915[5] was that of the painter and engraver Giulio Campagnola. Fiocco's evidence was based on the numerous episodes of *reconzatura* – works begun by Giorgione finished by Sebastiano del Piombo and Titian – observed by Marcantonio Michiel between 1525 and 1543, and referred to in his *Notizia d'opere del disegno*.

Fiocco surmises that the *Trial of Moses* was only 'sketched out' by Giorgione, 'who probably executed the central group and much of the landscape'. Campagnola seemed the ideal candidate for this partnership, considering the well-documented link between the two, as well as the replication of the female figure holding Moses in a fresco attributed to Campagnola, the *Birth of the Virgin* in the Scuola del Carmine in Padua.[6]

The hypothesis proposed in 1941 by Antonio Morassi and Pietro Zampetti, that the collaborator may have been Vincenzo Catena, lacks supporting evidence.[7]

According to Roberto Longhi, the distant figures in the landscape can be given to an unknown Ferrarese painter, either Ercole de' Roberti or Ludovico Mazzolino.[8] This new interpretation, proposed in 1946, led to the suggestion that Giorgione's training may have occurred outside Venice, in Bologna at the time of Lorenzo Costa for example;[9] this would tie the stylistic interpretation of the Uffizi painting to its hypothetical origins.[10] Others consider the painting to be 'entirely by Giorgione's own hand', with a proposed date of about 1496.[11] Stylistic similarity with *Homage to a Poet* in the National Gallery, London, is clear.

Scholars seem to agree on the innovative status of the landscape in the *Trial of Moses*, and its importance to the composition as a whole. It may well be this element – seen as an essential antecedent to *La Tempesta* (fig. 8) and *Il Tramonto* (cat. 19) – that has established such certainty when it comes to the presence of Giorgione's own hand in the painting.

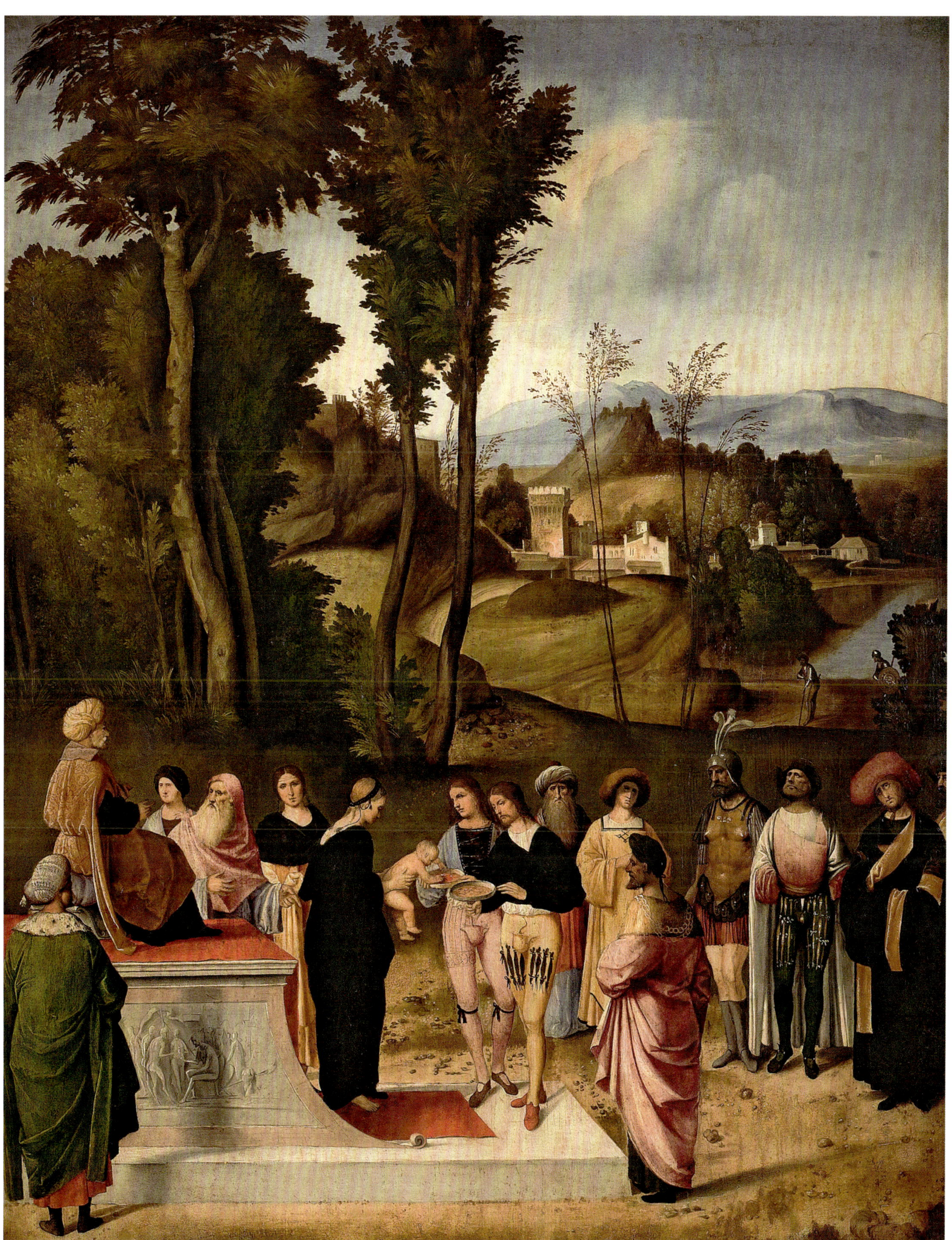

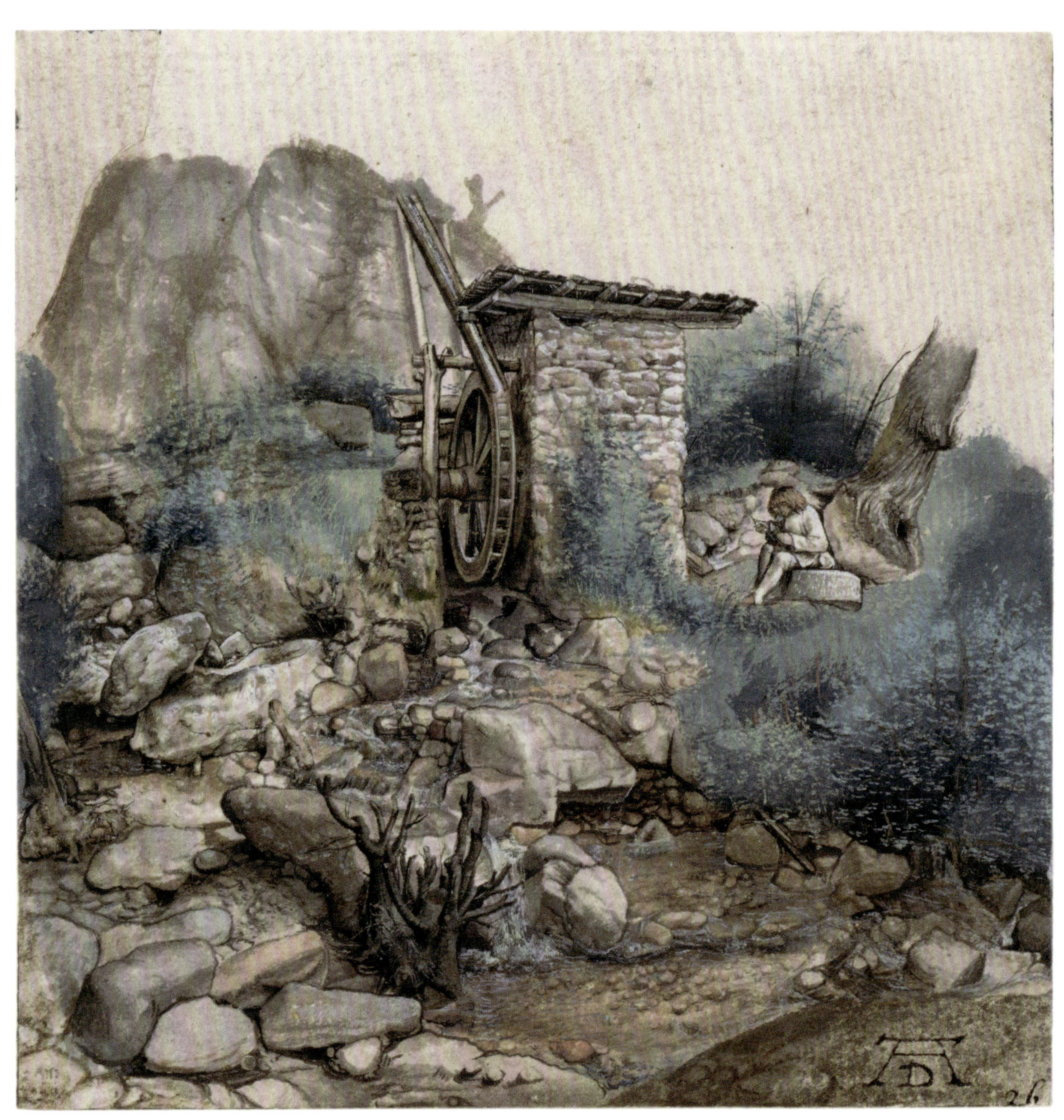

17

Watermill, *c.* 1494–95

ALBRECHT DÜRER NUREMBERG, 1471–1528

Pen and brown ink and watercolour on paper, 13.3 × 13.1 cm

Kupferstichkabinett, Staatliche Museen zu Berlin, inv. KdZ 3369

This small sheet, monogrammed in the lower right-hand corner, depicts a mill driven by water brought down from an outcrop by a wooden duct. The water emerges from the millwheel and continues across the rocks and stones of the mountainside. Dürer's impressive attention to detail captures even the reflections of the water as it flows into the sandy pool in the foreground. On the right, between thickets of conifers, sits a young man, notebook in hand. The figure is generally taken to be the artist himself.

The watercolour forms part of a series of works that Dürer produced during his first trip to Italy in 1494–95. The artist left Nuremberg to escape an outbreak of the plague; his destination was probably the city of Venice. Other watercolours produced during the journey include the *Courtyard of Innsbruck Castle* (Albertina, Vienna), the *View of the River Trent from the North* (Kupferstichkabinett, Kunsthalle, Bremen) and the *View of the Arco Valley* (Département des Arts graphiques, Musée du Louvre, Paris). Although the works in the series vary in size, they are stylistically consistent, and the present sheet has especially strong similarities, technically and stylistically, with the example in the Louvre.

Catherine Crawford Luber has suggested that Dürer did not travel to Italy in the middle of the 1490s. She attaches the works generally connected with that trip to the artist's Italian journey documented to between 1505 and 1507.[1] Giovanni Maria Fara has recently taken a strong line against Luber's radical hypothesis, and his observations strike us as indisputable.[2]

Antonio Rusconi had some success investigating the exact locations Dürer visited and recorded during his journey.[3] The present watercolour probably depicts Piazzo in Val di Cembra, close to the Castello di Segonzano. The stream could therefore be the Regnana, which flows into the Avisio, which in turn flows into the River Adige.[4]

NOTES

1 Luber 2005, pp. 40–76.

2 Fara 2014, pp. 1–2, n. 2.

3 Rusconi 1936, pp. 121–37.

4 Rome 2007 (Elena Filippo), p. 202, no. III.8. A more recent study by Marsilli (2015, pp. 102–03) concurs that this is the location.

18 Saint Jerome, 150[6?]

LORENZO LOTTO VENICE, c.1480 – LORETO, 1556

Oil on panel, 48 × 40 cm

Musée du Louvre, Paris, Département des Peintures, inv. MI 164

NOTES

1 Berenson 1901, p. 2.

2 Liberali 1981, pp. 75, 78, 83; Dal Pozzolo 1993, p. 38.

3 Fesch 1857, p. 17, no. 39.

4 Fesch 1841, p. 61, no. 1367.

5 Crowe and Cavalcaselle 1871, vol. 2, p. 501.

6 Morelli 1883, p. 31, note 2.

7 Longhi 1946, pp. 15, 56.

8 Wilde 1950, pp. 350–51.

9 Volpe 1981A, p. 128; Paris 1993 (Alessandro Ballarin), p. 309. They do so despite the problems of fitting the painting into the early years of Lotto's career.

10 Béguin 1981, pp. 99–101; Sgarbi 1981, p. 230; Romano 1991, p. 61; Dal Pozzolo 1993, pp. 37–38; Washington DC 1997 (David Alan Brown), pp. 88–90, no. 6.

11 Paris 1993 (Sylvie Béguin), pp. 274–75, no. 8.

Saint Jerome is seated on the ground with books around him, an allusion to his translation of much of the Bible into Latin, a version that became known as the Vulgate. His robe covers only the lower half of his body; his upper body is bare in readiness to receive self-inflicted penitential blows from the stone he holds in his right hand. In his left hand he holds a small crucifix to help him meditate on the Passion of Christ. Jerome's hermitage is an inhospitable place among rocky outcrops. At the left-hand side, almost invisible in the shadows, is a lion. According to tradition the lion kept Jerome company in the Syrian desert, near Aleppo, along with a second hermit who stands behind the animal and is thought to be Saint Anthony Abbot (as suggested by Bernard Berenson).[1] The colour of the sky suggests either dawn or dusk, and feeble rays of sunlight filter between the trees and rocks. In the distance a solitary horseman is making his way along the path that cuts across the valley. The painting is signed and dated 'Lotvs 150[6?]' on the dark spur of rock in the foreground, to the right of Saint Jerome. The last digit is rounded, but indistinct.

The earliest provenance of this painting is the subject of an interesting yet unverifiable hypothesis; the theory relates it to one of Lorenzo Lotto's major patrons, Bernardo de' Rossi, Bishop of Treviso (1468–1527). He possessed numerous works by Lotto: the *Allegory of Virtue and Vice* (1505; National Gallery of Art, Washington DC), the *Virgin and Child with Saint Peter of Verona* (1503) and the *Portrait of Bernardo de' Rossi* (1505; both Museo Nazionale di Capodimonte, Naples). In the inventories (dating from 1510 and 1511) in which these paintings are listed there also appears a 'Sancto Hieronimo', recognised by many art historians as the present painting.[2] The Louvre bought the picture in 1857 at the sale of the collection of Monsieur Moret,[3] which was composed of works from the collection of Cardinal Joseph Fesch (1763–1839).[4]

In the opinion of Joseph Archer Crowe and Giovanni Battista Cavalcaselle the painting was of unusual importance because of the central role played by the landscape in comparison with the figure, and the economy of the work's composition. The two scholars explained this innovation in light of Giorgione's impact on Lotto. They also drew attention to the signature, deeming it to be false.[5] As a result, Giovanni Morelli examined it in the closest detail, as did Gustavo Frizzoni, Clément de Ris and the Director of the Louvre at the time, Pierre-Paul Both de Tauzia; all agreed that it was genuine.[6]

If the inscription were to be genuine, and the date read as '1500', this painting would be the earliest in Lotto's known *œuvre*. Art historians have noted the novelty of a landscape painting at such an early time. In 1946 Roberto Longhi wrote of the picture: 'Lotto thinks that forms do not exist. He thinks that form, because of its internal uneasiness, is in continuous contention according to some new "animism" that does not involve only human beings.'[7] It is on the basis of this modern quality that Longhi compared Lotto with Rembrandt.

Johannes Wilde observed the inscription with even closer attention in 1950, and realised that the final digit of the date is irregular in shape and slightly smaller than the zero that precedes it.[8] He therefore interpreted it as 1506, citing strong stylistic similarities between *Saint Jerome* and Lotto's altarpiece in the cathedral at Asolo, in the region of Treviso, also dating from that year. In support of Wilde's theory, it is worth noting that in the Asolo painting the artist signs himself 'Lavrent Lotvs Iunior' ('still young') and that no paintings by him earlier than the year 1503 are known. In addition, the landscape depicted in the Asolo altarpiece bears undeniable similarities with the landscape in the Louvre work. Finally, the fractured rendering of Saint Jerome's clothing, executed in the same style as the faceting of the rocks, is derived from the *Altarpiece of Santa Cristina al Tiverone* (1504–06; Chiesa di Santa Cristina, Quinto di Treviso) rather than from the *Virgin and Child with Saint Peter of Verona*, mentioned previously, and dated to 1503.

Although a number of art historians continue to read the date as 1500,[9] Wilde's proposal has become the most accepted.[10] Sylvie Béguin maintained, however, that the final number of the date cannot be read with absolute conviction.[11]

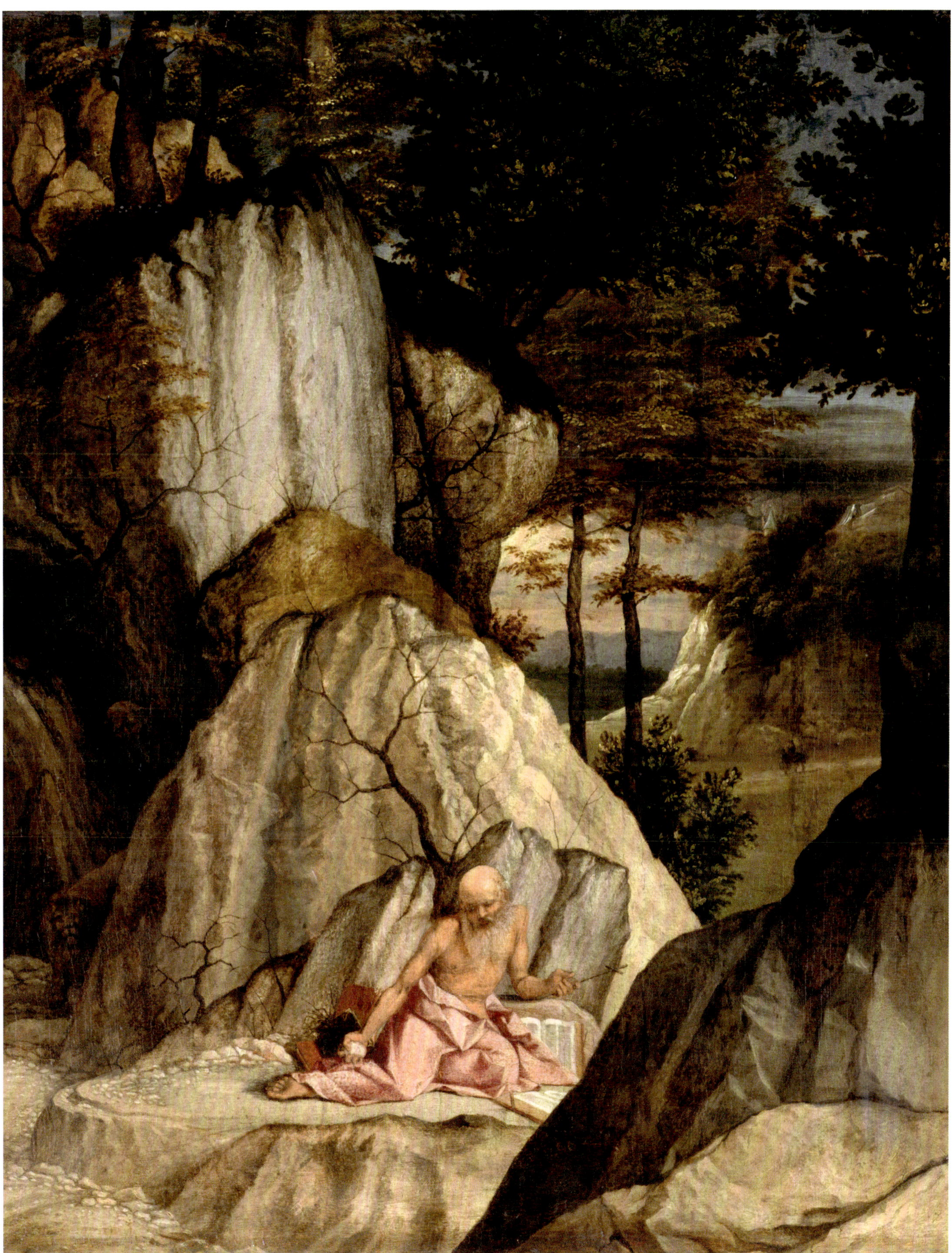

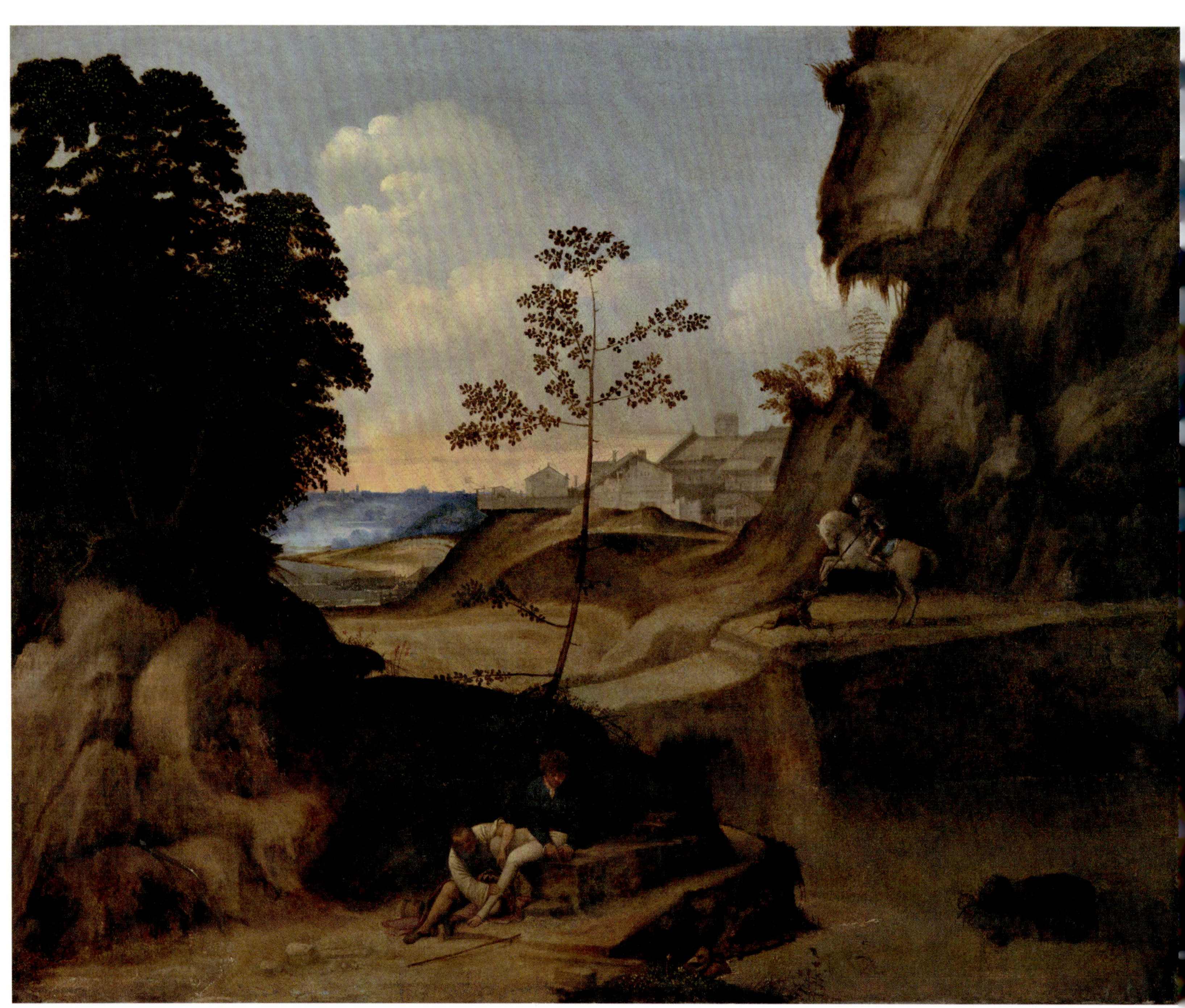

19 Il Tramonto, *c.* 1502–05

GIORGIONE (GIORGIO DA CASTELFRANCO) CASTELFRANCO VENETO, 1478 – VENICE, 1510

Oil on canvas, 73.3 × 91.4 cm

The National Gallery, London, bought 1961, inv. NG 6307

It has been suggested that one of the first owners of this painting was the celebrated Venetian connoisseur Marcantonio Michiel (1484–1552). From 1594 until the early twentieth century the Villa Garzoni at Pontecasale, near Padua, was home to Michiel's heirs. An inventory of the Michiel collection (made after his death in 1552) contains this entry: 'A painting in a landscape with two small figures framed in pure gold'; this has been tentatively identified as the picture now in the National Gallery.[1]

In 1933 this painting emerged at the Villa Garzoni, lending weight to the identification of the present work with the inventory entry. It was not immediately recognised as an autograph work, though its Giorgionesque character was apparent. The Director of the Museo Correr, Giulio Lorenzetti, played a crucial role in what followed: he noted the picture's Giorgionesque quality but did not identify Giorgione as the artist.[2] This oversight, caused partly by the work's poor state of conservation, was instrumental in allowing the landscape to be exported from Italy. Permission for this was granted in 1934 by a commission composed of Gino Fogolari, Ettore Modigliani and Carlo Gamba. Many years later Gamba recalled that the decision was made after direct comparison with Giorgione's *La Tempesta* (fig. 8), next to which the present work 'looked opaque and without chromatic perspective, like an imitation or a copy. And this we judged it to be.'[3]

Attempts at explaining the subject-matter of this painting are inevitably linked to its conservation history. The figure of Saint George slaying a dragon was an addition made in 1934 by Theodor Dumler, who was working under the supervision of the restorer Mauro Pellicioli, the art historian Roberto Longhi and the then owner of the painting, the Russian art historian, collector and dealer Vitale Bloch.[4] The addition of this scene was a result of the need to cover up a particularly badly damaged area of the canvas while providing a key to an understanding of the work. The title, *Il Tramonto* (*The Sunset*), was invented by Longhi,[5] who must have had in mind *La Tempesta*, another famously enigmatic painting.

Thus the only two figures who inform the interpretation of the original work are the men seated in the foreground: the younger one in a blue cloak and white breeches, the older with a beard. It appears that they have stopped near a spring to fill their cask. The older of the two inspects the younger man's leg: the stick in the foreground suggests that the seated youth might be having difficulty walking.

Various explanations have been proposed for the subject. One is that the painting illustrates the myth of Philoctetes.[6] According to Sophocles' tragedy *Philoctetes*, the eponymous hero was bitten on the foot by a snake after leaving for the siege of Troy with the Greek army, and was cruelly abandoned on the island of Lemnos. After ten years of war against the Trojans, the Greeks learnt from an oracle that victory would never be won without the bow and arrows of Philoctetes. On hearing this, Odysseus returned to Lemnos. Philoctetes agreed to rejoin the Greeks, and at Troy was cured by Machaon. This interpretation of the painting has the advantage of linking it to a convincing *terminus post quem*: Sophocles' tragedies were published by Aldus Manutius in Venice in August 1502.

Roberto Longhi published the first post-restoration photograph of the painting, and claimed that the work – along with Giorgione's *Three Philosophers* (fig. 7) – was typical of the 'chromatic classicism' that would become central to Titian's work.[7] On the basis of the photograph, Bernard Berenson also declared that the painting probably represented 'the most convincing of all attributions to Giorgione'.[8]

The painting first appeared in public in 1955, when it was included in the seminal exhibition 'Giorgione e i Giorgioneschi' in Venice. Following the exhibition the leading Italian scholars of the art of the Veneto were finally persuaded that the painting was by Giorgione.[9] The National Gallery in London acquired the painting from Bloch in 1961; since then, arguments over its attribution have diminished.

NOTES

1 Fletcher 1973, p. 384, no. 27; Lauber 2009, p. 190.

2 Lorenzetti and Planiscig 1934, p. VII.

3 Gamba 1954, p. 176.

4 Anderson 1996, pp. 181–83; Dunkerton 2010. It is likely that Dumler's skilful 'restoration' also included the addition of a hermit, who can be glimpsed inside a rocky hollow at the far right of the painting. The figure is generally believed to be Saint Anthony Abbot.

5 Longhi 1934, p. 79.

6 Castelfranco Veneto 2009 (Enrico Maria dal Pozzolo), pp. 431–33, no. 47.

7 Longhi 1946, pp. 19, 57.

8 Greer and Penny 2010, p. 365, no. 13.

9 Luigi Coletti, Vittorio Moschini, Antonio Morassi, Rodolfo Pallucchini, Lionello Venturi: see Venice 1955 (Pietro Zampetti), pp. 68–70, no. 30.

20, 21 Birth of Adonis, Death of Adonis, *c.* 1505–08

SEBASTIANO DEL PIOMBO (SEBASTIANO LUCIANI) VENICE, *c.* 1485 – ROME, 1547

Oil on panel,
each 40 × 48.5 cm

Museo Civico Amedeo Lia, La Spezia,
invs 164 and 165

NOTES

1 Votta 2001, pp. 19, 20.

2 Venice 1955 (Pietro Zampetti), p. 186, nos 86–87.

3 Ridolfi 1648, pp. 97–99.

4 Gentili 1995, p. 95; Dal Pozzolo 2009A, p. 46.

5 Venice 2012 (Santiago Arroyo), p. 82–83.

6 Joannides 2001, p. 77; Joannides 2009, p. 14.

7 Robertson 1955, p. 277; Pallucchini 1966, n.p.; 1981, pp. 528, 554; Lucco 1980, p. 90, nos 203; Rome 2008 (Mauro Lucco), p. 92, no. 1; Hope 1982, p. 637.

8 Quoted by Andrea G. De Marchi, in Zeri and De Marchi 1997, pp. 317–19, nos 141–42.

9 Richardson 1987, pp. 657–58.

10 Rome 2008 (Mauro Lucco), p. 92, no. 1.

These two panels illustrate the birth and death of the mythic figure Adonis. In the first, three female figures surround the tree of Myrrha. Myrrha, a daughter of the King of Cyprus, was turned into a myrrh tree to atone for the incestuous union she had formed with her father. The figure dressed all in white is Aphrodite; she extracts the infant Adonis, son of the king, from the bark of the tree. In the second panel Adonis, now grown up, is killed by a wild boar while out hunting. The artist has interpreted the legend somewhat freely, transforming the wild boar into a Sienese belted pig, a Cinta Senese, a breed distinguished by a white band around its middle.[1]

The two panels appeared for the first time in Venice, in the 1955 exhibition 'Giorgione e i giorgioneschi'; they were attributed to Sebastiano del Piombo.[2] This attribution was made by Roberto Longhi who, in a letter to the owner, associated the paintings with a passage in the life of Giorgione as narrated by the biographer Carlo Ridolfi in 1648:

> the fables painted by Giorgione on a number of chests [...] illustrating the loves of Apollo, of Hyacinth, of Venus and Adonis: and three of these panels are now the property of the Widmann family; one shows the birth of Adonis, the second a sweet embrace with Venus, and in the third he is killed by the wild boar; others of the chests described above were reduced to small paintings and were placed in various studios.[3]

According to Longhi, Ridolfi had quite understandably confused Sebastiano with Giorgione. Although this hypothesis cannot be supported with any hard evidence, it is nevertheless an ingenious idea, and has the advantage of addressing the probable function of the panels in the Museo Civico Amadeo Lia, which may be as the painted parts of a piece of furniture, possibly even a *cassone* (chest), as mentioned by Ridolfi. Unequivocal supporters of Longhi's hypothesis include Augusto Gentili and Enrico Maria Dal Pozzolo.[4] Many comparisons can be made, starting with the panels by Andrea Previtali now in the National Gallery, London. These illustrate episodes from the *Eclogues* by Antonio Tebaldeo, and date to about 1505–10, roughly contemporary with the present panels. It has been observed that the scene featuring Adonis and Venus, which would complete the series by Sebastiano, is missing.[5] Although establishing the age of the works in hand has proved difficult, they are generally considered to date from between 1505 and 1508; though to the present authors, a date prior to Giorgione's project at the Fondaco dei Tedeschi in Venice (1508) seems impossible.

The attribution of the La Spezia panels to Sebastiano has never been seriously challenged; only Paul Joannides remains unconvinced – he prefers to ascribe them to an anonymous contemporary of Titian.[6] The reference to Sebastiano was welcomed by Giles Robertson, Rodolfo Pallucchini, Mauro Lucco and Charles Hope.[7] Michael Hirst, after examining the paintings in the museum, also expressed his agreement (in a letter written to the museum on 1 July 1983).[8]

According to Francis Richardson,[9] the foreshortened figure of Adonis in the second panel could represent a preliminary idea for the same subject painted by Sebastiano in a later version, now in the Galleria degli Uffizi (and dated to 1511 or 1512). The comparison established by Lucco seems more convincing:[10] he likened the pose of the nymph in the foreground of the *Birth of Adonis* to that of the bad mother in the *Judgement of Solomon* (*c.* 1505–08) at Kingston Lacy. Lucco also observes the unusual pictorial values in the present panels, which are abbreviated and summarised – as might be expected of small works for the front of a *cassone*.

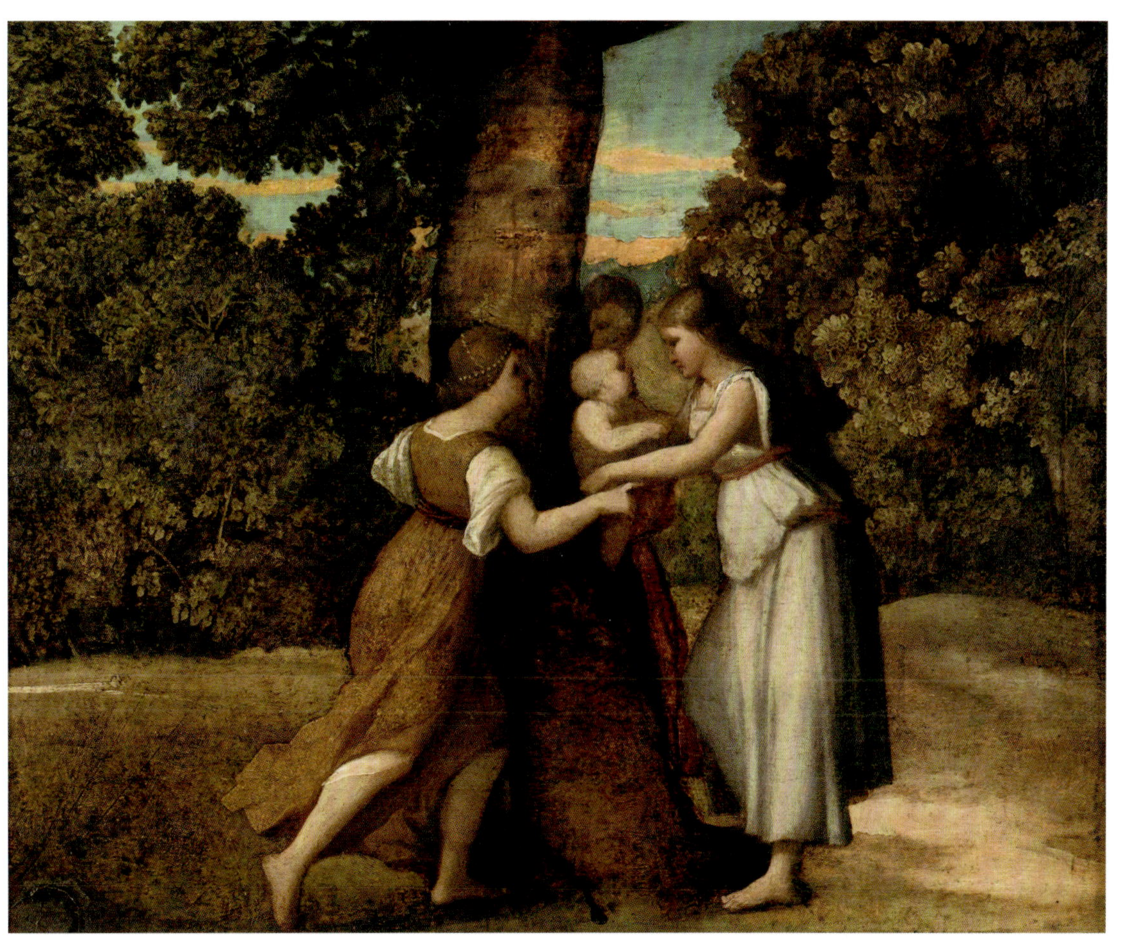

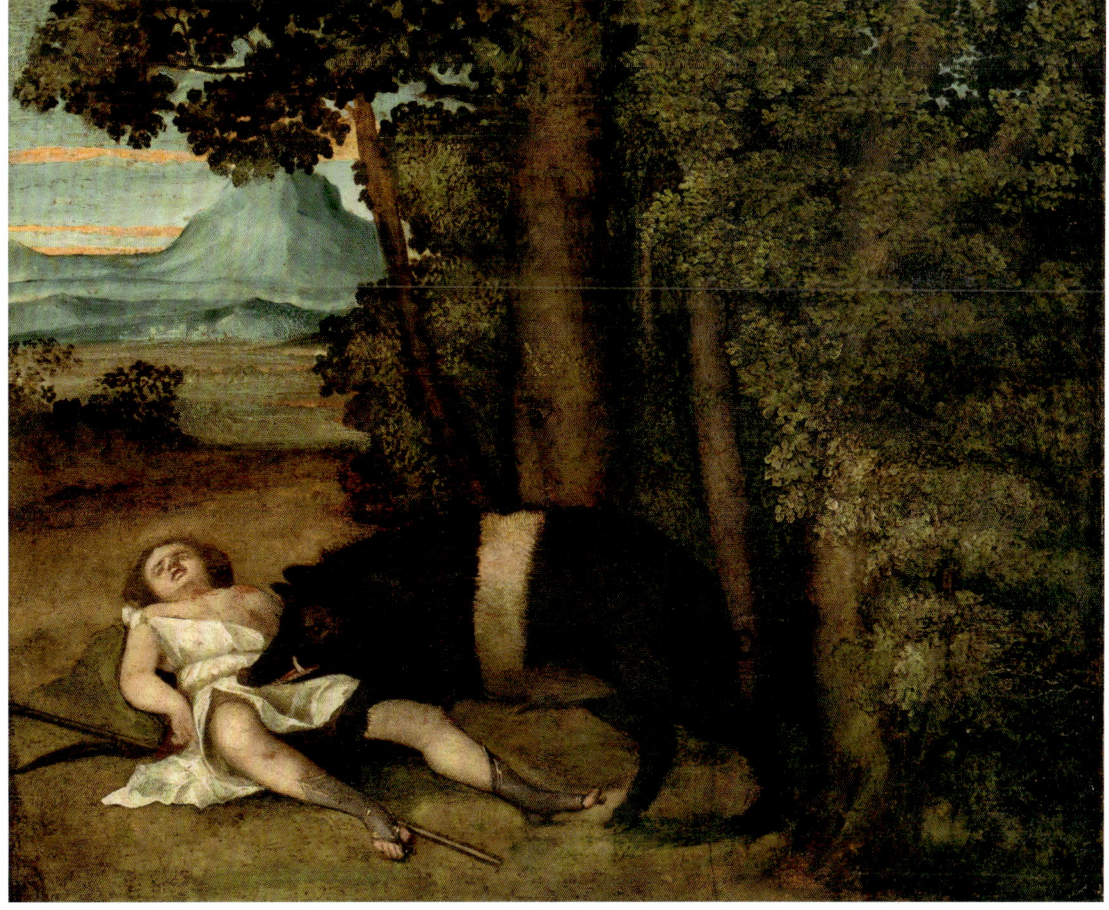

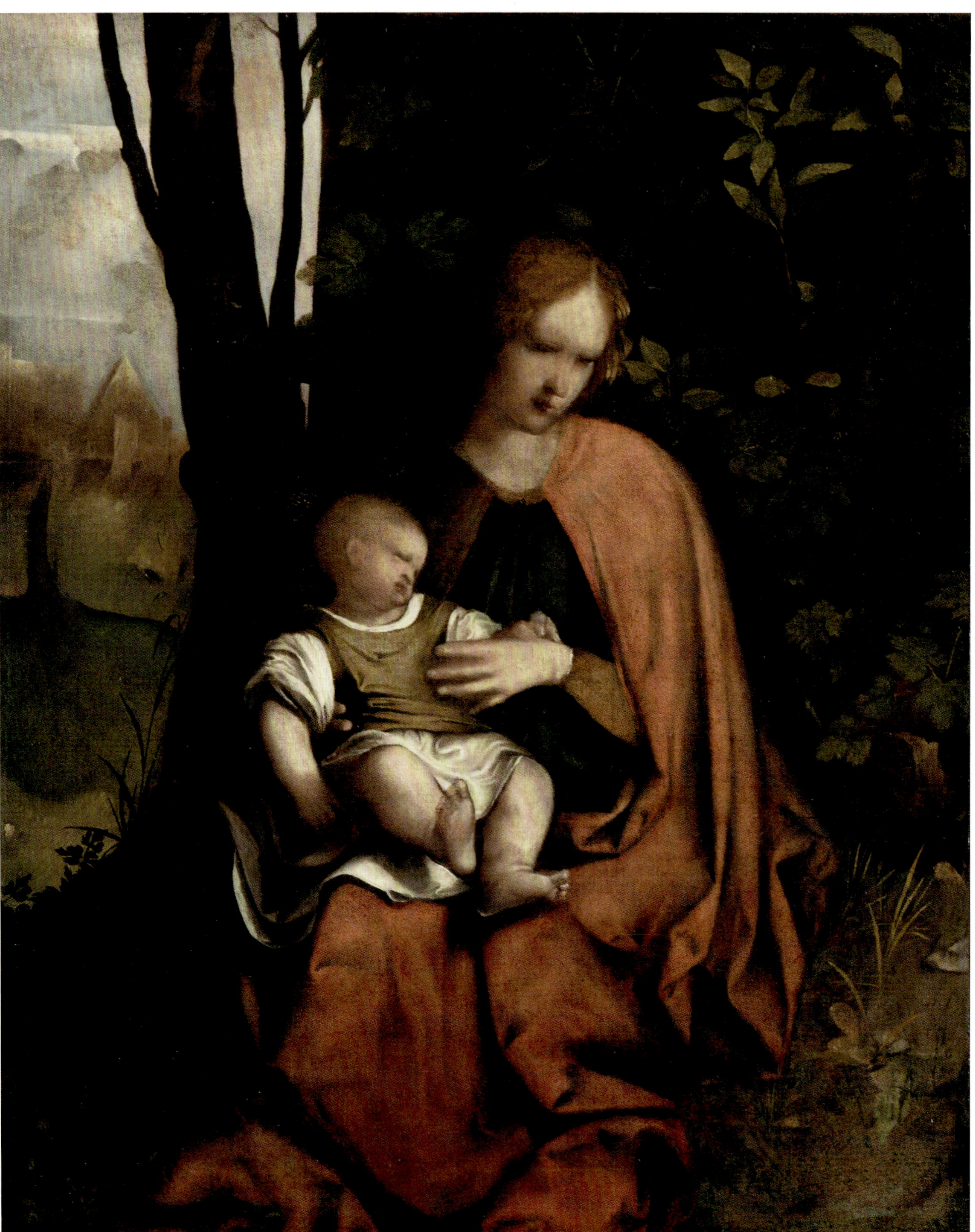

22

Virgin and Child, *c.* 1507

GIROLAMO ROMANINO BRESCIA, 1484/87 – BRESCIA, 1560

Oil on canvas,
76 × 61.2 cm

Musée du Louvre, Paris,
Département des Peintures,
inv. RF 1984.1

NOTES

1 Paris 1993 (Alessandro Ballarin), p. 443.

2 Paris 1987 (Sylvie Béguin), pp. 197–98.

3 Ballarin 1985, vol. 1, pp. 148–51.

4 Gregori 1986 (Francesco Frangi), pp. 168–69

5 Trento 2006 (Francesco Frangi), p. 88, no. 1.

6 Paris 1993 (Alessandro Ballarin), pp. 443–44, no. 68.

7 Nova 1994, p. 207, no. 1.

The subject of this painting is a Madonna of Humility: Mary is seated on a grassy bank screened by trees and bushes. The leaves of the laurel and the vine can be recognised, both attributes of the Virgin, known as '*regalis laurea*' ('royal laurel') and '*vitis superrima*' ('supreme vine').[1] The divided tree trunk to the left is a symbol of Christ's future Passion. Jesus is depicted moving His leg, His head heavily foreshortened. The Virgin holds Him closely and looks down at the ground with a melancholy gaze. In the distance a village can be seen, sketched in very rapidly. More vine leaves could originally be discerned against the light sky but these have almost disappeared. From this detail we can infer the degree of deterioration of the painting's surface. There is also significant damage to the flesh tones of the figures and Mary's red robe, which must originally have been enriched by a layer of glaze. To gain a more accurate impression of Girolamo Romanino's skill as a painter at this time, we should look to his *Narcissus at the Pool* (c. 1507; Städelsches Kunstinstitut und Städtische Galerie, Frankfurt).

The present painting was first recorded in the Parisian collection of Madame Cabanel, from which it was acquired by the Musée du Louvre in 1984. It was on this occasion that, independently of one another, Alessandro Ballarin, Sylvie Béguin and Mina Gregori all attributed the painting to Romanino.[2]

Ballarin conducted extensive research into the *Virgin and Child*;[3] he held it to be Romanino's earliest work, executed in Venice in about 1507. Stylistically, parallels with other artists are to be found, primarily Giorgione and also Giovanni Agostino da Lodi. Giorgione's so-called *Laura* (fig. 1) influenced the depiction of the Virgin's head, with the light falling on it but not on the greenery in the background. In 1986 the attribution of the painting was accepted by Francesco Frangi, who rightly highlighted the eccentric anti-classical choices made by Romanino.[4] The artist's predilection for Dürer – in addition to the influence of Giorgione's *Three Philosophers* (fig. 7) – has been noted in the irregular rendering of the Virgin's drapery, similar to that in Dürer's celebrated engravings. Comparison with the 1503 engraving *Virgin and Child on a Grassy Bench* by Dürer is indeed revealing.[5]

Ballarin returned to this painting in 1993 and endorsed the interpretation he had given in 1985;[6] Alessandro Nova declared himself in agreement with Ballarin's argument the following year.[7]

23

Daphnis, *c.* 1508–10

GIULIO CAMPAGNOLA PADUA, c.1482 – VENICE, AFTER 1515

Oil on panel,
19.6 × 16.4 cm

Alte Pinakothek, Bayerische Staatsgemäldesammlungen, Munich, inv. 76.

NOTES

1 Carradore 2010, p. 93.

2 Rylands 1988, p. 279, no. A.31.

3 Rylands 1988, p. 201, no. 14.

4 Mündler 1865, p. 365.

5 Morelli 1883, pp. 37, 40.

6 Morelli 1891, p. 198.

7 Thode 1898, p. 104; Venturi 1926, pp. 553–54.

8 Parma 1935, pp. 46–48, no. 33.

9 Schmidt 1900, p. 395; Phillips 1907, pp. 243–44; Berenson 1932, p. 410.

10 Phillips 1907, p. 243.

11 Longhi 1927C, p. 244, note 15.

12 Longhi 1946, p. 57, no. 104.

13 Venice 1955 (Pietro Zampetti), p. 64, no. 28.

14 Rylands 1988, p. 201, no. 14.

15 Christiansen 1994, pp. 341–45.

16 Dal Pozzolo 2009B, p. 344.

17 Brown 2010, pp. 90–92.

This lively young shepherd perches against a rock, playing his panpipes. The painter evidently wanted to depict a figure in motion; the blue cloak tied at the shepherd's shoulders appears just about to slip off his arm. There is a cithara leaning against the wall beside him. The immediate backdrop of rocks and trees opens onto a landscape in which a deer grazes. Visible in the distance is the outline of a group of dwellings and, on the horizon, a mountain painted in the sky's azure blue.

The figure has been identified as the mythical Sicilian shepherd Daphnis, accredited with the invention of pastoral poetry.[1] Another version of this painting is known, attributed either to Palma Vecchio or to the so-called 'Master of the Lansdowne *Concert*'.[2] In it the shepherd is clothed rather than naked, and is accompanied by a young woman who stands behind him and sings.

The present painting was first mentioned in an inventory of 1748; it was attributed to Vittore Carpaccio and was located at the Schloss Schleissheim, near Munich. When transferred to the Alte Pinakothek in 1836 it was ascribed to Antonio Allegri, known as Correggio.[3] The first to cast doubt on this attribution was the connoisseur Otto Mündler in 1865.[4] With admirable insight Mündler spotted the Venetian origin of the painting and proffered the names of the young Titian and Palma Vecchio. In 1883 Giovanni Morelli was persuaded by Mündler's authoritative opinion, and strove to associate the painting with Venice.[5] The only artist, in Morelli's opinion, who could have produced it was Lorenzo Lotto. Nevertheless, when he later revisited a photograph of the painting he was not totally convinced by this attribution, and reinstated the name of Correggio.[6] This attribution won an extraordinary body of support,[7] and the painting was exhibited in 1935 as part of Correggio's first monographic show.[8]

In the meantime, a number of scholars returned to Mündler's response and reassigned the work to Palma Vecchio.[9] Claude Phillips, in particular, lingered over the painting; in 1907 he highlighted its difference from the rest of Correggio's *œuvre* and emphasised its Venetian features: 'Even stronger evidence in favour of my argument is furnished by the landscape, which is not only typically Venetian, but to my thinking typically Palmesque.'[10]

Roberto Longhi's influential study of 1927, 'Cartella tizianesca', attributed the so-called *Laura* (fig. 1) in the Kunsthistorisches Museum in Vienna (inscribed 1506) to Giorgione for the first time. Longhi discussed the Munich painting in a footnote in the same essay, attributing it to Giorgione: 'The wonderful *Faunetto* in Munich [...] could serve to illustrate the transition from the timidity of the earliest paintings to the more sophisticated later works.'[11] Longhi reiterated the attribution in 1946, alongside chronological details that connect the panel with Giorgione's frescoes from about 1508 (fig. 2): 'With regard to the *Faunetto* in Munich, this is certainly related to the "formal gymnastics" of the Fondaco dei Tedeschi.'[12] The painting was included in the exhibition in Venice in 1955, with an attribution to Giorgione.[13] Many scholars have refused to accept the painting's promotion to Giorgione, preferring to return to the name of Palma Vecchio (see the 1988 summary by Ryland, who considers the work to be 'probably' an original by Palma).[14]

In 1994 a new line of research was opened by Keith Christiansen, who convincingly ascribed *Venus and Mars* in the Brooklyn Museum in New York to Giulio Campagnola.[15] This painting (previously thought to be by Palma Vecchio) has exactly the same measurements as the Munich painting. In 2009, on the basis of the analogies with *Venus and Mars*, Enrico Maria Dal Pozzolo tentatively suggested Campagnola as the artist,[16] and this was endorsed by David Alan Brown the following year.[17]

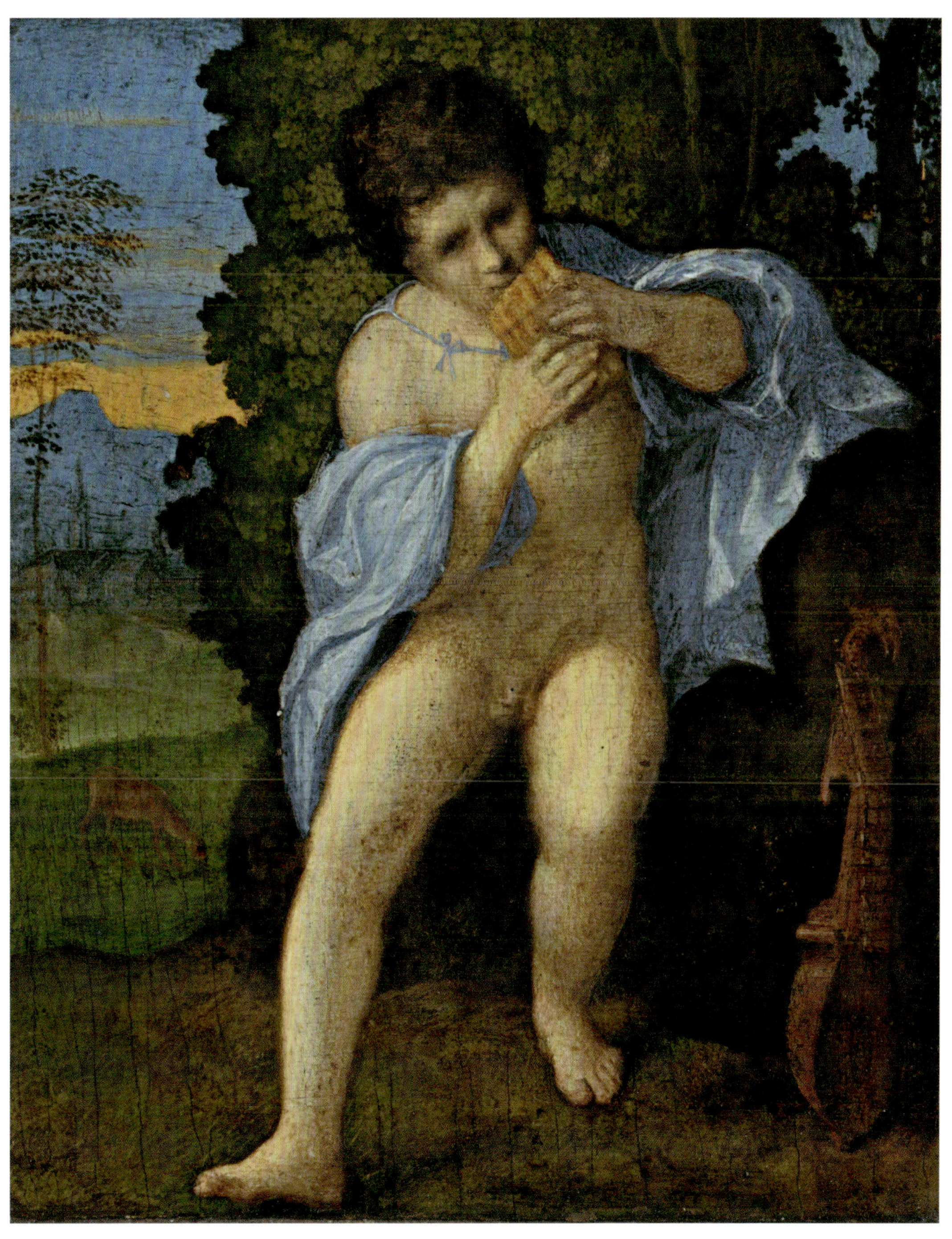

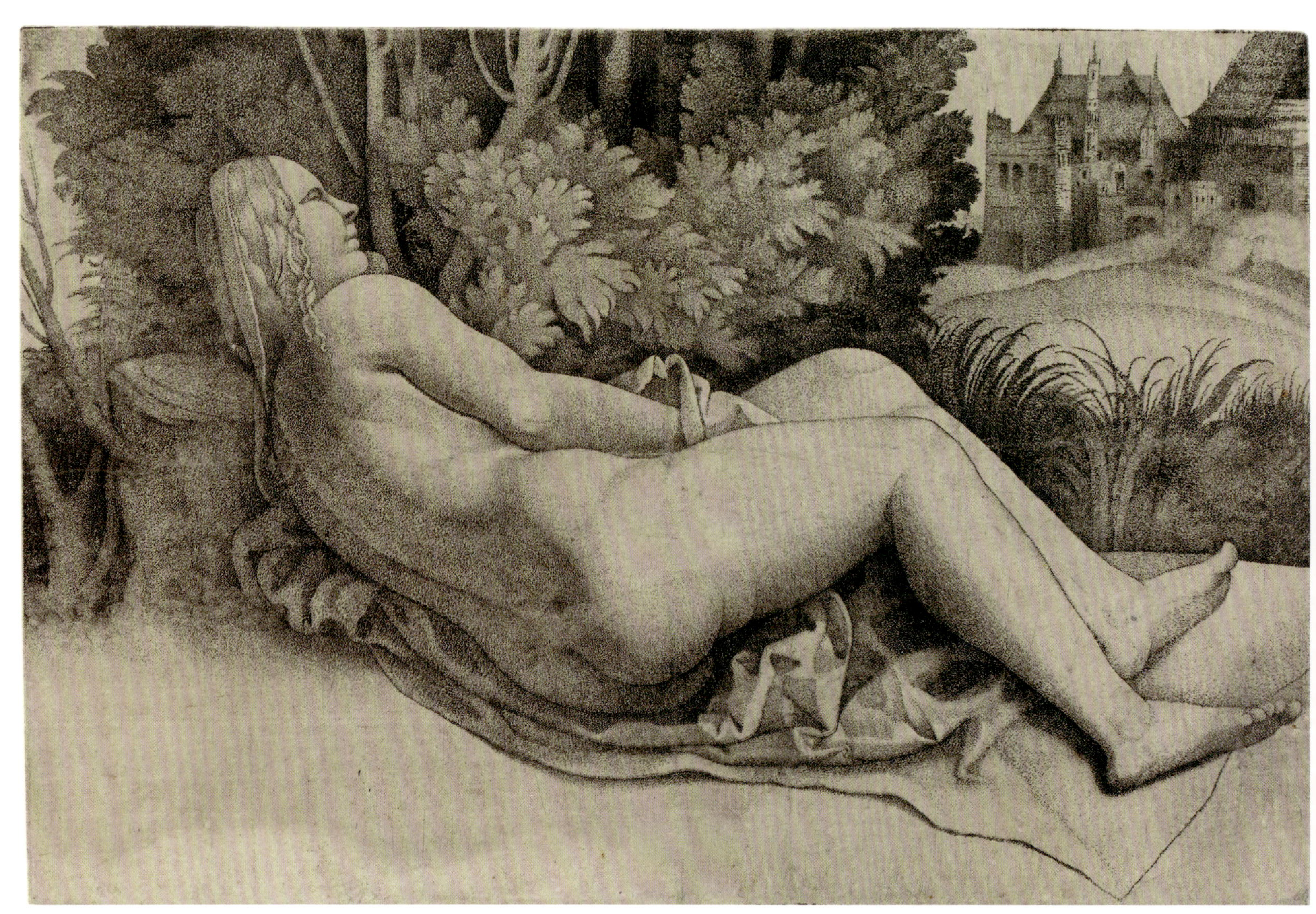

24 Venus Reclining in a Landscape, *c.* 1507–10

GIULIO CAMPAGNOLA PADUA, c. 1482 – VENICE, AFTER 1515

Engraving,
12.1 × 18.2 cm

Lent by the Trustees of the British Museum, London, Department of Prints and Drawings, inv. 1846,0509.136

A young woman reclines on ground that slopes down towards the viewer. She has chosen a sequestered spot, near a dense thicket, and lies on nothing more than a sheet. She appears asleep, her eyes closed, her head supported by a tree stump. The edge of the sheet is wound delicately around her head. Foliage shields her from a group of grand houses in the distance, reserving the role of voyeur for the viewer.

The engraving is known only in a single state, and is unanimously considered to be one of the best examples of Giulio Campagnola's work as an engraver. His extraordinary technical virtuosity can be seen in the seemingly infinite series of circular marks with which he creates a palpable, almost painterly chiaroscuro.

According to Mark J. Zucker the print was made after a *Venus* by Giorgione, a pendant to the *Sleeping Venus* in the Gemäldegalerie Alte Meister in Dresden (fig. 6),[1] but this hypothesis remains impossible to verify. The idea that the subject is a woman pleasuring herself is not totally convincing.[2] The proposal that she is a nymph, a female counterpart to the shepherds in Jacopo Sannazaro's pastoral poem *Arcadia* (Venice, 1502), seems more reasonable.[3] This interpretation is based on a painted copy of the print, made by Titian very late in his career, depicting a nymph with a shepherd (c. 1570–76; Kunsthistorisches Museum, Vienna). However, as has been observed, the iconography of the engraving is particularly difficult to interpret and cannot be explained with any certainty.[4]

The subject depicted here is apparently reminiscent of a miniature by Campagnola, copied by Giorgione, which during the first half of the sixteenth century was noted by the Venetian nobleman Marcantonio Michiel to be in the possession of the humanist Pietro Bembo: 'in the house of Messer Pietro Bembo the two small miniatures on vellum which were by the hand of Giulio Compagnola; the first is a nude taken from Zorzi, reclining and turned away.'[5] The most convincing hypothesis, and one that is generally accepted, is that Campagnola's print reproduces the same scene as that described by Michiel. Barbara Maria Savy has recently observed that Campagnola's miniature was cited as the pendant of 'a Nude (after Diana) giving water to a tree, with two small cherubs hoeing'.[6] Savy has suggested that Campagnola's miniatures juxtaposed subjects that the collector would consider complementary: a nude seen from the front and from behind (Dal Pozzolo wrote further on this subject in 2008[7]).

Philip Pouncey categorically rejected this idea in 1949, deducing instead from the woman's profile – which he compared with that of the bad mother in the Kingston Lacy *Judgement of Solomon* (c. 1505–08) – that the model from which the engraving was taken must have been by Sebastiano del Piombo.[8] Paul Joannides has since supported this theory.[9]

It is very difficult to suggest an exact date for the engraving. Konrad Oberhuber was convinced the work was based on an original by Giorgione,[10] as suggested by Michiel. If this is the case, Giorgione's original must date from around the execution of *La Tempesta* (fig. 8) and *Three Philosophers* (fig. 7). Campagnola is documented as being in Venice between 1507 and 1508. Barbara Maria Savy also suggested recently that *Venus Reclining in a Landscape* should be dated to between 1507 and 1510.[11] The style and technique of the present work have much in common with the undated engraving *Young Shepherd* by Campagnola, which is obviously inspired by the young man depicted in Giorgione's *Il Tramonto* (cat. 19).

NOTES

1 Zucker 1984, pp. 473–76, no. 008.

2 Emison 1992, p. 276.

3 Venice 1999 (Beverly Louise Brown), p. 444, no. 138; Sman 2003, p. 72, no. II.5; Korbacher 2015, pp. 5–7.

4 Sorce 2003, pp. 89–97.

5 Michiel 1521–43, p. 51; see the most recent transcription of the manuscript by Lauber 2013, p. 346.

6 Padua 2013 (Barbara Maria Savy), pp. 328–30, no. 5.7. 'Una Nuda che dà acqua ad uno albero, tratta dal Diana, cum dui puttini che zappano.'

7 Dal Pozzolo 2008, p. 117.

8 Pouncey 1949, p. 236.

9 Joannides 2001, p. 271; Joannides 2010A, p. 99.

10 Paris 1993 (Konrad Oberhuber), p. 523, no. 126; Rome 1995 (Konrad Oberhuber), p. 294, no. 74.

11 Padua 2013 (Barbara Maria Savy), pp. 328–30, no. 5.7.

25 Two Arcadian Musicians in a Landscape

ATTRIBUTED TO TITIAN (TIZIANO VECELLIO) PIEVE DI CADORE, c.1488/90 – VENICE, 1576

Black and brown ink
over black chalk on paper,
22.4 × 22.6 cm

Lent by the Trustees
of the British Museum, London,
Department of Prints and Drawings,
inv. 1895,0915.817

Two musicians are depicted in a landscape: the woman, seen from behind, is holding a pipe, the man a viola da gamba. The two do not appear to be in communication with one another. The man's eyes are lowered, the female figure outside his field of view is gazing at an inhabited landscape in the distance. Behind the man is a wooded scene with bushes, twisted trees and two sleeping sheep. The female figure is drawn with delicate, fine lines in black ink, and the male figure with more rapid, gestural strokes in brown ink.

The drawing was reproduced as a counterproof print, by Valentin Le Febre in 1682, as the work of Titian.[1] The inscription reads: 'V. le Febre de. et sculp. – TITIANVS IN. P. – I. Van Campen Formis Venetys'.[2] However in 1879 the original was exhibited at the Ecole des Beaux-Arts in Paris as by Giorgione. Philippe de Chennevières, in a review of the exhibition, was the first to associate the female figure with that in the *Concert champêtre* in the Louvre, at the time also believed to be by Giorgione.[3] For this reason he expressed particular regret that 'The drawing, which in other parts is in good condition and well preserved, unfortunately in the case of the interesting female torso is extensively reworked.'[4]

At around this time, attribution of the famous painting in Paris seems also to have been debated, with both Sebastiano del Piombo and Titian suggested as its author.

In 1883 Giovanni Morelli attributed the sheet to Domenico Campagnola;[5] Claude Phillips followed him in this in 1893, viewing it as a pastiche, liberally adapted from the *Concert champêtre*.[6] Betty Kurth followed the same line in 1926 and 1927, maintaining that the inspiration for Campagnola's drawing was a lost composition by Titian, which she had found.[7] Kurth's evidence was in fact only a later copy of the engraving that had been published by Le Febre, as Carl Justi seemed to realise.[8] Justi also made an interesting stylistic observation about the female figure, which he considered to be by Giorgione (a preparatory drawing for the *Concert champêtre*, fig. 15), and the male figure, which he thought a reworking by Campagnola. In 1930 Louis Hourticq considered the drawing to be the work of Titian,[9] and this fitted with his conviction that the *Concert champêtre* in the Louvre was by the same artist. In 1944 Hans Tietze and Erica Tietze-Conrat were the first to observe that the drawing had been executed in two differently coloured inks.[10] From this observation they hypothesised that the drawing could have been started in the first decade of the sixteenth century with the female figure in a landscape, and the rest added some time later. They discounted the name of Campagnola and suggested that the drawing had been executed by Titian at two different moments, and completed in the second decade of the sixteenth century.

In 1976 Konrad Oberhuber suggested that the sheet had been a preparatory drawing for the *Concert champêtre* in the Louvre by Titian, basing his opinion on various small differences between the drawn and painted female figures.[11] He later changed his opinion,[12] aligning himself with Fabio Benzi, who reconsidered the theory of the two periods launched by the Tietzes, claiming that the female figure was by Giorgione and that Titian had completed the drawing.[13] The same hypothesis was extended to the Louvre painting: that it was an unfinished work by Giorgione completed by his pupil.

As has been demonstrated here, the debate about the attribution of the present drawing is now so convoluted that it may never be resolved. For the sake of completeness, we should record the opinion of Maria Agnese Chiari, who in 1988 considered the drawing to be a 'pastiche in the manner of Titian, confused over time with the genuine article'.[14] Paul Holberton shared a similar opinion: he considered the drawing to have been executed in two phases (about 1510 and about 1530) by an anonymous Venetian artist.[15] Holberton drew attention to a print attributed to Giulio Campagnola (a work known via the sole surviving state in the Art Institute of Chicago), taken, in counterproof, from the right-hand figure in the *Concert champêtre*. Conversely, Antonio Mazzotta believed the drawing was planned and executed by Titian in about 1508.[16]

NOTES

1 Le Febre 1682, no. 20.

2 Chiari 1982, p. 111, no. 104.

3 Chennevières 1879, p. 530.

4 'Le dessin, qui dans ses autres parties, est sain et bien conservé, se trouve, par malheur, fort retouché dans cet intéressant torse de femme.'

5 Morelli 1883, p. 196.

6 Phillips 1893, p. 228.

7 Kurth 1926–27, p. 290.

8 Justi 1927–28, pp. 79–84.

9 Hourticq 1930, p. 98.

10 Tietze and Tietze-Conrat 1944, pp. 319–20, no. 1928.

11 Venice 1976 (Konrad Oberhuber), pp. 84–87, no. 32.

12 Paris 1993 (Konrad Oberhuber), pp. 507–08, no. 94; Rome 1995 (Konrad Oberhuber), pp. 280–81, no. 48.

13 Benzi 1982, pp. 183–87.

14 Chiari 1988, pp. 64–66, no. A 7.

15 Holberton 1993, p. 251.

16 Mazzotta 2012A, p. 74.

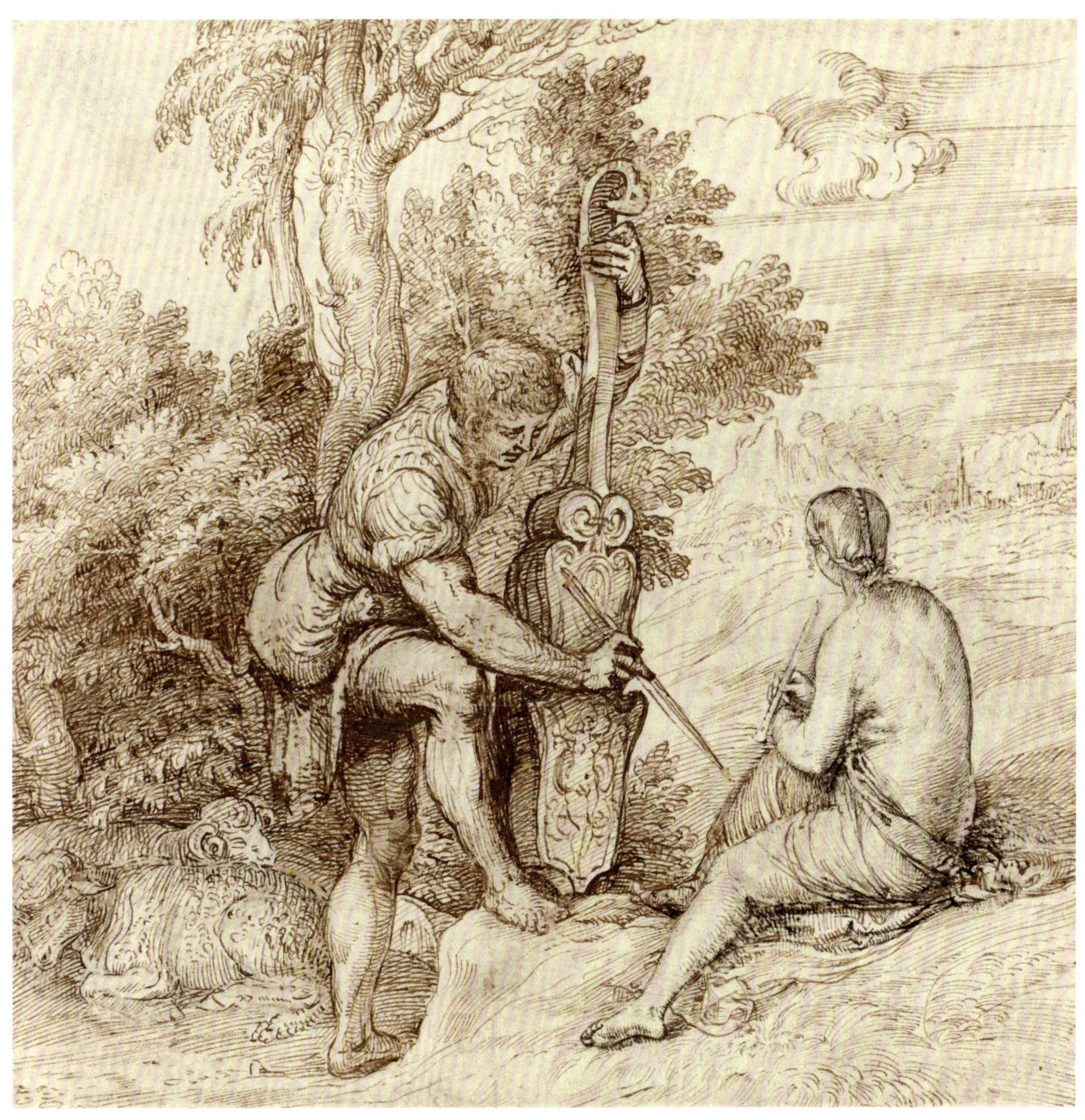

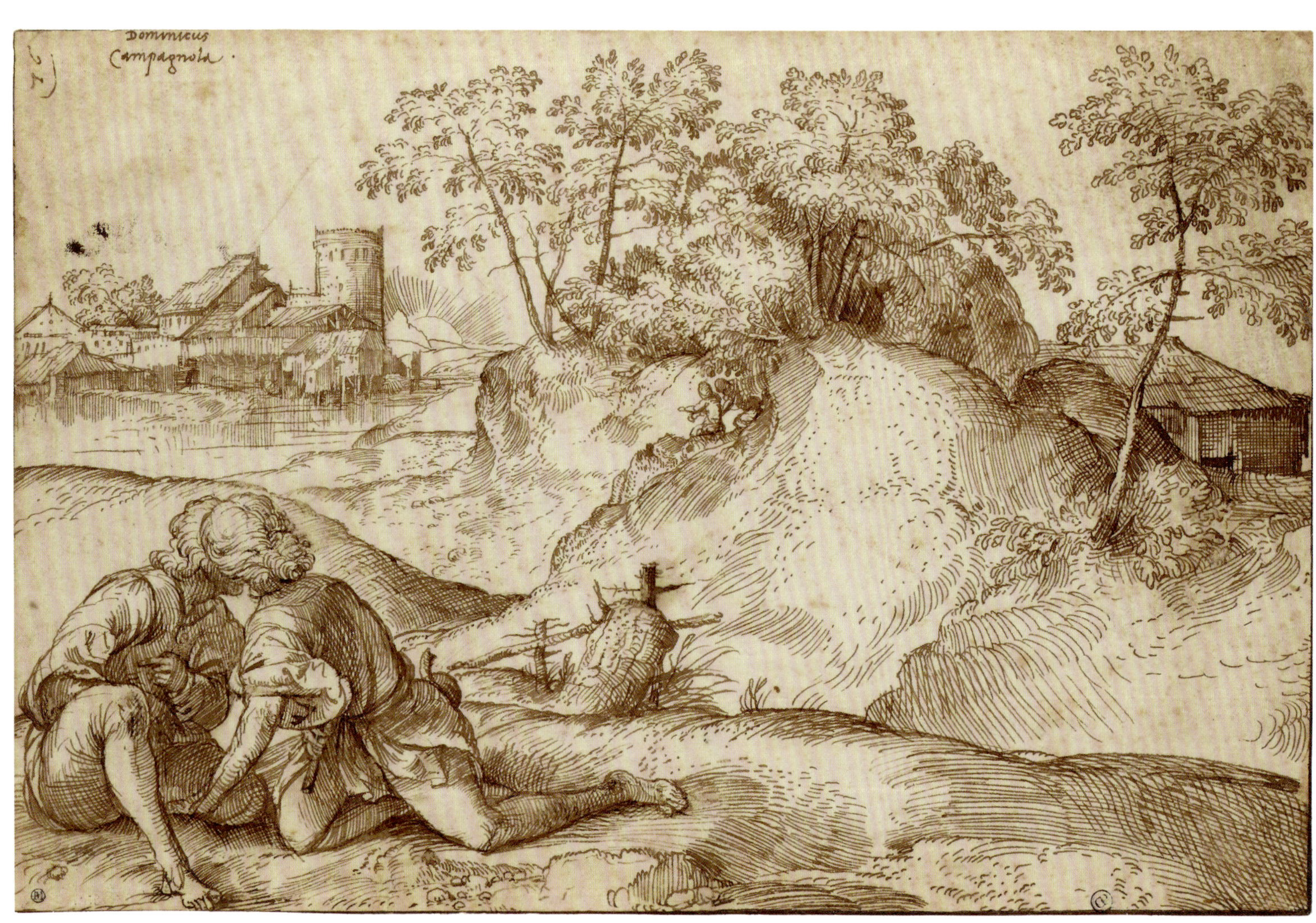
Dominicus
Campagnola

26 Two Kneeling Youths in a Landscape, *c.* 1515–20

DOMENICO CAMPAGNOLA VENICE, *c.* 1500 – PADUA, 1564

Pen and brown ink on paper, 18.2 × 27.3 cm

Lent by the Trustees of the British Museum, London, Department of Prints and Drawings, inv. 1895,0915.836

NOTES

1 Paris 1993 (Konrad Oberhuber), p. 514, no. 107.

2 Rearick 2001, p. 58.

3 Morelli 1891, p. 376.

4 Hourticq 1930, pp. 88–89.

5 Tietze and Tietze-Cronat 1939, p. 329.

6 Tietze and Tieze-Conrat 1944, p. 128, no. 487.

7 Venice 1976 (Konrad Oberhuber), p. 119, no. 63.

8 Paris 1993 (Konrad Oberhuber), p. 514, no. 107.

9 Rearick 2001, p. 58.

Two shepherds are depicted next to each other in a wide landscape, one sitting, one kneeling. They face away from the viewer, naturally arousing our curiosity. The right-hand shepherd, who holds a flute, seems to be whispering in the other's ear, perhaps to avoid being overheard. The shepherd to the left points his index finger at something outside the picture. In the middle distance two other shepherds can be seen, their attention caught by a far-flung figure emerging from under a hedge, or perhaps they are staring at the sun on the horizon. This subtle technique of connecting the figures with a network of glances invites the viewer to examine carefully every detail of the drawing, which is executed with extraordinary confidence and skill. It is signed at the top left in fine cursive script by its author: 'Dominicus / Campagnola'.

Konrad Oberhuber suggested the subject may be taken from Virgil's seventh *Eclogue*: these are the Arcadian shepherds Thyrsis and Corydon engaged in singing and playing the flute.[1] William R. Rearick was also convinced by this identification, and suggested that the two men in the foreground are exchanging a kiss.[2] However, the subject-matter of the drawing is difficult to ascertain with any accuracy.

In 1891 the drawing was studied in depth by Giovanni Morelli as the work of Domenico Campagnola, mainly on the basis of the signature.[3] Louis Hourticq, on the other hand, was convinced that the signature was a seventeenth- or eighteenth-century addition; he believed that the present work was by the same hand as the sheet at the British Museum (cat. 25), which he considered to be a preparatory drawing for the *Concert champêtre* (fig. 15) – in other words, by Titian.[4] This idea found no supporters, and the work was returned definitively to the catalogue of Campagnola. In 1939 Hans Tietze and Erica Tietze-Cronat remarked that the model for Campagnola's landscape was to be sought in the work of Giorgione or Giulio Campagnola rather than in the work of Titian.[5] Their proposed dating for the sheet was around 1515–16.[6] According to Oberhuber, writing in 1976, this date was to be brought forward a few years.[7] Oberhuber observed that the signature is located in the same position as works signed by Giulio Campagnola. The scholar also considered that the clear presence of the signature was an important declaration of authorship at a time when drawings were just starting to be collected.[8] In 2001 William R. Rearick followed a similar line of thought and emphasised the exquisite originality of the drawing, proposing a date of around 1520.[9]

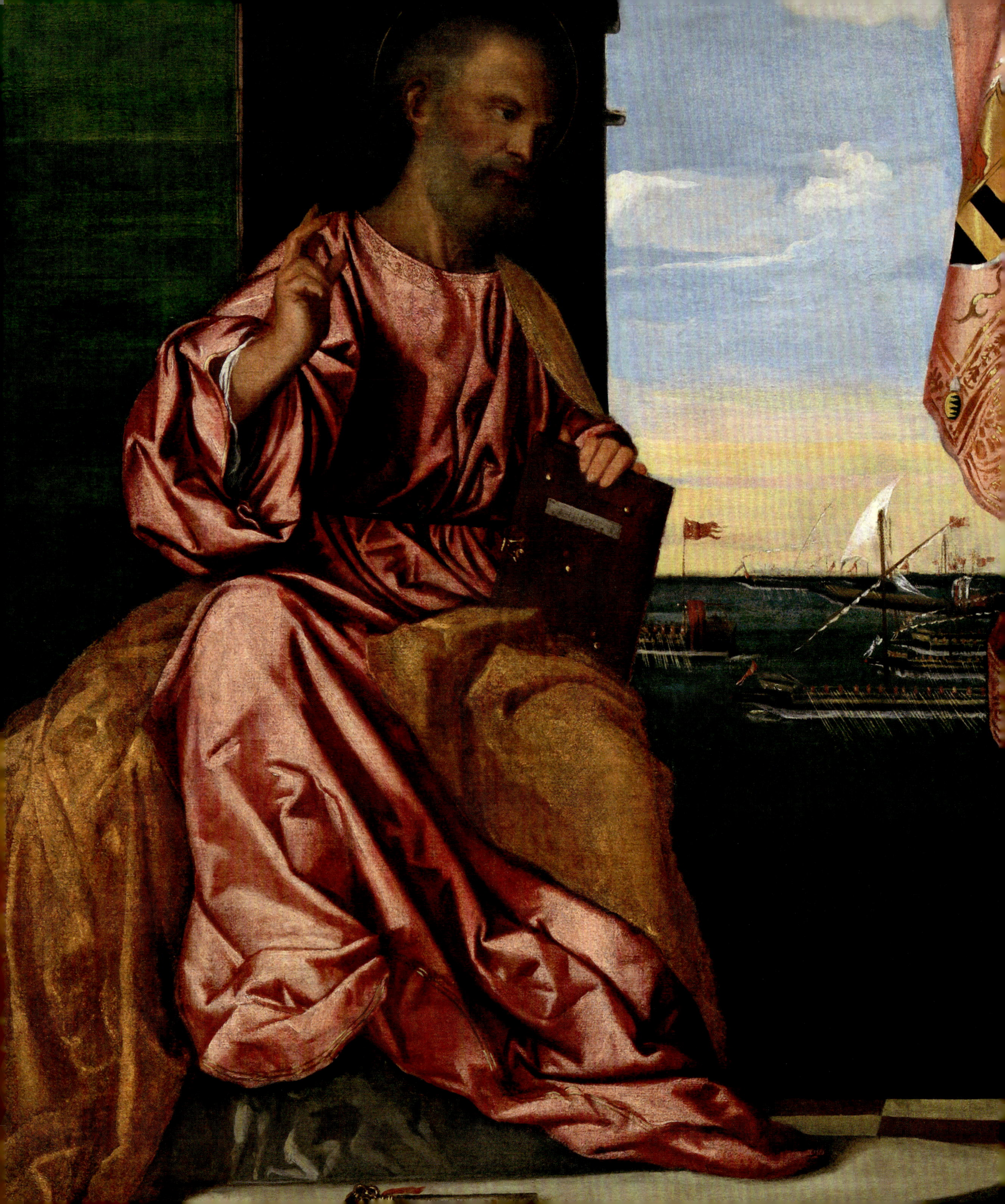

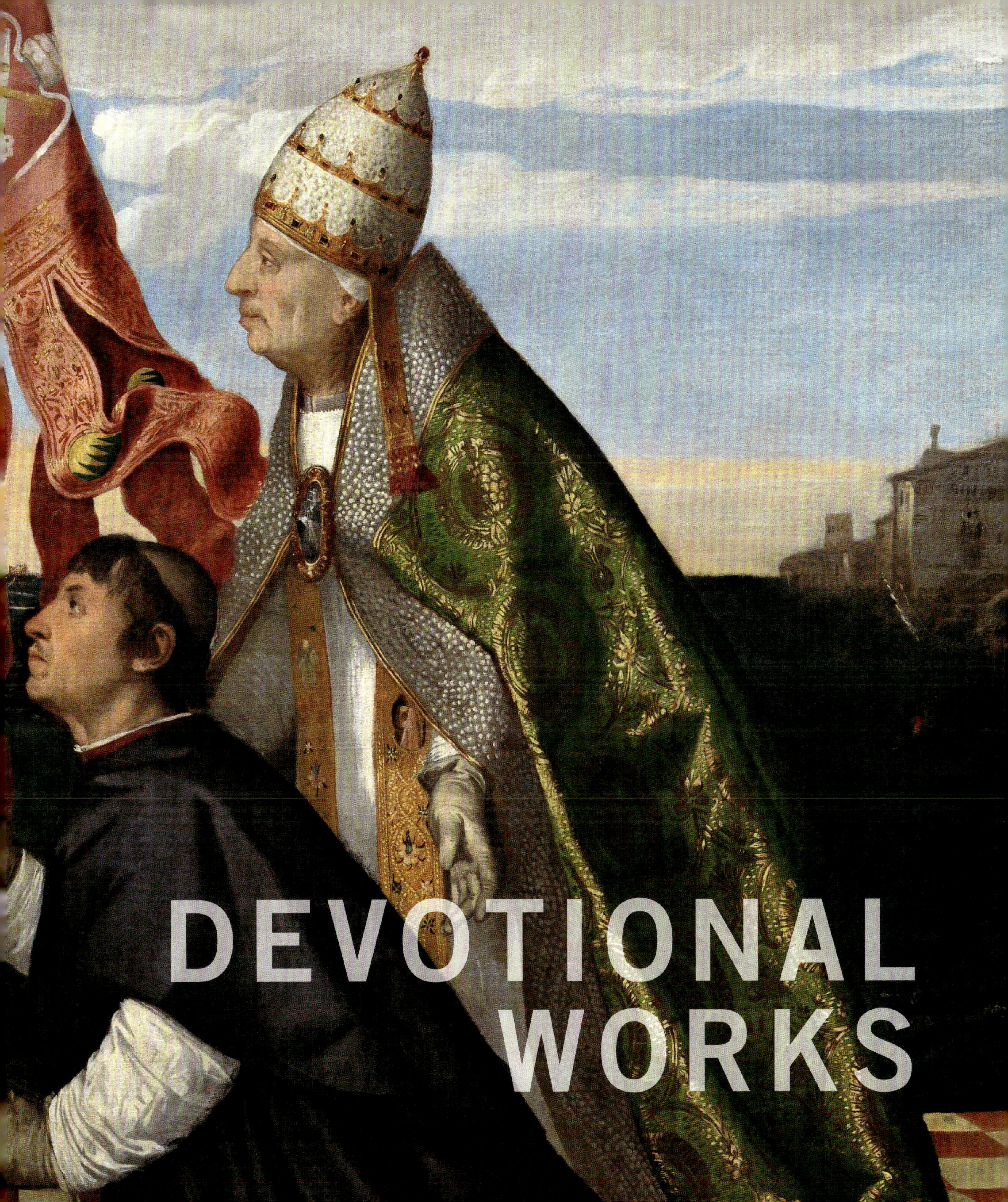

DEVOTIONAL WORKS

Fig. 17
GIORGIONE
***Virgin and Child with Saint Nicasius and Saint Francis of Assisi ('Castelfranco Altarpiece')*, c. 1500**
Oil on panel, 200 × 152 cm.
Duomo di Santa Maria Assunta e San Liberale, Castelfranco Veneto

Giorgione's arrival in Venice is described in sixteenth-century sources as a turning point for painting in the city. His celebrity was not solely due to his involvement in public works of art, although he contributed to the field with some noteworthy commissions. The first of these was one of his most celebrated, the *Castelfranco Altarpiece* (fig. 17), painted following the death of Matteo Costanzo and datable (almost certainly) to 1500.[1] The second is known through extremely valuable documentary information involving the Consiglio dei Dieci (Council of Ten) – the body in charge of state security and one of the most important agencies of the Venetian Republic. In 1507 the council paid Giorgione for a very large painting (whose subject is unknown) that was to be hung in the Sala del Maggior Consiglio in the Palazzo Ducale. The third was the façade of the Fondaco dei Tedeschi (fig. 2) on the Canal Grande; this building, the premises of the community of German merchants, was decorated by Giorgione in 1508.

These three examples give some idea of the painter's progress from the periphery to the centre, reaching his zenith with the official commission for the Palazzo Ducale. At the time, Giovanni Bellini was in charge of the painted decorative scheme inside the palazzo. Bellini was asked to name experts who would evaluate the work Giorgione had done on the Fondaco dei Tedeschi. Evidently Giorgione's success had not gone unnoticed by this senior figure of Venetian painting.

Despite these commissions, the greater part of Giorgione's work remained hidden from public view, jealously guarded by a small group of collectors. The most telling example of this dates from the year of the painter's death. In 1510 Isabella d'Este, Marchesa of Mantua, wrote a letter, now famous, describing her desire to possess a rare piece by Giorgione. She knew of the painter's untimely death and of the existence among his belongings of 'a night scene, very beautiful and unusual'.[2] Isabella wanted to acquire the work at any cost, and to this end prepared a meticulous plan of action; however, notwithstanding her careful calculations, the result was a failure. Her agent in Venice, Taddeo Albano, managed to find two paintings that matched her description but both were in the hands of collectors: 'And it has been given to me to understand that neither one nor the other is willing to sell at any price, for the reason that they wish to keep them for their own enjoyment.'[3] This episode reveals the nature of Venetian collectors of Giorgione's work: a closed group, impenetrable to outside persuasion.

As well as offering a description of the commissions available to artists working in Venice, the above paragraphs are intended as a reflection on the types of paintings included in this section: we have paintings intended for private devotion (such as cats 28, 29 and 30); paintings hung in private surroundings but with a representational function, as in the case of *Jacopo Pesaro Being Presented by Pope Alexander VI to Saint Peter* (cat. 31); and paintings intended for public display (such as cat. 35). Naturally, the dimensions and styles of paintings differed according to their purpose. With some exceptions, small- and medium-sized paintings were intended for private prayer within a domestic setting. This principle generally holds, although documentation proves the contrary in the case of *Christ Carrying the Cross* (fig. 4) in the Scuola Grande di San Rocco, to which we shall return.

Giorgione's versions of the Virgin and Child (cats 27 and 28) must have been painted earlier than Giovanni Bellini's *sacra conversazione* (cat. 29), although, given their compositions and styles, a viewer would be forgiven for thinking otherwise. Bellini's painting originally possessed two wings, now lost. By an unknown hand, these would have been painted inside and out; it was a portable altarpiece, to be opened or closed according to the devotional requirements of the owner, presumably the man kneeling before the Holy Family. Bellini's painting harks back to earlier models, in form and in structure; it seems less modern than the devotional works of Giorgione, which – by means of innovative, unmediated compositions – manage to eliminate the sense of remoteness and bring the viewer into the scene, transfiguring him or her as a worshipper. Also noticeable is that the landscape or view chosen for the background in Giorgione's paintings often depicts a place that held a particular significance for the patron who commissioned the painting (for example, cat. 28). The thoughtful, introspective demeanour of the Virgin in various of Giorgione's paintings was perhaps puzzling for the sixteenth-century viewer.

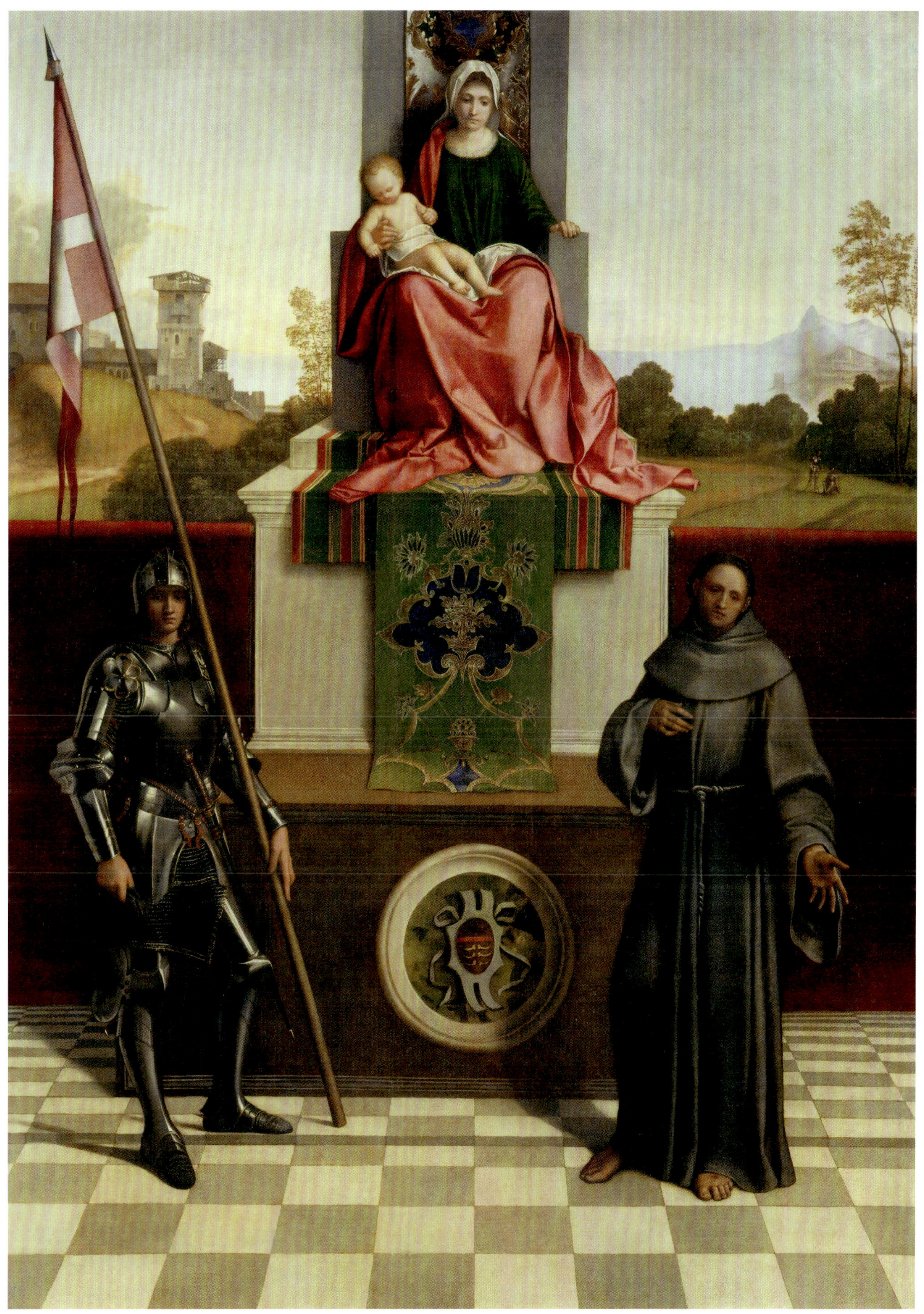

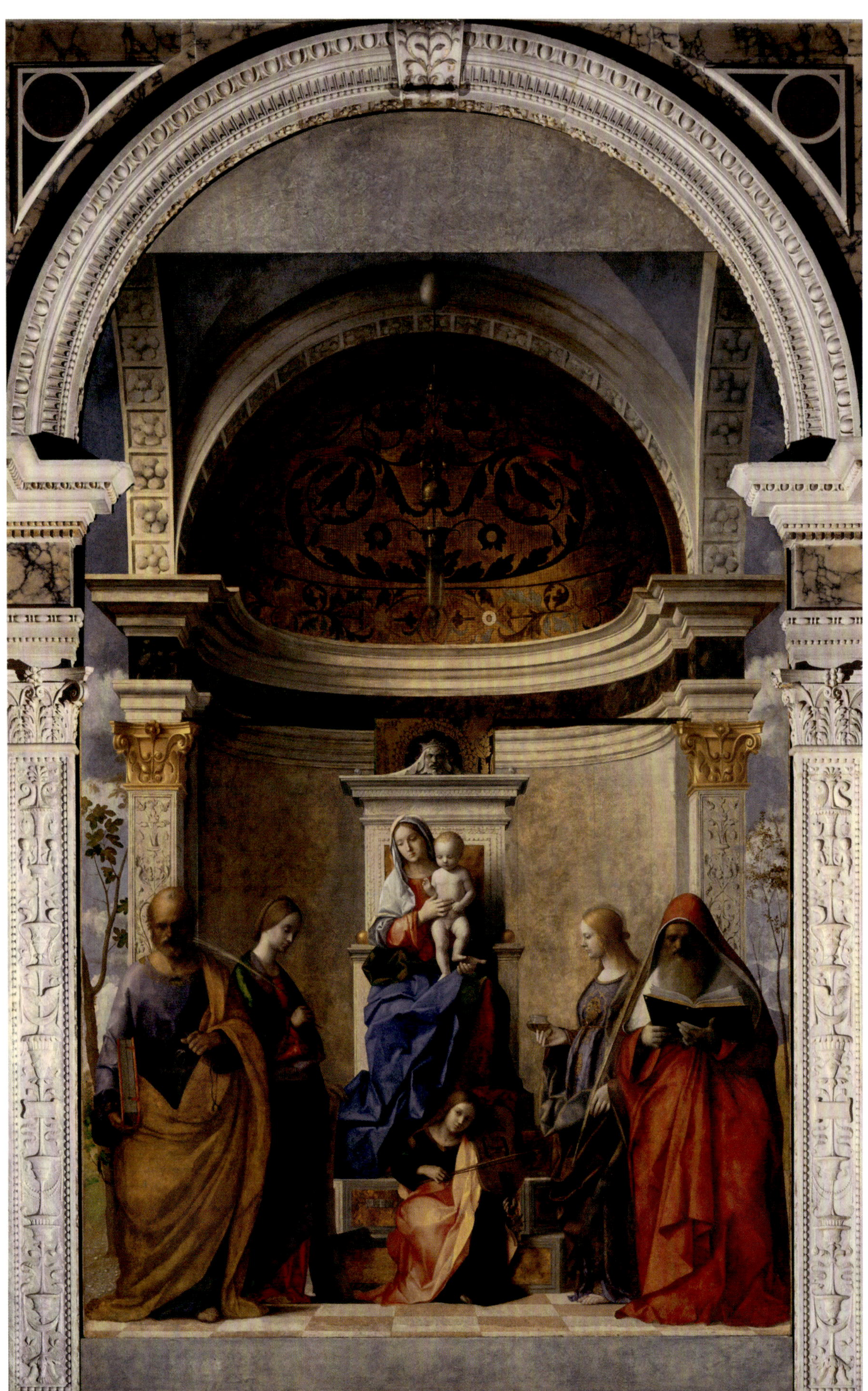

Fig. 18
GIOVANNI BELLINI
Virgin and Child with Saints Peter, Catherine of Alexandria, Lucy and Jerome, ('San Zaccaria Altarpiece'), 1505
Oil on panel, 500 × 235 cm
San Zaccaria, Venice

Fig. 19
DOMENICO MANCINI
Virgin and Child with Saint John the Baptist and Saint Peter, *c.* 1511
Oil on panel, 69 × 103 cm
Private collection

The panel by Domenico Mancini (cat. 35), signed and dated 1511, is a most unusual devotional object. It is all that remains of a triptych, a format that was already archaic in the period, having been superseded by the single-panel altarpiece. The choice of subject also betrays a backward-looking approach – it is a faithful copy of a celebrated altarpiece painted in Venice by Giovanni Bellini in 1505 (fig. 18). Yet, if we carefully examine the way the colour is applied, we notice a fluency of execution and an intensification of tone that go well beyond Bellini's example, pointing very clearly to the style of Titian. By 1511, only a year after the death of Giorgione, Titian was already a guiding light in Venetian painting, at least for Mancini, a painter whose only known work – apart from the scene formerly in the collection of the art historian Carlo Gamba (fig. 19) – is the exhibited panel from Lendinara.

The two years that separate the Fondaco dei Tedeschi project from Giorgione's sudden death are shrouded in mystery. Although the exterior fresco cycle painted by Giorgione and Titian has been almost entirely lost to damage and decay, we can still ponder the denouement of the association between the artists. According to Vasari, the collaboration saw the end of their relationship:

Titian then, seeing Giorgione's method, left Gian Bellini's manner, although he had spent a long time on it already, and adopted the new way, imitating it so well in a short time that

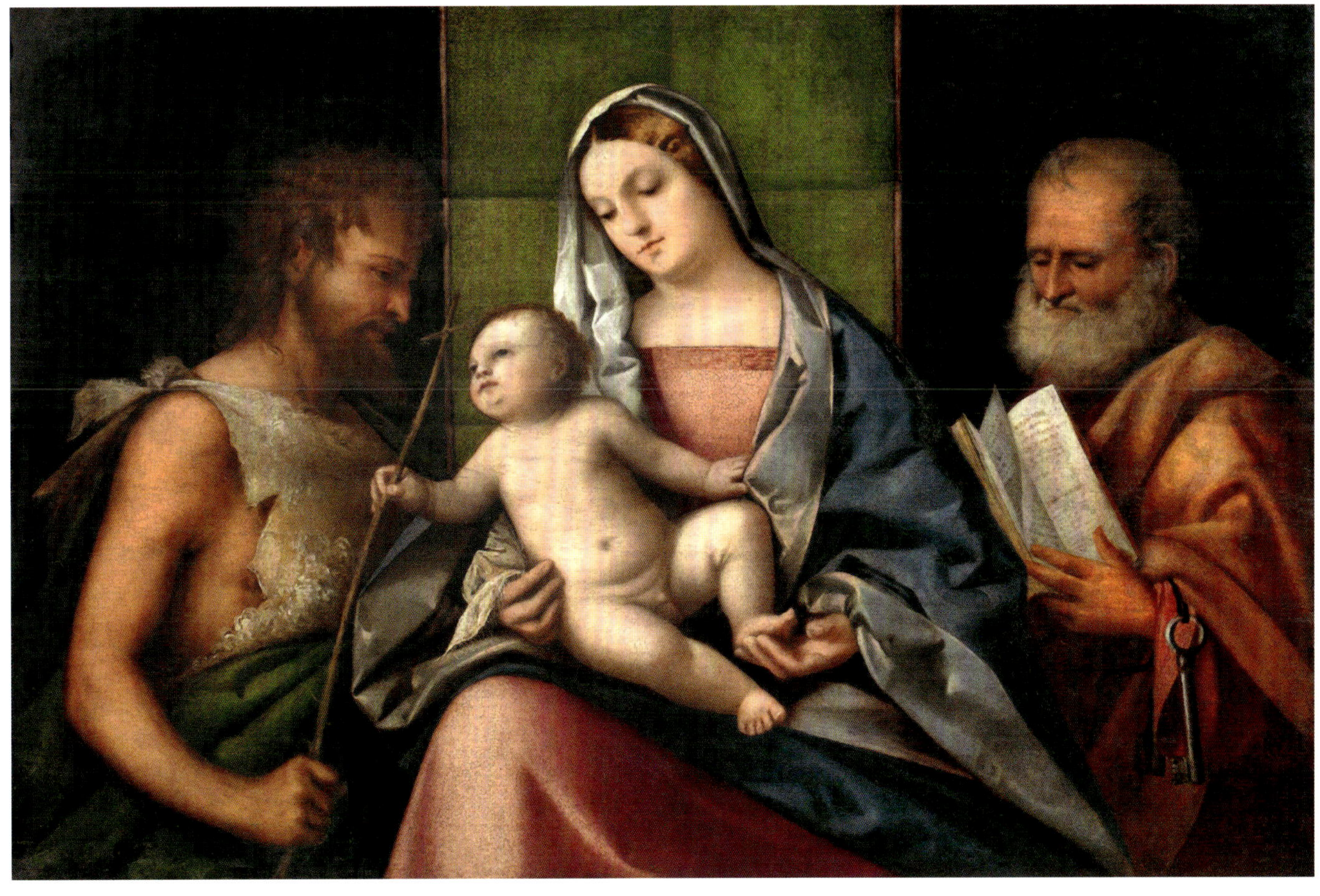

Fig. 20
TITIAN
The Miracle of the Newborn Child, 1511
Fresco, 340 × 355 cm
Scuola del Santo, Padua

> his pictures were mistaken for the works of Giorgione. [...] When Giorgione was employed upon the façade of the Fondaco dei Tedeschi through Barbarigo, part of the narrative was given to Titian, on the same building but above the Merceria. [...] Some gentlemen, not knowing that Giorgione had ceased to work there, and that Titian was employed upon it, meeting Giorgione one day, began to congratulate him, saying he was doing better on this façade than he had done on the one on the Grand Canal. And this vexed Giorgione so much that until the work was finished, and it was known that Titian had done that part, he would not be seen, and from that time forward he would not let Titian work with him or be his friend.[4]

The end of the story has the hallmarks of an exaggerated recollection; one can imagine it being recounted to Vasari by an ageing Titian, wishing to paint himself as the prodigy surpassing his mentor. It is, however, likely the two met on the scaffolding on the façade of the Fondaco.

From this moment, the attributions of some works of Giorgione and Titian became confused, resulting in a contested territory between their *œuvres* that is still disputed by art historians. Research on the period, historical and modern, is fuelled by doubts and queries. *Christ Carrying the Cross* best exemplifies this uncertainty. It is impossible to know which of the two, Giorgione or Titian, is the author of the work. Judgement depends on contradictory information from the sources, in particular from Vasari, who, in the two editions of the *Lives*, ascribes the painting first to Giorgione and then, as we see here, to Titian:

> For the church of Santo Rocho he [Titian] painted [...] a painting, Christ with the cross on his shoulder and a rope round his neck, pulled along by a Jew. This figure was thought by many to be by the hand of Giorgione, and is now the major devotional image in Venice.[5]

Recently the painting has been ascribed to Titian. This is because we know so little about Giorgione's final years, whereas Titian's career is much clearer, particularly after 1511, when all his early work culminates in the extraordinarily influential fresco cycle in the Scuola del Santo in Padua (fig. 20).

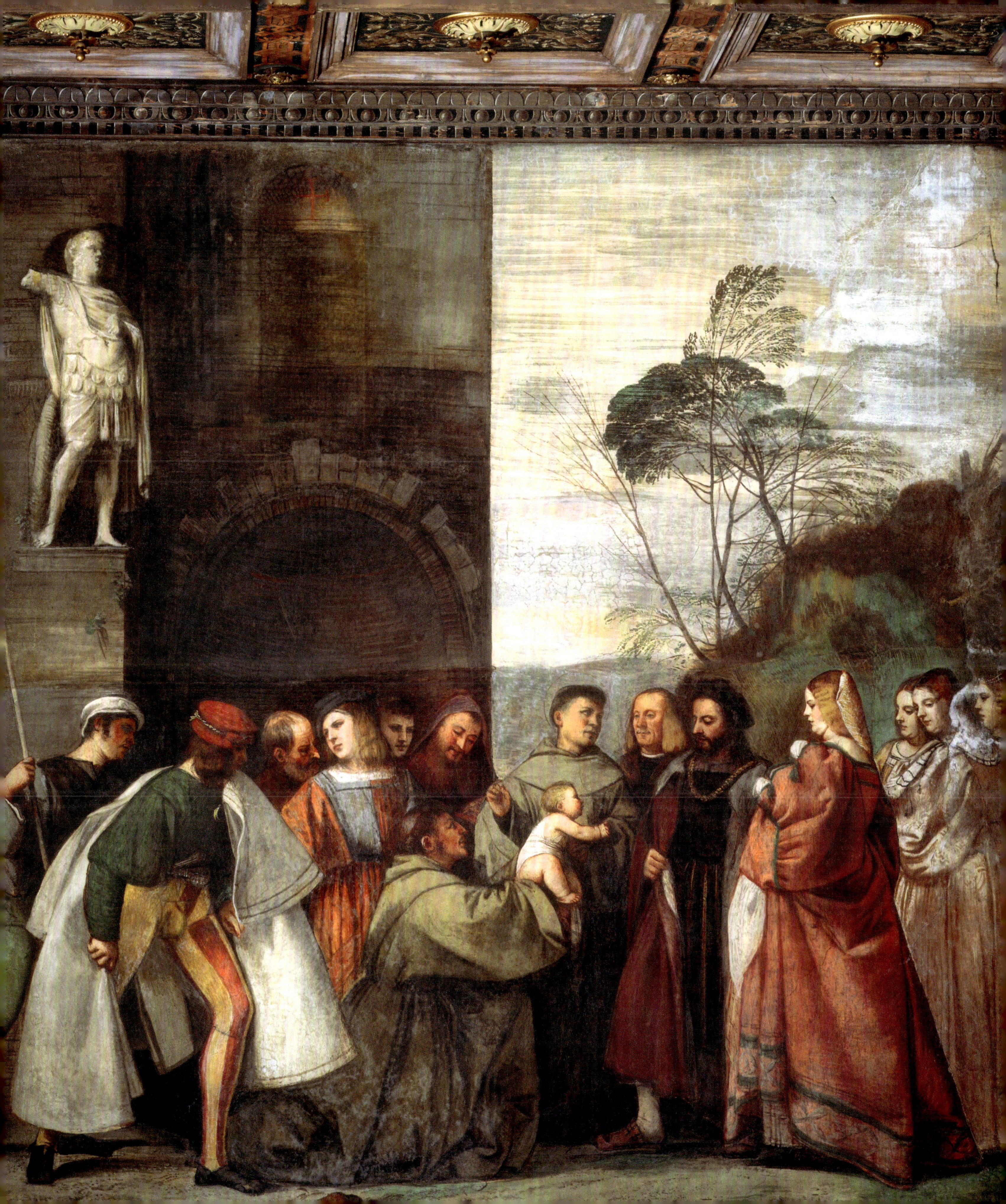

27 Virgin and Child in a Landscape, *c.* 1500–05

GIORGIONE (GIORGIO DA CASTELFRANCO) CASTELFRANCO VENETO, 1478 – VENICE, 1510

Oil on panel (transferred to canvas), 44 × 36.5 cm

The State Hermitage Museum, St Petersburg, inv. GE 185

NOTES

1 Formichova 1992, pp. 171–72.

2 Waagen 1864, p. 30.

3 Harck 1896, p. 423.

4 Somov 1899, p. 26, no. 6.

5 Phillips 1895, p. 347.

6 Phillips 1899, p. 467.

7 Cook 1900, p. 102.

8 Justi 1908, vol. 1, pp. 122–23.

9 Justi 1926, vol. 2, pp. 273–74.

10 Liphart 1910, p. 17.

11 Liphart 1916, no. 6.

12 Venturi 1912, pp. 134–35.

13 Richter 1937, p. 223, no. 40.

14 Berenson 1954, pp. 146–52; Berenson 1957, vol. 1, p. 54.

15 Zampetti 1955, pp. 59–60.

16 Pignatti 1969, pp. 100–01, no. 12; 1978, p. 104, no. 13; Tschmelitsch 1975, p. 97; Ballarin 1979, p. 231; Paris 1993 (Alessandro Ballarin), pp. 299–302, no. 17; Lucco 1980, pp. 132–33, no. 180; 1995, p. 38; Hornig 1987, pp. 176–77; Formichova 1992, pp. 171–72; Perissa Torrini 1993, p. 64, no. 15; Bassano del Grappa 2001 (Irina Artemieva), pp. 54–55, no. 4, Castelfranco Veneto 2009 (Irina Artemieva), pp. 416–18, no. 38; Dal Pozzolo 2009B, pp. 156, 158. For alternative attributions, see Heinemann 1962, vol. 1, p. 116, no. 185; Freedberg 1971, p. 91; Anderson 1996, p. 341.

Mary is shown seated on a rock, in a landscape that falls steeply down to a small village. The hill behind has two caves, probably used for quarrying stone. The Christ Child is resting on Mary's lap, trying to keep His balance by propping Himself up on an arm. His mother tenderly supports His head. In her other hand she clutches a book to her chest while she intently watches her child, who gazes beyond the picture frame. Mary seems to have just finished nursing, which is indicated by the opening in her dress that would reveal her breast.

The painting entered the State Hermitage in 1817 from the collection of the court doctor, one Creighton, with an attribution to Benvenuto Garofalo of Ferrara.[1] In 1864 Gustav Waagen was the first to challenge this attribution, ascribing the work to the school of Giovanni Bellini.[2] Towards the end of the nineteenth century, scholars proposed a variety of pupils known to have worked in Bellini's studio; however, neither Andrea Previtali[3] nor Francesco Bissolo[4] was an entirely convincing suggestion. The name of Giorgione was first introduced by Claude Phillips in 1895.[5] Phillips later retracted his opinion, describing the present work as a copy of a lost original.[6] Herbert Cook preferred to remain impartial.[7] Ludwig Justi also changed his opinion regarding the attribution. In 1908 he initially declared himself convinced that the *Virgin and Child in a Landscape* was an autograph work by Giorgione – dating it to around 1495 and basing his hypothesis on a comparison with the *Trial of Moses* (cat. 16) and the *Judgement of Solomon* in the Uffizi;[8] later he expressed doubts regarding the authenticity of the work.[9] Ernst von Liphart accepted the attribution to Giorgione in 1910[10] but later suggested the name of Bartolomeo Veneto.[11] Lionello Venturi, like Waagen, ascribed the painting to an imitator of Giovanni Bellini.[12]

In 1937 Jean Paul Richter in turn declared himself convinced by the attribution to Giorgione, dating the panel to 1500.[13] His argument was based on the position of Mary's hand supporting the Christ Child's head, which recalls the *Holy Family* in the National Gallery of Art, Washington DC.

Bernard Berenson associated the *Virgin and Child in a Landscape* with the so-called *Tallard Madonna* (cat. 28) and the *Virgin and Child with Saint Catherine and Saint John the Baptist* in the Gallerie dell'Accademia (cat. 30), pointing the group in the direction of Giovanni Cariani.[14] No one has followed him in this assumption. On the contrary, since the painting's inclusion in the exhibition 'Giorgione e i Giorgioneschi' in 1955, opinion in favour of Giorgione gathered strength.[15] More recently Terisio Pignatti, Günther Tschmelitsch, Alessandro Ballarin, Mauro Lucco, Christian Hornig, Tamara Formichova, Annalisa Perissa Torrini, Irina Artemieva and Enrico Maria Dal Pozzolo have supported the attribution to Giorgione, with variations in dating from 1495 to 1507.[16]

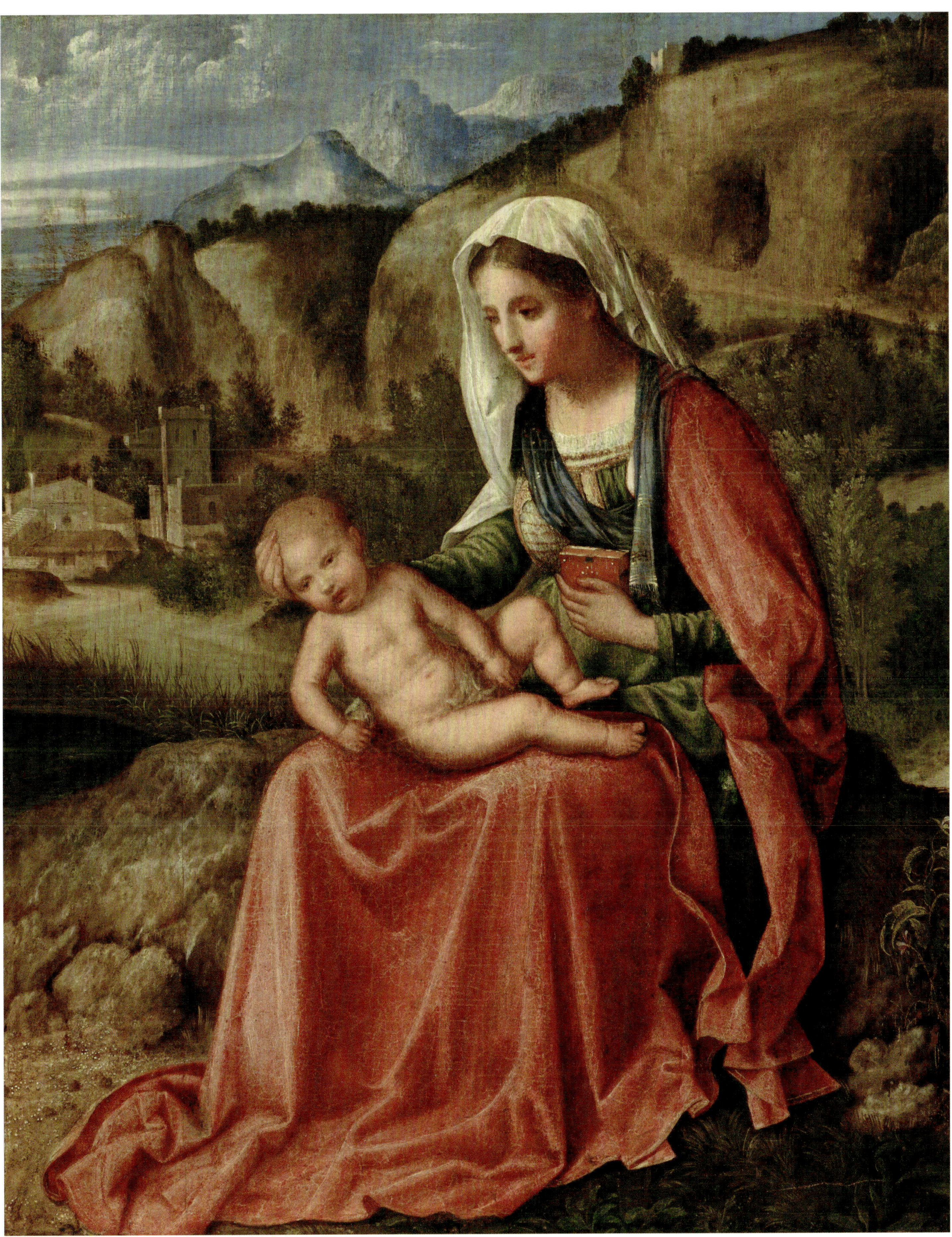

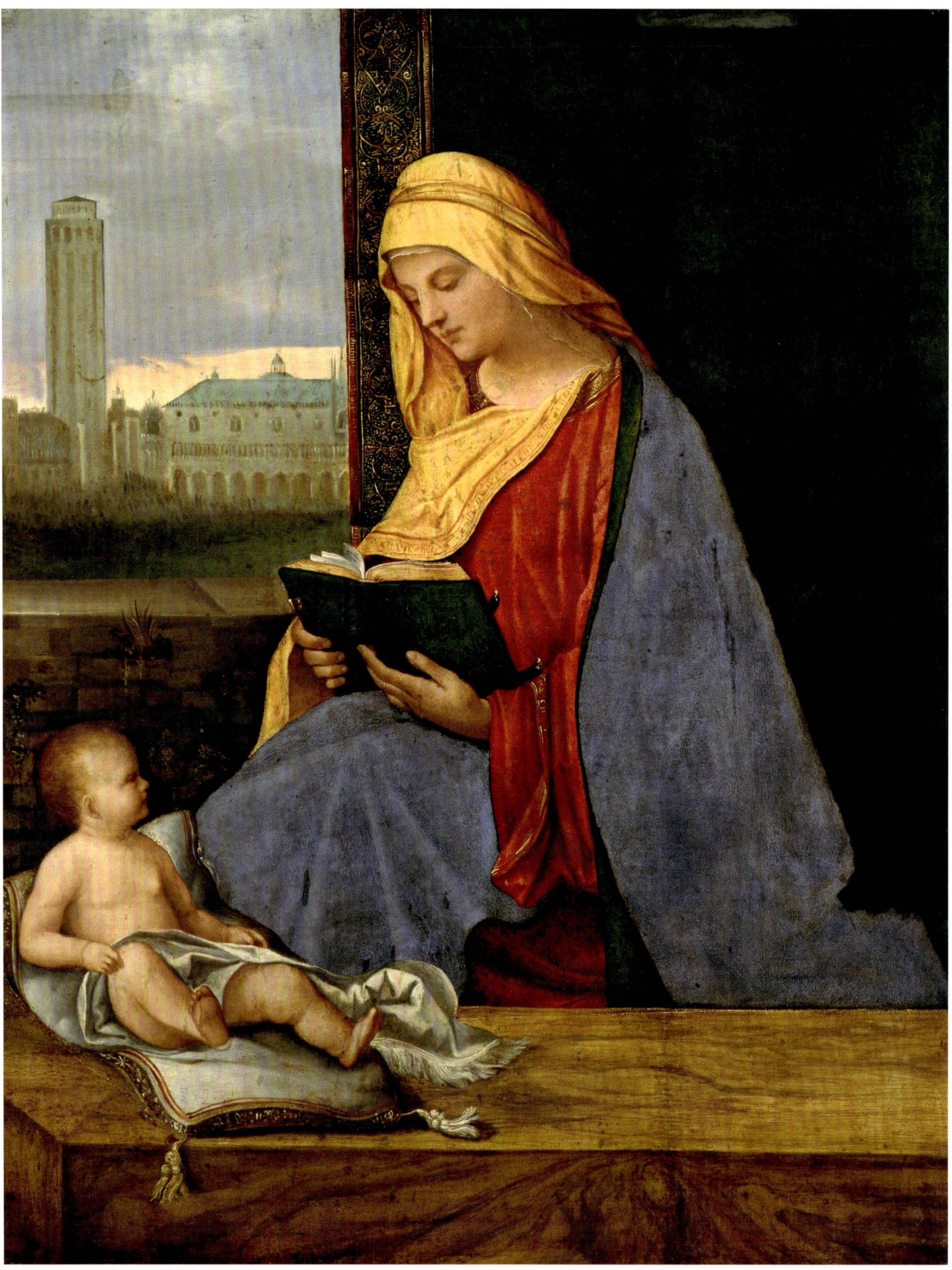

28

Virgin and Child ('Tallard Madonna'), *c.* 1500–05

ATTRIBUTED TO GIORGIONE (GIORGIO DA CASTELFRANCO) CASTELFRANCO VENETO, 1478 – VENICE, 1510

Oil on panel, 76.7 × 60.2 cm

The Ashmolean Museum, Oxford. Purchased 1949, inv. WA1949.222

The Virgin and Child are depicted outside the usual enclosed and protected interior. An elegant green fabric and a weed-covered low wall frame a view of the area around Saint Mark's Basilica, seen from the island of San Giorgio Maggiore. The campanile, the two columns on the Molo, the Torre dell'Orologio (glimpsed in the distance) and the broad façade of the Palazzo Ducale facing the Bacino are all clearly visible.

We can assume that the clear, dark brush strokes of paint against Saint Mark's Square are not intended to represent a large throng of people (pre-empting the style of the Futurist painter Umberto Boccioni as Mauro Lucco suggests, or painted in a 'freely impressionistic' manner, as described by Jaynie Anderson).[1] Rather, they are a naturalistic representation of a stormy lagoon buffeting the Molo. Perhaps this is what prompted the commission of a devotional image such as this, which could be invoked to afford protection from potential catastrophe.

The protagonists are independently absorbed: Mary reads, while Christ, seated comfortably on a cushion, is distracted by something happening beyond the picture frame.

The *Tallard Madonna* takes its name from its earliest documented owner, Marie-Joseph, Duc de Tallard (1683–1755). In the sale catalogue of his collection, published a year after his death, the painting is listed as by 'Giorgione da Castel Franco, called Giorgione. The Virgin sitting reading; The child Jesus is before her. We see Piazza S. Mark of Venise.'[2] As has been observed, the dimensions given in the Parisian catalogue match the dimensions of the Oxford painting.[3] A distinguished spectator at the 1756 sale, Pierre-Jean Mariette, considered to be the 'greatest connoisseur of the eighteenth century',[4] noted: 'It seems to me to be by Giovanni Bellini.'[5] Ever since its first appearance, the painting's attribution has divided experts.

A similar situation occurred when the painting reappeared on the market in London in 1949.[6] It was attributed to Giovanni Cariani and acquired – through the dealers Colnaghi – by the Ashmolean Museum in Oxford, whose Keeper at the time, Karl Parker, attributed the work to Giorgione with the support of James Byam Shaw, the drawings specialist and Director of Colnaghi.[7] From this moment, the majority of scholars in the field have considered the attribution to Giorgione valid; supporters have included Hans D. Gronau, Rodolfo Pallucchini, Antonio Morassi, Lionello Venturi, Pietro Zampetti and Paola Della Pergola.[8]

Bernard Berenson's suggestion that the *Tallard Madonna* is instead by Giovanni Cariani[9] needs to be reconsidered in light of later studies that render this attribution untenable. Most scholars have noted the almost identical profiles of the *Tallard Madonna* and the Virgin in the so-called *Allendale Nativity* in the National Gallery of Art, Washington DC. This has had an effect on the chronological interpretation of the two paintings, which are usually thought to date from near the beginning of Giorgione's career. It has also been observed that the Oxford work features the top of the Torre dell'Orologio, which was completed in 1497. This has enabled Alessandro Ballarin to date the painting to 1498–99, slightly earlier than Giorgione's *Castelfranco Altarpiece* (fig. 17), which is ascribed to about 1500.[10]

Those favouring a slightly later date, around 1505–08, include Antontio Morassi, Rodolfo Pallucchini and Teresio Pignatti.[11] In addition, Lionello Puppi believed that this date was correct, citing as proof the presence of the wings on either side of the Torre dell'Orologio – structures that were not completed until 1506.[12] This theory has also been adopted by Filippo Pedrocco and Enrico Maria Dal Pozzolo.[13] These additions do not strike the present authors as clearly visible.

Jaynie Anderson disagrees with the attribution to Giorgione, describing its creator as a 'young painter trained in the studio of Bellini but familiar with the new fashionable style, the style of Giorgione in about 1506'.[14]

NOTES

1 Lucco 1995, p. 64; Anderson 1996, p. 335.

2 Tallard 1756, p. 51, no. 88. 'Giorgione da Castel Franco, dit le Giorgion. La Vierge assise lisant; L'Enfant Jésus est devant elle. Dans le fond, on apperçoit la Place de S. Marc de Venise.'

3 Lloyd 1977, p. 78, no. 3.

4 Haskell 1981, p. 601.

5 Jervis 1989, pp. 559–61: 'Il me paroit de Jean Bellin.' Mariette's copy of the catalogue is now in the National Art Library, at the Victoria and Albert Museum, London.

6 Christie's, 13 May 1949, lot 119.

7 Parker 1949, p. 43.

8 Gronau 1949, p. 183; Pallucchini 1949; Morassi 1951; Venturi 1954, pp. 42–43; Venice 1955 (Pietro Zampetti), pp. 20–22, no. 10; Della Pergola 1955A, p. 36.

9 Berenson 1954, pp. 146–52.

10 Ballarin 1979, p. 229; Ballarin 1993A, p. 283; Paris 1993 (Alessandro Ballarin) p. 300.

11 Morassi 1951, p. 212; Pallucchini 1955, p. 3; Pignatti 1969, p. 104, no. 17; and Pignatti 1978, p. 108, no. 18.

12 Puppi 1981, p. 357.

13 Pedrocco 1999, p. 156, no. 23; Dal Pozzolo 2009B, pp. 279–81.

14 Anderson 1996, pp. 334–35. 'Un jeune peintre instruit dans l'atelier de Bellini mais au courant du nouveau style en vogue, celui de Giorgione vers 1506.'

29

Virgin and Child with Saint Peter and Saint Mark and a Donor ('Cornbury Park Altarpiece'), 1505

GIOVANNI BELLINI VENICE, c.1430 – 1516

Oil on panel,
91.4 × 81.3 cm

Lent by Birmingham Museums Trust on behalf of Birmingham City Council, inv. 1977P227

NOTES

1 Ridolfi 1648, p. 72.

2 Dal Pozzo 1718, p. 283.

3 Cannon-Brookes 1977, unnumbered.

4 Douglas-Scott 1996, pp. 5–21.

5 Gronau 1909, p. 263; Gibbons 1962, pp. 46–47.

6 Tempestini 1992, pp. 258–60; Rome 2008 (Peter Humfrey), p. 294, no. 51.

7 Berenson 1957, vol. 1, p. 30; Robertson 1968, pp. 115–16; Agosti 2009, pp. 126–27; Mazzotta, 2012, pp. 43–44.

The Virgin and Child sit on a throne placed on a large marble platform. The throne is made of precious materials: its marble back is set inside a border finely carved with plants and animals. Two stylised dolphins in bronze surmount the throne. The donor, portrayed in profile, kneels on a particularly elegant paving of chequered, coloured tiles, and stares fixedly forwards.

The donor's immobility contrasts with the dynamism of the saints. Saint Peter is depicted standing with his weight on his right foot, and his head turned towards the Holy Family. He appears to be gesturing towards the devout donor with his right hand. Saint Mark leans forward, one hand on the donor, the other on the throne. His mouth is open and he appears to be conversing with the Virgin and Child. It looks as if only the saints have access to the sacred vision, and their direct experience is denied to the donor. The detailed characterisation of the faces of the saints, painstakingly painted, contrasts with the indistinct quality of the features of the Virgin and Child. Mary in particular looks little more than a young girl, with a body that is perceptibly smaller than those of the saints. She wears a broad blue mantle lined with green. The throne is located in the open air, in a landscape that becomes more mountainous as it recedes into the distance.

This small altarpiece, designed for private devotional use, formerly had two side wings. The shadow that falls, reaching as far as the donor, must be that of a figure from the missing panel on the left. The painter has handled the effect of the shadow darkening the marble paving with great skill. The lower step of the platform bears a label inscribed in Roman capitals with the signature and date of execution: 'Joannes Bellinvs / MCCCCCV'.

The earliest reference to this painting occurred in 1648 by Carlo Ridolfi, who locates it in the collection of Giacomo Muselli (1569–1641) in Verona, and describes it as follows:

> Signor Christoforo and Signor Francesco Musel[l]i in Verona have, among the many items collected by their Father, by this Author [Giovanni Bellini] two exceptionally rare Paintings, one in the shape of an altar containing the Queen of Heaven, it has on either side Saints Peter and Paul and someone standing dressed in old-fashioned clothes; in the cover Saint Francis and Saint Vincent Ferrer.[1]

A later, more detailed description of the small altarpiece was found in the 1662 inventory of the Muselli collection; this report also contained the measurements of the work (expressed in the *braccia* of Modena), which are compatible with those of the present painting. It is easy to understand the misidentification of Saint Mark as Saint Paul. It is less easy to explain the presence of the two saints, belonging to different religious orders, who apparently adorned the two lost wings. Who knows in what posture they were depicted? Perhaps they were turned towards the viewer, as are the outer figures in the altarpiece at San Zaccaria in Venice (fig. 18), painted by Bellini in 1505. The two side panels were not mentioned in 1718 when the painting was recorded in the collection of the Sereghi family in Verona,[2] indicating that by this time the altarpiece had been broken up. Birmingham Museums and Art Gallery acquired the central panel in 1977, prior to which it is documented as having been in the United Kingdom from 1801 without interruption.[3]

Michael Douglas-Scott's 1996 hypothesis concerning the possibility that this painting might be that presented by Hieronimo Olivier to the Chiesa della Madonna dell'Orto in Venice is not convincing.[4] The description in the will is too general – it mentions only a Virgin and Child and the portrait of Marco Olivier by Giovanni Bellini.

The extent of Bellini's participation in this painting has been widely discussed by scholars. Some have expressed their belief in the involvement of Bellini's studio. The names of the 'Pseudo-Basaiti' and of Marco Bello have been suggested in particular.[5] The areas of the painting of especial interest to critics are the apparent disproportion – in comparison to the other figures – of the portrait of the donor, and the generic expressions of the Virgin and Child. X-rays have revealed a detailed drawing beneath this group, with no pentimenti. The figures on either side, however, conceal many corrections made during execution. These indications have been viewed as evidence that an assistant painted the central section on top of the maestro's drawing.[6] Yet the quality of the painting is so high that the contribution of the workshop, should it exist, is almost impossible to detect. Many scholars, past and present, share this opinion.[7]

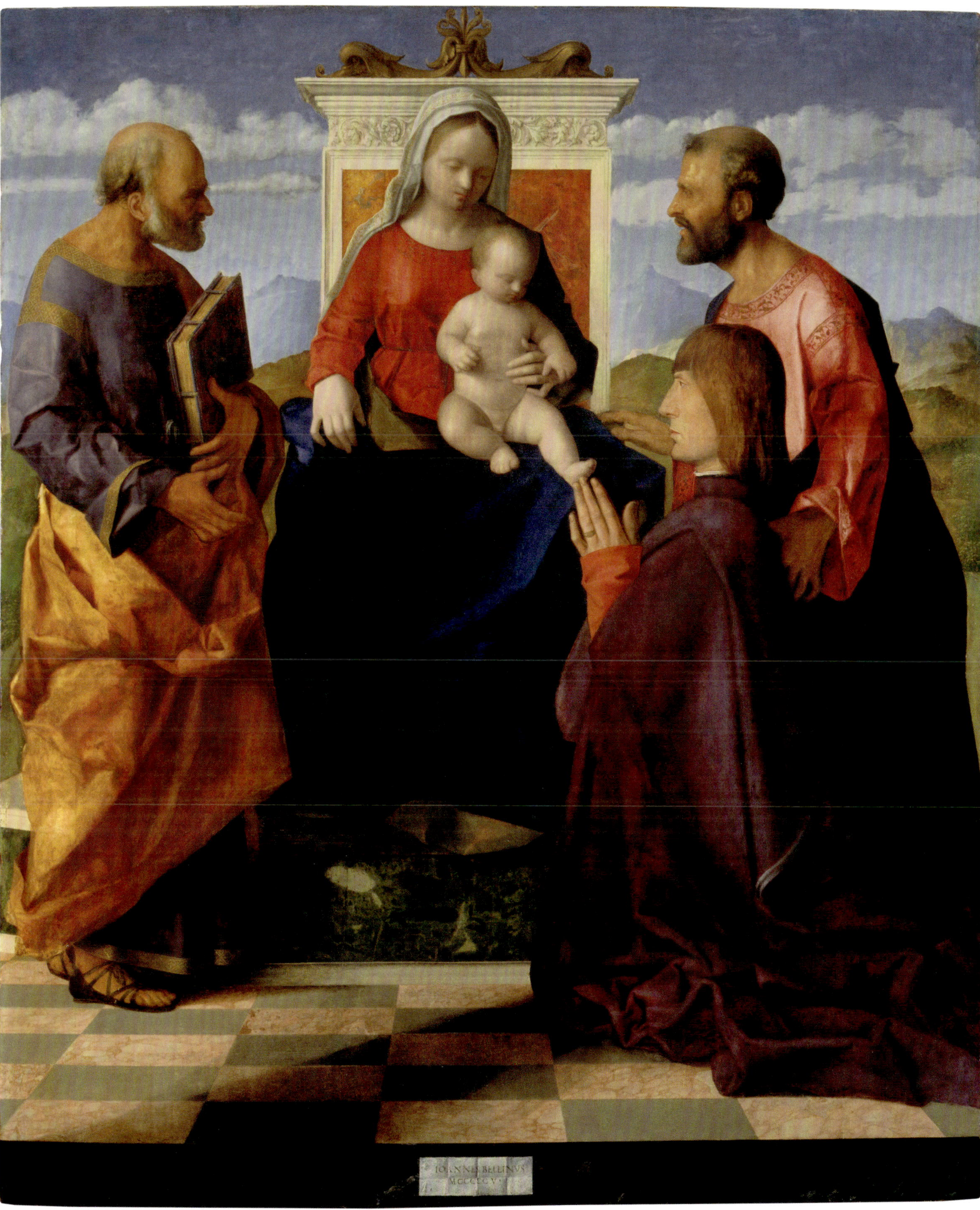
IOANNES BELLINVS
MCCCCCV

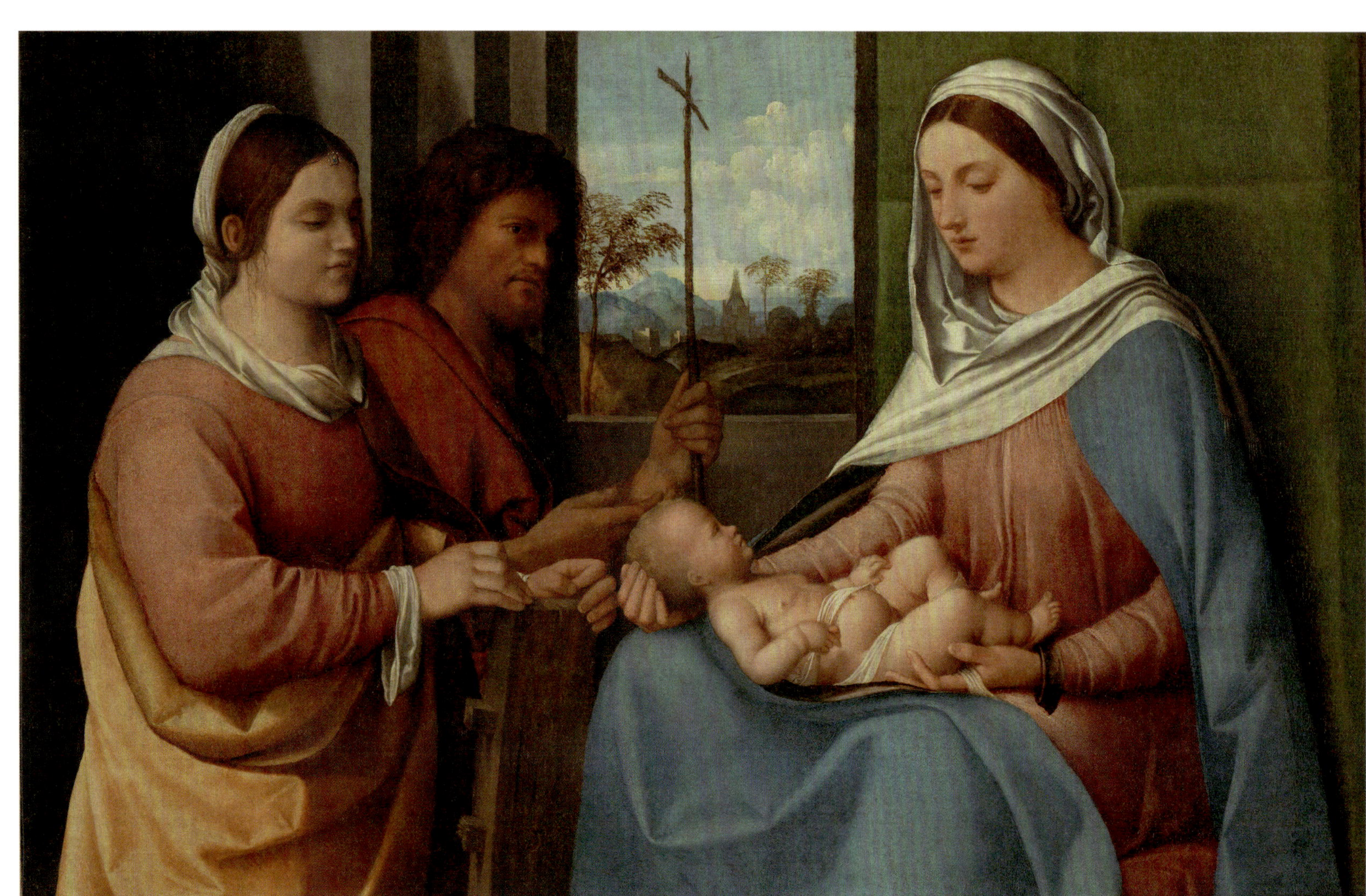

30 Virgin and Child with Saint Catherine and Saint John the Baptist, *c.* 1505–08

ATTRIBUTED TO SEBASTIANO DEL PIOMBO (SEBASTIANO LUCIANI) VENICE, c. 1485 – ROME, 1547

Oil on panel,
51 × 81 cm

Gallerie dell'Accademia, Venice,
inv. 70

The Virgin is depicted before a large open window, through which can be seen a landscape and a distant village. She sits at an angle to the viewer, with a green cloth behind her. The placement of the two saints gives the painting depth, breaking completely with the conventional composition of sacred paintings destined for private devotion in Venice in the early sixteenth century. The Baptist stares into the distance, and points to the cross. Mary and Saint Catherine fix their thoughtful gazes on Christ.

The earliest documented reference to this painting records it as being in the collection of Girolamo Contarini (1770–1843), originally in the Palazzo Contarini degli Scrigni in Venice. Contarini presented the work to the Gallerie dell'Accademia in 1838, with 187 other paintings; while in the Contarini collection, the painting was attributed to Andrea Previtali, a pupil of Giovanni Bellini.[1] This was resolutely rejected by Giovanni Battista Cavalcaselle, who considered it instead to be a work combining 'all the elements of the progress in the Venetian school at the opening of the career of Giorgione and Titian'.[2]

In 1908 Georg Gronau introduced the name of Vincenzo Catena, creating a group of works consisting of the *Allendale Nativity*, the *Benson Holy Family* (both National Gallery of Art, Washington DC) and the *Adoration of the Kings* (National Gallery, London).[3] In 1932 Bernard Berenson linked the painting to Bernardino Licinio;[4] two decades later he changed his attribution to Giovanni Cariani,[5] connecting the painting with the *Madonna* in Oxford (cat. 28) and that in St Petersburg (cat. 27).

Roberto Longhi intervened decisively, returning the group assembled by Gronau to Giorgione's catalogue, 'around the time of the *Castelfranco Altarpiece* [fig. 17], around 1505'.[6] Longhi's proposal (reiterated in 1946)[7] met with widespread approval and remains popular today.[8]

Rodolfo Pallucchini took a different stance in 1935; he considered the painting to be the work of Sebastiano del Piombo, Giorgione's most faithful follower.[9] Pallucchini made a convincing case,[10] and over time his reasoning gained a number of supporters.[11]

The question of attribution seems destined to remain open. The case of the *Three Philosophers* (fig. 7), mentioned in 1525 by Marcantonio Michiel as a work 'begun by Zorzi da Castelfranco and finished by Sebastiano', is highly significant due to the level of collaboration between the two artists. It is impossible to establish which part of the Vienna painting can be ascribed to Sebastiano, and in general the work is regarded as exclusively the work of Giorgione – a comfortable simplification.

The case of the present panel is different. Anyone thinking to ascribe the painting to Sebastiano will encounter numerous 'Morellian' clues demonstrating that this work belongs to the painter's early career. It is the authors' opinion that these elements are sufficiently well defined to allow the work to be compared with others created by Sebastiano in about 1505, the period preceding his *sacra conversazione* in the Louvre and his altarpiece at San Giovanni Crisostomo in Venice, the latter of which is documented to 1509.

NOTES

1 Pinacoteca Contarini 1841, p. 7.

2 Crowe and Cavalcaselle 1871, vol. 1, p. 277, note 2.

3 Gronau 1908, p. 509.

4 Berenson 1932, p. 284; 1936, p. 243.

5 Berenson 1954; Berenson 1958, vol. 1, p. 57.

6 Longhi 1927C, p. 236.

7 Longhi 1946, pp. 16–17.

8 Suida 1935, pp. 76–78; Morassi 1942, p. 64; Morassi 1951, p. 215; Ballarin 1979, p. 229; Lucco 1980, p. 142, no. 248; Ballarin 1993A, pp. 283–84; Lucco 1995, p. 21; Lucco 2008, p. 28, no. 11.

9 Pallucchini 1935, pp. 43–44.

10 Pallucchini 1941, p. 455; Pallucchini 1944A, pp. 17–18, 25, 153; Pallucchini 1981, vol. 2, pp. 525–27, 554.

11 Fiocco 1948, p. 20; Pignatti 1969, p. 134; Hirst 1981, pp. 4–6, 26, 94; Nepi Scirè 1991, p. 144; Perissa Torrini 1993, pp. 139–40, no. 14A; Holberton 1994, p. 33; Filippo Pedrocco, in Pignatti and Pedrocco 1999, p. 210, no. A20; Castelfranco Veneto 2009 (Enrico Maria Dal Pozzolo), pp. 434–35, no. 48; Tempestini 2012, p. 229.

31 Jacopo Pesaro Being Presented by Pope Alexander VI to Saint Peter, *c.* 1508–11

TITIAN (TIZIANO VECELLIO) PIEVE DI CADORE, *c.* 1488/90 – VENICE, 1576

Oil on canvas,
147.5 × 189 cm

Koninklijk Museum voor Schone Kunsten, Antwerp, inv. 357

NOTES

1 Wittkower 1938–39, pp. 194–205.

2 Saxl 1935 [1957], vol. 1, pp. 163–64.

3 Ozzola 1932, pp. 128–30.

4 Brown 2013, pp. 51–59.

5 Panofsky 1969, pp. 178–79.

6 'Jacobus Pisaurus Paphi Ep[iscop]us Qui / Turcas Bello Seipsu[m] Pace Vincebat.'

7 Crowe and Cavalcaselle 1877, vol. 1, pp. 60–64.

8 Hope 1980, p. 26; London 1984 (Giles Robertson), p. 219, no. 113; Brown 1990, pp. 59–60.

9 Ballarin 1993B, pp. 357–66; Paris 1993 (Alessandro Ballarin), pp. 368–75, no. 40.

10 Longhi 1927C, p. 235.

11 Pallucchini 1981, vol. 2, pp. 538–39; Naples 2006 (Caroline Campbell), p. 106, no. 1.

12 Aikema 2013, p. 24; Brown 2013, pp. 60–61.

At the centre of the lower edge of the painting an inscription (probably added in the seventeenth century) describes the scene: 'Ritratto di vno di ca^{sa} Pesaro / in Venetia che fv fatto / generale di s^{ta} chiesa. / Titiano f.' ('Portrait of one of the Pesaro family in Venice who was made [a] general of the holy church painted [by] Titian'). The gentleman on his knees is Jacopo Pesaro (1464–1547), Bishop of Paphos, Cyprus; he is holding a standard bearing a coat of arms associated with the Borgia family. Pope Alexander VI – who here accompanies Pesaro – was himself a Borgia. Saint Peter is seated on a throne; he holds a gospel in one hand, while with his other he makes a gesture spelling out Christ's name. The two high steps of his throne are decorated with narrative bas-reliefs. The female figure on the right of the lower relief can be recognised as Venus Genetrix, the patroness of victory; she is the protagonist of an allegorical story based on the triumph of Christianity over paganism.[1] This reference further emphasises Pesaro's affiliation with Paphos; Venus was believed to be the owner of the island in antiquity.[2]

Bishop Pesaro has removed a heavy helmet – the study of which has yielded one presumed date for the work, about 1505–10[3] – and has placed it on the chequered floor tiles. From Saint Peter's terrace we can see a shoreline facing open sea, on which a fleet of warships sails under red flags, similar to that held by Pesaro. In 1502 Alexander VI appointed Pesaro to lead twenty papal galleys in a crusade against the Turks. In the final days of August that year, thanks to the support of the Venetian and Spanish fleets, victory was won near the Ionian island of Santa Maura (ancient Leucas). The following year, however, saw not only the death of the Borgia pope, but also the loss of Christian control over the island. The iconography of the painting, which is interwoven with the biography of Pesaro, has been studied by Brown.[4]

Anthony van Dyck made a copy of this painting in his Italian sketchbook in Venice in 1622. In 1639 the work appeared in the inventory of King Charles I of England; it was sold in 1651, following his execution in 1649. After changing hands a number of times the painting was acquired in Paris by William I of Holland, and presented to the museum in Antwerp in 1823.

The main debate concerning the painting is its date, and thus the work's chronological position among Titian's works. Evidently the story of the 1502 victory played a key role in the evaluation of this painting, and according to the authoritative opinion of Erwin Panofsky:

> It is hard to believe that the Antwerp picture, clearly intended to glorify the events of 1502, was commissioned when these events had become a thing of the remote past. [...] I am therefore inclined to believe that the Antwerp altarpiece was commissioned no later than 1503, perhaps as a memorial to Alexander VI who died on 18 August of that year ...[5]

We know that his victory over the Turks in 1502 was the high point of Pesaro's life. The standard displayed here also appears in the so-called *Pesaro Madonna* in Santa Maria Gloriosa dei Frari in Venice, commissioned from Titian by the same bishop in 1519 and completed in 1526. Furthermore, Pesaro's tomb, also in the Frari, bears the epitaph: 'Jacopo Pesaro Bishop of Paphos conquered the Turks in battle and himself in Peace.'[6]

Despite the problems of reconstructing the chronology of Titian's early career, Joseph Archer Crowe and Giovanni Battista Cavalcaselle deduced from the painting's style that it was indeed executed in about 1502,[7] which coincides with the documentary evidence. An alternative proposal of around 1506 (also derived from the painting's style) corresponds with the biography of Pesaro, who was apparently in Venice that year.[8] The comprehensive reconstruction of Titian's early years by Alessandro Ballarin accorded an extremely prominent position to the Antwerp canvas, based on the artist's later involvement in the project at the Fondaco dei Tedeschi in Venice, and dated the painting to around 1506.[9]

Although Ballarin's proposal is appealing, a more tentative suggestion made by Roberto Longhi in 1927 is to be preferred.[10] He ascribed to the work a date of between 1508 and 1511, the years within which Titian's fresco cycle in the Scuola del Santo, Padua (fig. 20), was documented. With some exceptions, recent scholars – ourselves included – accept this position.[11] Also worth noting are recent attempts to extend the chronological window to 1510–15, with proposals focused on 1512–13, after the Paduan frescoes.[12]

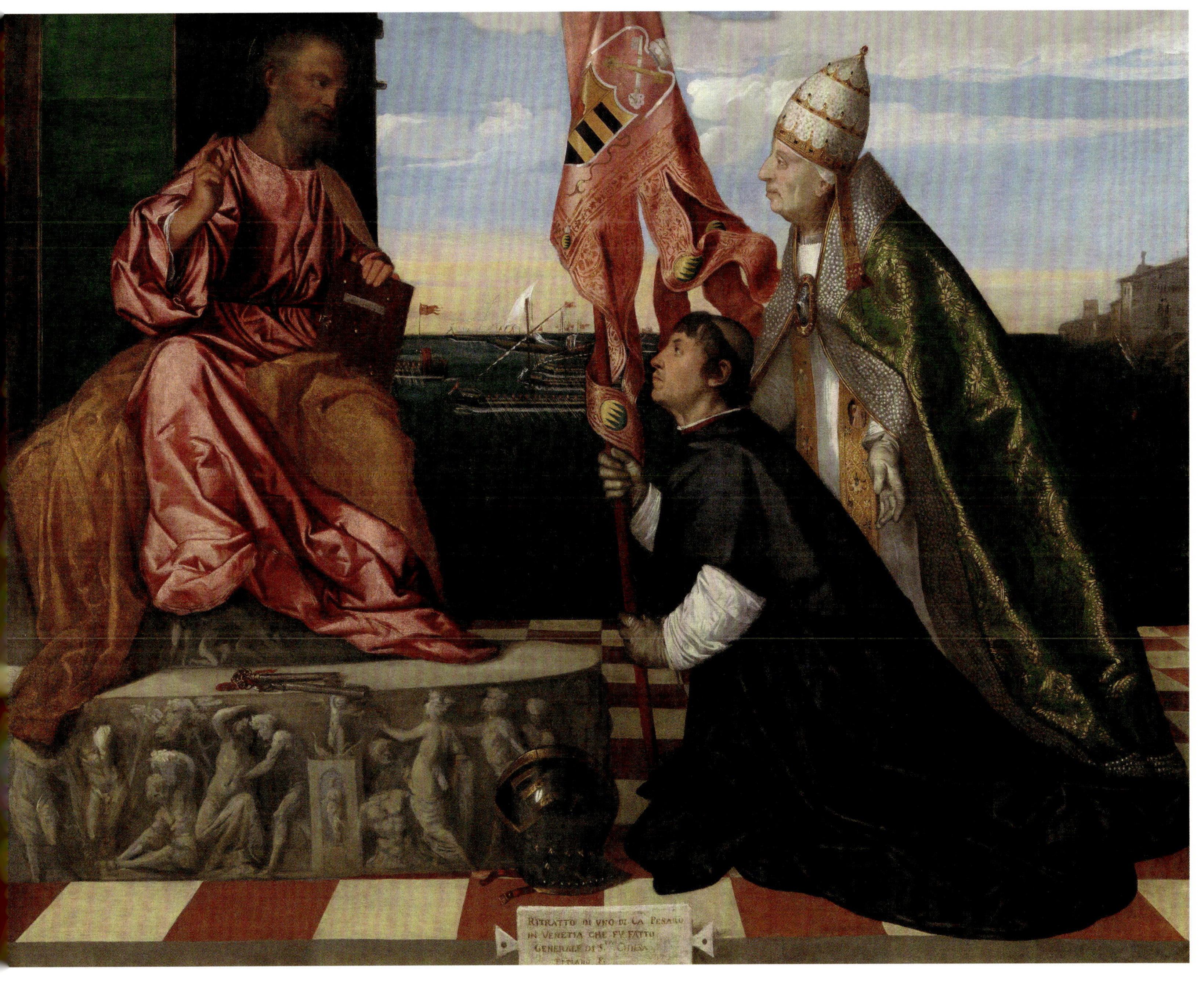
RITRATTO DI VNO DI CA PESARO
IN VENETIA CHE FV FATTO
GENERALE DI STA CHIESA

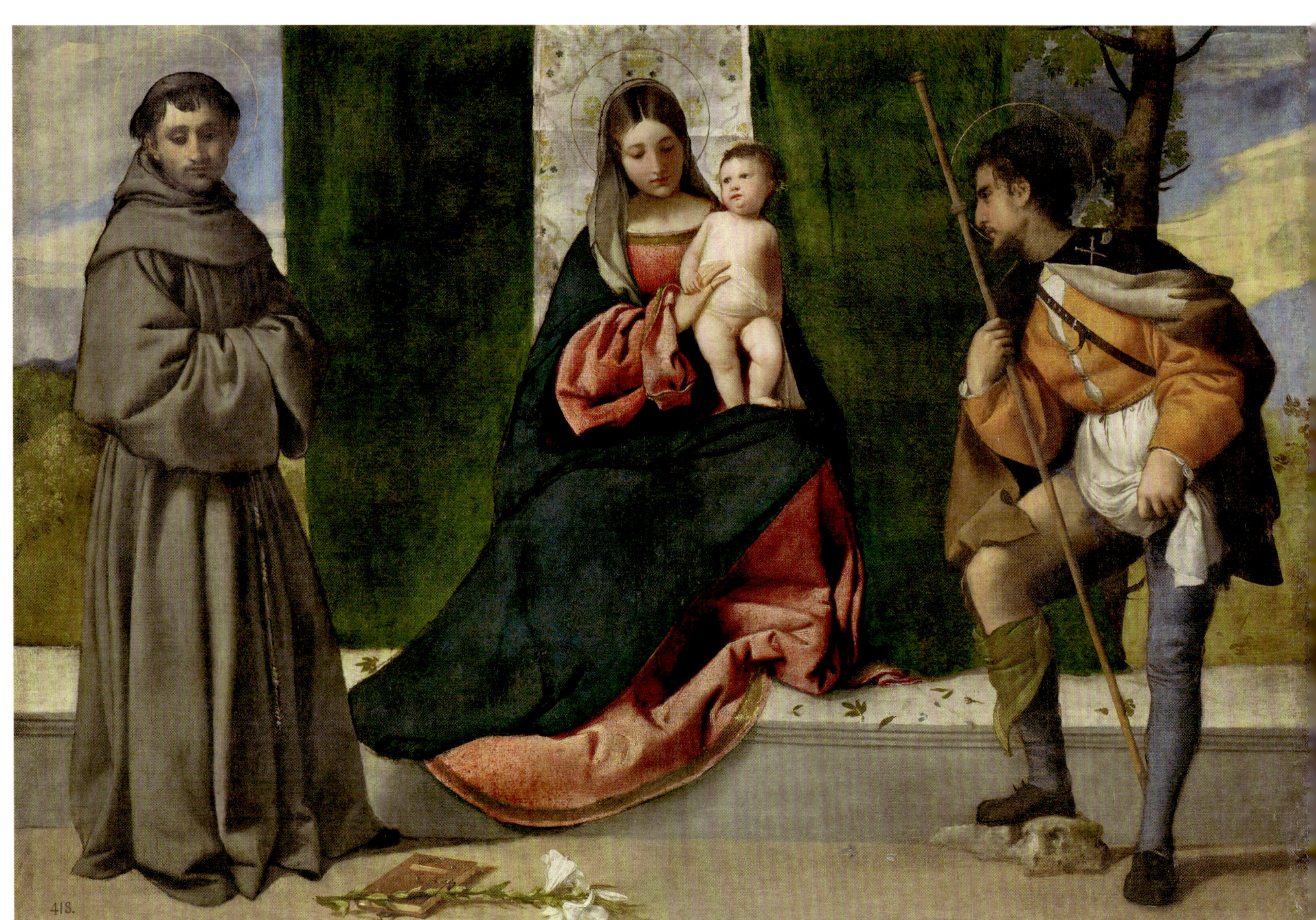
418.

32

Virgin and Child with Saint Anthony of Padua and Saint Roch, *c.* 1509–10

TITIAN (TIZIANO VECELLIO) PIEVE DI CADORE, *c.* 1488/90 – VENICE, 1576

Oil on canvas,
92 × 133 cm

Museo Nacional del Prado, Madrid,
inv. 288

NOTES

1 Brown 2002, pp. 66–67; Madrid 2003 (Miguel Falomir), pp. 142–43, no. 3.

2 Santos 1657, p. 46v.

3 Velasco and Santos 1746, p. 48.

4 Crowe and Cavalcaselle 1871, vol. 2, p. 292.

5 Frizzoni 1894, pp. 65–66.

6 Morelli 1880, p. 216; 1886, p. 162.

7 Berenson 1894, p. 100; Cook 1900, pp. 45–46; Justi 1908, p. 140; Gronau 1908, pp. 425–26.

8 Schmidt 1904, p. 160.

9 Berenson 1932, p. 233; Berenson 1957, vol. 1, p. 84.

10 Richter 1937, pp. 228–29, no. 50.

11 Hourticq 1919, pp. 38, 112.

12 Suida 1933, pp. 21–22; Pallucchini 1981, vol. 2, pp. 539–40; Paris 1993 (Alessandro Ballarin), pp. 400–03, no. 44; Joannides 2001, pp. 125–27; Washington DC 2006 (Peter Humfrey), pp. 82–83, no. 7.

13 Madrid 2003 (Miguel Falomir), pp. 142–43, no. 3; Lucco 2013, p. 52.

14 Hope 1980, p. 40, note 19; Hope 2003, p. 740.

15 London 1983 (Francis L. Richardson), pp. 168–69, no. 34.

16 Holberton 1993, p. 257.

This *sacra conversazione* takes place in the open air, in a landscape bordered at the front by a broad stone terrace. On the terrace stands a throne, behind it a panel of white fabric embroidered with thistle leaves, which is itself backed by a broad green curtain. The painter has emphasised the importance of the Virgin and Child by placing them at the centre of the composition. Mary is lost in thought, eyes downcast, and her child gazes at a distant spot on the horizon. The saints are depicted in contrasting poses. Saint Anthony of Padua is detached and introspective, hands hidden in his ample Franciscan habit. His attributes, the book and the lily, lie before him on the ground. Saint Roch cuts a livelier figure. He leans on his pilgrim's staff, raising the hem of his shirt to show a boil – symptom of the plague – on his inner thigh. He looks intently towards the Virgin and Child.

Attempts have been made to identify this painting as that acquired in 1654 by the Spanish nobleman Alonso de Cárdenas from the heirs of Alethea Talbot, widow of the Earl of Arundel, on behalf of King Philip IV of Spain. The identification is questionable, the purchased work being described as 'large, on canvas' with 'life-sized figures', whereas the present picture is modest in scale, and the figures are certainly not life-sized.[1]

The painting was first mentioned in 1657, when Francisco de los Santos's description places it in El Escorial: 'by the hand of Bordonon; Our Lady seated on a Throne, with the Infant Jesus standing on her knee, to her right Saint Anthony of Padua, on the other side Saint Roch; medium-sized figures, very well painted, and it pleases me greatly.'[2] 'Bordonon' is rendered as 'Pordenone' (the byname of Giovanni Antonio de Sacchis) in a later edition of the description.[3] In 1839 the painting entered the Museo Nacional del Prado with this attribution, yet Joseph Archer Crowe and Giovanni Battista Cavalcaselle rejected Pordenone in favour of Francesco Vecellio, Titian's brother and collaborator.[4] Giovanni Morelli made notes on this picture during his first trip to Spain:

> Pordenone: no. 341. This painting, in my opinion one of the most interesting of all the wonderful examples of the Venetian school possessed by this richly stocked Gallery, bears all the traits typical of Giorgione's brush. In addition, I detect in the style of this Virgin the same style that is to be found in the large painting by Giorgione in the church in Castelfranco [fig. 17].[5]

The attribution to Giorgione began to circulate,[6] and was soon accepted by the leading specialists.[7]

In 1904 Wilhelm Schmidt launched a different interpretation, suggesting that the painting was the work of the young Titian, pre-dating his *Gypsy Madonna* (*c.* 1510; Kunsthistorisches Museum, Vienna).[8] Schmidt's intuition was confirmed by later studies, and the attribution stands today. The influence of Morelli, however, was such that followers such as Bernard Berenson[9] and George Martin Richter[10] continued to give the work to Giorgione.

An attribution to Titian was supported by Louis Hourticq, who compared the Prado painting with the *Concert champêtre* (fig. 15), as well as with Titian's frescoes in the Scuola del Santo in Padua (fig. 20), which date from 1511.[11] This was generally accepted, with some minor differences in the dating. Most scholars recognised a lack of stylistic coherence between the work of Titian from 1511 and the present picture, and so ascribed it to an earlier year.[12] Recently Miguel Falomir and Mauro Lucco have made attempts to date the painting to 1511.[13] In the present authors' opinion, a date of about 1509–10 is still to be preferred. Charles Hope was convinced that the work was executed by a lesser-known artist,[14] and at 'The Genius of Venice' (1983) at the Royal Academy it was exhibited as 'Circle of Giorgione. Attributed to Titian'.[15] In 1993 Paul Holberton suggested that the artist might be Domenico Mancini.[16]

33 Virgin and Child ('Lochis Madonna'), *c.* 1511

TITIAN (TIZIANO VECELLIO) PIEVE DI CADORE, *c.* 1488/90 – VENICE, 1576

Oil on panel,
38 × 47 cm

Accademia Carrara, Bergamo,
inv. 81 LC 00232

This form of nativity, in which Mary appears seated on the ground, is known as a Madonna of Humility. The Virgin and Child are settled before a low wall, and the Christ Child reaches up to touch His mother's hair. This intimate moment takes place against a rural landscape with a small flock of sheep grazing in a field; further in the distance buildings and mountains take on the same intense shade of blue as the sky. The painting was immediately successful: Bernardino Licinio[1] and Francesco Prata da Caravaggio[2] are known to have made copies (with some variations).

Guglielmo Lochis was the earliest documented owner of the painting, and it remained in his possession until 1833. The following year it was referred to, in the catalogue of his collection, as 'a marvellous painting by Titian'.[3] Joseph Archer Crowe and Giovanni Battista Cavalcaselle summarily put the attribution to Titian to one side and viewed the work more modestly, as by Sante Zago, a follower of Titian.[4]

In 1900 Herbert Cook took an opposite view, thinking the *Lochis Madonna* unusually important.[5] He considered it one of Giorgione's paintings, of a quality equivalent to the *Gypsy Madonna* (c. 1511; Kunsthistorisches Museum, Vienna) and the *Bache Madonna* (*c.* 1508–10; The Metropolitan Museum of Art, New York).[6] At that time, debate about the painting focused on its position within the grey area between Giorgione and Titian. In some respects the Bergamo painting has followed the controversial critical history of the *Christ and the Adulteress* in Glasgow (cat. 34), which is similar in style. The present work has also been attributed, erroneously, to Giovanni Cariani.[7]

A turning point was reached in 1933 when Wilhelm Suida revived the attribution to Titian.[8] Roberto Longhi also defended the reference to Titian, suggesting a date prior to the 1511 frescoes in the Scuola del Santo in Padua (fig. 20).[9]

Although both Giuseppe Fiocco and Bernard Berenson proposed Francesco Vecellio as the artist,[10] the attribution to Titian has not been seriously queried since the 1950s, and debate has moved to the presumed dating of the painting.

Rodolfo Pallucchini proposed a date of around 1510–11.[11] Alessandro Ballarin's interpretation was different: he ascribed it to 1507, before Titian began the project at the Fondaco dei Tedeschi in Venice.[12] This chronology is difficult to accept – despite the support of Luisa Attardi[13] – because there are so few verifiable, documented works in the catalogue of Titian's early career. Bert Meijer preferred a date of around 1511,[14] and Paul Joannides suggested around 1510.[15]

NOTES

1 Joannides 2001, p. 96.
2 Lucco 2013, p. 42.
3 Lochis 1834, p. 30, no. XXXVIII.
4 Crowe and Cavalcaselle 1877, vol. 2, p. 438.
5 Cook 1900, pp. 97, 101–02.
6 Today the *Gypsy Madonna* and the *Bache Madonna* are attributed to Titian.
7 Phillips 1937, pp. 44, 59.
8 Suida 1933, pp. 55, 155.
9 Longhi 1946, p. 48.
10 Fiocco 1955, p. 79; Berenson 1957, vol. 1, p. 85.
11 Pallucchini 1969, vol. 1, p. 237.
12 Ballarin 1993B, p. 360. He ascribed *Christ and the Adulteress* (cat. 34) to the same year.
13 Rome 2013 (Luisa Attardi), pp. 70–71, no. 1.
14 Venice 1999 (Bert Meijer), p. 506, no. 506.
15 Joannides 2001, pp. 96–98.

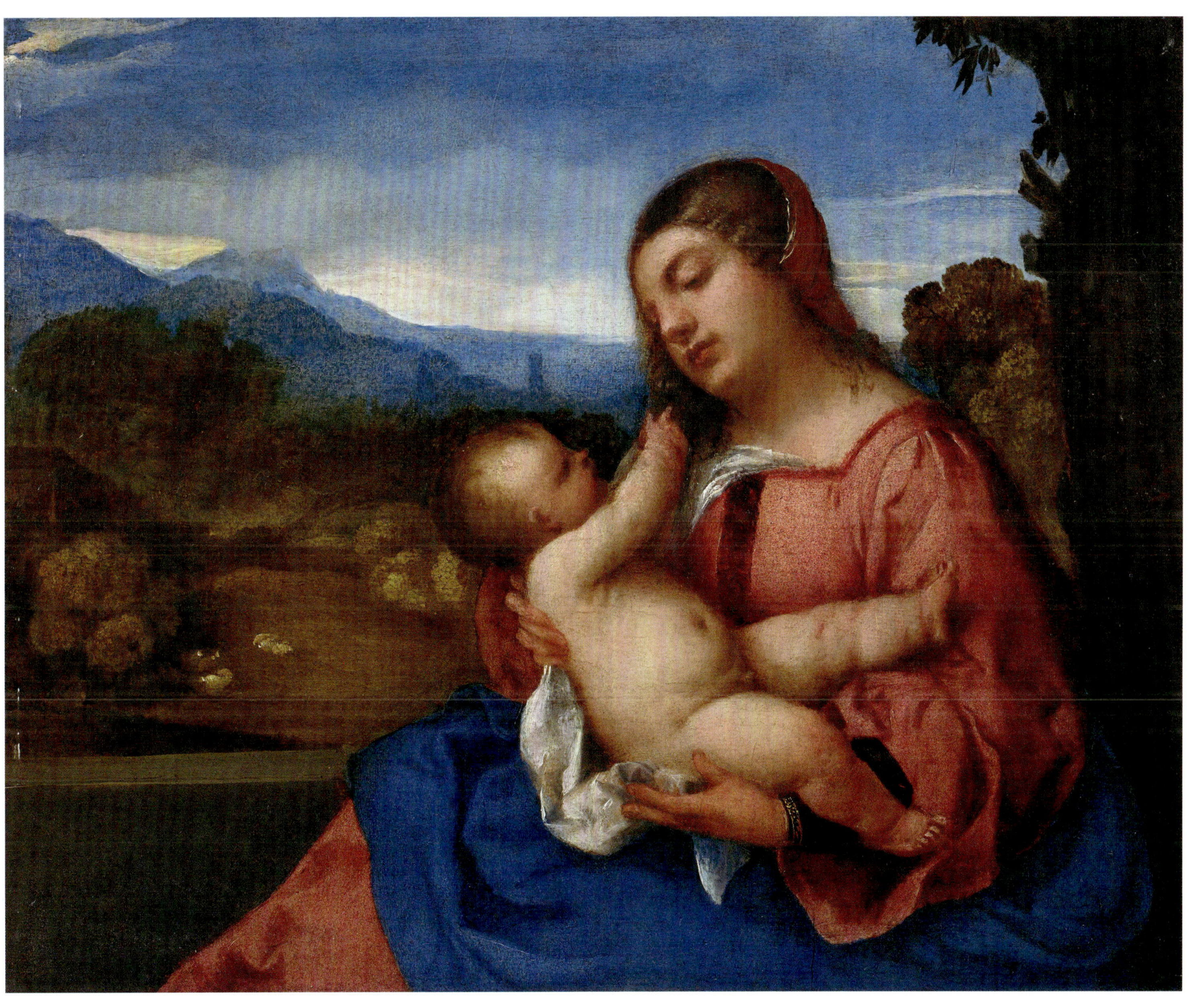

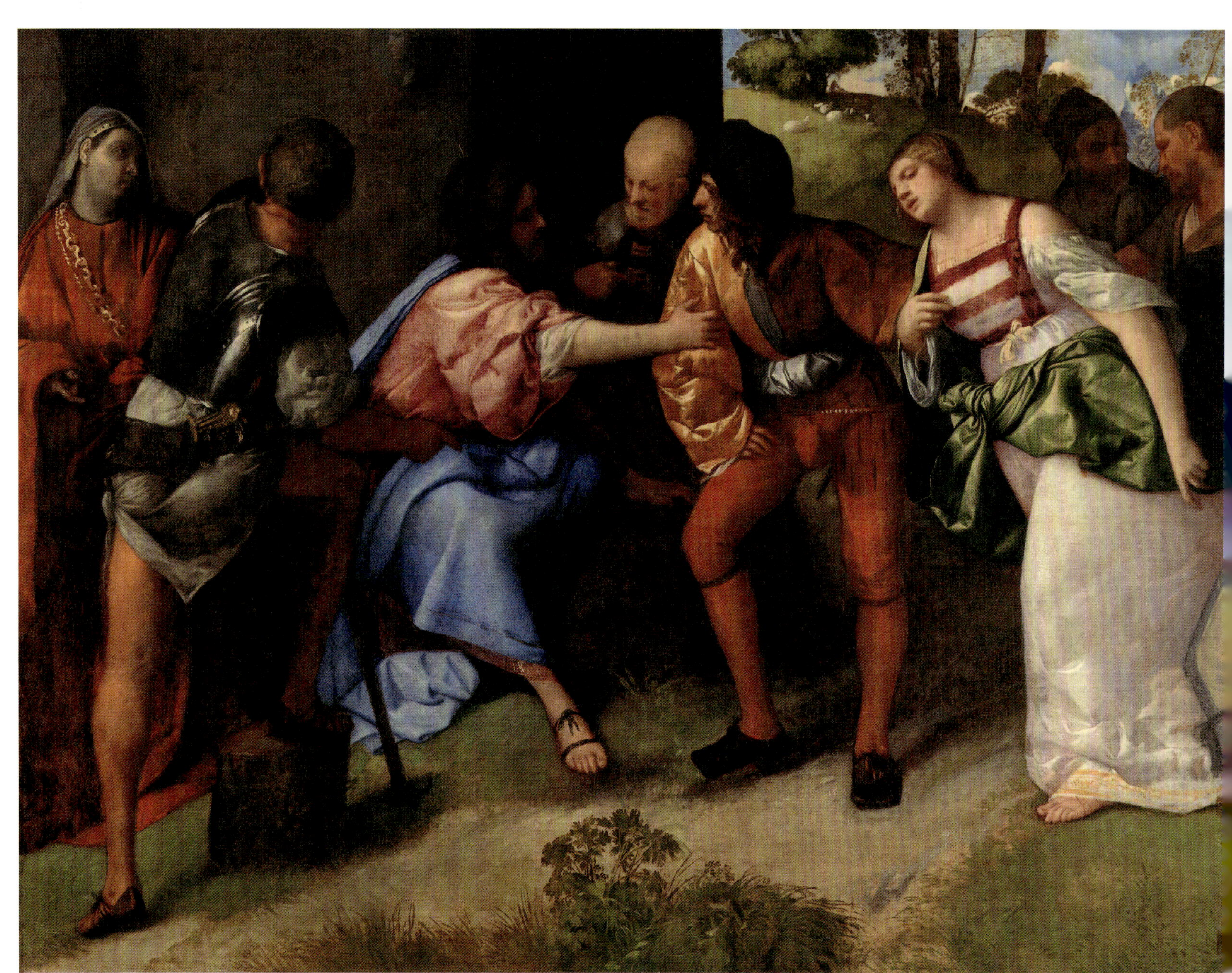

34 Christ and the Adulteress, *c.* 1511

TITIAN (TIZIANO VECELLIO) PIEVE DI CADORE, *c.* 1488/90 – VENICE, 1576

Oil on canvas,
139.2 × 181.7 cm

Glasgow Life (Glasgow Museums) on behalf of Glasgow City Council. Archibald McLellan Collection, purchased 1856, inv. 181

The dynamic appearance of this scene is due in part to the artist's use of a diagonal composition. The figures all converge on the centre, although each is engaged in an individual conversation. Originally there was a full-length male figure on the far right, as can be seen in a copy of the original now in the Accademia Carrara in Bergamo.[1] It is not known when this part of the painting was cut down.

The painting illustrates a passage in the Gospel of John (VIII, 2–7). At the centre of the scene is Christ. He wears a red robe with a blue mantle, and is the only figure dressed in clothing of the biblical era. He is seated outside a temple, in animated conversation with a young man who listens with rapt attention. The other figures have overheard the debate, and Christ's words about the adulterous woman, 'He that is without sin among you, let him cast the first stone at her,' have caused an outcry.

All the figures apart from Christ are dressed in the fashions of the first decade of the sixteenth century. The story illustrates a moral conflict of perennial interest. For this reason it has been suggested that the painting might have been hung in a public space where justice was dispensed.[2] It is also quite possible that it adorned the portico of a private palace in Venice.[3]

The earliest documented owner of the painting was Archibald McLellan (1797–1854), who bequeathed it, with the rest of his collection, to the Museum of Glasgow. It was at the time attributed to Bonifacio de' Pitati.

In terms of attribution, the work's history has been as controversial as that of the *Concert champêtre* (fig. 15). The two paintings have frequently been compared on stylistic grounds, and have shared interpretations concerned in a general way with the blurred boundary that separates late Giorgione from the young Titian.

Gustav Friedrich Waagen's opinion of 1857 was extraordinarily lucid for the period: 'Judging from the highly original conception of the characters, and from the feeling and depth of colour, I am inclined to consider this picture a fine work of the middle period of Giorgione.'[4] In 1871 Joseph Archer Crowe and Giovanni Battista Cavalcaselle compared the work with the copy in the Accademia Carrara, reversing the received wisdom by suggesting that the Glasgow painting was not the prime version: 'probably, by Cariani. […] It is a replica or copy of Cariani's similar picture in the Carrara collection at Bergamo.'[5] Correspondence between Giovanni Morelli and Jean Paul Richter revealed the thoughts of the latter, at the time a young student, who was convinced that this was the work of Domenico Campagnola.[6] In 1893 the name of Campagnola was published by Richter and reiterated by Claude Phillips.[7] In 1894 Georg Gronau also supported the attribution, finding some surprising analogies in the *Concert champêtre*.[8] Meanwhile, in 1900, the name of Giorgione was given new lustre by Herbert Cook: 'Nay, if gorgeousness of colour, splendour of glow, mastery of chiaroscuro, and brilliancy of technique are qualities which go to make up great painting, then the Glasgow picture must take high rank, even in a school where such qualities found their grandest expression.'[9] Ludwig Justi also thought of Giorgione.[10]

One critical moment in the history of the attribution of this painting was the 1919 essay by Louis Hourticq in which he transferred the *Concert champêtre*, as well as that of the Glasgow picture, to the young Titian.[11] Roberto Longhi and Bernard Berenson were convinced by Hourticq's idea.[12] George Martin Richter returned to the traditional attribution to Giorgione with great conviction in 1937,[13] and was supported by others such as Giles Robertson and Ellis Waterhouse.[14] Some scholars even thought of ascribing the painting to Domenico Mancini.[15]

Today, no one questions the attribution to Titian, although the painting's date is still disputed. The opinion of Alessandro Ballarin is worth noting; he saw it as dating from 1507, before Titian was employed to decorate the Fondaco dei Tedeschi in Venice.[16] The majority of scholars prefer a date of about 1511 because of similarities with the frescoes in the Scuola del Santo in Padua, documented in that year (fig. 20).[17] This is practically the same idea as that proposed by Hourticq when he bravely removed two of Giorgione's most famous works from the artist's *œuvre*.

NOTES

1 Illustrated in Rossi 1983, pp. 262–64, no. A7. For a fragment of the upper-right portion of the painting, see Glasgow Museums, inv. 3283.

2 Brown 2007, pp. 97–98.

3 Lucco 2006, p. 102.

4 Waagen 1857, pp. 459–60, no. 95.

5 Crowe and Cavalcaselle 1871, vol. 2, pp. 159, 547–48.

6 In particular the letter of 15 July 1855: Richter 1960, p. 420.

7 Richter 1893, p. 310; Phillips 1893, p. 227.

8 Gronau 1894, p. 331

9 Cook 1900, p. 103.

10 Justi 1908, vol. 1, pp. 157–63; Justi 1926, vol. 1, pp. 173.

11 Hourticq 1919, p. 38.

12 Longhi 1927C, p. 235; Berenson 1928, pp. 147–54.

13 Richter 1937, pp. 219–20, no. 33.

14 Robertson 1955, p. 276; Waterhouse 1974, pp. 3–4, 22–25.

15 Hope 1980, p. 40; Brown 1990, p. 66, no. 19; Holberton 1993, pp. 257–58.

16 Paris 1993 (Alessandro Ballarin), pp. 379–91, no. 42a.

17 Joannides 2001, pp. 89–94; Edinburgh 2004 (Peter Humfrey), pp. 80–82, no. 13; Lucco 2013, p. 52.

35

Virgin and Child with an Angel, 1511

DOMENICO MANCINI fl. VENICE, 1511

Oil on panel,
166 × 98 cm

Duomo di Santa Sofia, Lendinara

NOTES

1 Silvestri 1755.

2 Brandolese 1795, p. 32.

3 Brandolese 1795, p. 33; Brandolese 1795 (Vittorio Sgarbi and Paola Pizzamano), p. 69.

4 Brandolese 1795, pp. 32–33.

5 Crowe and Cavalcaselle 1871, vol. 2, p. 235.

6 Tempestini 2010, pp. 93–95.

7 Longhi 1927B, p. 87.

8 Sorce 2007, pp. 474–76.

9 Tempestini 2010, pp. 97–98.

10 London 1983 (Francis L. Richardson), pp. 169–71, no. 35.

11 Holberton 1993, pp. 257–58; Hope 2003, p. 14.

The marble throne is placed in the centre of an opulent octagonal plinth; it stands in the open air, enclosed by an apse-shaped wall with wild plants growing from it. Mary holds the Christ Child with her right hand; her left palm is extended, ready to support a step forwards He has started to take. Both look down at an awestruck angel who is playing a lute and seems to be singing.

The painting originally comprised three panels side by side. Two side panels, now lost, depicted Saint John the Evangelist and Saint James, and Saint Jerome and another saint whose identity is unknown. It was to the left-hand pairing, Saint John and Saint James, that the angel's gaze was directed. On the lower step of the plinth is painted a card bearing the date of the picture's execution and the name of the artist: 'opus dominicj mancinj / venetj p[inxit] / 1511'.

The painting was first mentioned in 1562, when it was described (in a manuscript compendium of 1755[1]) as being in the church of San Francesco in Lendinara, where the triptych adorned the altar of the Immaculate Conception. In 1769, after the suppression of the Franciscans in Lendinara, the central panel was moved to its present location.[2] The two side panels were stored in the church of Santa Maria Elisabetta in Lendinara and were later acquired by Pietro Brandolese.[3] The first person to praise Domenico Mancini was Brandolese himself: 'I challenge the boldest baptiser to guess the author who, however much he appears to have belonged originally to the timid school of Giambellino, also knew very well how to take advantage of the new beauty that had been introduced into art.'[4]

Joseph Archer Crowe and Giovanni Battista Cavalcaselle confirmed Brandolese's intuition in 1871 when they were the first to identify the painting that had inspired Mancini's *Virgin and Child with an Angel*: the altarpiece in San Zaccaria (fig. 18), painted by Giovanni Bellini in 1505.[5] Among the many copies – partial or whole – made of the celebrated Venetian altarpiece,[6] here we are looking at a truly exceptional interpretation. Roberto Longhi certainly viewed it in this way:

below the Madonna, weightless – at least in an iconographic sense – from a Bellini-esque model, the pictorial freedom of the angel musician is surprising for the year 1511. The impasto, and the brushwork bring us a little farther forward in that year than were Palma or even Titian.[7]

Mancini seems to have been familiar at an early date with the work of the young Titian who, in 1511, was known for the astonishing frescoes in the Scuola del Santo in Padua (fig. 20).

During the twentieth century the excitement engendered by the Lendinara painting gave birth to a genuine 'Mancini affair', stoked by innumerable scholars, from Johannes Wilde to Carlo Gamba and Bernard Berenson.[8] At present only one other painting can be attributed to this mysterious painter with any degree of certainty: the *Madonna and Child with Saint John the Baptist and Saint Peter* (fig. 19), formerly owned by Carlo Gamba, and now in a private collection.[9] Mancini has had a great impact on the imaginations of art historians, even until quite recently. In particular, a number of works currently considered key examples of Titian's early output, such as the *Virgin and Child with Saint Anthony of Padua and Saint Roch* in Madrid (cat. 32) and *Christ and the Adulteress* in Glasgow (cat. 34), have been associated with his name.[10] The notion that Mancini could be the author of the celebrated *Concert champêtre* (fig. 15) – an attribution generally contested between Giorgione and Titian – has also been considered.[11]

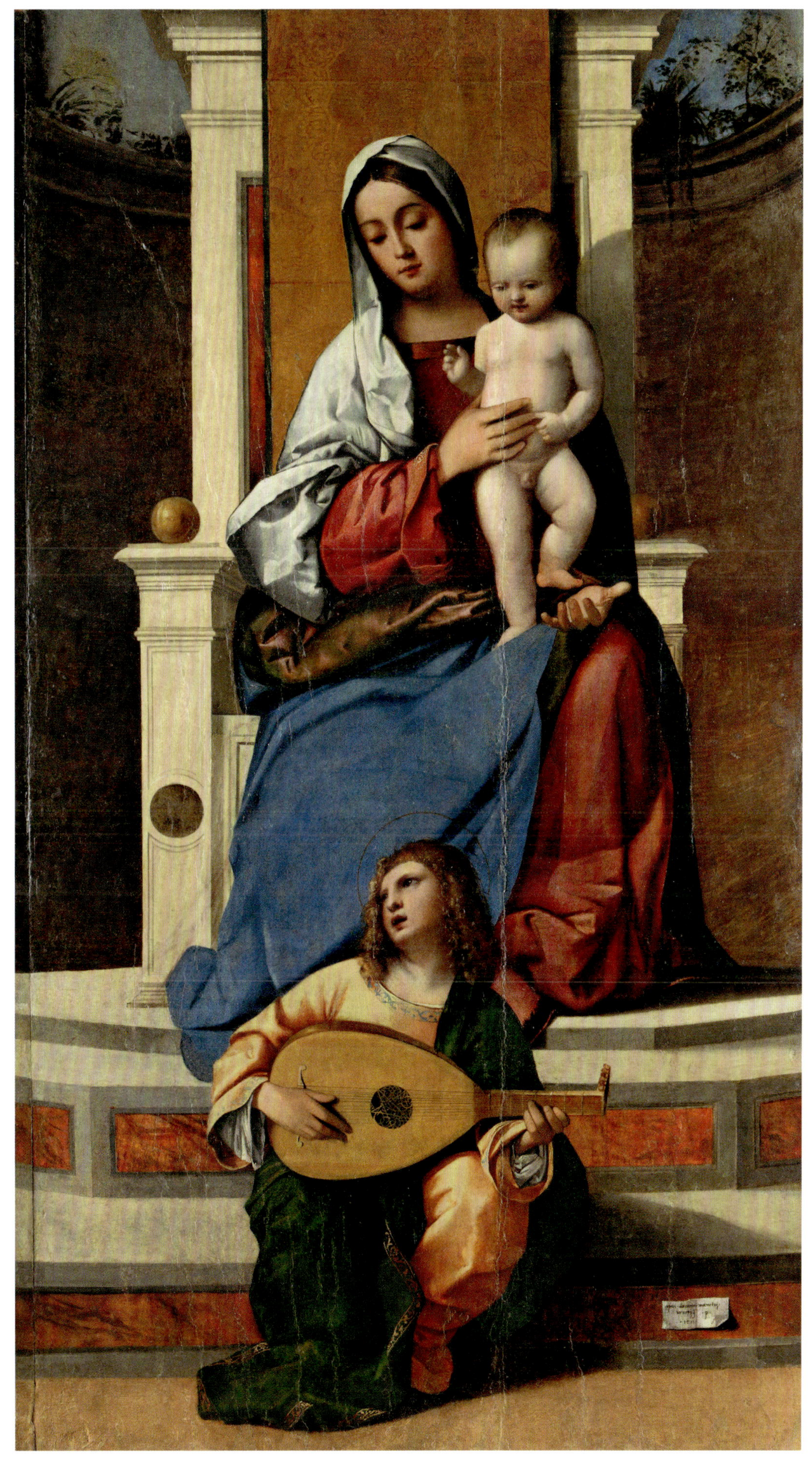

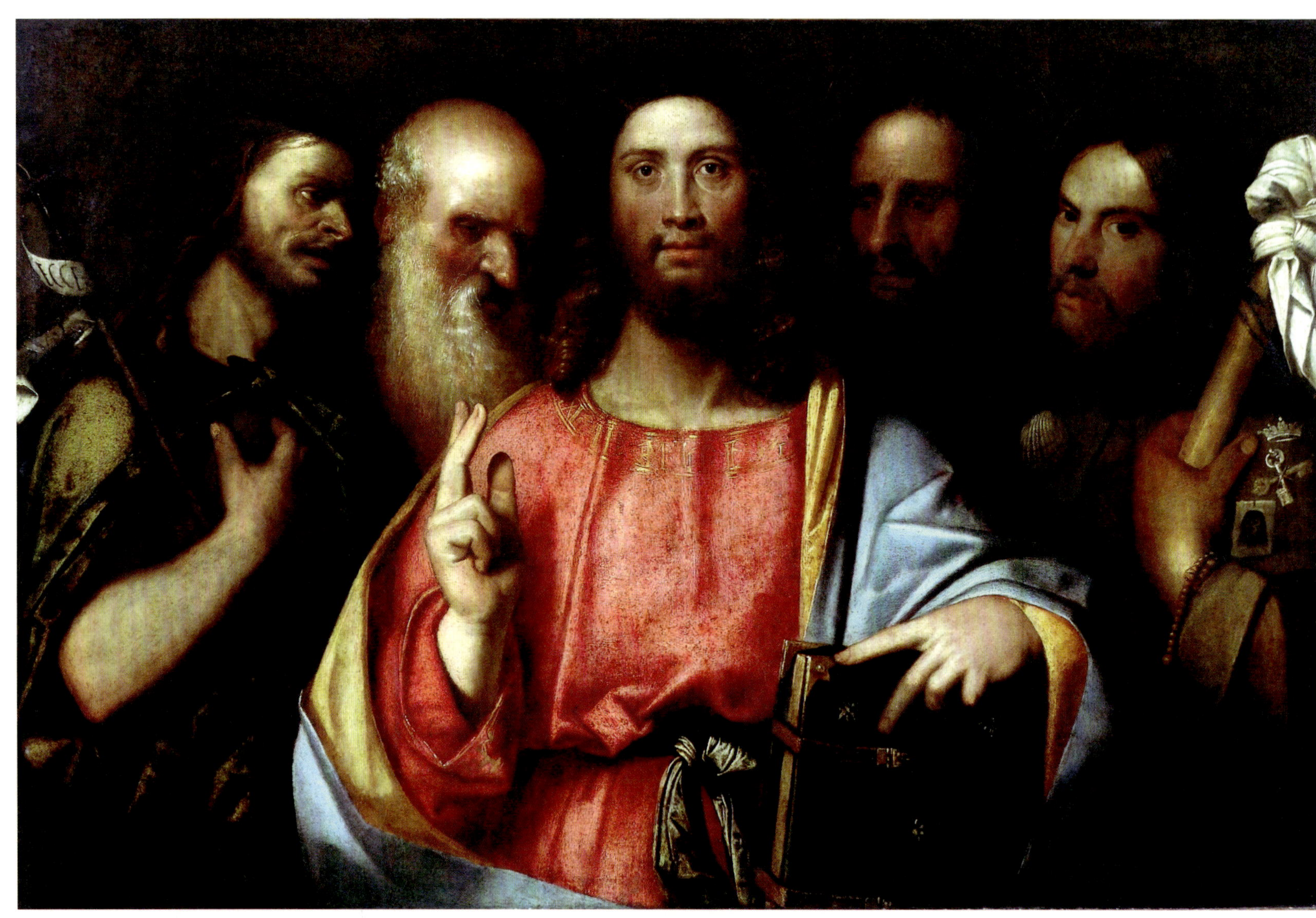

36 Christ Blessing, *c.* 1510–15

GIOVANNI CARIANI FUIPIANO AL BREMBO, BERGAMO, *c.* 1485 – VENICE, AFTER 1547

Oil on panel,
65 × 100 cm

Private collection

NOTES

1 Carotti 1901, pp. 55–56.

2 Carotti 1901, p. 56.

3 Heinemann 1962, vol. 1, p. 59, no. j.

4 Dal Pozzolo 1997, pp. 22, 25.

5 Pallucchini 1983, p. 37.

6 Paris 1993 (Alessandro Ballarin), p. 438.

7 Milan 2001 (David Alan Brown), p. 292, no. 114.

8 Paris 1993 (Alessandro Ballarin), pp. 437–38.

A shaft of sunlight shining from the left fully illuminates Christ, while the skilful handling of light and shade allows the four saints standing behind Him to emerge gradually from the background. Christ is depicted frontally, and physically dominates the scene. He wears a red robe adorned with delicate gold embroidery around the neck and sleeves. A green fabric belt is tied at His waist and a blue cloak lined with yellow hangs from His shoulders. He holds a heavy book in one hand and with the other makes the gesture of benediction that spells out His name.

The saints behind him are carefully studied, each expressing a different mood. Only one saint tries to engage with the viewer, otherwise all eyes are fixed on Christ. This right-hand figure, thought to be Saint Roch (or perhaps Saint James), is dressed as a pilgrim; he holds a staff and wears the scallop shell of Saint James of Compostela. Stitched to his cloak are symbols of the Christian shrines he has visited; the crossed keys of Saint Peter and Saint Veronica's veil indicate that he has been to Rome. The realism and precise detail of this figure suggest that it might be a portrait of the man who commissioned the painting. The panel's dimensions make it clear it was designed for private devotion.

The work was first published in the catalogue recording the collection in the Milanese residence of Joséphine Melzi d'Eril-Barbò, widow and second wife of Lodovico Melzi d'Eril.[1] It is not known whether this painting, as well as the earliest group of works inherited by Lodovico, came from the collection assembled by his ancestor Giacomo Melzi (1721–1802).

The salient features of the painting are outlined in the first description of the work: 'The finest figure is that of the Redeemer, generously painted, imposing, Giorgionesque. The style of the Master of Castelfranco, whose pupil Marconi is considered to have been, appears again in the head of Saint Roch (or Saint James the Greater) drawn and modelled on a grand scale.'[2] It cannot be determined whether the saint on the far right is Saint Roch or Saint James – there is no distinctive sign that would confirm either identification. The attribution to Rocco Marconi was later discounted, although Fritz Heinemann did revisit it in 1962.[3] (Other instances of confusion between Marconi and Giovanni Cariani have occurred: for example, in the case of the extraordinary altarpiece of Saint John the Baptist in the church of San Cassiano in Venice, now correctly ascribed to the period Cariani spent in Venice.[4])

The attribution of *Christ Blessing* to Cariani was made in 1983 by Rodolfo Pallucchini,[5] who emphasised the painting's Düreresque elements. A decade later Alessandro Ballarin took the same line, comparing the work with *Christ Among the Doctors* (Thyssen-Bornemisza Museum, Madrid),[6] which Dürer painted in Venice in 1506. On this basis, Ballarin proposed a date of about 1510 for the panel. The Melzi d'Eril panel has been previously exhibited on only one occasion, in 2001. At that time it was carefully examined by David Alan Brown, who related the work to Cariani's first stay at Bergamo, from 1517 to 1523, suggesting that it might be the outcome of a delayed reaction to seeing Leonardo's *Last Supper* (*c.* 1494–98; Santa Maria delle Grazie, Milan).[7] This proposal is not convincing, particularly in light of the recent rearrangement of Cariani's early works, primarily a result of earlier observations made by Ballarin.[8]

The present painting's debt to Dürer is easy to identify: character is given to the faces of the saints through intense realism that, by the time of the Edinburgh *Saint Agatha* (cat. 46), seems to have diminished.

37 Virgin and Child with Saint Peter, c. 1510–15

GIOVANNI CARIANI FUIPIANO AL BREMBO, BERGAMO, c. 1485 – VENICE, AFTER 1547

Oil on canvas,
72 × 92 cm

Galleria Borghese, Rome,
inv. 164

The Christ Child does not seem overly worried by the risk of falling over the edge of the parapet. His gaze is focused on the aerobatics of a goldfinch, which is secured to the boy's right hand by a fine thread. The only person aware of the impending danger is the Virgin, who has moved to protect the infant by delicately placing a hand on His leg. Behind the parapet is the imposing figure of Saint Peter, who does not actively participate in the scene, but seems lost in his own thoughts. Behind the Virgin a green ceremonial cloth edged with gold embroidery defines the interior space. An open, round-headed window shows an urban skyline in the distance.

The presence of Saint Peter – Saint Joseph would have been more usual in a composition of this nature – could be explained by the fact that the painting was perhaps commissioned by someone of that name.[1] Pears are usually included as an explicit reference to maternity: the two on the parapet imply that the canvas may have been intended as a wedding gift.

The earliest description of the painting can be found in the inventory of the Borghese collection in Rome in 1693: 'A painting on canvas, three *palmes* in size, of the Madonna and Child and Saint Peter, no. 98, gold frame, by Palma Vecchio.' In the Borghese Fedecommesso of 1833 the painting reappears as attributed to Giovanni Bellini.[2]

Joseph Archer Crowe and Giovanni Battista Cavalcaselle, and, independently, Otto Mündler attributed the painting to Giovanni Cariani.[3] Crowe and Cavalcaselle especially demonstrated the painting's affinity with the work of Palma Vecchio and Lorenzo Lotto: 'The Roman Madonna reminds us of Palma in the mould of its faces, and more of Lotto in the golden tinge of its colour. Palma and Lotto – both of them Bergamasques and sixteenth-century craftsmen – were just the sort of men to whom Cariani would naturally lean.' Their attribution was later endorsed by Giovanni Morelli and since then has never been disputed.[4]

Debate subsequently moved to the work's dating. Ludwig Baldass and Alessandro Ballarin supposed that it must originate from the early years of Cariani's career, in 1515.[5] The majority of scholars, however, noting the influence of Palma Vecchio, preferred a date of after 1525.[6] Conversely Rodolfo Pallucchini and Francesco Rossi agreed that the work belonged to the artist's time in Bergamo, and dated it to between 1520 and 1523.[7]

Baldass was the first to point out stylistic similarities between the present painting and Sebastiano del Piombo's *Holy Family with Saint Catherine, Saint Sebastian and a Donor* (c. 1510–15; Musée du Louvre, Paris),[8] both paintings being similar in format as well as in style. These works are also comparable in style to Cariani's *Saint Agatha* in Edinburgh (cat. 46), a work that dates from around 1510.

Stylistic affinity with Sebastiano would place the work between 1508 and 1510, a period in which Giorgione had great impact on both Sebastiano and Cariani. The close relationship of the present painting and *Saint Agatha*, both by Cariani, with Sebastiano's *sacra conversazione* in the Musée du Louvre cannot be ignored. Sebastiano's painting is generally viewed as a reaction to Giorgione's celebrated decoration of the Fondaco dei Tedeschi (fig. 2) in Venice, and can thus be ascribed to a similar date of about 1508.

The unusual arrangement of the Christ Child's legs in the present canvas closely echoes that of Giovanni Bellini's altarpiece in San Zaccaria (fig. 18), dated 1505. Bellini's model was evidently still popular in 1511, when Domenico Mancini made a faithful copy of it in the Lendinara panel (cat. 35).

NOTES

1 Pallucchini 1983, p. 37.

2 Della Pergola 1955B, vol. 1, p. 109, no. 196.

3 Mündler 1869, p. 310; Crowe and Cavalcaselle 1871, vol. 2, p. 547.

4 Morelli 1890, p. 315.

5 Baldass 1929, p. 91; Ballarin 1968, p. 244; London 1988 (Alessandro Ballarin), p. 30; Ballarin 2007, p. 67.

6 Troche 1934, p. 122; Martini 1978, p. 68.

7 Pallucchini 1983, p. 37; Rossi 1983, p. 137, no. 67.

8 Baldass 1929, p. 91.

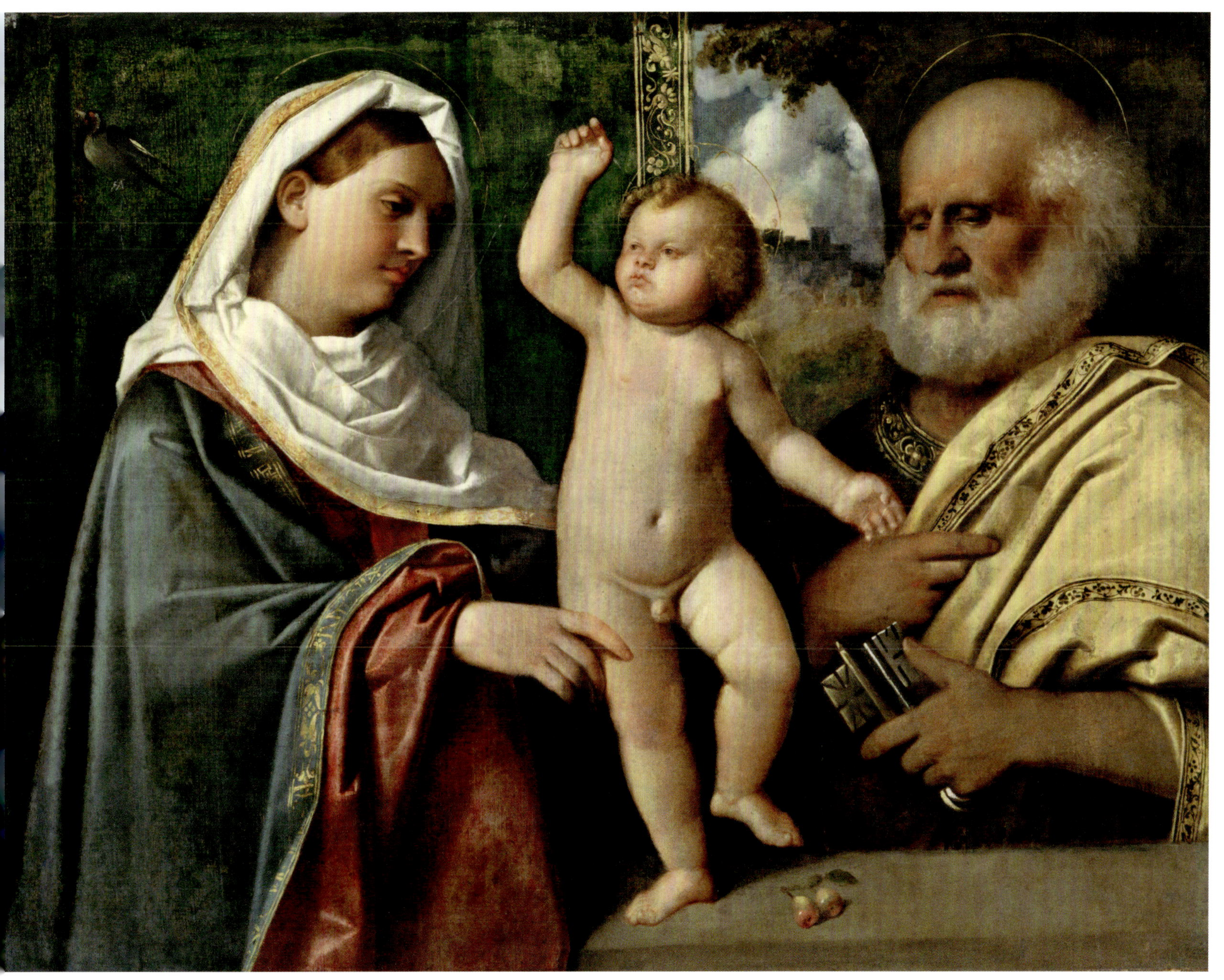

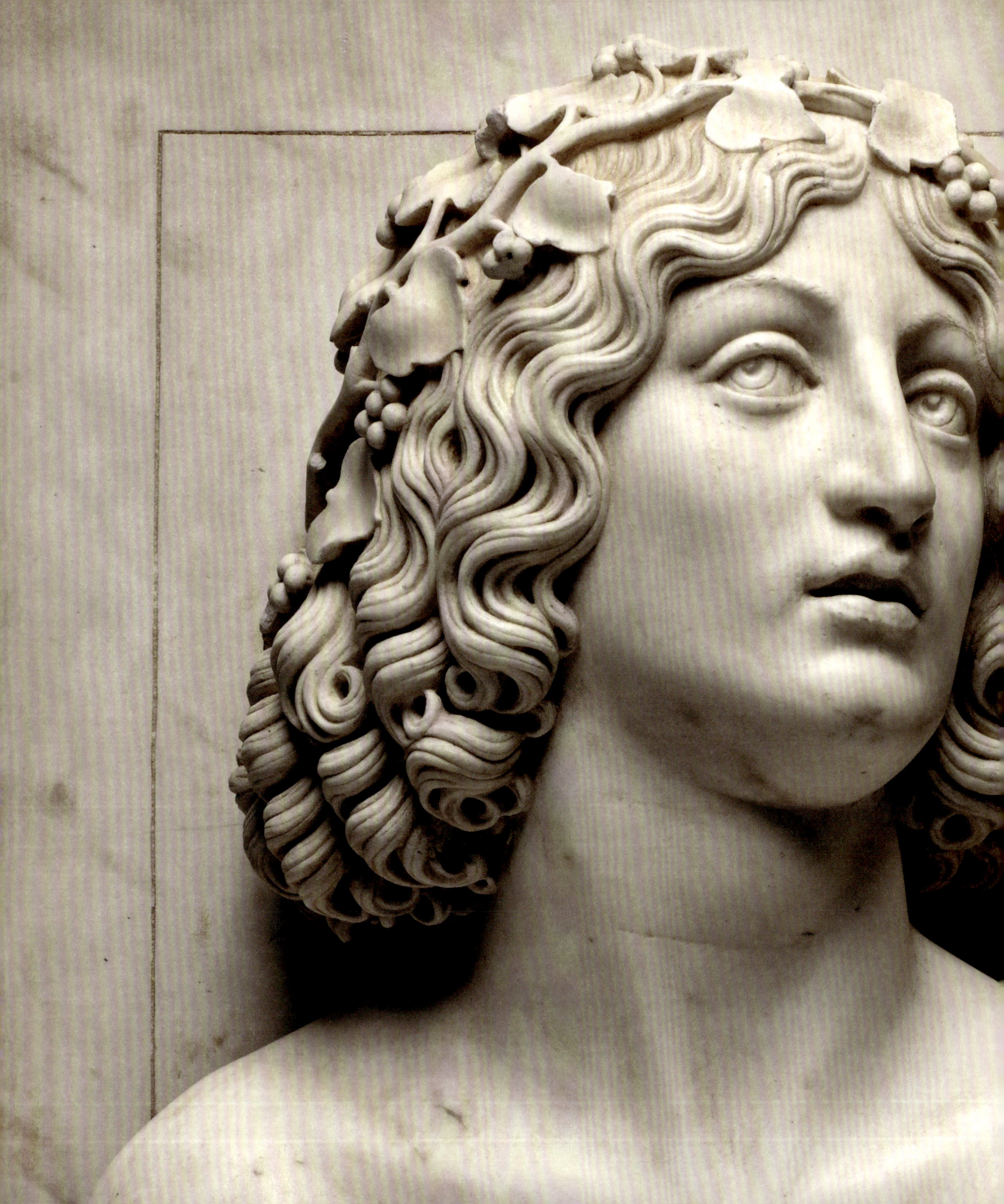

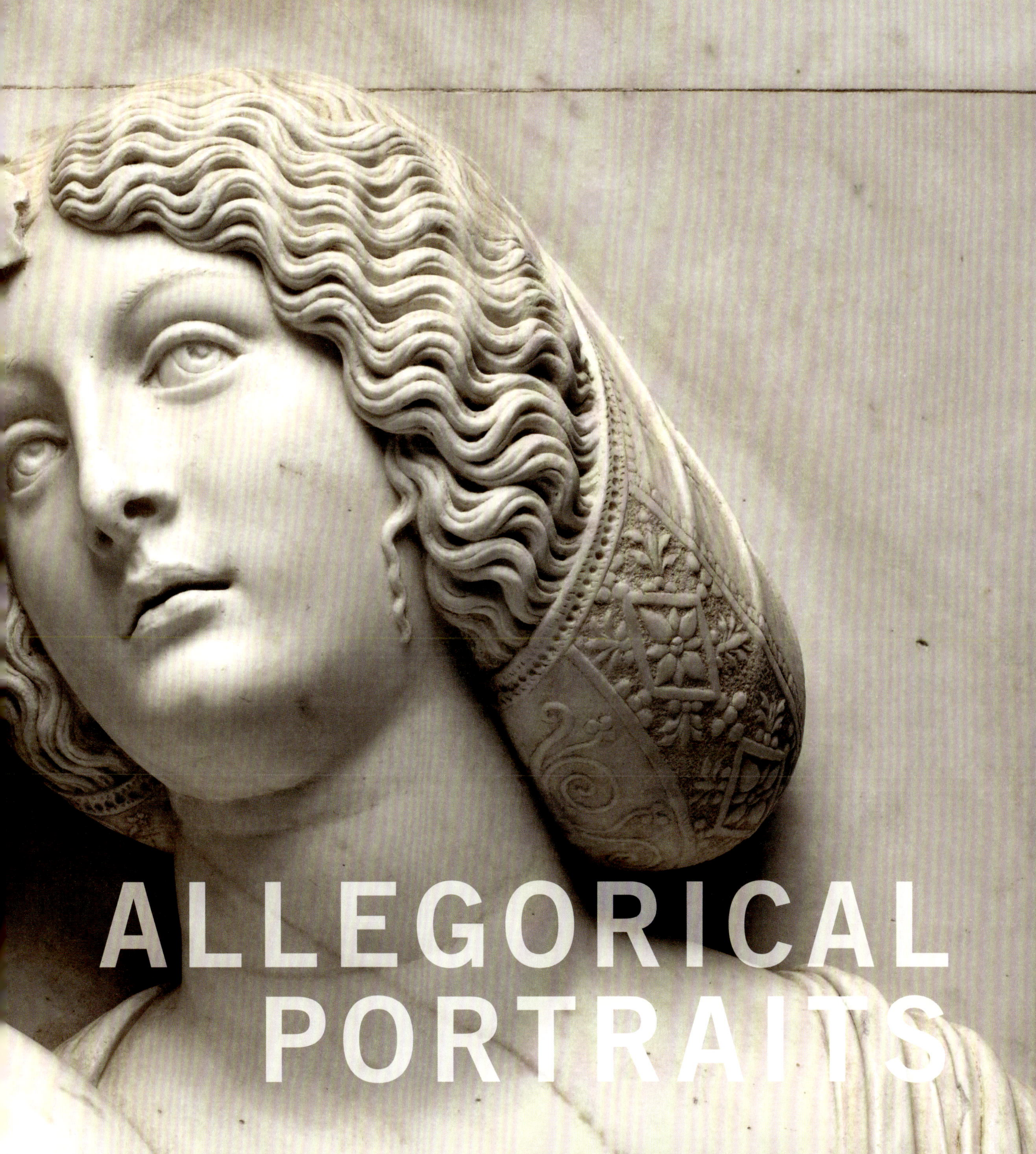

ALLEGORICAL PORTRAITS

To reduce the rich and complex heritage of early sixteenth-century portraiture to an inexorable march towards the supremacy of a depersonalised form would be too schematic. The questions thus aroused would be far more numerous than such a schema could comprehend, and anyway, to justify a 'depersonalising' reaction, an existing 'personalised' schema would have to be assumed. […] An important factor, one that is never forgotten, is the introduction of psychological characterisation, and beyond it, as a rider, the expression of a particular state of mind at a given moment, rather than as an indication of universal character.[1]

Leonardo da Vinci played a central role in the introduction of what Enrico Castelnuovo, writing in 1973, termed 'psychological characterisation'. Leonardo left the Duchy of Milan in 1499 after the fall of Ludovico Sforza, known as Ludovico il Moro. He made his way to Mantua, where he portrayed Isabella d'Este (Musée du Louvre, Paris), and at the beginning of 1500 spent several months in Venice, where he was called up to serve as a military engineer. Vasari tells us (possibly with slight exaggeration) that Giorgione was much influenced by Leonardo's work:

Giorgione had seen some things by the hand of Leonardo with a beautiful gradation of colours and with extraordinary relief effected […] by means of dark shadows, and this manner pleased him so much that he was for ever studying it as long as he lived, and in oil painting he imitated it greatly.[2]

There seems no doubt that the *Three Ages of Man* in Palazzo Pitti (cat. 38) can be explained by this influence; in particular, the figure of the old man who turns slowly towards the viewer. He possesses particularly characterful physical features, and resembles closely a figure in one of Leonardo's most celebrated works, the *Last Supper* in the convent of the Chiesa di Santa Maria delle Grazie in Milan. Giorgione may have become familiar with this through its many preparatory drawings. Even the composition of Giorgione's painting, with the figures' subtle interactions, follows the composition of this celebrated model. After this life-changing encounter Giorgione seems to have attained a greater degree of artistic independence, and began creating the more moving and mysterious material for which he is remembered best.

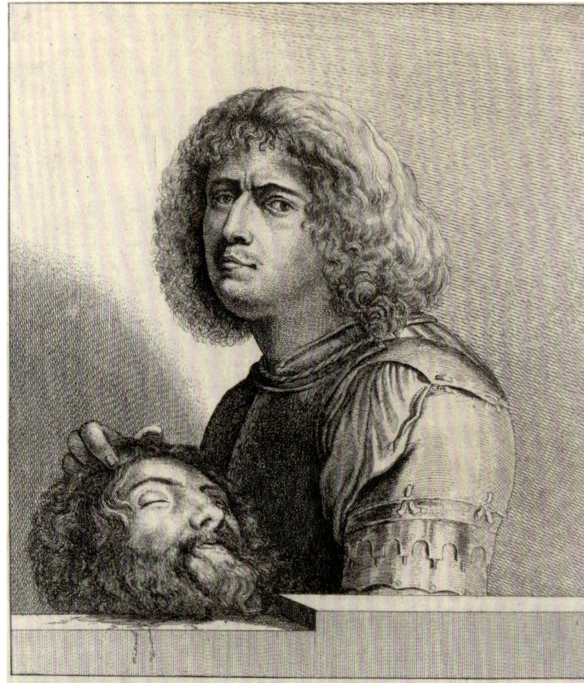

Fig. 21
WENCESLAUS HOLLAR, after GIORGIONE
Self-portrait as David, 1650
Engraving, 22.8 × 19.5 cm
British Museum, London

Fig. 22
Attributed to GIORGIONE
Self-portrait as David
Oil on canvas, 52 × 43 cm
Herzog Anton Ulrich-Museum, Brunswick

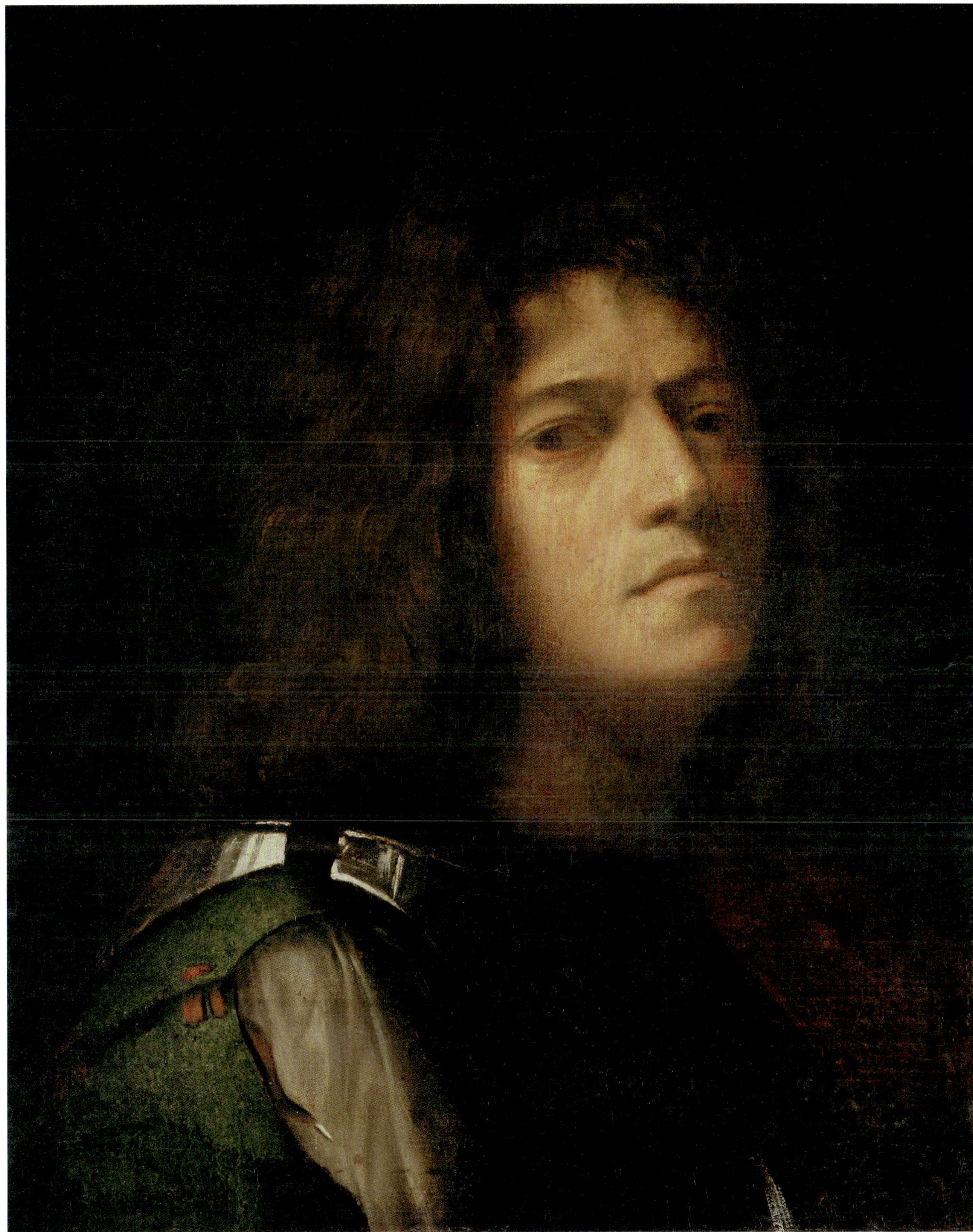

Fig. 23
GIOVANNI BELLINI
***Fra Teodoro of Urbino as Saint Dominic*, 1515**
Oil on canvas, 63.9 × 49.5 cm
National Gallery, London, inv. L1115.
On loan from the Victoria and Albert Museum, London

Giorgione dealt with psychological characterisation in portraiture, especially self-portraiture, in a most radical manner. If we compare the way in which, at more or less the same time, Raphael represented himself, such as in his *Self-portrait* (c. 1506; Galleria degli Uffizi, Florence) with the partial copy Giorgione is thought to have executed of his own self-portrait (fig. 22) we notice a great difference. It is almost possible to talk of a clean break with the established figurative tradition epitomised by Raphael's painting.

Vasari described the prime Giorgione self-portrait in the collection of Domenico Grimani:

> In his youth he executed in Venice many pictures of Our Lady and other portraits from nature, which are very lifelike and beautiful, of which we still have proof in three most beautiful heads in oils by his hand, which are in the study of the Very Reverend Grimani, Patriarch of Aquileia. One represents David and it is reported to be his own portrait with long locks reaching to the shoulders, as was the custom of those times. It is so vivacious and so fresh in colouring that it seems to be living flesh. And there is armour on the breast, as there is on the arm with which he is holding the severed head of Goliath.[3]

We know the painting via the probable partial copy, and also by a print reproduction (fig. 21) that likely follows the original, larger, composition (which included the Philistine's severed head). The painting is listed in the 1528 inventory of the collection of Grimani as 'Portrait of Zorzon by his own hand for David and Goliath'.[4]

Where before have we encountered a painter who chooses to portray himself wearing the panoply of the biblical hero, displaying the head of Goliath trickling blood? To find anything at all similar we have to leap forward a century to Caravaggio in Rome. The tradition of depicting sitters in the guise of saints existed in Giorgione's day, but never had it been carried to such extreme lengths. Some examples found in the output of Giovanni Bellini are useful here because they emphasise the unusual nature of Giorgione's case. The *Virgin and Child with Saint Paul and Saint George* (Gallerie dell'Accademia, Venice) contains a portrait of the commander of the fleet of the Venetian Republic, Giorgio Dragan, dressed as his namesake Saint George.[5] Bellini's portrait of Fra Teodoro of Urbino (fig. 23) shows the sitter dressed in the black cloak of the founder of his order, Saint Dominic. The inclusion of Dominic's attribute, a stalk of lilies, makes the association clear. In these cases, however, we are within a clear and acceptable framework justified by a spiritual and devotional tradition. Bellini's work bears no relation to the expressive exuberance, nor to the deliberate choice of an Old Testament narrative of violence, on which Giorgione based his self-portrait as David.

We should bear in mind that none of the examples examined so far was intended for public display – on the contrary, they were aimed at quite restricted domestic circles. This makes it difficult for us to imagine how much deviation from the allegorical framework a contemporary viewer might have detected in the painting. If we remain within the close circle of Giorgione and examine Sebastiano del Piombo's *Portrait of a Young Woman as a Wise Virgin* (fig. 24), we are left with lingering doubts about the painting's exact significance. The immediate impression is that it is a portrait: we deduce this from the lack of idealisation of the Virgin's face, and from the hairstyle and clothes, all borrowed from contemporary fashion. Various paintings by Giovanni Cariani appear to have been influenced by Sebastiano, including the Edinburgh *Saint Agatha* (cat. 46) and the extraordinary *Judith* (cat. 45). In these works Cariani clearly wished to produce a 'natural portrait'.

Current research suggests a particular appetite in Venice at this time for such crypto-portraits for private clients – the proof is that so many examples have survived, a larger number than anywhere else in Italy.[6]

On the verso of *Portrait of a Young Woman* (*'Laura'*) (fig. 1) the following inscription can be read: 'On 1 June 1506 this was made by the hand of master Giorgio from Castelfranco, the colleague of master Vincenzo Catena, at the instigation of misser Giacomo.'[7] The painting is not an idealised representation; on the contrary, it is a commissioned portrait of striking naturalism. The young woman is portrayed with her body turned a little to the right and her gaze focused on a spot beyond the picture's edge. The sitter in the so-called

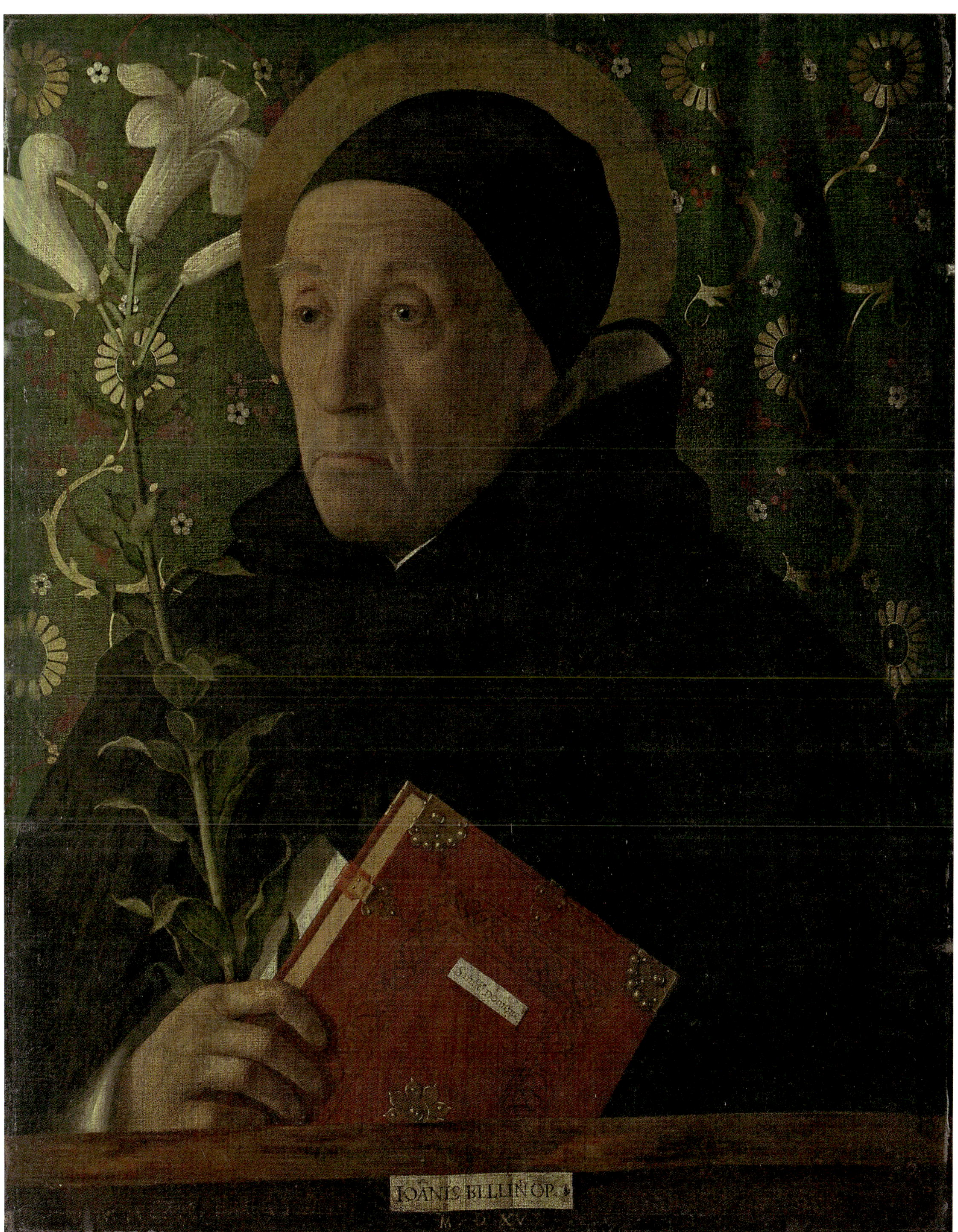
IOANES BELLIN OP.
M D XV

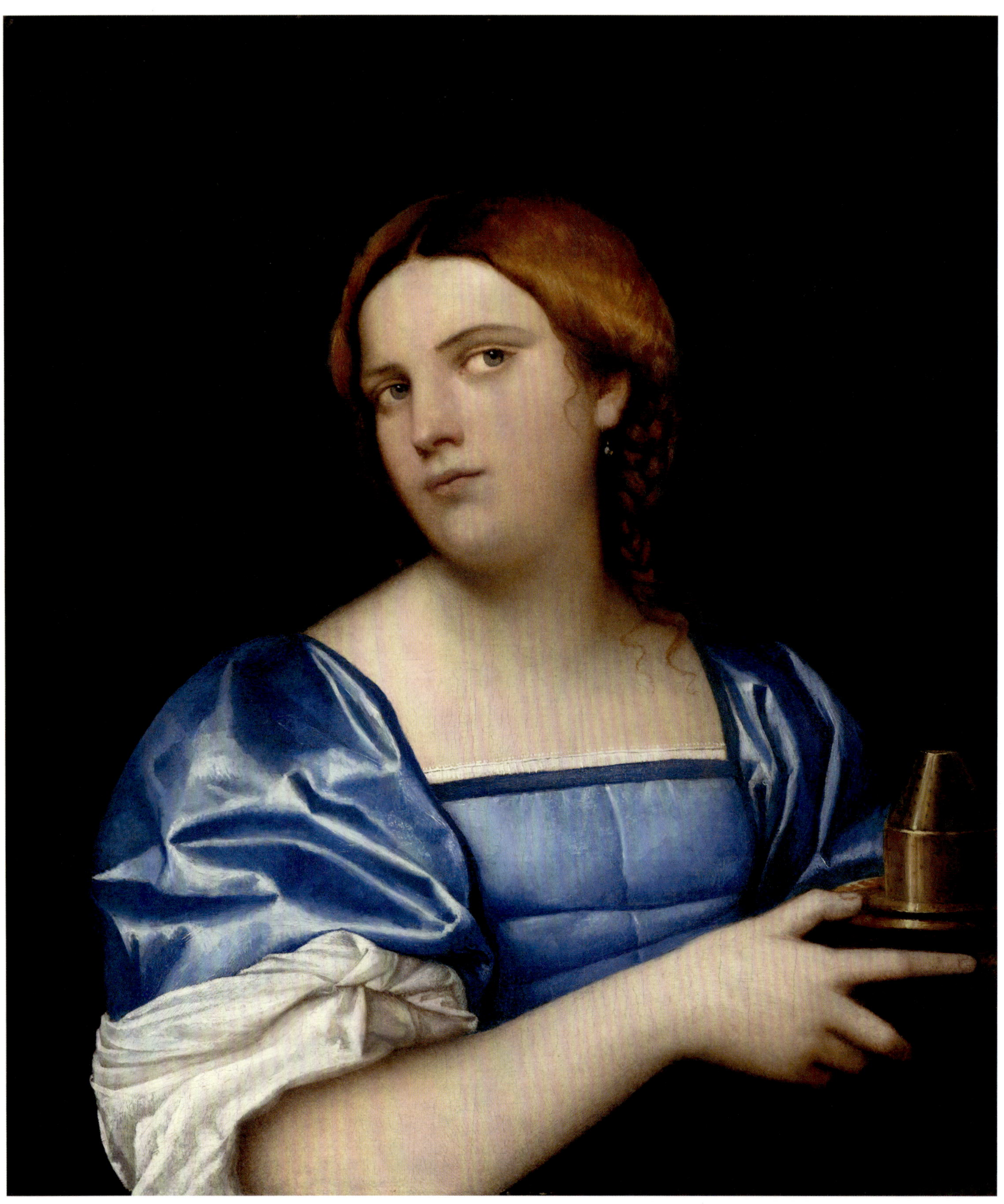

Fig. 24
SEBASTIANO DEL PIOMBO
Portrait of a Young Woman as a Wise Virgin, c.1510
Oil on panel (transferred to hardboard), 54.7 × 47.5 cm
National Gallery of Art, Washington DC, Samuel H. Kress Collection

Laura has an attitude of detachment. One edge of her red, fur-lined gown is deliberately pulled back to reveal her breast, delicately draped in translucent fabric. Laurel leaves emerge from behind her shoulders and are silhouetted against a black background. It is clear that the painting conceals a message – but what is the message? For many years it was said to portray the Laura beloved by Petrarch and celebrated in his poetry. There have also been suggestions that the young woman may be a courtesan, or a lover. The most convincing hypothesis to date is that the picture was a commission, by the 'Giacomo' named in the inscription, for a bridal portrait to be enjoyed in a domestic context.[8] The portrait lost its original meaning after 1636, when it left Venice on a ship bound for England, where it eventually joined the collection of King Charles I.

The case of Giorgione's *La Vecchia* (cat. 39) in the Gallerie dell'Accademia is quite different. There is no doubt about the subject-matter of the painting, even if uncertainties remain about its specific purpose and original location. The allegory of ageing is outweighed by the portrait's extraordinary and merciless realism: it shows all too clearly the visible traces left on the body by the passing of time. Unsurprisingly, no one was to follow Giorgione's lead in this direction, at least not in the immediate future.

38 Three Ages of Man, *c.* 1500

GIORGIONE (GIORGIO DA CASTELFRANCO) CASTELFRANCO VENETO, 1478 – VENICE, 1510

Oil on panel, 62 × 78 cm

Galleria Palatina, Palazzo Pitti, Florence, inv. 110

The three figures stand out from a black background thanks to light from the top left. The youngest of the three wears a cap that shades his eyes. He looks fixedly at a sheet of music, part of which is visible to the viewer. The half-open mouth and the position of the hand of the man dressed in green seem to indicate that he and the boy are engaged in communication from which the older man is momentarily excluded. The oldest figure, positioned diagonally within the picture, has turned to meet the gaze of the viewer. The subject-matter is usually interpreted allegorically, with the musical education of the young boy seen as a metaphor for the attempt to reach a form of universal harmony.

The earliest reference to the painting was made in 1698, when it was listed in the collection of Ferdinando II de' Medici, Grand Duke of Tuscany: 'A painting on panel in an excellent Lombard style, which represents three naturalistic heads, signifying the three ages of man.'[1] Various attempts have been made to unearth an earlier provenance. The most likely hypothesis is that the work can be identified as the painting sold in Venice in 1666 by the Flemish artist and collector Nicolas Régnier. It was attributed to Palma Vecchio and described as 'A Marcus Aurelius studying between two philosophers, half figures as natural, on panel, five *quarte* wide, four *quarte* high, in a gold frame.'[2] Shortly before the sale, the merchant and collector Paolo del Sera had in fact offered the painting to Ferdinando's brother, Leopoldo de' Medici, accompanied by the following note: 'I judge this to be by Giorgione's hand, in his middle style, and it is very fine.'[3] Bearing in mind that many of the paintings in the Régnier sale came from the Vendramin family, it has been suggested that the present picture might be identified as that mentioned in the inventory of the possessions of Gabriele Vendramin, drawn up between 1567 and 1569: 'Another painting with three people singing with gilded frame.'[4] Jaynie Anderson and Rosella Lauber, among others, supported this hypothesis.[5]

The name Giorgione appears for the first time in connection with this painting in a print entitled *La Leçon de Chant*, executed between 1799 and 1815 by Antoine Claessens, after a drawing by Jacques Touzé.[6] During this period the painting itself was transferred – as war booty – to the Musée Napoléon in Paris, before being returned permanently to the Galleria Palatina in 1815. For much of the nineteenth century the name Lorenzo Lotto was associated with the work,[7] and Joseph Archer Crowe and Giovanni Battista Cavalcaselle repeated this attribution.[8] Giovanni Morelli, however, expressed a different belief: 'Even without documents to hand to support my opinion, I make bold to attribute this painting to Giorgione.'[9] Morelli's view was not to be accepted seriously for almost another century.

Reservations expressed by Roberto Longhi in 1927 and 1949 – he considered the work to belong to 'the very last years of Giovanni Bellini, I believe, but Giorgionesque' – fail to address his own desire to minimise, if not exclude, the influence of Leonardo in the development of the *maniera moderna* (modern style) in Venice.[10]

The Florentine panel has been attributed to a large number of painters in the circle of Giorgione, including Lorenzo Luzzo (known as Morto da Feltre),[11] Francesco Torbido[12] and Domenico Mancini.[13] In 1932 Bernard Berenson named the artist 'The Master of the *Three Ages of Man*'; active around 1510, between Giovanni Bellini and Giorgione. However he conceded 'we could be looking at Giambellino as an octogenarian'.[14]

Alessandro Ballarin considered more closely the impact on Giorgione of Leonardo's sojourn in Venice during 1499 and 1500, particularly in relation to the *Three Ages of Man*.[15] Detailed comparison of the painting with Leonardo's drawings – especially with *Head of a Young Woman* (1483; Biblioteca Reale, Turin) and *Head of Saint Philip in the Last Supper* (c. 1495; Royal Collection, London) – has given credence to his insight and resulted in a date of around 1500 for the painting (the suggestion was published by Ballarin in 1990 and 1993).[16] Since then, all studies have followed this line, in particular Mauro Lucco's publication, which broadened the investigation to include the works Giovanni Agostino da Lodi produced while he was in Venice – *Christ Washing the Feet of the Disciples* (1500; Gallerie dell'Accademia, Venice), for example – further supporting Ballarin's argument.[17] In 1992 David Alan Brown also accepted this proposal, although he chose to date the painting to the final phase of Giorgione's career.[18]

NOTES

1 Lucco 1989, p. 26, no. 2.
2 Garas 1979, p. 167.
3 Mazza 1987, p. 7.
4 Ravà 1920, p. 177.
5 Anderson 1979, p. 643; Lauber 2002B, p. 103.
6 Garas 1979, p. 169, no. 11.
7 Inghirami 1828, p. 40, no. 9.
8 Crowe and Cavalcaselle 1871, vol. 2, p. 502.
9 Morelli 1880, pp. 162–63.
10 Longhi 1927A, p. 182; Longhi 1949, p. 107.
11 Logan 1894, p. 1.
12 Pallucchini 1944B, p. XVI.
13 Gamba 1949, p. 212.
14 Berenson 1932, p. 349.
15 Ballarin 1979, pp. 230–32.
16 Ballarin 1990, vol. 1, pp. 12–13; Paris 1993 (Alessandro Ballarin), pp. 309–13, no. 21.
17 Lucco 1989, pp. 18–26.
18 Venice 1992 (David Alan Brown), p. 338, no. 66; Pignatti 1969, p. 110, no. 28.

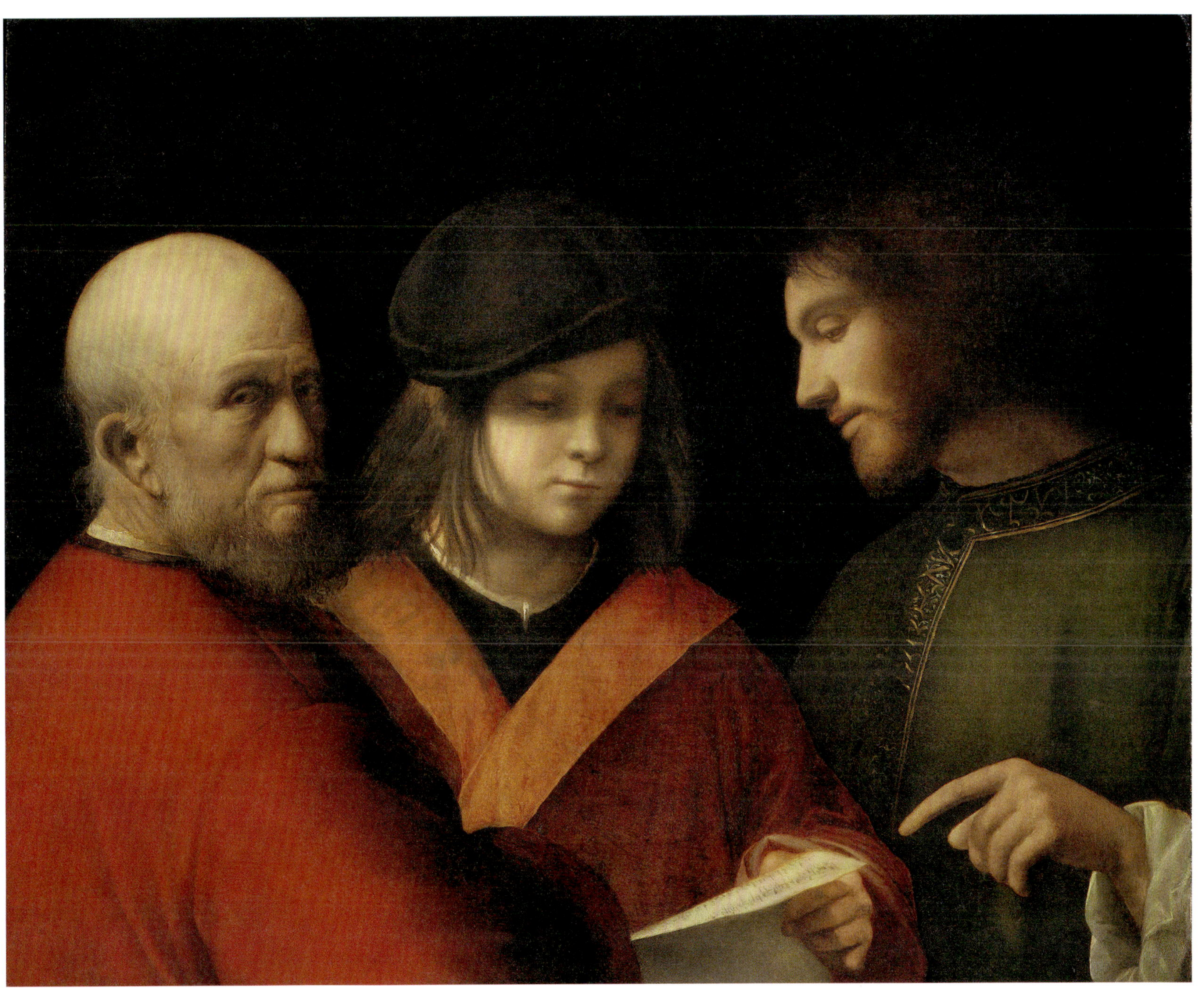

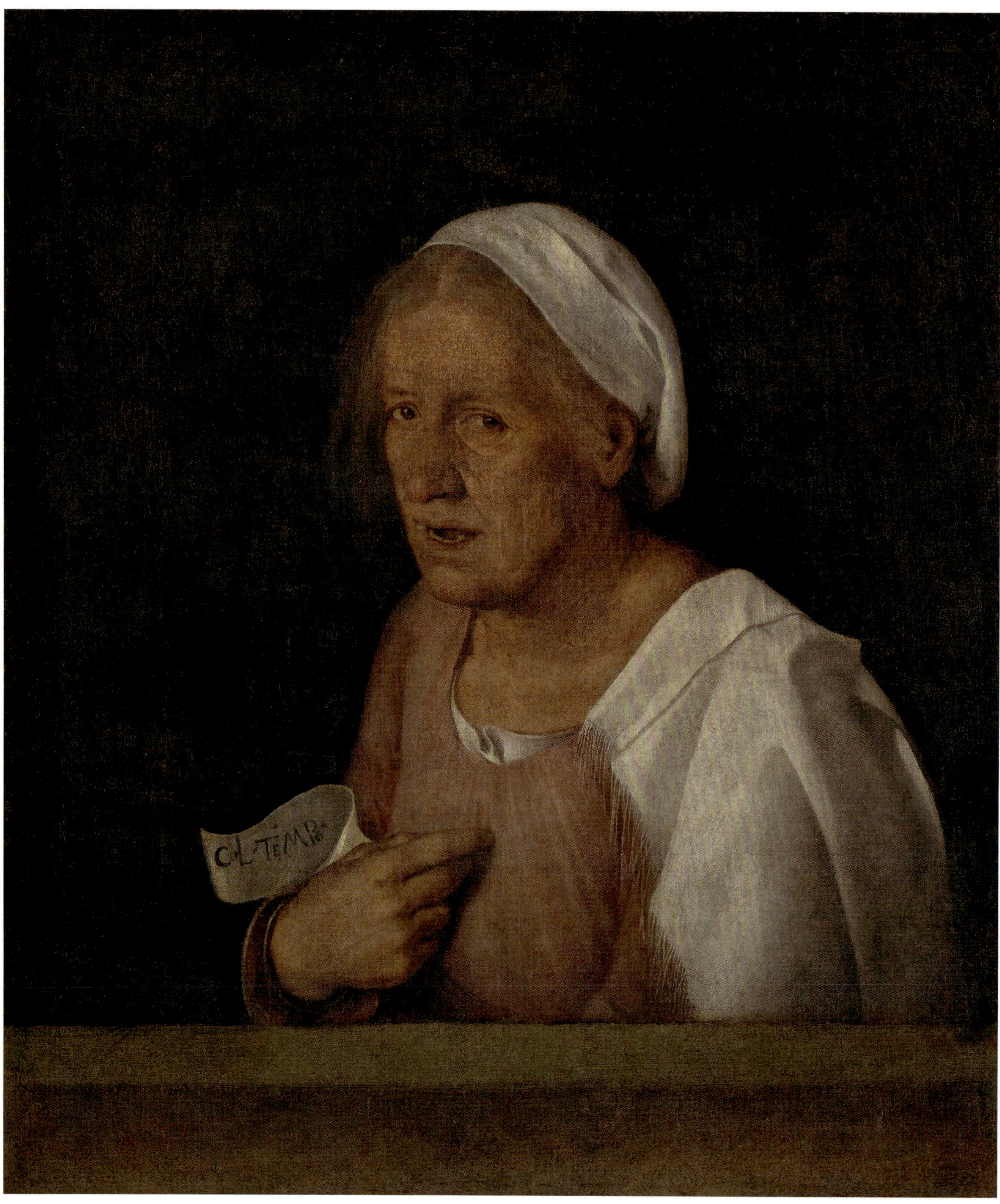
CoL·TEMPO

39

La Vecchia, *c.* 1508–10

GIORGIONE (GIORGIO DA CASTELFRANCO) CASTELFRANCO VENETO, 1478 – VENICE, 1510

Tempera and oil on canvas, 68 × 59 cm

Gallerie dell'Accademia, Venice, inv. 272

NOTES

1 Panofsky 1969, pp. 90–91.

2 Ravà 1920, p. 178.

3 Anderson 1979, pp. 643, 647, nos VII, IX; a third inventory, dated 1602, has been traced by Rosella Lauber, in Castelfranco Veneto 2009, pp. 401–02, no. 19.

4 Michiel 1521–43, p. 217.

5 Anderson 1979, p. 642.

6 Borean and Mason 2002, p. 137.

7 Venice 2003 (Giovanna Nepi Sciré), p. 162.

8 Della Rovere [1888], p. 36.

9 Viana 1933, pp. 25–26, 72, no. 21; Fiocco 1941, pp. 30, 45; Pallucchini 1944B, p. XVI.

10 Berenson 1932, p. 233. This despite his initial belief that the painting was by Cariani: Berenson 1894, p. 95.

11 Anderson 1979, p. 647, no. VII.

12 Panofsky 1969, p. 70.

13 Paris 1993 (Alessandro Ballarin), pp. 320–24, no. 24.

14 Aikema 2003, pp. 76–80.

15 Salvini 1961, pp. 231–33.

An old woman, body and head partly turned towards the viewer, is set against a dark background. Although the high sill creates a clear divide between the viewer and the sitter, the old woman is full of life. It feels as though, if you were to get close to the painting, you might hear her breathing. This lifelike quality is created by a series of tiny, directly observed details transferred to the canvas: for example, the stray hairs escaping from her cap, or the white shawl flung over her shoulder. Without making a full analysis of her face, we should highlight the intensity of the eyes, and the toothless mouth. The latter, half-open, invites us to listen to what she is saying while her hand held upon her chest emphasises the message: 'Col Tempo' ('With Time'). The link between the text and the image is the idea of the *memento senescere*, a reminder of ageing.[1]

La Vecchia (*The Old Woman*) is listed in the inventory of the collection of Gabriele Vendramin (1484–1552) in the second half of the 1560s: 'portrait of the mother of Giorgione by the hand of Giorgione, its frame painted with the arms of Vendramin's family'.[2] From a later inventory, dated 1601, we learn that the painting had a cover featuring the portrait of a man: 'A painting of an Old Woman with her frame of Walnut five and a half *quarte* in height and about five *quarte* wide with the arms of the Vendramin family painted in the frame, the cover of the said painted with the picture of a man wearing a black leather jacket.' The cover painting, with the same measurements, is listed next: 'A painted portrait of a man dressed in black with the frame of Walnut five and a half *quarte* in height and about five *quarte* wide.'[3] We know nothing of this male portrait listed in the inventory; it could be the lost portrait of Vendramin himself, painted by Giovanni Cariani and mentioned by Marcantonio Michiel.[4] The hypothesis put forward by Anderson,[5] who claimed to recognise it as *Man with a Glove*, a painting in the Musée Fesch, Ajaccio, has received no support (and, moreover, that work has been attributed to Titian).

Between 1648 and 1657 the painting was sold by one of the heirs of Vendramin, Andrea di Zuanne, to Cristoforo Orsetti. Description of the subject remained the same: 'Portrait of the old mother of Giorgione said to be by Giorgione himself.'[6] However, at the end of the eighteenth century, when the painting entered the collection of Girolamo Manfrin (1742–1801), it was imaginatively listed as: 'Old woman known as the mother of Titian in the manner of Giorgione.'[7] Finally, in 1856, the Emperor Franz Josef acquired it, along with other works that formed the core of the Galleria Manfrin, all of which were destined for the Gallerie dell'Accademia in Venice.

La Vecchia has also been attributed to Francesco Torbido on the basis of a proposed resemblance to the figure of Saint Anne in the *sacra conversazione* at San Zeno, Verona.[8] This attribution won a certain amount of approval.[9] However we owe the recovery of the name of Giorgione to Bernard Berenson,[10] whose attribution has gradually become accepted, partly due to the discovery of the 1601 Vendramin inventory mentioned earlier. The dimensions given in 1601 for the painting and the frame correspond almost exactly with those of *La Vecchia*.[11]

A few scholars have refused to accept this attribution because the image of the old woman does not match their conception of Giorgione's style. For example in 1969 Erwin Panofsky claimed the work's 'forcefulness, this inexorable veracity in the depiction of features once beautiful but now distorted and corroded [...] by old age, endows it with *terribilità* which, in my and at least one other scholar's opinion, militates against its attribution to the gentle master of Castelfranco'.[12] With this in mind, Panofsky prefers to ascribe it to the young Titian.

Despite occasional dissenting voices such as these, the attribution to Giorgione has generally been accepted. Debate has shifted to the date of the painting, with strong opinions that range from 1500 to 1510. In 1993 Alessandro Ballarin suggested the work dates from around 1502–03 and is closely related to the *Three Ages of Man* (cat. 38) and to Leonardo's Venetian period.[13] In 2003 Bernard Aikema provided a different interpretation by relating the painting to Albrecht Dürer's *Avarice* and *Portrait of a Young Man* (both 1507; Kunsthistorisches Museum, Vienna).[14]

The uncertainties surrounding Giorgione's catalogue make a level of caution advisable, yet within the sequence that includes Berlin (cat. 1), Florence (cat. 38) and San Diego (cat. 5), *La Vecchia* in Venice probably occupies the final position.

40 David Between Saul and Jonathan (?)

ATTRIBUTED TO GIORGIONE (GIORGIO DA CASTELFRANCO) CASTELFRANCO VENETO, 1478 – VENICE, 1510

Oil on canvas,
86 × 70 cm

Mattioli Collection

The figure in the foreground is depicted from slightly below eye level, with his head angled to one side; his half-open mouth reveals his tongue and an upper row of teeth. The man's eyes are directed away from the tilt of his head, which makes his appearance even more expressive. In his right hand he carries an object that has been identified as a treble lyre, held upside down, of which only the resonating chamber can be seen. Over his white shirt he wears a brightly embroidered tunic; the fringed edge of an undergarment can be seen on his arm.

This central figure stands between two others: the man on the left looks to him; while his companion on the right, old and bearded, seems detached and preoccupied with his own thoughts. Both the peripheral figures wear dark caps of a similar style.

A recent interpretation identified the right-hand figure as King Saul of Israel, the central figure as David, Saul's armour-bearer, and the younger figure on the left as Jonathan, son of Saul.[1] The scene appears to illustrate the episode described in I Samuel XVI, 21–23: 'And it came to pass, when the evil spirit from God was upon Saul, that David took his harp and played with his hand: so Saul was refreshed, and was well, and the evil spirit departed from him.'

Since the painting was first recorded, its subject has been interpreted in a number of different ways. It has been identified as one in the collection of Gabriele Vendramin (1484–1552) of Venice, which was described in an inventory drawn up between 1567 and 1569, after the owner's death: 'Painting by the hand of Zorzon de Castelfranco, with three large singing heads.'[2] In a later Vendramin inventory of 1601 a little more detail was provided: 'A painting with one large head, and two other heads one in shadow.'[3] Some of the paintings in this collection were later acquired by the painter and dealer Nicolas Régnier (1591–1667), and the present work was mentioned in the catalogue of his sale in Venice in 1666. However, the subject was interpreted in a very different manner: 'A painting by Giorgione of Castelfranco in which a figure of Samson, half-length and full-face, supporting himself with one hand on a rock; he is vexed because his hair has been cut off. Behind him, two figures are making fun of him.'[4] After that there was no mention of the work until 1944.

In 1946 Roberto Longhi was the first to suggest the present painting as the work of Giorgione.[5] Longhi also mentioned the subject in a letter of 1944, the year that the painting was acquired by the Milanese collector Gianni Mattioli (1903–1977). In this letter he gave his reasons for the attribution to Giorgione:

> The almost gigantic dimensions of Samson's head do not strike me only as requirements of the subject, but also, and more so, as the natural disposition of someone who was still pulsing, one might almost say, with the grandiose rhythm of the figure on the Fondaco; the unusual difficulty of the foreshortening of the main protagonist's head appears to have inspired the young Titian (in about 1510).[6]

The painting was included in the 1955 exhibition 'Giorgione e i Giorgioneschi', with a putative reference to Giorgione himself.[7] The attribution caused some controversy and was not accepted by Lionello Venturi, Pietro Zampetti or Giles Robertson,[8] all of whom considered it to be a much later work, dating from the second half of the sixteenth century.

In 1963 Carlo Volpe reintroduced the name of Giorgione, suggesting that the painting provided essential evidence of the progress of 'Ferrarese Giorgionism', in other words, the influence of Giorgione on the earliest work of Dosso Dossi.[9] In 1994 Mauro Lucco expressed the same opinion.[10] Other recent positions on the painting's attribution have proved fairly diverse. Giulio Bora, Alessandro Ballarin and Giorgio Fossaluzza can all be counted among those who believe Giorgione to be the artist,[11] while Terisio Pignatti, Annalisa Perissa Torrini and Jaynie Anderson disagree.[12]

The main problem is the impossibility of reconstructing the catalogue of Giorgione's late work with any degree of certainty. The so-called *Impassioned Singer* in Rome's Galleria Borghese, usually invoked in support of Longhi's attribution of the present painting to Giorgione, is in reality stylistically very different and its own attribution is much discussed. The profoundly Giorgionesque quality of the work under discussion, which contains some very unusual characterisation, can in our opinion be explained by an attribution to Dosso Dossi who in about 1510–15 was just starting out in Venice.

NOTES

1 Castelfranco Veneto 2009 (Giorgio Fossaluzza), p. 441.

2 Ravà 1920, p. 177.

3 Anderson 1979, p. 647, no. XIV.

4 Ordeni 1666, no. G 7.

5 Longhi 1946, p. 57.

6 Venice 1992 (Giulio Bora), pp. 378–79.

7 Venice 1955 (Pietro Zampetti), p. 88, no. 39.

8 Venice 1955 (Pietro Zampetti), p. 88, no. 39; Zampetti 1955, pp. 66–67; Robertson 1955, p. 276.

9 Volpe 1963, unnumbered.

10 Lucco 1994B, p. 37.

11 Venice 1992 (Giulio Bora), pp. 378–79, no. 82; Paris 1993 (Alessandro Ballarin), pp. 341–44, no. 29; Castelfranco Veneto 2009 (Giorgio Fossaluzza), pp. 439–42, no. 50.

12 Pignatti 1978, p. 129, no. A29; Perissa Torrini 1993, p. 132, no. 11A; Anderson 1996, p. 333.

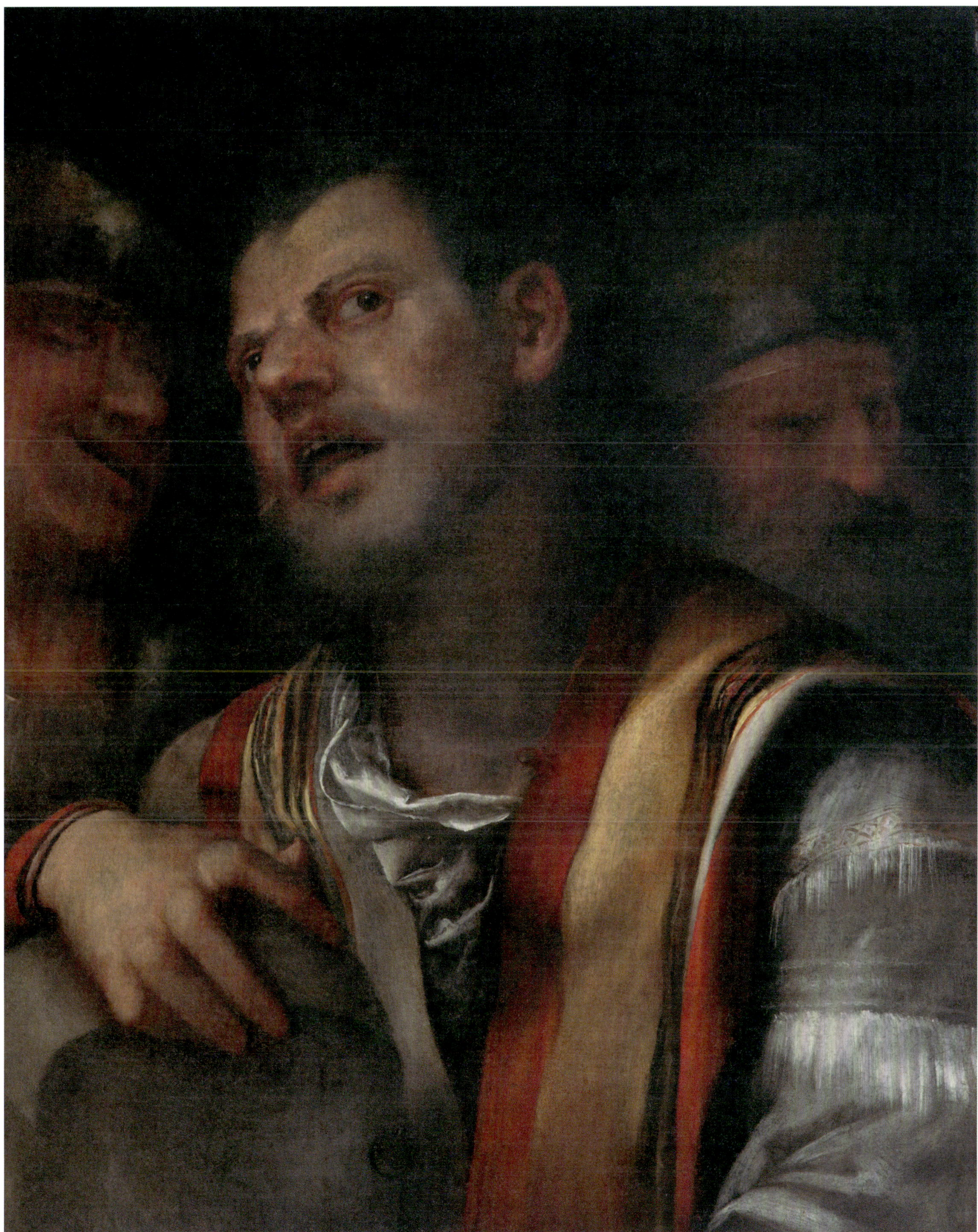

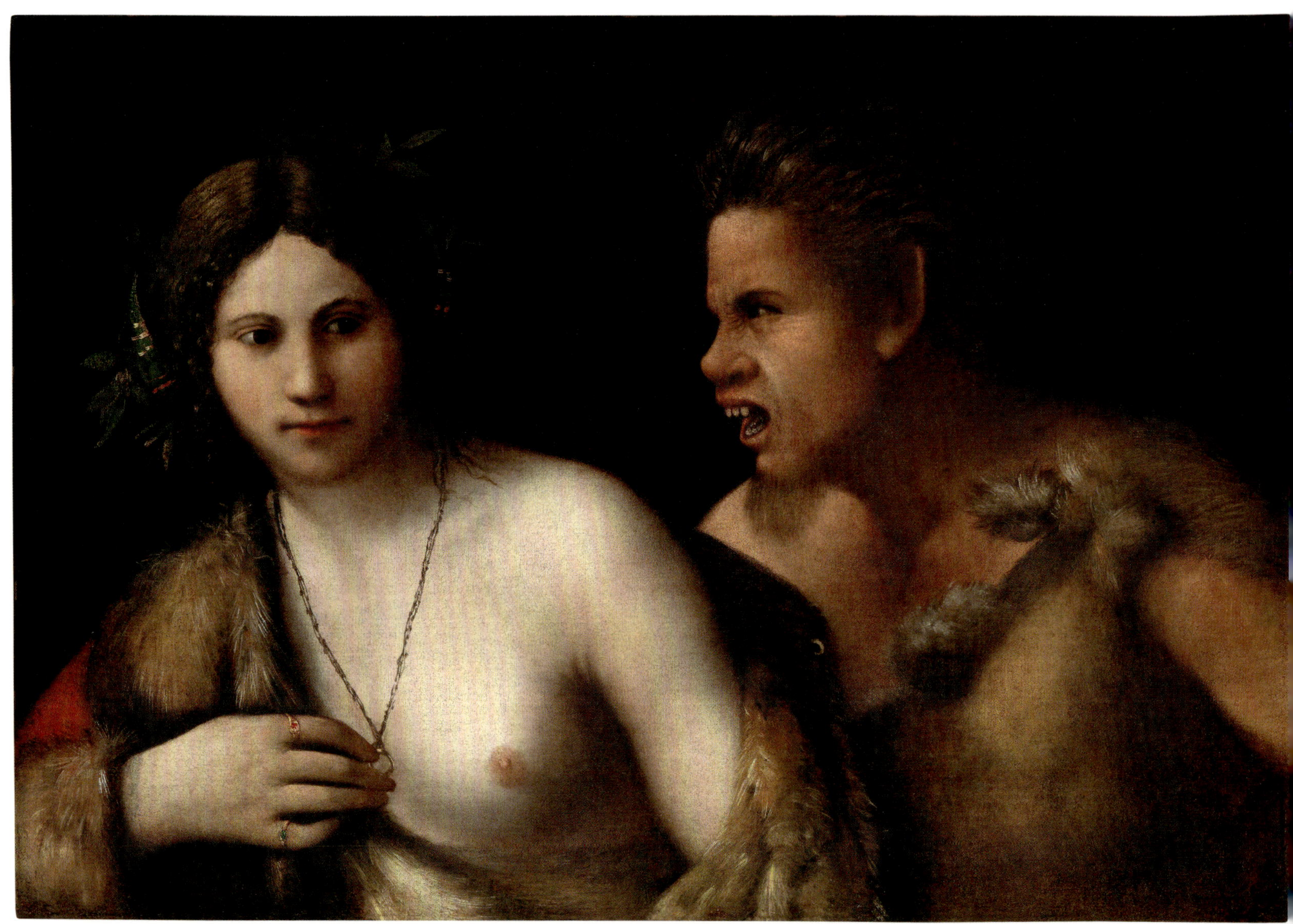

41

Angelica and Orlando (?), *c.* 1515

DOSSO DOSSI (GIOVANNI FRANCESCO LUTERI) TRAMUSCHIO, 1486/87 – FERRARA, 1541/42

Oil on canvas,
57.8 × 83.2 cm

Galleria Palatina,
Palazzo Pitti, Florence,
inv. 147

The painting shows two figures emerging from a dark background. The young woman is luxuriously dressed in a red, fur-lined gown; her raven-black hair is parted and tied with a green ribbon that bears a few sprigs of laurel. A sudden movement, perhaps one of fear, has caused the gown to slip from her shoulder, uncovering her breast. She is reaching for the ring that hangs from her necklace. Standing behind her, seen in profile, is a male figure with the beast-like features of a satyr. His skin is dark – contrasting with the dazzlingly pale skin of the woman – and his snarl suggests some kind of mental distress.

The title *Nymph and Satyr* is generally used, following the description given in early inventories, though there are other suggestions as to the painting's subject. An episode related by the poet Moschus describing the love of a satyr for the nymph Lyda has been considered,[1] as has the meeting of Jupiter and Antiope;[2] however, neither of these interpretations explains the presence of the ring, which seems a key element of the composition.

Edmund Gardner's idea, revived by Maria Matilde Simari, is that Ludovico Ariosto's epic *Orlando Furioso* may have inspired the work.[3] Perhaps here we see an event from the twenty-ninth canto, in which Angelica uses a magic ring to avoid the crazed Orlando. The ring, though cursed, protects her from magic spells when worn on the finger, and causes her to vanish when it is placed in the mouth. This interpretation need not necessarily impose on the painting a date of 1516 (the year Ariosto's poem was published in Ferrara); *Orlando Furioso* was circulating in manuscript form in the courts of Ferrara and Mantua by 1507.[4]

The earliest reference to the work dates from 1675, when it was listed as the work of Andrea Schiavone in the collection of Leopoldo de' Medici (1617–1675) in Florence.[5] An inventory of 1691 noted it as by Giorgione,[6] and this attribution was repeated until the nineteenth century. In 1871 Joseph Archer Crowe and Giovanni Battista Cavalcaselle considered it the work of 'a follower of Titian and Giorgione'.[7]

In 1885 Adolfo Venturi put forward the definitive attribution to Dosso Dossi, convinced that this was the painting acquired by Hans von Aachen on behalf of the Emperor Rudolf II in 1604,[8] and described as Dosso's depiction of 'a Satyr and a woman who has a shawl thrown over her shoulders'.[9] After initial disagreements,[10] the attribution to Dosso Dossi gained acceptance.

The style of the painting is given as proof of Giorgione's influence on Dosso's early career, and Bernard Berenson and Roberto Longhi upheld this interpretation.[11] Lionello Venturi perhaps summed up the artist's ambition when he wrote: 'It is an attempt to compete with Giorgione's palette, on a Giorgionesque subject: as far as can be gauged the effort has managed to deceive connoisseurs ancient and modern.'[12]

Amalia Mezzetti is alone in dating the canvas to the early 1530s.[13] Scholars in general agree on a date of between 1508 and 1516. An even earlier date is endorsed by Peter Humfrey – based on his theory about the work's similarities with Giorgione's *Laura* (fig. 1)[14] – and Alessandro Ballarin.[15]

NOTES

1 Eisler 1948, pp. 83–84.

2 Gibbons 1968, p. 175.

3 Florence 1986 (Maria Matilde Simari), pp. 303–04, no. 11.

4 Trent 2014 (Federica Caneparo), p. 56, no. 2.

5 Florence 1982 (Marilena Mosco), p. 40.

6 Florence 1982 (Marilena Mosco), p. 41, n. 20.

7 Crowe and Cavalcaselle 1871, vol. 2, p. 162.

8 Venturi 1885, p. 12.

9 'Einen Satyr und ein Weib, das sich ein Tuch über di Schultern wirft.'

10 Herbert Cook (1900, pp. 44, 155), for example, repeated the reference to Giorgione.

11 Berenson 1907, p. 209; Longhi 1934, p. 86.

12 Venturi 1913, p. 196.

13 Mezzetti 1965, p. 86.

14 Ferrara 1998 (Peter Humfrey), pp. 84–86, no. 1.

15 Ballarin 2001, pp. 24–25.

42

Bacchus and Ariadne, *c.* 1510

TULLIO LOMBARDO *c.* 1455 – VENICE, 1532

Marble,
56 × 71.5 × 22 cm

Kunsthistorisches Museum,
Kunstkammer, Vienna,
inv. 7471

NOTES

1 Egger and Hermann 1906, p. 75.

2 Kryza-Gersch 2007, pp. 69–79.

3 Luchs 1995, pp. 70–71; Rome 1995 (Wendy Sheard Stedman), pp. 262–65, no. 30; Ceriana 2004, p. 275; Washington 2009 (Sarah Blake McHam), pp. 70–73, no. 2.

4 Schulz 2014, p. 104.

A man and a woman, both very young, are portrayed half-length; their heads rest together, just touching. Around his head the young man wears a wreath of vine leaves (sometimes identified as ivy). The young woman wears a net into which the dense tangle of her hair is gathered in a fashion popular in the early sixteenth century. Both are barechested, although the girl wears a *mantello* (a light cloak) over her shoulders and upper arms. Both gaze upwards and into the distance; the viewer can only guess at what they see. The young man's mouth is slightly open and his teeth can be glimpsed.

The carving, in high relief, emerges from a rectangular marble slab that creates a background as well as a frame for the composition. A few traces of a red can be seen, particularly on the young woman's hairnet; this could be a residue of bole, suggesting that originally parts of the sculpture were gilded.

The piece comes from the collection of Tommaso degli Obizzi (1750–1803) and was kept at the Castello di Catajo, near Padua. The Obizzi heirs transported the collection to Vienna, and the present sculpture entered the Kunsthistorisches Museum in 1896. It has always been assumed that the Obizzi were its original owners. In 1470 Antonio degli Obizzi was involved in the commissioning of a new chapel dedicated to Saint Anthony in the Basilica del Santo in Padua. Much later Tullio Lombardo was to make two reliefs for the same chapel, the *Miracle of the Repentant Son* (1500–01) and the *Miracle of the Miser Heart* (1520–25). Antonio's son Girolamo donated a considerable sum of money to the Basilica del Santo in 1506 to be used for marble sculpture to decorate the façade separating the votive chapel of the Madonna Mora from the adjoining chapel of Saint Anthony of Padua.

The sculpture was first attributed to Lombardo in 1906 by Julius Hermann, who compared it with the double portrait at the Ca' d'Oro in Venice, signed by Lombardo.[1] Hermann also suggested that the figures in the present work are Bacchus and Ariadne; this hypothesis, almost unanimously accepted at the time, was based on the wreath of vine leaves or ivy, both attributes of Bacchus. Ariadne was the daughter of the King of Crete. Her lover Theseus abandoned her on the island of Naxos, where Bacchus discovered and married her. Despite their mythical status, the figures have a naturalistic appearance. Recently it has been suggested that the ivy could identify the young man as a poet, reciting his verse with such inspiration that the young woman listens, enraptured.[2]

Based on stylistic analysis, scholars have dated the work to the first decade of the sixteenth century.[3] Anne Markham Schulz disagrees, preferring a much later date of around 1520.[4]

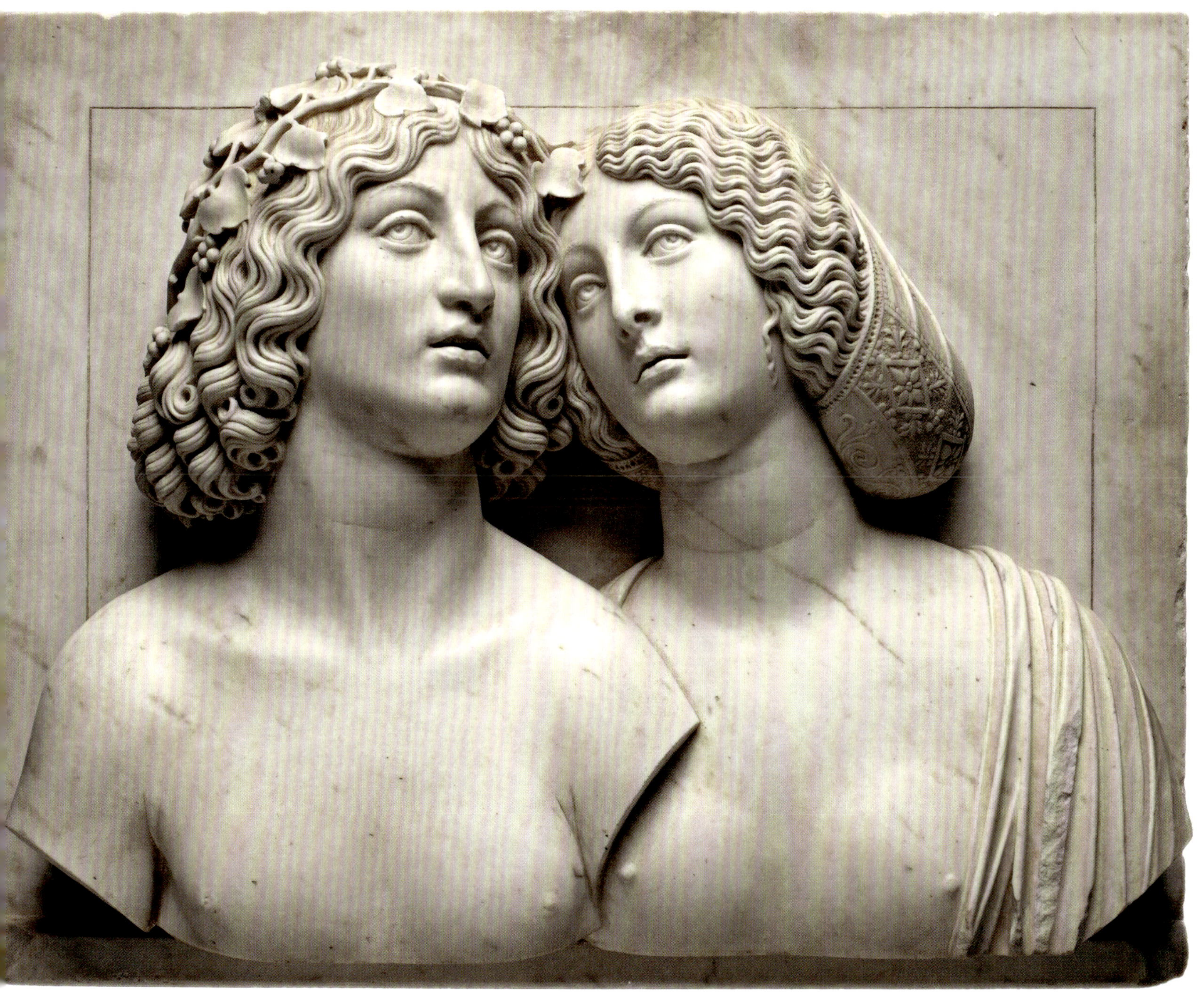

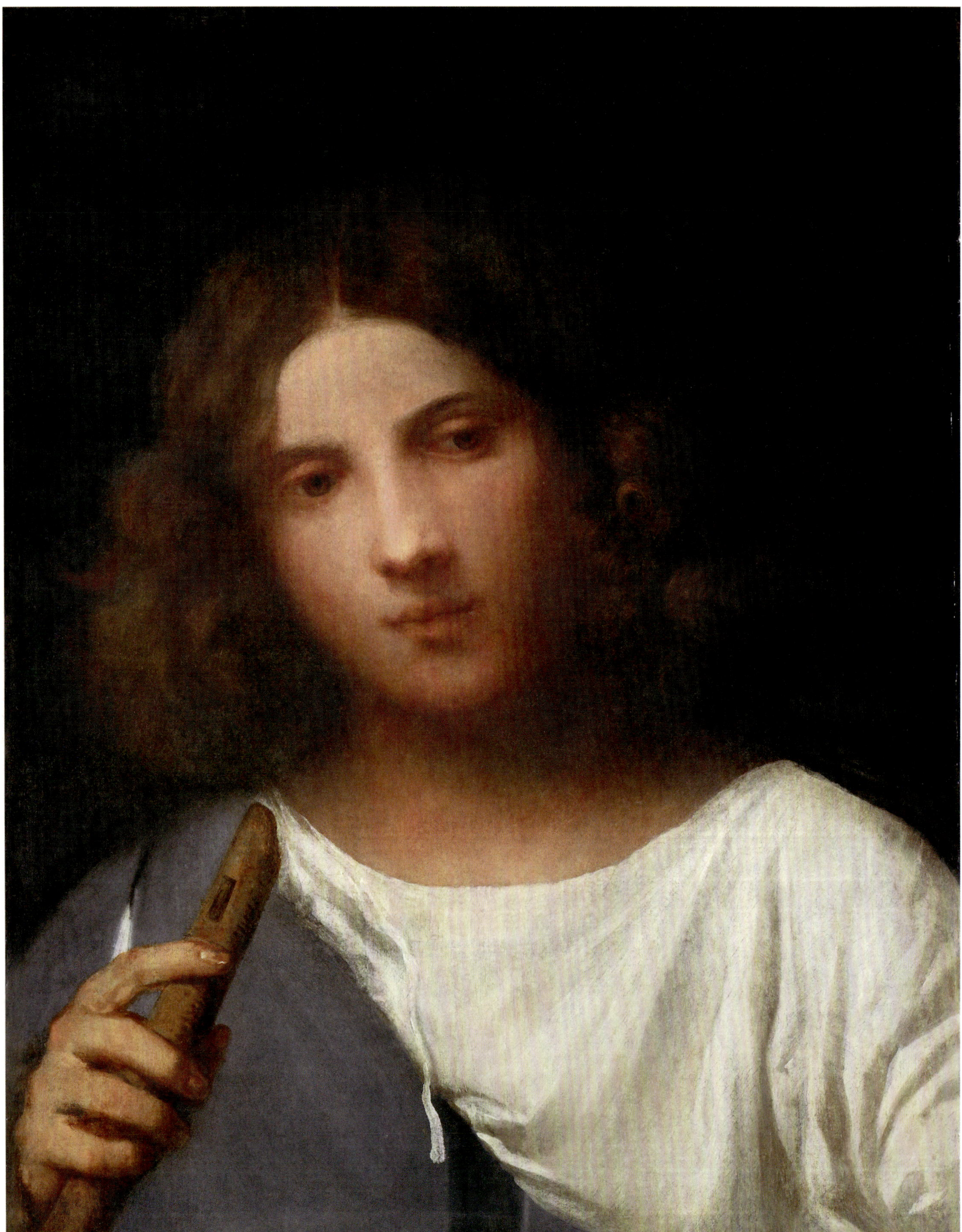

43

Boy with a Pipe ('Shepherd'), *c.* 1510–12

ATTRIBUTED TO TITIAN (TIZIANO VECELLIO) PIEVE DI CADORE, *c.* 1488/90 – VENICE, 1576

Oil on canvas, 62.4 × 49.2 cm

The Royal Collection, RCIN 405767

NOTES

1 Joannides 2010A, p. 107.

2 Millar 1960, p. 39; on the subsequent fortunes of the painting see Shearman 1983, p. 253.

3 Crowe and Cavalcaselle 1871, vol. 2, p. 164.

4 Richter 1960, p. 149.

5 Morelli 1891, pp. 285–86; Morelli 1893, p. 219.

6 Berenson 1894, p. IX.

7 Berenson 1897, p. 269.

8 Cook 1900, p. 49.

9 Venturi 1913, pp. 74, 210; Venturi 1928, p. 916.

10 Ballarin 1981, p. 151; Lucco 1995, p. 126.

11 Justi 1926, vol. 2, p. 276; Richter 1937, pp. 220–21, no. 35.

12 Fiocco 1948, p. 36.

13 Venice 1955 (Pietro Zampetti), pp. 38–40, nos 17–18.

14 Shearman 1983, pp. 253–56, no. 271.

15 Anderson 1996, pp. 327–28; Joannides 2001, pp. 254–55; London 2007 (Lucy Whitaker and Martin Clayton), pp. 185–87, no. 58; Joannides 2010A, p. 107.

A boy, dressed simply in a white shirt with a blue mantle over his shoulder, is seen before a dark background. The pipe in his hand gives a clue to the interpretation of the subject; we are in the pastoral world, a world described in Jacopo Sannazaro's *Arcadia* (Venice, 1502). It has recently been suggested that the boy may be tentatively identified as Paris.[1] The most striking elements of the composition are his languid gaze and introspective, withdrawn air.

The painting matches a description in the inventory of the collection of Charles I of England (1600–1649), drawn up by Abraham van der Doort (*c.* 1575/80–1640): 'done By Georgzone […] Item a Shipheard without a beard with long hanging hare Houlding a pipe in his right hand Being Some part *bing his* white Shirt.'[2]

The critical history of the painting is fraught with controversy, which can be traced back to 1871, when Joseph Archer Crowe and Giovanni Battista Cavalcaselle discussed the subject of the repetition of Giorgionesque subjects by painters of later generations, from Rocco Marconi to Pietro della Vecchia:

> Especially interesting in connection with these is the frequent repetition of one subject, a bust of a man in a hat with a flageolet in his hand, of which one example is registered in the Catalogue of James II's collection. Though none of the extant replicas can be admitted as genuine Giorgiones, they may have been all derived from an original that has been lost.[3]

Giovanni Morelli's reaction to the painting was quite different, as we learn from a letter sent to him by Jean Paul Richter on 28 February 1881.[4] Richter congratulated himself (and Morelli) on the convincing attribution to Giorgione of the *Three Ages of Man* at the Palazzo Pitti (cat. 38), and on the no less dazzling attribution of the present painting. Morelli's attribution to Giorgione proved popular and was accepted by his closest followers.[5] Bernard Berenson reproduced the painting as the frontispiece to his *Venetian Painters of the Renaissance* (1894), with the following words of justification: 'a picture which perhaps better than any other expresses the Renaissance at the most fascinating point of its course'.[6] A few years later Berenson returned to the debate, comparing the painting with the *David with the Head of Goliath* (Kunsthistorisches Museum, Vienna), held to be a copy of a lost original by Giorgione:

> The head of the David and the head of the Shepherd are, in everything but quality, identical – but in quality what a difference! How sweet is the mouth in the Hampton Court picture; how sensitive the nostrils; how the eyes glow under the smooth broad brow! – and the hair has the magic of a summer sunset seen through a long stretch of forest.[7]

Berenson's inspired prose failed to convince Herbert Cook who in 1900 demoted the work, attributing it to Francesco Torbido;[8] Lionello Venturi and Adolfo Venturi shared this view.[9]

Plenty of scholars continued to attribute the painting to Giorgione – among them, relatively recently, Alessandro Ballarin and Mauro Lucco.[10] Doubts remained however, until the painting was eventually discarded from the catalogue of the autograph works by Giorgione.[11] It was held to be a copy after a lost original,[12] as Crowe and Cavalcaselle had suspected.

At the exhibition in Venice in 1955 the juxtaposition was made between the *Boy with an Arrow* (fig. 9) and the present painting.[13] The two share undeniable affinities of composition even though their stylistic divergence is quite clear.

John Shearman proposed another alternative. Acknowledging that the painting exhibits certain fundamentally Giorgionesque characteristics, he noticed that the figure bears a certain similarity to the two shepherds painted by Giorgione in the lost *Birth of Paris*, mentioned by Marcantonio Michiel and known today thanks to a faithful copy (Private collection) made by David Teniers the Younger in the seventeenth century. In addition, Shearman drew attention to the peerless stylistic quality of the painting, suggesting an attribution to Titian and a date of about 1512, adding that 'the most Giorgionesque of Titian's works are not necessarily the earliest'.[14] The attribution to Titian was greeted favourably by numerous scholars.[15]

44

Portrait of a Young Woman, *c.* 1508–10

GIOVANNI CARIANI FUIPIANO AL BREMBO, BERGAMO, *c.* 1485 – VENICE, AFTER 1547

Oil on panel,
52.5 × 42.8 cm

Szépművészeti Múzeum, Budapest,
gift of Mrs György Ráth, 1906
inv. 51.879

NOTES

1 Frangi 2014 (Giorgio Fossaluzza), pp. 124, 126.

2 Budapest 1888, p. 42, no. 353.

3 Frimmel 1892, p. 258.

4 London 2010 (David Ekserdjian), p. 32, no. 24.

5 Berenson 1894, p. 110; Berenson 1957, vol. 1, p. 96.

6 Radisics 1906, pp. 6, 58, no. 208.

7 Gombosi 1925–26, pp. 57–66.

8 Venturi 1928, pp. 83–84; Pallucchini 1935–36, p. 42; 1944, pp. 15, 20, 22, 112, 154; Dussler 1942, pp. 17–19, 129, no. 8; Lucco 1980, pp. 90–91, no. 4; and Hirst 1981, pp. 4, 29, 31, 93–94.

9 Rome 2008 (Mauro Lucco), p. 94, no. 2

10 Facchinetti 2010, p. 11.

11 Frangi 2014 (Giorgio Fossaluzza), pp. 124–31.

The young woman's glance, directed at the viewer, is carefully posed to appear spontaneous. It is not known for whom this painting was intended, but it is likely that the recipient was a potential suitor. Similar portraits – alike in subject-matter and in composition – were painted during the second decade of the sixteenth century by Titian and Palma Vecchio; these bear traditional poetic titles such as *Violante* or *La Bella*. With the present work we are certainly not confronted with transfigured beauty but by a truthful and unidealised image.

The young woman gathers her shawl in her hand (X-ray analysis shows that her thumb was originally painted beneath the fabric, and that what we see at present is the result of later repainting[1]); with this gesture, she draws attention to the bold décolleté of her blouse. The sense of movement created by the slight forwards tilt of the head, seen in three-quarter profile, is emphasised by her gaze, which is directed at the viewer. Thanks to the woven ribbons that hold back her hair, the young woman can show off both her neck as well as her valuable earrings.

In 1869 the painting was purchased by György Ráth (1828–1905). From 1907 until 1949 it was displayed as part of the Hungarian national collection, until it was transferred to the Szépművészeti Múzeum in 1949.

The eighteenth- and nineteenth-century critical history of the portrait focuses almost exclusively on the name of Sebastiano del Piombo, and the earliest bibliographical reference to the painting dates from its first public exhibition in 1888.[2] Soon after, Theodor Frimmel was at pains to state that the painting certainly belonged to the artist's Venetian period, which ended in 1511 with his departure for Rome.[3] David Ekserdjian recently repeated the attribution to Sebastiano, with a few nuances of interpretation and chronology.[4] The only influential scholar never to have accepted the attribution to Sebastiano was Bernard Berenson, who in 1894 proposed Bernardino Licinio as the artist.[5] The dissident opinion of Jenö Radisics, who in 1906 gave the portrait to Palma Vecchio, has received no support.[6]

The study that most contributed to the success of the attribution to Sebastiano is undoubtedly that published in the 1920s by György Gombosi. He suggested some convincing visual comparisons, in particular with two unchallenged paintings from Sebastiano's Venetian period: *Portrait of a Young Woman as a Wise Virgin* (fig. 24) and the *Daughter of Herodias* (1510; National Gallery, London).[7] On the basis of the chronology proposed by Gombosi, the Budapest painting acquired a prominent position in the sequence of Sebastiano's works. Dated to before 1510 (with some disagreement as to the precise year), the work appears in all the major monographs devoted to Sebastiano.[8] More recently, Mauro Lucco revived Gombosi's original proposition: 'of all the work known to us, this may be the earliest painting by the Master, about 1505–06'.[9]

A recent suggestion by the present author, that this is a work from Giovanni Cariani's youth,[10] was debated at length and accepted by Giorgio Fossaluzza.[11] Fossaluzza suggests a date of immediately after 1510. This means acknowledging the connection between the portrait and Cariani's *Woman Reclining in a Landscape*, (*c.* 1510–15; Gemäldegalerie, Berlin). The suggestion also requires us to reconsider Cariani's role among Giorgione's closest followers, alongside Sebastiano. In this early phase of the painter's activity, around 1505, his works range from the *Holy Family Between Saints Lucy and Mary Magdalene* in the Gallerie dell'Accademia, Venice, and *Christ and the Adulteress* in the Musée Condé, Chantilly. Subsequent stylistic developments in the painter's work, represented by the *Saint Agatha* in Edinburgh (cat. 46), indicate that the present painting should be dated to before 1510.

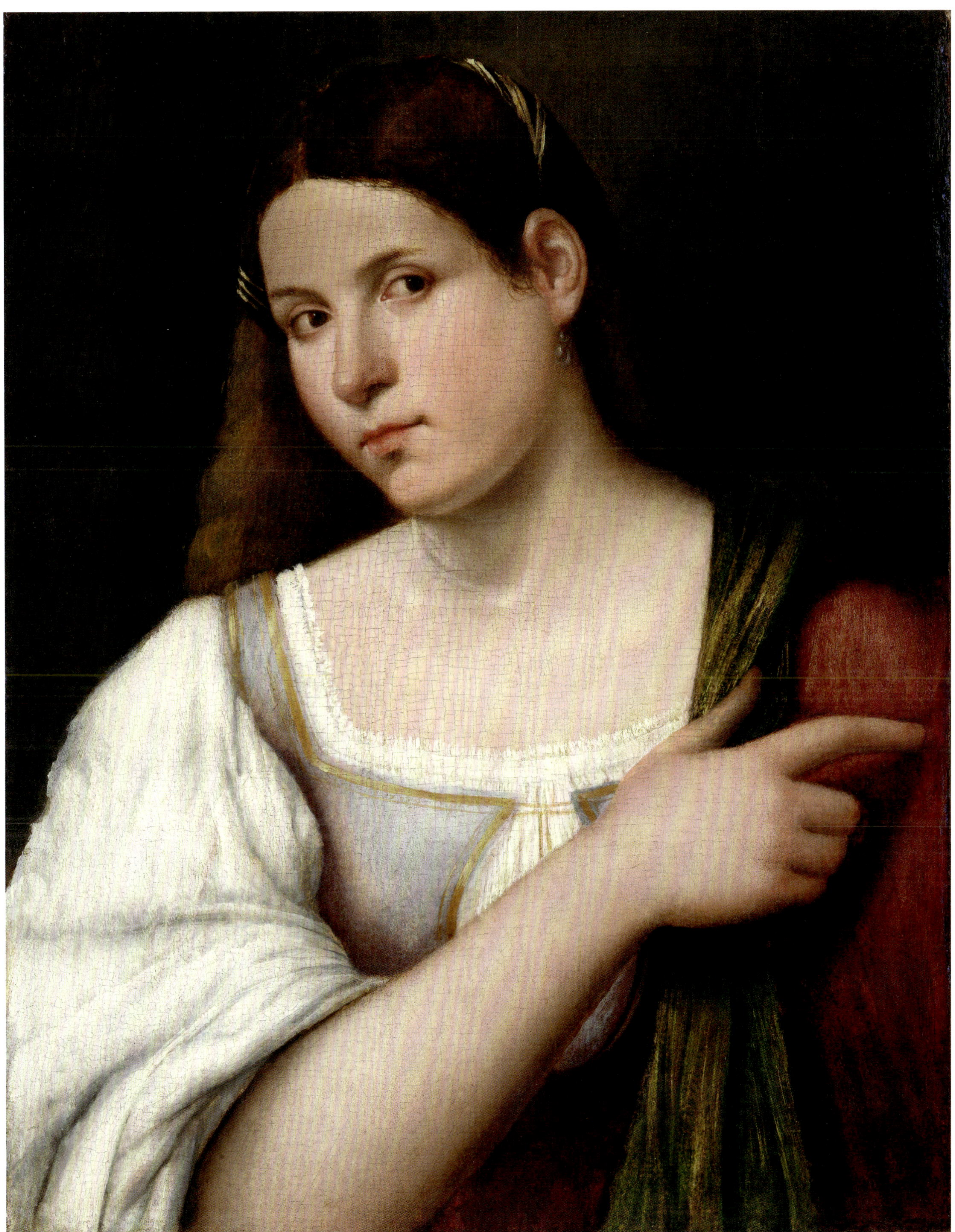

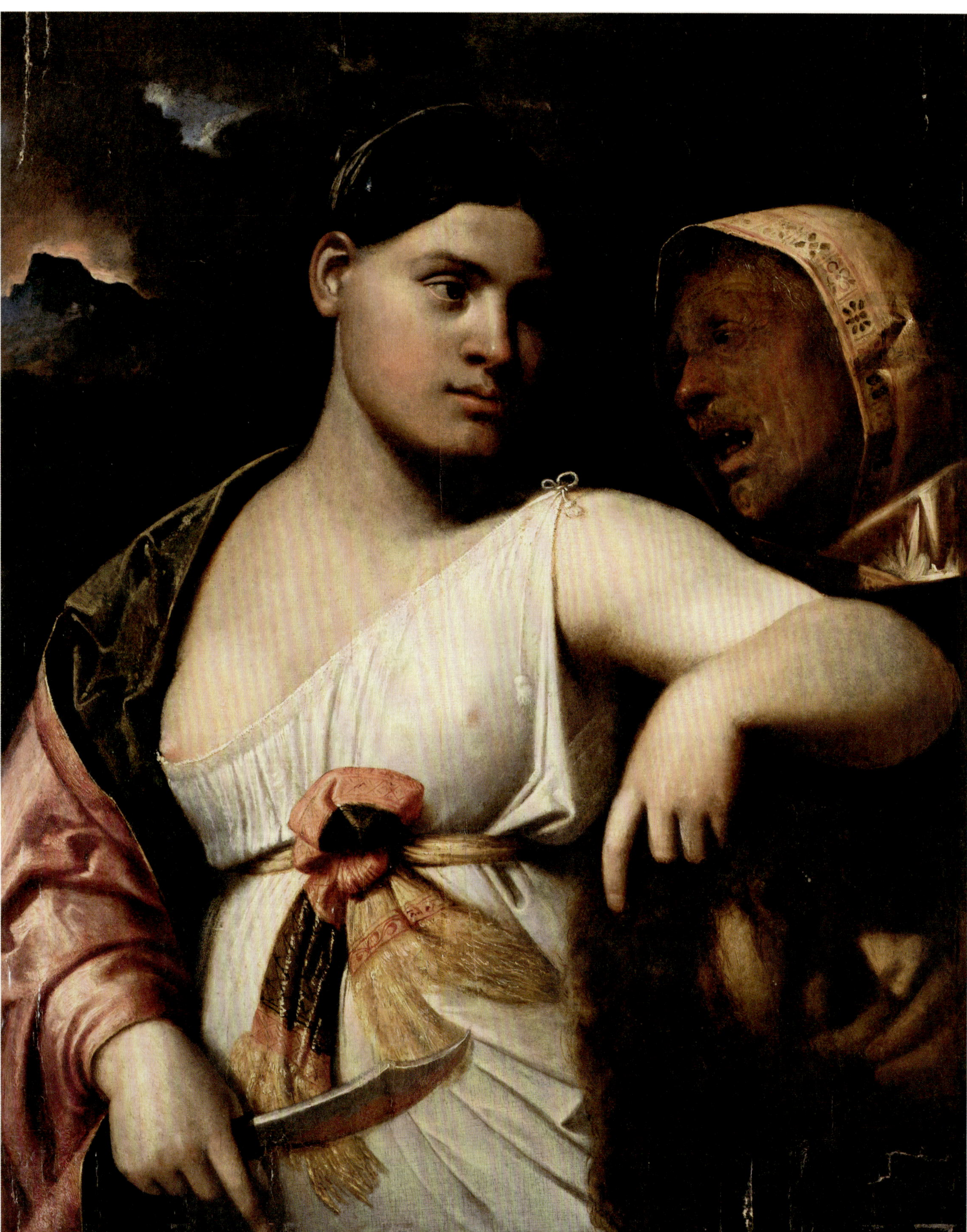

45

Judith, *c.* 1510–15

GIOVANNI CARIANI FUIPIANO AL BREMBO, BERGAMO, *c.* 1485 – VENICE, AFTER 1547

Oil on panel,
69 × 56.5 cm

Francesca and Massimo Valsecchi

NOTES

1 Cristina di Svezia 1689, p. 347.

2 Couché 1786, no. 111.

3 Couché 1808, no. 111; Furlan 1982, p. 12.

4 Berenson 1904, p. 158.

5 London 1914, p. 28, no. 30.

6 Troche 1934, p. 109.

7 Gallina 1954, p. 108.

8 London 1982 (Clovis Whitfield), p. 22, no. 10.

9 Dal Pozzolo 2008, p. 46.

10 Pallucchini 1983, p. 29; Rossi 1983, p. 120, no. 36.

11 London 1988 (Alessandro Ballarin), pp. 30–32.

12 Paris 1993 (Alessandro Ballarin), p. 438; Ballarin 2007, pp. 65–66.

13 Frangi 2014 (Giorgio Fossaluzza), p. 129.

Judith, heroine of the Israelites, is depicted as a raven-haired young woman, and dressed in a light white shift tied at the waist with an embroidered sash. Over one shoulder she wears a red cloak lined with green. Her bare breast is an allusion to the desire she inspired in Holofernes, general of the enemy Assyrian troops. Holofernes invited her into his tent, where he drank a surfeit of wine. After he fell asleep Judith struck off his head.

Judith seems to be in meditative mood, perhaps thinking of the man she has just killed. Her maid is close, her mouth open, perhaps in speech. A glow in the distant sky silhouettes a mountain, increasing the dramatic impact of the scene. The image manages to be attractive and repellent at the same time.

The painting is generally reported to have come from the collection of Queen Christina of Sweden (1626–1689), although the inventory description does not exactly match: 'A painting of a Judith with an old woman, holding a lighted candle in front of her with the head of Holofernes in a cloth.'[1] The painting is mentioned in the collection of Philippe II, duc d'Orléans (1674–1723), where it is believed to be by Pordenone.[2] It also appears as attributed to Pordenone in the version engraved by Christian Wilhelm Ketterlinus.[3]

The painting was attributed to Giovanni Cariani for the first time in 1904 by Bernard Berenson, who saw it at Grittleton House, the home of Sir Audley D. Neeld near Chippenham in Wiltshire. Berenson considered it 'an admirable female portrait by Cariani showing Judith with an old hag by her side, the hag carrying the head of Holofernes. Energetic, almost brutal in the deed, in a curious way the painting resembles the work of Sebastiano del Piombo.'[4] The painting's provenance in private collections has prevented research into the reference to Sebastiano. (Apart from the 1914 exhibition at the Burlington Fine Arts Club, London,[5] it did not reappear in public until 1982.) Debate about the dating of the painting has followed the same critical course as that of a considerable number of early works by Cariani. In 1934 Ernst Günter Troche pinpointed the work to the years Cariani spent in Bergamo, between 1517 and 1524.[6] Twenty years later Luciano Gallina further refined this date as being between 1516 and 1518.[7]

According to Clovis Whitfield, writing in 1982, the high visibility of the yellow sash – a distinctive element of the clothing of Venetian prostitutes at the time – alludes to 'Judith's role as a courtesan'.[8] Whitfield did not take into consideration that in the Book of Judith, a deuterocanonical text, she is described as an irreproachable widow.[9] More relevant is Whitfield's comparison of the figure of the servant with Giorgione's *La Vecchia* (cat. 39), a work clearly of fundamental importance to Cariani's composition.

In 1983 Rodolfo Pallucchini and Francesco Rossi fixed the presumed date of the painting at around 1516–17.[10] After the rediscovery of *Saint Agatha* (cat. 46) in 1986, the *Judith* received renewed scholarly attention in light of this new insight into Cariani's early career.[11] As Berenson had already surmised, parallels between the *Judith* and Sebastiano's early development – in particular his *Salome* (1510; National Gallery, London) – are quite striking. Nor should we forget the painting's affinities with the late work of Giorgione, or with Titian's early career. Alessandro Ballarin returned to the subject on several occasions, and dated the *Judith* to a little after 1510;[12] Giorgio Fossaluzza welcomed this suggestion.[13]

46 Saint Agatha, *c.* 1510–15

GIOVANNI CARIANI FUIPIANO AL BREMBO, BERGAMO, *c.* 1485 – VENICE, AFTER 1547

Oil on canvas,
69 × 58 cm

Scottish National Gallery, Edinburgh,
inv. NG 2494

It is probable that this is a portrait of a sitter in the guise of Saint Agatha. Perhaps it depicts a young Venetian woman who shared the saint's name and decided to pose with the attributes of the Christian martyr slain for refusing to renounce her faith.

We are inclined to accept this hypothesis because of the contemporary clothing worn by the young woman and because of her facial features, which are rendered in a highly individual – rather than idealised – manner.[1] She poses in an interior next to an open, round-headed window that looks out onto a landscape with a town in the distance.

The viewer cannot fail to be struck by the unconventional way the artist has presented the saint's attributes: two breasts on a glass dish with the palm of martyrdom between them. Agatha is believed to have perished in Catania in the mid-third century, during the persecution of the Christians carried out by the Roman proconsul Quintian. The saint underwent torture, remaining steadfast even when her breasts were severed. The base of the plinth on the left is decorated with a battle scene in which a horseman and a foot soldier face one another, perhaps taken from a Roman sarcophagus.[2] The allusion to the victory of Saint Agatha over persecution by the pagans seems clear.

There is no record of the painting prior to its appearance in a saleroom in London in 1986, when it was correctly attributed to Giovanni Cariani.[3] Alessandro Ballarin's stylistic analysis published soon after is convincing.[4] His comparison of this painting with the Venetian work of Sebastiano del Piombo led him to propose a date around 1510. Ballarin particularly highlighted the formal links between the present work and Cariani's *Judith* (cat. 45), comparing both with Sebastiano's *Daughter of Herodias* (1510; National Gallery, London). In a more extended analysis, aimed at revisiting Cariani's style in around 1510, Ballarin proposed some additions to this extraordinary period in the artist's career, among them the intense *Christ Blessing* (cat. 36).[5]

The date Ballarin suggested for the present painting – around 1510 – has been widely accepted.[6] Alternative opinions have been expressed by Peter Humfrey, who gives a date of around 1516–17, and Aidan Weston-Lewis, who proposed that the portrait belongs to the period the painter spent in Bergamo (1517–23).[7]

The earliest date seems the most convincing, especially considering the overwhelmingly emotional style of Saint Agatha's depiction, something that would be unthinkable far from Venice. Comparison with the earlier portrait in Budapest (cat. 44) shows a stylistic development. The present painting also reveals an intense use of colour, attributable to the influence of Sebastiano and Titian in around 1510. The drapery is more nuanced with *sfumatura*, more richly articulated and voluminous – similar to the work of Sebastiano, but also to the Venetian experiments of the young Dosso Dossi.

NOTES

1 Tokyo 1993 (Aidan Weston-Lewis), p. 145, no. 1.

2 A similar bas-relief appears in another of Cariani's paintings, *Portrait of a Woman* (1518–20; Accademia Carrara, Bergamo).

3 Sotheby's 1986, lot 22.

4 London 1988 (Alessandro Ballarin), pp. 30–32.

5 Paris 1993 (Alessandro Ballarin), pp. 437–38.

6 Brigstocke 1993, p. 49; Lucco 1996, p. 115, no. 204; Bergamo 2001 (Francesco Rossi), p. 152, no. IV.1; Amerigo 2009, p. 54; Frangi 2014 (Giorgio Fossaluzza), p. 129.

7 Edinburgh 2004 (Peter Humfrey), p. 98, no. 22; Tokyo 1993 (Aidan Weston-Lewis), p. 145, no. 1.

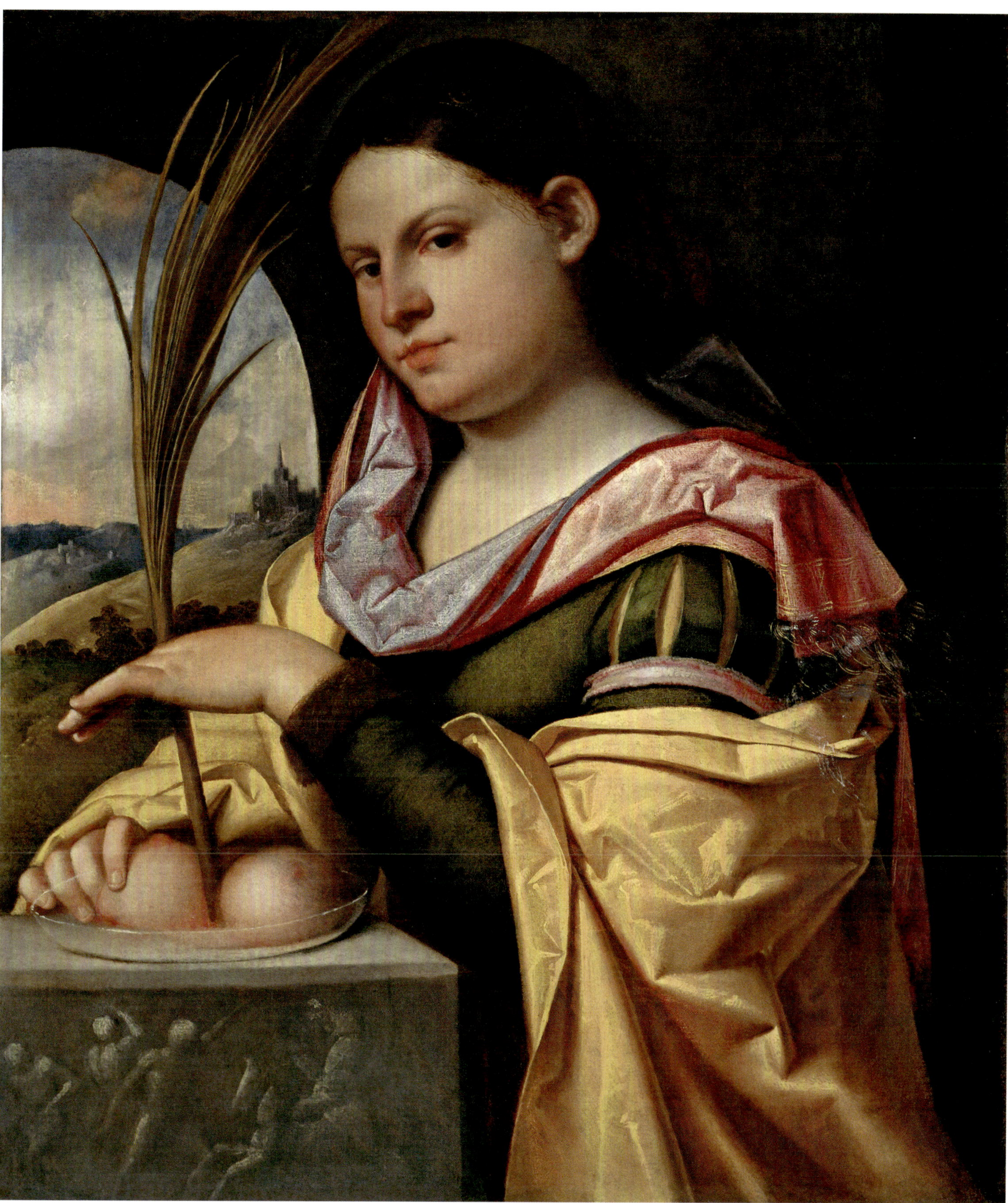

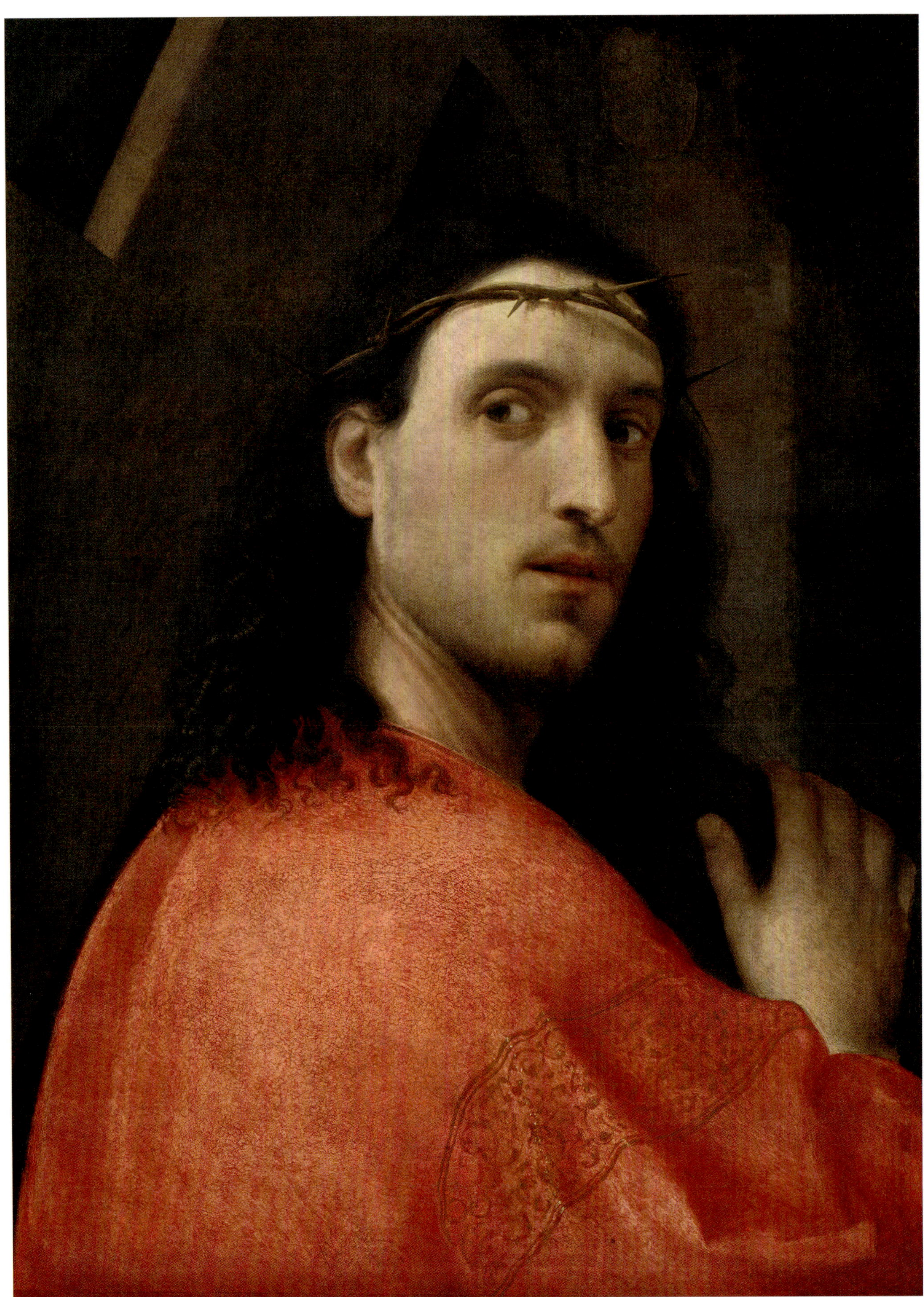

47

Christ Carrying the Cross

ATTRIBUTED TO PORDENONE (GIOVANNI ANTONIO DE SACCHIS) PORDENONE, c. 1483 – FERRARA, 1539

Oil on panel,
63 × 46 cm

Kunsthistorisches Museum, Vienna, Gemäldegalerie, inv. GG 280

NOTES

1 Engerth 1882, p. 119, no. 163.

2 Berenson 1894, p. 95.

3 Gallina 1954, p. 120.

4 Suida 1931, p. 139.

5 Wilde 1933, p. 121.

6 Rylands 1988, p. 299, no. A73; Rome 2008 (Mauro Lucco), p. 124, no. 14.

7 Heinemann 1962, vol. 1, p. 202, no. 819.

8 Volpe 1975, pp. 100–03.

9 Lucco 1982, p. 40; Lucco 1994A, p. 33.

10 Furlan 1988, pp. 63–68, no. 12.

11 Cohen 1996, vol. 1, p. 493.

12 Washington DC 2006 (Mauro Lucco), pp. 110–11, no. 15.

Christ is about to enter one of the gates of Jerusalem – just visible behind – and walk along the Via Dolorosa on His way to Golgotha. The weight of the cross does not seem to bother Him too greatly, and despite the crown of sharp thorns, there is no trace of blood on His face. He wears a red robe with a delicately embroidered plant design on the shoulder. His head and shoulders are portrayed at close quarters, involving the viewer in the scene. This impression is emphasised by Christ's farewell glance: He has stopped suddenly and looked back, mouth half open. It is difficult for the viewer to avoid meeting His questioning gaze. Most surprising is the absence of idealisation in the depiction of Christ's face, to the extent that the work resembles a portrait of a real sitter.

The painting came from the Count Althmann collection and passed into the Viennese imperial collection in 1785 with an attribution to Correggio.[1] This ascription may be connected to a former provenance in northern Italy.

Giovanni Cariani was first proposed as the artist by Bernard Berenson in 1894,[2] an attribution that was endorsed by Luciano Gallina in 1954[3] and may have been influenced by the existence of a painting of the same subject signed by Cariani, now in the Accademia Carrara in Bergamo.

The present work has been the subject of numerous comparisons with *Portrait of a Man* (c. 1515–20) in the Alte Pinakothek, Munich. According to Wilhelm Suida, writing in 1931, both works are by Palma Vecchio, on account of their close compositional and stylistic similarities.[4] Johannes Wilde on the other hand, writing shortly after, ascribed the two paintings to an artist he names the 'Master of the Self-portraits', assembling a small group of paintings around this figure, including Titian's so-called *Il Bravo* (Kunsthistorisches Museum, Vienna).[5]

To this day there is no generally accepted attribution for the Alte Pinakothek portrait, which is usually ascribed either to Palma Vecchio or to Sebastiano del Piombo, although both Philip Rylands and Mauro Lucco have voiced contrasting opinions.[6]

If we disregard the misleading attribution by Heinemann – who in 1962 compared the work to that of the 'Master of the *Three Ages of Man*' (cat. 38)[7] – most studies of the present painting incline towards Giovanni Antonio de Sacchis, known as Pordenone. Carlo Volpe was first to suggest this: 'the link between the Munich portrait […] and the Vienna *Christ* is, on closer inspection, soon broken and makes no sense […]. If you look harder at the exceptional *Christ* in Vienna, it more closely resembles a fine Roman portrait from the circle of Raphael or Sebastiano than any version of a contemporary Venetian portrait.'[8] This new direction was accepted by Lucco[9] and by Caterina Furlan[10] but not by Charles Cohen in the most recent monograph on Pordenone;[11] however Lucco recently reconsidered his position, exercising greater caution and preferring to keep the attribution open: 'Venetian artist, sixteenth century (Pordenone?).'[12] It is difficult to suggest an alternative name.

A prototype must have existed to explain the close relationship between a series of paintings that all emanate from the circle of Giorgione; this could be *Portrait of an Archer* in Edinburgh (cat. 7). In addition to the paintings from Vienna and Munich, *Shepherd with a Flute* in the Lansdowne Collection at Bowood House may also belong to the group; however, the latter is probably a sixteenth-century copy of a lost original by Sebastiano. This copy is likely to be the most faithful version of an image that was then repeated countless times. Worth noting is the effect of the turning head on the skin of the neck in the Lansdowne painting. This detail also appears in the present work, where it is painted with more finesse. From this prototype, Titian may have borrowed the trick of involving the viewer in a portrait by depicting a surprised expression. The immediacy of Titian's *Portrait of a Musician* in the Galleria Spada, Rome, seems to spring from this Giorgionesque invention.

ENDNOTES

The Biography of a Myth
pp. 18–31

1 Berenson 1895, p. 136.

2 D'Annunzio 1895, p. 79.

3 Luzio 1888, p. 47.

4 The artist's place of death is revealed in Isabella's letter.

5 Segre 2011, p. 386. The garments were for men and women, suggesting that Giorgione may have lived with a woman.

6 Luzio 1888, p. 47.

7 Segre 2012–13, p. 86. The document in question is an inventory of the assets of Giorgione requested by his heir Francesco Fisoli. It is dated 14 March 1511.

8 '1506 adj primo zugno fo fatto questo de ma[n] de maestro zorzi da chastelfr[anco] / cholega de maestro vizenzo chaena ad istantia de mis giac[o]mo.'

9 '15[06] / Di man de m° zorzi da castel franco.'

10 Castiglione 1528, p. 80.

11 Martin 1993, pp. 57–56.

12 Conte 2007, pp. 66–102; Hope 2008, pp. 15–37.

13 Vasari 1550 and 1568, vol. 4, p. 41.

14 Vasari 1550 and 1568, vol. 4, p. 42.

15 Vasari 1550, vol. 4, p. 45; Vasari 1568, vol. 4, p. 550.

16 Vasari 1568, vol. 6, p. 157.

17 Vasari 1550 and 1568, vol. 4, pp. 45–46.

18 Vasari 1568, vol. 6, p. 160.

19 Bernasconi 1864, pp. 107–17.

20 Lauber 2002B, pp. 99–115.

21 Bologna 1992, p. 73.

22 Michiel 1521–43, pp. 168–70. In this quotation and those that follow it, we have indicated wherever possible the paintings by Giorgione that Michiel mentions.

23 Michiel 1521–43, pp. 164–65, 167. The *Birth of Paris* is known through a copy by David Teniers the Younger in a private collection in London.

24 Michiel 1521–43, p. 185.

25 Michiel 1521–43, p. 218.

26 Michiel 1521–43, p. 208.

27 Michiel 1521–43, p. 162.

28 Michiel 1521–43, p. 230.

29 Michiel 1521–43, p. 149. The 'Christ in S. Rocco' is the *Christ Carrying the Cross* in the Scuola Grande di San Rocco, Venice (fig. 4).

30 Haskell 1981, pp. 583–614.

31 Couché 1786, vol. 1.

32 Pater 1873, pp. 117–18.

33 Zampetti 1955, p. 54.

34 Berenson 1897, p. 274. 'L'un des exploits le plus mémorable de la critique moderne.'

35 Morelli 1883, pp. 164–65. Michiel is described as 'Anonymous' only out of habit.

36 Morelli 1892, pp. 248–49.

37 Gamba 1912, pp. IV–V.

38 Gamba 1954, p. 172.

39 Berenson 1954, p. 145.

40 Hourticq 1919, pp. 1–31.

41 Venice 1955, p. XXXIX.

42 Lucco 1994B, p. 33.

43 Venice 2003; Vienna 2004.

44 Washington DC 2006.

45 Castelfranco Veneto 2009.

Portraits
pp. 34–39

1 Fara 2007, p. 33.

2 Vasari 1568, vol. 3, p. 430.

3 Vasari 1568, vol. 3, pp. 438–39.

4 Bembo 1548, vol. 1, pp. 53–55, n. XX.

O imagine mia celeste et pura,
che splendi più che 'l sole agli occhi miei
et mi rassembri il volto di colei
che scolpita ho nel cor con maggior cura,
credo che 'l mio Bellin con la figura
t'habbia dato il costume ancho di lei,
che m'ardi, s'io ti miro, et per te sei
freddo smalto cui giunse alta sventura.

Et come donna in vista dolce humile,
ben mostri tu pietà del mio tormento;
poi, se merce' ten' prego non rispondi.
In questo hai tu di lei men fero stile,
né spargi sì le mie speranze al vento,
ch'almen, quando ti cerco, non t'ascondi.

5 Vasari 1568, vol. 4, p. 155.

6 Michiel 1521–43, p. 217.

Landscape
pp. 70–75

1 Gombrich 1966, p. 109. On the subject of landscape in Venice at the time of Giorgione see Lucco 2012, pp. 17, 35; Mariuz 2012, pp. 25–39 and Mazzotta 2012A.

2 Michiel 1521–43, p. 189.

3 Michiel 1521–43, p. 168.

4 Michiel 1521–43, pp. 169, 230.

5 Michiel 1521–43, pp. 167, 218.

6 Shearman 1967, p. 50.

7 Dal Pozzolo 2009B, pp. 230–36.

8 Fletcher 1973, p. 384, n. 27.

9 Michiel 1521–1543, p. 162. 'El San Hieronimo nudo che siede in un deserto al lume delle luna.'

10 Michiel 1521–43, p. 162.

11 Castiglione 1528, p. 382.

Devotional Works
pp. 96–103

1 Cortesi Bosco 2009, pp. 113–22.

2 Luzio 1888, p. 47: 'una pictura de una nocte, molto bella et singolare'.

3 Luzio 1888, p. 47. 'M'è stato afirmato né l'una né l'altra non sono da vendere per pretio nesuno, però che li hanno fatte fare per volerli godere per loro.'

4 Vasari 1568, vol. 6, pp. 156–57. 'Tiziano dunque, veduto il fare e la maniera di Giorgione, lasciò la maniera di Gianbellino, ancorché vi avesse molto tempo consumato, e si accostò a quella, così bene imitando in brieve tempo le cose di lui, che furono le sue pitture talvolta scambiate e credute opere di Giorgione, come di sotto si dirà. [...] Intanto, avendo esso Giorgione condotta la facciata dinanzi del Fondaco de' Tedeschi, per mezzo del Barbarigo furono allogate a Tiziano alcune storie che sono nella medesima sopra la Merceria. [...] Nella quale facciata non sapendo molti gentiluomini che Giorgione non vi lavorasse più, né che la facesse Tiziano, il quale ne aveva scoperto una parte, scontrandosi in Giorgione, come amici si rallegravano seco, dicendo che si portava meglio nella facciata di verso la Merceria che non aveva fatto in quella che è sopra il Canal Grande; della qual cosa sentiva tanto sdegno Giorgione, che infino che non ebbe finita Tiziano l'opera del tutto, e che non fu notissimo che esso Tiziano aveva fatta quella parte, non si lasciò molto vedere, e da indi in poi non volle che mai più Tiziano praticasse o fusse amico suo.'

5 Vasari 1568, vol. 6, pp. 159–60. 'Per la chiesa di Santo Rocho fece un quadro, Christo con la croce in spalla et con una corda al collo, tirata da un Ebreo. La qual figura che hanno molti creduta sia di mano di Giorgione è hoggi la maggior divozione di Venezia.'

Allegorical Portraits
pp. 126–33

1 Castelnuovo 1973, p. 1,066.

2 Vasari 1568, vol. 4, p. 42.

3 Vasari 1568, vol. 4, p. 43.

4 Paschini 1927, p. 171.

5 Fletcher 2009, p. 30.

6 Frangi (forthcoming).

7 '1506 adj primo zugno fo fatto questo de ma[n] de maestro zorzi da chastelfr[anco] / cholega de maestro vizenzo chaena ad istantia de mis giac[o]mo.'

8 Dal Pozzolo 2008, pp. 31–53.

BIBLIOGRAPHY

Agosti 2009
Giovanni Agosti, *Un amore di Giovanni Bellini*, Milan, 2009

Aikema 2003
Bernard Aikema, 'Giorgione: i rapporti con il nord e una nuova lettura della *Vecchia* e della *Tempesta*', in Venice 2003, pp. 73–89

Aikema 2013
Bernard Aikema, 'Tiziano, Venezia e il papa Borgia. Le ragioni e gli esiti di una mostra: dati, proposte e qualche provocazione', in Pieve di Cadore 2013, pp. 19–37

Ajaccio 2010
Titien, l'étrange homme au gant, exh. cat., Palais Fesch-musée des Beaux-Arts, Ajaccio, 2010

Amerigo 2009
Simone Amerigo, *Giovanni Busi detto il Cariani*, Bergamo, 2009

Anderson 1979
Jaynie Anderson, 'A Further Inventory of Gabriel Vendramin's Collection', *The Burlington Magazine*, CXXI, 1979, pp. 639–48

Anderson 1981
Jaynie Anderson, 'Mito e realtà di Giorgione nella storiografia artistica: dal senatore Giovanni Morelli ad oggi', in *Giorgione e l'umanesimo veneziano, Atti del corso d'alta cultura (Venise, 26 agosto – 16 settembre 1978)*, Rodolfo Pallucchini (ed), vol. 2, Florence, 1981, pp. 637–53

Anderson 1996
Jaynie Anderson, *Giorgione, peintre de la 'brièveté poetique'*, Paris, 1996

Anderson 2000
Jaynie Anderson, *I Taccuini manoscritti di Giovanni Morelli*, Milan, 2000

Andrews 1947
Julia Gethman Andrews, *A Catalogue of European Paintings: 1300–1870*, San Diego, 1947

Anzelewsky 1991
Fedja Anzelewsky, *Albrecht Dürer. Das malerische Werk* (second edition), 2 vols, Berlin, 1991

Arslan 1932
Edoardo Arslan, 'Contributi alla storia della pittura veronese', in *Bollettino della Società letteraria di Verona*, XII, 1932, pp. 5–8

Baldass 1929
Ludwig Baldass, 'Ein unbekanntes Hauptwerk des Cariani. Studie über den Entwicklungsgang des Künstlers', *Jahrbuch der Kunsthistorischen Sammlungen in Wien*, 1929, pp. 91–110

Baldass and Heinz 1964
Ludwig Baldass and Gunther Heinz, *Giorgione*, Vienna and Munich, 1964

Ballarin 1968
Alessandro Ballarin, 'Pittura veneziana nei musei di Budapest, Dresda, Praga, Varsavia', *Arte Veneta*, XXII, 1968, pp. 237–55

Ballarin 1970
Alessandro Ballarin, 'Tre disegni: Palma il Vecchio, Lotto, Romanino', *Arte Veneta*, XXIV, 1970, pp. 47–62

Ballarin 1970–71
Alessandro Ballarin, 'La *Salomè* del Romanino. Corso di lezioni sulla giovinezza del pittore bresciano' [1970–71], in *La Salomè del Romanino ed altri studî sulla pittura bresciana del Cinquecento*, Barbara Marie Savy (ed.), vol. 1, Cittadella, 2006, pp. 45–121

Ballarin 1979
Alessandro Ballarin, 'Una nuova prospettiva su Giorgione: la ritrattistica degli anni 1500–03', in *Giorgione, Atti del convegno internazionale di studi per il quinto centenario della nascita (Castelfranco Veneto, 29–31 maggio 1978)*, Venice, 1979, pp. 227–52

Ballarin 1980
Alessandro Ballarin, 'Tiziano prima del Fondaco dei Tedeschi', in *Tiziano e Venezia, atti del convegno (Venise, 26 settembre 1 ottobre 1976)*, Venice, 1980, pp. 493–99

Ballarin 1981
Alessandro Ballarin, 'Giorgione: per un nuovo catalogo e una nuova cronologia', in *Giorgione e la cultura Veneta tra '400 e '500, atti del convegno (Roma, novembre 1978)*, Rome, 1981, pp. 26–30

Ballarin 1983
Alessandro Ballarin, 'Giorgione e la Compagnia degli Amici: Il "Doppio ritratto" Ludovisi', in *Storia dell'arte italiana*, vol. 1, *Dal Medioevo al Quattrocento*, Turin, 1983, pp. 479–541

Ballarin 1985
Alessandro Ballarin, 'La *Salomè* del Romanino quindici anni dopo: addenda et corrigenda' [1985], in *La Salomè del Romanino ed altri studî sulla pittura bresciana del Cinquecento*, Barbara Maria Savy (ed.), vol. 1, Cittadella, 2006, pp. 125–55

Ballarin 1990
Alessandro Ballarin, 'Attorno a Giorgione l'anno 1500: Boccaccio Boccaccino' [1990], in Ballarin 1994–95, vol. 1, pp. 3–21

Ballarin 1993A
Alessandro Ballarin, 'Une nouvelle perspective sur Giorgione: les portraits des années 1500–03', in Paris 1993, pp. 281–94

Ballarin 1993B
Alessandro Ballarin, 'Le problème des œuvres de la jeunesse de Titien. Avancées et reculs de la critique', in Paris 1993, pp. 357–67

Ballarin 1994–95
Alessandro Ballarin, *Dosso Dossi. La pittura a Ferrara negli anni del ducato di Alfonso I*, 2 vols, Cittadella, 1994–95

Ballarin 2001
Alessandro Ballarin, 'L'arrivo di Bacco nell'isola di Nasso' [2001], in *Il camerino delle pitture di Alfonso I*, Alessandro Ballarin (ed.), vol. 1, Cittadella, 2007, pp. 15–47

Ballarin 2007
Alessandro Ballarin, 'Ancora sulla giovinezza del Cariani', in *Il cielo, o qualcosa di più*, Adriano Mariuz and Elisabetta Seccomani (eds), Cittadella, 2007, pp. 65–69

Ballarin 2010
Alessandro Ballarin, *Leonardo a Milano. Problemi di leonardismo milanese tra Quattrocento e Cinquecento: Giovanni Antonio Boltraffio prima della Pala Casio* (with the collaboration of Maria Lucia Menegatti and Barbara Maria Savy), vol. 2, Verona, 2010

Banti 1953
Anna Banti, *Lorenzo Lotto*, Florence, 1953

Bätschmann 2008
Oskar Bätschmann, *Giovanni Bellini*, London, 2008

Béguin 1981
Sylvie Béguin, 'A propos des peintures de Lorenzo Lotto au Louvre', in *Lorenzo Lotto: Atti del convegno internazionale di studi per il V centenario della nascita (Asolo, 18–21 settembre 1980)*, Pietro Zampetti and Vittorio Sgarbi (eds), Venice, 1981, pp. 99–105

Bembo 1548
Pietro Bembo, *Le Rime* [1548], Andrea Donnini (ed.), 2 vols, Rome, 2008

Benzi 1982
Fabio Benzi, 'Un disegno di Giorgione a Londra e il "Concerto Campestre" del Louvre', *Arte Veneta*, XXXVI, 1982, pp. 183–87

Berenson 1894
Bernard Berenson, *The Venetian Painters of the Renaissance*, New York and London, 1894

Berenson 1897
Bernard Berenson, 'De quelques copies d'après des originaux perdus de Giorgione', *Gazette des Beaux-Arts*, XVIII, 1987, pp. 265–82

Berenson 1901
Bernard Berenson, *Lorenzo Lotto: An Essay in Constructive Art Criticism*, London, 1901

Berenson 1904
Bernard Berenson, 'Scoperte e primizie artistiche', *Rassegna d'Arte*, IV, 1904, pp. 156–58

Berenson 1907
Bernard Berenson, *The North Italian Painters of the Renaissance*, New York and London, 1907

Berenson 1928
Bernard Berenson, 'The Missing Head of the Glasgow *Christ and Adulteress*', *Art in America*, XVI, 1928, pp. 147–54

Berenson 1932
Bernard Berenson, *Italian Pictures of the Renaissance: A List of the Principal Artists and Their Works with an Index of Places*, Oxford, 1932

Berenson 1936
Bernard Berenson, *Pitture italiane del Rinascimento. Catalogo dei principali artisti e delle loro opere con un indice dei luoghi*, Milan, 1936

Berenson 1954
Bernard Berenson, 'Notes on Giorgione', *Arte Veneta*, VIII, 1954, pp. 146–52

Berenson 1956
Bernard Berenson, *Lorenzo Lotto*, London, 1956

Berenson 1957
Bernard Berenson, *Italian Pictures of the Renaissance: Venetian School*, 2 vols, London, 1957

Berenson 1968
Bernard Berenson, *Italian Pictures of the Renaissance: Central and North Italian School*, 3 vols, London, 1968

Bergamo 2001
Bergamo. L'altra Venezia. Il Rinascimento negli anni di Lorenzo Lotto, 1510–1530, Francesco Rossi (ed.), exh. cat., Accademia Carrara, Bergamo, 2001

Bernasconi 1864
Cesare Bernasconi, *Studj sopra la storia della pittura italiana dei secoli XIV e XV e della scuola pittorica veronese dai medij tempi fino a tutto il secolo XVIII*, Verona, 1864

Berti 1980
Gli Uffizi. Catalogo generale, Luciano Berti (ed.), Florence, 1980

Boccia 1980
Lionello G. Boccia, 'L'armatura lombarda tra il XIV e il XVII secolo', in *Armi e armature lombarde*, Lionello G. Boccia, Francesco Rossi and Marco Morin (eds), Milan, 1980, pp. 13–177

Bologna 1992
Ferdinando Bologna, *La coscienza storica dell'arte in Italia*, Turin, 1992

Bologna 2008
Amico Aspertini 1474–1552: artista bizzarro nell'età di Dürer e Raffaello, Andrea Emiliani and Daniela Scaglietti Kelescian (eds), exh. cat., Pinacoteca Nazionale, Bologna, 2008

Bordeaux 2005
Splendeur de Venise, 1500–1600: peintures et dessins des collections publiques françaises, Oliver Le Bihan and Patrick Ramade (eds), exh. cat., Musée des Beaux-Arts, Bordeaux, and Musée des Beaux-Arts, Caen, 2005

Borean and Mason 2002
Linda Borean and Stefania Mason, 'Cristoforo Orsetti e i suoi quadri di "perfetta mano"', in *Figure di collezionisti a Venezia tra Cinque e Seicento*, Linda Borean and Stefania Mason (eds), Udine, 2002, pp. 119–57

Borenius 1913
Tancred Borenius, *A Catalogue of the Painting at Doughty House, Richmond, and Elsewhere in the Collection of Sir Frederick Cook*, vol. 1, *Italian Schools*, London, 1913

Brandolese 1795
Pietro Brandolese, *Del genio de' Lendinaresi per la pittura e di alcune pregevoli pitture di Lendinara* [1795], Vittorio Sgarbi (ed.), Rovigo, 1990

Brescia 1990
Giovanni Gerolamo Savoldo tra Foppa, Giorgione e Caravaggio, exh. cat., Monastero di Santa Giulia, Brescia, and Schirn Kunsthalle, Frankfurt, 1990

Brigstocke 1993
Hugh Brigstocke, *Italian and Spanish Paintings in the National Gallery of Scotland* (second edition), Edinburgh, 1993

Brown 2007
Beverly Louise Brown, 'Corroborative Detail: Titian's Christ and the Adulteress', *Artibus et Historiae*, XXVIII, 56, part 2, 2007, pp. 73–105

Brown 2013
Beverly Louise Brown, 'In hoc signo vinces. Il vescovo Jacopo Pesaro e papa Alessandro VI davanti a san Pietro di Tiziano', in Pieve di Cadore 2013, pp. 47–89

Brown 1990
David Alan Brown, 'Bellini e Tiziano', in Venice 1990, pp. 57–67

Brown 2010
David Alan Brown, 'Giulio Campagnola: The Printmaker as Painter', *Artibus et Historiae*, XXXI, 61, 2010, pp. 83–97

Brown 2013
David Alan Brown, 'Bembo and Bellini', in *Pietro Bembo e le arti*, Guido Beltramini, Howard Burns and Davide Gasparotto (eds), Vicenza, 2013, pp. 309–27

Brown 2002
Jonathan Brown, 'Artistic Relations between Spain and England 1604–1655', in *The Sale of the Century: Artistic Relations between Spain and Great Britain, 1604–1655*, Jonathan Brown and John Elliott (eds), New Haven and London, 2002, pp. 41–68

Budapest 1888
Tárgymutató a budapesti I. gyermekmenhely javára a Mucsarnokban magántulajdondan levo, régi és modern képerbol rendezzett kiállitáshoz, exh. cat., Mucsarnok, Budapest, 1888

Burroughs 1938
Alan Burroughs, *Art Criticism from a Laboratory*, Boston, 1938

Byam Shaw and Robertson 1962
James Byam Shaw and Ian Robertson, 'Sir Karl Parker and the Ashmolean', *The Burlington Magazine*, CIV, 1962, pp. 428–33

Campori 1870
Giuseppe Campori (ed.), *Raccolta di cataloghi ed inventari inediti di quadri, statue, disegni, bronzi, dorerie, smalti, medaglie, avorii, ecc. dal secolo XV al secolo XIX*, Modena, 1870

Cannon-Brookes 1977
Peter Cannon-Brookes, *The Cornbury Park Bellini: A Contribution Towards the Study of the Late Paintings of Giovanni Bellini*, Birmingham, 1977

Carotti 1901
Giulio Carotti, *Capi d'arte, appartenenti a S. E. la duchessa Joséphine Melzi d'Eril-Barbò*, Bergamo, 1901

Carradore 2010
Antonio Carradore, 'Giulio Campagnola, un artista umanista', *Venezia Cinquecento*, XX, 40, 2010, pp. 55–134

Castelfranco Veneto 2009
Giorgione, Enrico Maria Dal Pozzolo and Lionello Puppi (eds), exh. cat., Museo Casa Giorgione, Castelfranco Veneto, 2009

Castelnuovo 1973
Enrico Castelnuovo, 'Il significato del ritratto pittorico nella società', in *Storia d'Italia*, vol. 5, part 2, *I documenti*, Turin, 1973, pp. 1,034–94

Castiglione 1528
Baldassare Castiglione, *Il libro del Cortegiano* [1528], Walter Barberis (ed.), Turin, 1998

Caterino 2012
Antonello Fabio Caterino, 'Il ricordo di Alcippo (Antonio Brocardo) tra le rime di Niccolò Franco', in *Banca Dati 'Nuovo Rinascimento'*, 2012, pp. 2–12

Ceriana 2004
Matteo Ceriana, 'La scultura veneziana al tempo di Giorgione', in *Da Bellini a Veronese. Temi di arte veneta*, Gennaro Toscano and Francesco Valcanover (eds), Venice, 2004, pp. 253–97

Chennevières 1879
Philippe de Chennevières, 'Les dessins de maîtres anciens exposés à l'Ecole des Beaux-Arts en 1879', *Gazette des Beaux-Arts*, XIX, 1879, pp. 505–35

Chiari 1982
Maria Agnese Chiari, *Incisioni da Tiziano. Catalogo del fondo grafico a stampa del Museo Correr*, Venice, 1982

Chiari 1988
Maria Agnese Chiari, 'Per un catalogo ragionato dei disegni di Tiziano', *Saggi e Memorie di Storia dell'Arte*, 16, 1988, pp. 21–99

Christiansen 1994
Keith Christiansen, 'A Proposal for Giulio Campagnola Pittore', in *Hommage à Michel Laclotte. Etudes sur la peinture du Moyen Age et de la Renaissance*, Paris, 1994, pp. 344–55

Cohen 1996
Charles Cohen, *The Art of Giovanni Antonio Pordenone: Between Dialect and Language*, 2 vols, Cambridge, 1996

Coletti 1955
Luigi Coletti, *Tutta la pittura di Giorgione*, Milan, 1955

Collins Baker 1929
Charles Henry Collins Baker, *Catalogue of the Pictures at Hampton Court*, Glasgow, 1929

Conte 2007
Floriana Conte, 'Osservazioni sulle varianti della Vita di Giorgione di Vasari', *Annali della Critica d'Arte*, 3, 2007, pp. 61–102

Cook 1900
Herbert Cook, *Giorgione*, London, 1900

Cook 1906
Herbert Cook, 'Some Venetian Portraits in English Possession', *The Burlington Magazine*, VIII, 1906, pp. 338–44

Cook 1908
Herbert Cook, 'Notizie d'Inghilterra. L'esposizione invernale al Burlington Fine Arts Club', *L'Arte*, XI, 1908, pp. 57–59

Cook 1910
Herbert Cook, 'Venetian Portraits, and Some Problems', *The Burlington Magazine*, XVI, 1910, pp. 328–34

Cortesi Bosco 2005
Francesca Cortesi Bosco, 'L' avventura della ricerca. Per la data della Pala di Castelfranco di Giorgione', *La Rivista di Bergamo*, 42, 2005, pp. 54–57

Cortesi Bosco 2009
Francesca Cortesi Bosco, 'Matteo Costanzo nella guerra del Casentino. Considerazioni sull'esecuzione della tavola di Giorgione a Castelfranco', in Castelfranco Veneto 2009, pp. 113–22

Couché 1786
Jacques Couché, *Galerie du Palais Royal gravée d'après les tableaux des différentes écoles qui la composent, avec une abrégé de la vie des peintres et une description historique de chaque tableau par m.r l'abbé de Fontenai*, vol. 1, Paris, 1786

Couché 1808
Jacques Couché, *Galerie du Palais Royal gravée d'après les tableaux des différentes écoles qui la composent, avec une abrégé de la vie des peintres et une description historique de chaque tableau par m.r l'abbé de Fontenai*, vol. 2, Paris, 1808

Cremona 2001
Dipingere la musica. Strumenti in posa nell'arte del Cinque e Seicento, Sylvia Ferino-Pagden (ed.), exh. cat., Santa Maria della Pietà, Cremona, 2001

Cristina di Svezia 1689
'Inventario della raccolta della Regina Cristina di Svezia' [1689], in Campori 1870, pp. 336–376

Crowe and Cavalcaselle 1871
Joseph Archer Crowe and Giovanni Battista Cavalcaselle, *A History of Painting in North Italy*, 2 vols, London, 1871

Crowe and Cavalcaselle 1877
Joseph Archer Crowe and Giovanni Battista Cavalcaselle, *Titian: His Life and Times*, 2 vols, London, 1877

Cust 1928
Lionel Cust, 'A Portrait by Giovanni Bellini at Hampton Court Palace', *Apollo*, VII, 47, 1928, p. 247

Dal Pozzo 1718
Bartolomeo Dal Pozzo, *Le vite de' pittori, degli scultori, et architetti veronesi*, Verona, 1718

Dal Pozzolo 1993
Enrico Dal Pozzolo, 'Osservazioni sul catalogo di Lorenzo Lotto. 1503–1516', *Arte Veneta*, XLV, 1993, pp. 32–49

Dal Pozzolo 1997
Enrico Maria Dal Pozzolo, 'Tra Cariani e Rocco Marconi', *Venezia Cinquecento*, VII, 13, 1997, pp. 5–37

Dal Pozzolo 2008
Enrico Maria Dal Pozzolo, *Colori d'amore. Parole, gesti e carezze nella pittura veneziana del Cinquecento*, Treviso, 2008

Dal Pozzolo 2009A
Enrico Maria Dal Pozzolo, 'Ipotesi per un esordio', in Castelfranco Veneto 2009, pp. 37–50

Dal Pozzolo 2009B
Enrico Maria Dal Pozzolo, *Giorgione*, Milan, 2009

D'Annunzio 1895
Gabriele D'Annunzio, 'Omaggio a Venezia' (1895), in Paola Barocchi, *Testimonianze e polemiche figurative in Italia. Dal Divisionismo al Novecento*, Florence, 1974, pp. 73–79

Della Pergola 1955A
Paola Della Pergola, *Giorgione*, Milan, 1955

Della Pergola 1955B
Paola Della Pergola, *Galleria Borghese, i dipinti*, Rome, 1955

Della Rovere [1888]
Antonio Della Rovere, *Guida alla R. Galleria di Venezia con note storiche e critiche*, Venice [1888]

De Marchi 2004
Andrea G. De Marchi, *Scrivere sui quadri. Ferrara e Roma. Agucchi e alcuni ritratti rinascimentali*, Florence, 2004

Doetsch 1895
Catalogue of the Highly Important Collection of Pictures by Old Masters of Henry Doetsch, London, 1895

Douglas-Scott 1996
Michael Douglas-Scott, 'Giovanni Bellini's *Madonna and Child with Two Saints and a Donor* at Birmingham: A Proposal', *Venezia Cinquecento*, VI, 11, 1996, pp. 5–21

Dunkerton 2010
Jill Dunkerton, 'Giorgione and Not Giorgione: The Conservation History and Technical Examination of *Il Tramonto*', *National Gallery Technical Bulletin*, 31, 2010, pp. 42–63

Dussler 1942
Luitpold Dussler, *Sebastiano del Piombo*, Basel, 1942

Edinburgh 2004
The Age of Titian: Venetian Renaissance Art from Scottish Collections, Aidan Weston-Lewis (ed.), exh. cat., National Galleries of Scotland, Edinburgh, 2004

Egger and Hermann 1906
Otto Egger and Julius Hermann, 'Aus den Kunstsammlungen des Hauses Este in Wien', *Zeitschrift für Bildende Kunst*, XLI, 1906, pp. 84–105

Eisler 1948
Robert Eisler, 'Luca Signorelli's School of Pan', *Gazette des Beaux-Arts*, 33, 1948, pp. 77–92

Emison 1992
Patricia Emison, 'Asleep in the Grass of Arcady: Giulio Campagnola's Dreamer', *Renaissance Quarterly*, XLV, 2, 1992, pp. 271–92

Engerth 1882
Eduard R. von Engerth, *Kunsthistorischen Sammlungen des allerhöchsten Kaiserhauses. Gemälde. I Band. Italienische, spanische und französische Schulen*, Vienna, 1882

Facchinetti 2010
Simone Facchinetti, *Intorno ai Santacroce*, Bergamo, 2010

Fara 2007
Albrecht Dürer, Lettere da Venezia, Giovanni Maria Fara (ed), Milan, 2007

Fara 2014
Giovanni Maria Fara, *Albrecht Dürer nelle fonti italiane. 1508–1686*, Florence, 2014

Farr 1987
Dennis Farr, *100 Masterpieces from the Courtauld Collections: Bernardo Daddi to Ben Nicholson. European Painting and Drawings from the Fourteenth to the Twentieth Century*, London, 1987

Ferino-Pagden 2008
Sylvia Ferino-Pagden, 'Giorgione ins 21. Jahrhundert', in *Giorgione entmythisiert*, Sylvia Ferino-Pagden (ed), Turnhout, 2008, pp. 1–14

Ferrara 1998
Dosso Dossi. Pittore di corte a Ferrara nel Rinascimento, Andrea Bayer (ed), exh. cat., Palazzo dei Diamanti, Ferrara, 1998

Fesch 1841
Catalogue des tableaux composant la galerie de feu son éminence le Cardinal Fesch, Rome, 1841

Fesch 1857
Catalogue de tableaux anciens provenant de la galerie du cardinal Fesch et composant celle de M. Moret, Paris, 1857

Fiocco 1915
Giuseppe Fiocco, 'La giovinezza di Giulio Campagnola', *L'Arte*, XVIII, 1915, pp. 137–56

Fiocco 1929
Giuseppe Fiocco, 'Pier Maria Pennacchi', *Rivista del R. Istituto d'Archeologia e Storia dell'Arte*, I, 1929, pp. 97–135

Fiocco 1941
Giuseppe Fiocco, *Giorgione*, Bergamo, 1941

Fiocco 1948
Giuseppe Fiocco, *Giorgione* (second edition), Bergamo, 1948

Fiocco 1955
Giuseppe Fiocco, 'Profilo di Francesco Vecellio – II', *Arte Veneta*, IX, pp. 71–79

Fletcher 1973
Jennifer Fletcher, 'Marcantonio Michiel's Collection', *Journal of the Warburg and Courtauld Institutes*, 36, 1973, pp. 382–85

Fletcher 2009
Jennifer Fletcher, 'Donors' Portraits in Venetian and Veneto Altarpieces During the Renaissance', in London 2009, pp. 25–57

Florence 1982
La Galleria Palatina. Storia della quadreria granducale di Palazzo Pitti, Marilena Mosco (ed.), exh. cat., Palazzo Pitti, Florence, 1982

Florence 1986
Capolavori e Restauri, exh. cat., Palazzo Vecchio, Florence, 1986

Florence 1989
'Le Tre età dell'uomo' della Galleria Palatina, exh. cat., Palazzo Pitti, Florence, 1989

Florence 2001
Disegni del rinascimento in Valpadana, Giovanni Agosti, exh. cat., Gabinetto Disegni e Stampe degli Uffizi, Florence, 2001

Formichova 1992
Tamara D. Formichova, *The Hermitage. Catalogue of Western European Painting. Venetian Painting. Fourteenth to Eighteenth Centuries*, Florence, 1992

Frangi 2014
Francesco Frangi (ed.), *Dipinti in Valpadana tra Medioevo e Rinascimento. Studi al Museo di Belle Arti di Budapest in ricordo di Miklös Boskovits*, Milan, 2014

Frangi (forthcoming)
Francesco Frangi, *Come se li fossi presente. A proposito di Giovan Girolamo Savoldo* (forthcoming)

Freedberg 1971
S. J. Freedberg, *Painting in Italy: 1500–1600*, Harmondsworth, 1971

Frimmel 1892
Theodor Frimmel, *Kleine Galeriestudien*, vol. 1, Bamberg, 1892

Frizzoni 1894
Gustavo Frizzoni, 'Appunti del senatore Giovanni Morelli a proposito della Galleria del Prado e dell'arte spagnuola', *Archivio Storico dell'Arte*, VII, 1, 1894, pp. 63–66

Furlan 1982
Caterina Furlan, 'Tra Giorgione e il Pordenone: a proposito di alcuni dipinti già nella collezione del duca d'Orléans', in *Giornata di studio per il Pordenone (Piacenza, 26 settembre 1981)*, Paola Ceschi Lavagetto (ed.), Parma, 1982, pp. 12–23

Furlan 1988
Caterina Furlan, *Il Pordenone*, Milan, 1988

Gallina 1954
Luciano Gallina, *Giovanni Cariani (Materiale per uno studio)*, Bergamo, 1954

Gamba 1905
Carlo Gamba, 'Paolo Morando detto il Cavazzola', *Rassegna d'Arte*, IV, 3, 1905, pp. 33–40

Gamba 1912
Carlo Gamba, 'Necrologio di Enrico Costa', *Rassegna d'Arte*, XII, 1–2, 1912, pp. IV–V

Gamba 1949
Carlo Gamba, 'Contributi alla conoscenza di Domenico Mancini', *La Critica d'Arte*, VIII, 3, 1949, pp. 211–17

Gamba 1954
Carlo Gamba, 'Il mio Giorgione', *Arte Veneta*, VIII, 1954, pp. 172–77

Garas 1964
Klára Garas, 'Giorgione et giorgionisme au XVIIe siècle. I', *Bulletin du Musée Hongrois des Beaux-Arte*, 25, 1964, pp. 51–80

Garas 1967
Klára Garas, 'The Ludovisi Collection of Pictures in 1633. II', *The Burlington Magazine*, CIX, 771, 1967, pp. 339–48

Garas 1972
Klára Garas, 'Bildnisse der Renaissance: II, Dürer und Giorgione', *Acta histariae artium Academiae Scientiarum Hungaricae*, XVIII, 1–2, 1972, pp. 125–35

Garas 1973
Klára Garas, *The Budapest Gallery. Paintings in the Museum of Fine Arts* (second edition), Budapest, 1973

Garas 1979
Klára Garas, 'Giorgione e il Giorgionismo: ritratti e musica', in *Giorgione, Atti del convegno internazionale di studi per il quinto centenario della nascita (Castelfranco Veneto, 29–31 maggio 1978)*, Venice, 1979, pp. 165–70

Gardner 1906
Edmund G. Gardner, *The King of Court Poets: A Study of the Work, Life and Times of Ludovico Ariosto*, New York, 1906

Gentili 1990
Augusto Gentili, 'Savoldo, il ritratto e l'allegoria musicale', in Brescia 1990, pp. 65–70

Gentili 1995
Augusto Gentili, 'Amore e amorose persone: tra miti ovidiani, allegorie musicali, celebrazioni matrimoniali', in Rome 1995, pp. 82–105

Gentili 2001
Augusto Gentili, 'Di musica e d'amore: accordi, richiami, tentazioni (e rimozioni)', in Cremona 2001, pp. 69–73

Gibbons 1962
Felton Gibbons, 'Giovanni Bellini and Rocco Marconi', *The Art Bulletin*, XLIV, 1962, pp. 127–31

Gibbons 1968
Felton Gibbons, *Dosso and Battista Dossi: Court Painters at Ferrara*, Princeton, 1968

Gnaccolini 1996
Laura Paola Gnaccolini, 'La donazione Pyrker', *Arte Lombarda*, 117, 1996, pp. 116–26

Gombosi 1925–26
György Gombosi, 'Un ritratto giovanile di Sebastiano del Piombo', *Dedalo*, VI, 1925–26, pp. 57–66

Gombosi 1932
György Gombosi, 'Palma il vecchio', in *Thieme-Becker, Allgemeines Lexikon der Bildenden Künstler*, XXVI, Leipzig, 1932

Gombosi 1937
György Gombosi, *Palma Vecchio, des meisters gemälde und zeichnungen*, Berlin and Stuttgart, 1937

Gombrich 1966
Ernst H. Gombrich, 'The Renaissance Theory of Art and the Rise of Landscape', in *Norm and Form: Studies in the Art of the Renaissance*, London, 1966, pp. 107–21

Greer and Penny 2010
Elena Greer and Nicholas Penny, 'Giorgione and the National Gallery', *The Burlington Magazine*, CLII, 2010, pp. 364–75

Gregori 1986
Pittura del Cinquecento a Brescia, Mina Gregori (ed.), Cinisello Balsamo, 1986

Gronau 1894
Georg Gronau, 'Notes sur les dessins de Giorgione et des Campagnola', *Gazette des Beaux-Arts*, XII, 1894, pp. 322–34

Gronau 1908
Georg Gronau, 'Kritische Studien zu Giorgione', *Repertorium für Kunstwissenschaft*, XXXI, 1908, pp. 403–36, 503–21

Gronau 1909
Georg Gronau, 'Bellini, Giovanni', in *Thieme-Becker, Allgemeines Lexikon der Bildenden Künstler*, vol. 3, Leipzig, 1909, p. 263

Gronau 1922
Georg Gronau, 'Über Bildnisse von Giovanni Bellini', *Jahrbuch der Preussischen Kunstsammlungen*, XLIII, 1922, pp. 97–105

Gronau 1928
Georg Gronau, *Spätwerke des Giovanni Bellini*, Strasburg, 1928

Gronau 1936
Georg Gronau, 'Alcuni quadri di Tiziano illustrati da documenti', *Bollettino d'Arte*, XXX, 1936, pp. 289–96

Gronau 1949
Hans D. Gronau, 'Pitture veneziane in Inghilterra', *Arte Veneta*, III, 1949, pp. 182–84

Hadeln 1925
Detlev von Hadeln, *Venezianische Zeichnungen der Hochrenaissance*, Berlin, 1925

Haitovsky 1990–91
Dalia Haitovsky, 'Giorgione's *Trial of Moses*: A New Look', *Jewish Art*, XVI–XVII, 1990–91, pp. 20–29

Harck 1896
Fritz Harck, 'Notizen über italienische Bilder in Petersburger Sammlungen', *Repertorium für Kunstwissenschaft*, XIX, 1896, pp. 413–36

Haskell 1981
Francis Haskell, 'La sfortuna critica di Giorgione', in *Giorgione e l'umanesimo veneziano, Atti del corso d'alta cultura (Venise, 26 agosto – 16 settembre 1978)*, Rodolfo Pallucchini (ed), vol. 2, Florence, 1981, pp. 583–614

Heinemann 1962
Fritz Heinemann, *Giovanni Bellini e i Belliniani*, 2 vols, Venice, 1962

Hendy and Goldscheider 1945
Philip Hendy and Ludwig Goldscheider, *Giovanni Bellini*, Oxford, 1945

Hirst 1981
Michael Hirst, *Sebastiano del Piombo*, Oxford, 1981

Holberton 1993
Paul Holberton, 'The *Pastorale* or *Fête Champetrê* in the Early Sixteenth Century', in *Titian 500*, Joseph Manca (ed.), Washington DC, 1993, pp. 245–62

Holberton 1994
Paul Holberton, 'Varieties of Giorgionismo', in *New Interpretations of Venetian Renaissance Painting*, Francis Ames-Lewis (ed.), London, 1994, pp. 31–41

Holmes 1909
Charles John Holmes, '"The School of Giorgione" at the Grafton Galleries', *The Burlington Magazine*, XVI, 1909, pp. 72–74

Hope 1980
Charles Hope, *Titian*, London and New York, 1980

Hope 1982
Charles Hope, 'Review of *Sebastiano del Piombo* by Michael Hirst and *L'opera completa di Sebastiano del Piombo* by Carlo Volpe and Mauro Lucco', *The Burlington Magazine*, CXXIV, 1982, pp. 637–38

Hope 2003
Charles Hope, 'Titian's Life and Times', in *Titian*, David Jaffé (ed.), exh. cat., National Gallery, London, 2003, pp. 11–28

Hope 2008
Charles Hope, 'Giorgione in Vasari's *Vite*', in *Giorgione entmythisiert*, Sylvia Ferino-Pagden (ed.), Turnhout, 2008, pp. 15–37

Hornig 1976
Christian Hornig, *Cavazzola*, Munich, 1976

Hornig 1987
Christian Hornig, *Giorgiones Spätwerk*, Munich, 1987

Hourticq 1919
Louis Hourticq, *La Jeunesse de Titien*, Paris, 1919

Hourticq 1930
Louis Hourticq, *Le problème de Giorgione: sa légende, son oeuvre, ses élèves*, Paris, 1930

Hourticq 1935
Louis Hourticq, 'L'art italien au Petit Palais et au Jeu de Paume', *La revue de l'art ancient et modern*, LXVIII, 1935, pp. 15–34

Inghirami 1828
Francesco Inghirami, *L'Imperiale e Reale Palazzo Pitti*, Fiesole, 1828

Janitschek 1890
Hubert Janitschek, *Die städtische Sammlung von Gemälden alter Meister*, Strasbourg, 1890

Jervis 1989
Simon Jervis, 'Mariette's Annotated Copies of the Tallard and Julienne Sale Catalogues', *The Burlington Magazine*, CXXXI, 1989, pp. 559–61

Joannides 2001
Paul Joannides, *Titian to 1518: The Assumption of Genius*, New Haven and London, 2001

Joannides 2009
Paul Joannides, 'Sebastiano's *Venus and Adonis*', in *La Pietà di Sebastiano a Viterbo. Storia e tecniche a confronto*, Costanza Barbieri, Enrico Parlato and Simona Rinaldi (eds), Rome, 2009, pp. 12–16

Joannides 2010A
Paul Joannides, 'Titian, Giorgione and the Mystery of Paris', *Artibus et Histariae*, XXXI, 61, part 1, 2010, pp. 99–114

Joannides 2010B
Paul Joannides, *Le jeune Titien portraitiste*, in Ajaccio 2010, pp. 13–83

Justi 1908
Ludwig Justi, *Giorgione*, 2 vols, Berlin, 1908

Justi 1926
Ludwig Justi, *Giorgione* (second edition), 2 vols, Berlin, 1926

Justi 1927–28
Ludwig Justi, 'Giorgione oder Campagnola', *Zeitschrift für bildende Kunst*, LXI, 1927–28, pp. 79–84

Kákay-Szabó 1960
Kákay-Szabó, György, 'Giorgione o Tiziano?', *Bollettino d'Arte*, XLV, 1960, pp. 320–24

Köpl 1889
Karl Köpl, 'Urkunden, Alten Registers und Inventare aus dem K. K. Statthalterei-Archiv in Prag', *Jahrbuch der Kunsthistorische Sammlungen der Allerhöchsten Kaiserhause*, X, 1889, pp. LXIII–CC

Korbacher 2015
Dagmar Korbacher, 'Poetic Printmaking: Arcadia and the Engravings of Giulio Campagnola', *Art in Print*, IV, 5, 2015, pp. 5–7

Kryza-Gersch 2007
Claudia Kryza-Gersch, '"Il poeta cantore e l'amata". Una nuova interpretazione per il Doppio ritratto di Vienna come Allegoria della musica', in *Tullio Lombardo, atti del convegno di studi (Venise, Fondazione Giorgio Cini, 4 – 6 aprile 2006)*, Matteo Ceriana (ed.), Verona 2007, pp. 69–79

Kurth 1926–27
Betty Kurth, 'Ein verschollenes Gemälde Tizians', *Zeitschrift für Bildende Kunst*, 60, 1926–27, pp. 288–92

Lauber 2002A
Rosella Lauber, 'Per un ritratto di Gabriele Vendramin. Nuovi contributi', in *Figure di collezionisti a Venezia tra Cinque e Seicento*, Linda Borean and Stefania Mason (eds), Udine, 2002, pp. 25–75

Lauber 2002B
Rosella Lauber, '"Et è il nudo che ho io in pittura de l'istesso Zorzi." Per Giorgione e Marcantonio Michiel', *Arte Veneta*, LIX, 2002, pp. 99–115

Lauber 2009
Rosella Lauber, 'Una lucente linea d'ombra. Note per Giorgione nel collezionismo veneziano', in Castelfranco Veneto 2009, pp. 189–206

Lauber 2013
Rosella Lauber, 'Note per Marcantonio Michiel e Pietro Bembo', in Padua 2013, pp. 344–47

Law 1898
Ernest Law, *The Royal Gallery of Hampton Court Illustrated*, London, 1898

Le Febre 1682
Valentin Le Febre, *Opera Selectiora quae Titianus Vecellius Cadubrensis et Paulus Caliari Veronensis...*, Venice, 1682

Liberali 1981
Giuseppe Liberali, 'Gli inventari delle suppellettili del vescovo Bernardo de Rossi nell'Episcopio di Treviso (1506–1524)', in *Lorenzo Lotto. Atti del convegno internazionale di studi per il V centenario della nascita, Asolo (18–21 settembre 1980)*, Pietro Zampetti and Vittorio Sgarbi (eds), Treviso, 1981, pp. 73–92

Liphart 1910
Ernst von Liphart, 'La peinture italienne', in *Les Anciennes écoles de peinture dans les palais et collections privées russes, représentées à l'exposition organisée à St-Pétersbourg en 1909 par la Revue d'Art Ancien 'Staryé Gody'*, Brussels, 1910, pp. 17–39

Liphart 1916
Ernst von Liphart, *Kratjij katalog kartinnoj galerej*, Petrograd, 1916

Lloyd 1977
Christopher Lloyd, *A Catalogue of the Earlier Italian Paintings in the Ashmolean Museum*, Oxford, 1977

Lochis 1834
Guglielmo Lochis, *Cento quadri della Galleria Lochis in Bergamo*, Bergamo, 1834

Loeser 1896
Carlo Loeser, 'I quadri italiani nella Galleria di Strasburgo', *Archivio Storico dell'Arte*, II, 1896, pp. 277–87

Logan 1894
Mary Logan, *Guide to the Italian pictures at Hampton Court*, London, 1894

London 1907
Catalogue of a Collection of Pictures, Decorative Furniture and Other Works of Art, exh. cat., Burlington Fine Arts Club, London, 1907

London 1914
Catalogue of a Collection of Pictures of the Venetian School Including Works by Titian and His Contemporaries, exh. cat., Burlington Fine Arts Club, London, 1914

London 1982
Discoveries from the Cinquecento, Clovis Whitfield (ed.), exh. cat., Colnaghi & Co., London, 1982

London 1983
The Genius of Venice 1500–1600, Jane Martineau and Charles Hope (eds), exh. cat., Royal Academy of Arts, London, 1983

London 1988
Gothic to Renaissance: European Painting 1300–1600, exh. cat., Colnaghi and Co., London, 1988

London 1991
Master Drawings from the Courtauld Collections, William Bradford and Helen Braham (eds), exh. cat., Courtauld Institute of Art, London, 1991

London 2007
The Art of Italy in the Royal Collection: Renaissance and Baroque, Lucy Whitaker and Martin Clayton (eds), exh. cat., The Queen's Gallery, Buckingham Palace, London, 2007

London 2009
Paolo Veronese: The Petrobelli Altarpiece, Xavier Salomon (ed.), exh. cat., Dulwich Picture Gallery, London, 2009

London 2010
Treasures from Budapest: European Masterpieces from Leonardo to Schiele, David Ekserdjian (ed.), exh. cat., Royal Academy of Arts, London, 2010

London 2011
The Northern Renaissance: Dürer to Holbein, Kate Heard and Lucy Whitaker (eds), exh. cat., The Queen's Gallery, Buckingham Palace, London, 2011

Longhi 1927A
Roberto Longhi, 'Un chiaroscuro e un disegno di Giovanni Bellini' [1927], in Longhi 1967, vol. 1, pp. 179–88

Longhi 1927B
Roberto Longhi, 'Un problema del Cinquecento ferrarese (Dosso giovane)' [1927], in Longhi 1967, vol. 1, pp. 306–11

Longhi 1927C
Roberto Longhi, 'Cartella tizianesca' [1927], in Longhi 1967, vol. 1, pp. 233–44

Longhi 1934
Roberto Longhi, 'Officina ferrarese' [1934], in *Edizione delle opere complete di Roberto Longhi*, vol. 5, *Officina ferrarese 1934, seguita dagli ampliamenti 1940 e dai nuovi ampliamenti 1940–55*, Florence, 1956, pp. 7–122

Longhi 1946
Roberto Longhi, 'Viatico per cinque secoli di pittura veneziana' [1946], in Longhi 1978, pp. 1–63

Longhi 1949
Roberto Longhi, 'The Giovanni Bellini Exhibition' [1949], in Longhi 1978, pp. 99–109

Longhi 1967
Roberto Longhi, *Edizione delle opere complete di Roberto Longhi*, vol. 2, *Saggi e ricerche, 1925–28*, 2 vols, Florence, 1967

Longhi 1978
Roberto Longhi, *Edizione delle opere complete di Roberto Longhi*, vol. 10, *Ricerche sulla pittura veneta, 1946–69*, Florence, 1978

Lorenzetti and Planiscig 1934
Giulio Lorenzetti and Leo Planiscig, *La collezione dei conti Donà dalle Rose a Venezia*, Venice, 1934

Luber 2005
Katherine Crawford Luber, *Albrecht Dürer and the Venetian Renaissance*, Cambridge, 2005

Lucco 1980
Mauro Lucco, *L'opera completa di Sebastiano del Piombo, presentazione di Carlo Volpe*, Milan, 1980

Lucco 1982
Mauro Lucco, 'La giovinezza del Pordenone (nuove riflessioni su vecchi studi)', in *Giornata di studio per il Pordenone (Piacenza, 26 settembre 1981)*, Paola Ceschi Lavagetto (ed.), Parma, 1982, pp. 26–42

Lucco 1989
Mauro Lucco, 'Le cosiddette Tre età dell'uomo di Palazzo Pitti', in Florence 1989, pp. 11–28

Lucco 1990
Mauro Lucco, 'Review of Giovanni Gerolamo Savoldo, tra Foppa, Giorgione e Caravaggio, exhibition catalogue', *Osservatorio delle Arti*, V, 1990, pp. 88–93

Lucco 1994A
Mauro Lucco, 'Review of the Palma il Vecchio by Philip Rylands', *The Burlington Magazine*, CXXXVI, 1994, pp. 32–33

Lucco 1994B
Mauro Lucco, 'Le siècle de Titien', *Paragone*, XLV, 47–48, 1994, pp. 26–47

Lucco 1995
Mauro Lucco, *Giorgione*, Milan, 1995

Lucco 1996
Mauro Lucco, 'Venezia, 1500–1540', in *La Pittura nel Veneto. Il Cinquecento*, vol. 1, Milan, 1996, pp. 13–146

Lucco 2006
Mauro Lucco, 'Sacred Stories', in Washington DC 2006, pp. 100–07

Lucco 2008
Mauro Lucco, 'Sebastiano del Piombo a Venezia', in Rome 2008, pp. 23–29

Lucco 2012
Mauro Lucco, 'Da "paese" a "paesaggio": le molte facce della natura veneta', in Milan 2012, pp. 17–35

Lucco 2013
Mauro Lucco, 'Tiziano dai succhi dei fiori al colore selvaggio', in Rome 2013, pp. 41–69

Luchs 1995
Alison Luchs, *Tullio Lombardo and Ideal Portrait Sculpture in Renaissance Venice, 1490–1530*, Cambridge, 1995

Luzio 1888
Alessandro Luzio, 'Isabella d'Este e due quadri di Giorgione', *Archivio Storico dell'Arte*, I, 1888, pp. 47–48

Macola 2007
Novella Macola, *Sguardi e scritture. Figure con libro nella ritrattistica italiana della prima metà del Cinquecento*, Venice, 2007

Madrid 2003
Tiziano, Miguel Falomir (ed.), exh. cat., Museo Nacional del Prado, Madrid, 2003

Mariuz 2012
Adriano Mariuz, 'Il Paesaggio veneto del Cinquecento', in Venice 2012, pp. 25–39

Marciari 2015
John Marciari, *Italian, Spanish, and French Paintings Before 1850 in the San Diego Museum of Art*, San Diego, 2015

Marsilli 2015
Pietro Marsilli, 'Per una topografia düreriana in Trentino', in *Dürerweg. Artisti in viaggio tra Germania e Italia da Dürer a Canova, Convegno di studi (Cembra e Segonzano, 7–8 marzo 2015)*, Roberto Pancheri (ed), Trent, 2015, pp. 93–116

Martin 1993
Andrew John Martin, 'Giorgione e Baldassar Castiglione. Proposte per l'interpretazione di un passo fondamentale del Cortegiano', *Venezia Cinquecento*, III, 5, 1993, pp. 57–66

Martini 1978
Egidio Martini, 'Opere inedite del Cariani con alcune osservazioni', *Notizie da Palazzo Albani*, VII, 1978, pp. 61–69

Mazza 1987
Miriam Fileti Mazza (ed.), *Archivio del collezionismo mediceo. Il cardinal Leopoldo. Rapporti con il mercato veneto*, vol. 1, Milan and Naples, 1987

Mazza 2004
Cristiana Mazza, *I Sagredo. Committenti e collezionisti d'arte nella venezia del sei e settecento*, Venice, 2004

Mazzotta 2012A
Antonio Mazzotta, *Titian: A Fresh Look at Nature*, London, 2012

Mazzotta 2012B
Antonio Mazzotta, *Giovanni Bellini's Dudley Madonna*, London, 2012

Mechel 1783
Christian von Mechel, *Verzeichnis der Gemälde der Kaiserlich Königlichen Bilder Gallerie in Wien*, Vienna, 1783

Mezzetti 1965
Amalia Mezzetti, *Il Dosso e Battista ferraresi*, Ferrara, 1965

Michiel 1521–43
[Marcantonio Michiel], *Notizia d'opere di disegno* [1521–1543], Gustavo Frizzoni (ed.), Bologna, 1884

Milan 2001
Il Genio e le Passioni. Leonardo e il Cenacolo. Precedenti, innovazioni, riflessi di un capolavoro, Pietro C. Marani (ed.), exh. cat., Palazzo Reale, Milan, 2001

Milan 2012
Tiziano e la nascita del paesaggio moderno, exh. cat., Palazzo Reale, Milan, 2012

Millar 1960
'Abraham van der Doort's Catalogue of the Collections of Charles I', Oliver Millar (ed.), *The Journal of the Walpole Society*, vol. 37, 1958–60, Glasgow, 1960

Morassi 1942
Antonio Morassi, *Giorgione*, Milan, 1942

Morassi 1951
Antonio Morassi, 'The Ashmolean "Madonna Reading" and Giorgione's Chronology', *The Burlington Magazine*, XCIII, 1951, pp. 212–16

Morelli 1880
Giovanni Morelli, *Die Werke italienischer Meister in den Galerien von München, Dresden und Berlin*, Leipzig, 1880

Morelli 1883
Giovanni Morelli, *Italian Masters in German Galleries. A Critical Essay on the Italian Pictures in the Galleries of Munich–Dresden–Berlin*, London, 1883

Morelli 1886
Giovanni Morelli, *Le opere dei maestri italiani nelle Gallerie di Monaco, Dresda e Berlino*, Bologna, 1886

Morelli 1890
Giovanni Morelli [Ivan Lermolieff], *Kunstkritische Studien über Italienische Malerei. Die Galerien Borghese und Doria Panfili in Rom*, Leipzig, 1890

Morelli 1891
Giovanni Morelli, *Kunstkritische Studien über Italienische Malerei. Die Galerie zu München und Dresden*, Leipzig, 1891

Morelli 1892
Giovanni Morelli, *Italian Painters: Critical Studies of Their Works: The Borghese and Doria-Pamfili Galleries in Rome*, London, 1892

Morelli 1893
Giovanni Morelli, *Italian Painters: Critical Studies of Their Works: The Galleries of Munich and Dresden*, London, 1893

Mündler 1855–58
Otto Mündler, 'The Travel Diary 1855–58', Carol Togneri Dowd (ed.), *Journal of the Walpole Society*, vol. 51, 1985

Mündler 1865
Otto Mündler, 'Die Apokryphen der Münchner Pinakothek und der neue Katalog', *Recensionen und Mittheilungen über bildende Kunst*, 4, 1865, pp. 363–65

Mündler 1869
Otto Mündler, 'Beiträge zu Jacob Burckhardt's Cicerone', *Jahrbücher für Kunstwissenschaft*, II, 1869, pp. 259–324

Mutini 1972
Claudio Mutini, 'Brocardo, Antonio', in *Dizionario biografico degli italiani*, vol. 9, Rome, 1972, pp. 383–84

Naples 2006
Tiziano e il Ritratto di Corte da Raffaello ai Carracci, Museo e Gallerie Nazionali di Capodimonte, exh. cat., Museo di Capodimonte, Naples, 2006

Nepi Scirè 1991
Giovanna Nepi Scirè, *I capolavori dell'arte veneziana. Le Gallerie dell'Accademia*, Venice, 1991

Nova 1994
Alessandro Nova, *Girolamo Romanino*, Turin, 1994

Offner 1924
Richard Offner, 'A Remarkable Exhibition of Italian Paintings', *The Arts*, V, 1924, pp. 261–64

Ordeni 1666
Ordeni et regole stabilite dall'Illustrissimi Proveditori di Commun li 4 Decembre 1666 […] in materia d'un Lotto de Quadri de D. Nicolò Renieri, Venice, 1666

Ozzola 1932
Leandro Ozzola, 'Il S. Pietro di Tiziano al Museo di Anversa e la sua data', *Bollettino d'Arte*, XXVI, 1932, pp. 128–30

Padua 2013
Pietro Bembo e l'invenzione del Rinascimento, Guido Beltramini, Davide Gasparotto and Adolfo Tura (eds), exh. cat., Palazzo del Monte di Pietà, Padua, 2013

Pallucchini 1935
Rodolfo Pallucchini, 'La formazione di Sebastiano del Piombo', *La Critica d'Arte*, I, 1, 1935, pp. 40–47

Pallucchini 1941
Rodolfo Pallucchini, 'Vicende delle ante d'organo di Sebastiano del Piombo per S. Bartolomeo a Rialto', *Le Arti*, III, 6, pp. 448–55

Pallucchini 1944A
Rodolfo Pallucchini, *Sebastian Viniziano*, Milan, 1944

Pallucchini 1944B
Rodolfo Pallucchini, *La pittura veneziana del Cinquecento*, Novara, 1944

Pallucchini 1949
Rodolfo Pallucchini, 'Un nuovo Giorgione a Oxford', *Arte Veneta*, III, 1949, pp. 178–80

Pallucchini 1955
Rodolfo Pallucchini, *Giorgione*, Milan, 1955

Pallucchini 1966
Rodolfo Pallucchini, *Sebastiano del Piombo*, Milan, 1966

Pallucchini 1969
Rodolfo Pallucchini, *Tiziano*, Florence, 1969

Pallucchini 1978
Rodolfo Pallucchini, 'I due "creati" di Giorgione: Sebastiano e Tiziano', in Venice 1978, pp. 15–33

Pallucchini 1981
Rodolfo Pallucchini, 'Due eccellenti suoi creati: Sebastiano Viniziano… e Tiziano da Cadore', in *Giorgione e l'umanesimo veneziano, Atti del corso d'alta cultura (Venise, 26 agosto – 16 settembre 1978)*, Rodolfo Pallucchini (ed.), vol. 2, Florence, 1981, pp. 513–54

Pallucchini 1983
Rodolfo Pallucchini, 'Giovanni Cariani', in Pallucchini and Rossi 1983, pp. 9–92

Pallucchini and Rossi 1983
Rodolfo Pallucchini and Francesco Rossi, *Giovanni Cariani*, Cinisello Balsamo, 1983

Panofsky 1943
Erwin Panofsky, *The Life and Art of Albrecht Dürer*, 2 vols, Princeton, 1943

Panofsky 1969
Erwin Panofsky, *Problems in Titian, Mostly Iconographic*, London and New York, 1969

Paris 1935
Exposition de l'art italien de Cimabue à Tiepolo, exh. cat., Petit Palais, Paris, 1935

Paris 1965
Le XVIe siècle européen. Peintures et dessins dans les collections publiques françaises, exh. cat., Petit Palais, Paris, 1965

Paris 1987
Nouvelles acquisitions du Département des Peintures (1983–86), exh. cat., Musée du Louvre, Paris, 1987

Paris 1993
Le siècle de Titien. L'âge d'or de la peinture à Venise, Michel Laclotte (ed.), exh. cat., Grand Palais, Paris, 1993

Parker 1949
Karl Parker, 'The Tallard Madonna', *Ashmolean Museum. Report of the Visitors*, 1949, pp. 43–45

Parker 1956
Karl Parker, *Catalogue of the Collection of Drawings in the Ashmolean Museum*, vol. 2, Oxford, 1956

Parma 1935
Mostra del Correggio, Armando Ottaviano Quintavalle (ed.), exh. cat., Palazzo della Pilotta, Parma, 1935

Paschini 1927
Pio Paschini, 'Le collezioni archeologiche dei prelati Grimani del Cinquecento', in *Atti della Pontificia Accademia Romana di Archeologia*, V, 1927, pp. 149–90

Pater 1873
Walter Pater, *The Renaissance*, New York, 1873

Pedrocco 1999
Filippo Pedrocco, 'Tavole. Opere autografe. Bibliografia alle Tavole autografe. Opere attribuite', in Pignatti and Pedrocco 1999, pp. 91–222

Pelli Bencivenni (before 1793)
Giuseppe Pelli Bencivenni, *Inventario dei disegni, MS. 102*, 4 vols, Florence, n.d.

Perissa Torrini 1993
Annalisa Perissa Torrini, *Giorgione. Catalogo completo*, Florence, 1993

Perissa Torrini 2004
Annalisa Perissa Torrini, 'Documents and Sources', in Vienna 2004, pp. 21–30

Phillips 1893
Claude Phillips, 'L'Exposition des maîtres anciens à la Royal Academy', *Gazette des Beaux-Arts*, IX, 1893, pp. 221–37

Phillips 1895
Claude Phillips, 'A Probable Giorgione', *Magazine of Art*, vol. 3, 1895, pp. 120–22

Phillips 1899
Claude Phillips, 'The Picture Gallery of The Ermitage. I', *The North American Review*, CLXIX, 1899, pp. 454–72

Phillips 1907
Claude Phillips, 'Notes on Palma Vecchio', *The Burlington Magazine*, XLVI, 1907, pp. 243–52

Phillips 1937
Duncan Phillips, *The Leadership of Giorgione*, Washington DC, 1937

Pieve di Cadore 2013
Tiziano. Venezia e il papa Borgia, Bernard Eikema (ed.), exh. cat., Palazzo Cosmo, Pieve di Cadore, 2013

Pignatti 1969
Terisio Pignatti, *Giorgione*, Venice, 1969

Pignatti 1978
Terisio Pignatti, *Giorgione. L'opera completa* (seconda edition), Venice, 1978

Pignatti 1981
Terisio Pignatti, 'Il "corpus" pittorico di Giorgione', in *Giorgione e l'umanesimo veneziano, Atti del corso d'alta cultura (Venise, 26 agosto – 16 settembre 1978)*, Rodolfo Pallucchini (ed.), vol. 1, Florence, 1981, pp. 131–60

Pignatti 1990
Terisio Pignatti, *Giorgione e Tiziano*, in Venice 1990, pp. 68–76

Pignatti and Pedrocco 1999
Terisio Pignatti and Filippo Pedrocco, *Giorgione*, Milan, 1999

Pinacoteca Contarini 1841
Pinacoteca Contarini, aggiunta a quella dell'Imperiale Regia Accademia, Venice, 1841

Pincus 2008
Debra Pincus, 'Giovanni Bellini's Humanist Signature: Pietro Bembo, Aldus Manutius and Humanism in Early Sixteenth-century Venice', *Artibus et Historiae*, XXIX, 58, 2008, pp. 89–119

Popham 1931
Arthur E. Popham, *Italian Drawings Exhibited at the Royal Academy, Burlington House, London, 1930*, Oxford, 1931

Pope-Hennessy 1966
John W. Pope-Hennessy, *The Portrait in the Renaissance*, Princeton, 1966

Pordenone 2000
Da Pordenone a Palma il Giovane. Devozione e pietà nel disegno veneziano del Cinquecento, Caterina Furlan (ed), exh. cat., Chiesa di san Francesco, Pordenone, 2000

Pouncey 1949
Philip Pouncey, 'Review of A. M. Hind, Early Italian Engraving', *The Burlington Magazine*, XCI, 1949, pp. 234–36

Pouncey 1965
Philip Pouncey, *Lotto disegnatore*, Vicenza, 1965

Puerari 1957
Alfredo Puerari, *Boccaccino*, Milan, 1957

Puppi 1981
Lionello Puppi, 'Giorgione e l'architettura', in *Giorgione e l'umanesimo veneziano, Atti del corso d'alta cultura (Venise, 26 agosto – 16 settembre 1978)*, Rodolfo Pallucchini (ed.), vol. 1, Florence, 1981, pp. 343–71

Radisics 1906
Jenö Radisics, *Az Orzágos Ráth György Múzeum kalauza*, Budapest, 1906

Ravà 1920
Aldo Ravà, 'Il "Camerino delle antigaglie" di Gabriele Vendramin', *Nuovo Archivio Veneto*, XXXIX, 1920, pp. 155–81

Ravaglia 1922
Emilio Ravaglia, 'Un quadro inedito di Sebastiano del Piombo', *Bollettino d'Arte*, XV, 1922, pp. 474–77

Rearick 1979
William Roger Rearick, 'Chi fu il maestro di Giorgione?', in *Giorgione, Atti del convegno internazionale di studi per il quinto centenario della nascita (Castelfranco Veneto, 29–31 maggio 1978)*, Venice, 1979, pp. 187–93

Rearick 1981
William Roger Rearick, 'Lorenzo Lotto: The Drawings, 1500–1525', in *Lorenzo Lotto: Atti del convegno internazionale di studi per il V centenario della nascita (Asolo, 18–21 settembre 1980)*, Pietro Zampetti and Vittorio Sgarbi (eds), Venice, 1981, pp. 23–36

Rearick 2001
William Roger Rearick, *Il disegno veneziano del Cinquecento*, Milan, 2001

Ricci 1914
Corrado Ricci, *Disegni delle Scuole Emiliana e Cremonese nei secoli XV e XVI*, Florence, 1914

Richardson 1987
Francis Richardson, 'Review of Sebastiano del Piombo, by Michael Hirst', *The Art Bulletin*, LXIX, 1987, pp. 657–58

Richter 1893
Jean Paul Richter, 'Die Winterausstellung der Londoner Akademie', *Kunstchronik*, IV, 19, 1893, pp. 305–10

Richter 1937
George Martin Richter, *Giorgio da Castelfranco, Called Giorgione*, Chicago, 1937

Richter 1960
Irma and Gisela Richter (eds), *Italienische Malerei der Renaissance im Briefwechsel von Giovanni Morelli und Jean Paul Richter 1876–91*, Baden-Baden, 1960

Ridolfi 1648
Carlo Ridolfi, Le *maraviglie dell'arte, overo le vite de gl'illustri pittori veneti, e dello stato* [1648], critical edition by Detlev von Hadeln, vol. 1, Berlin, 1914

Robertson 1955
Giles Robertson, 'The Giorgione Exhibition in Venice', *The Burlington Magazine*, XCVII, 1955, pp. 272–79

Robertson 1968
Giles Robertson, *Giovanni Bellini*, Oxford, 1968

Robertson 1971
Giles Robertson, 'New Giorgione Studies', *The Burlington Magazine*, CXIII, 1971, pp. 475–77

Romano 1991
Studi sul paesaggio. Storia e immagini, Turin, 1991

Rome 1995
Tiziano. Amor sacro e amor profano, Maria Grazia Bernardini (ed), exh. cat., Palazzo delle Esposizioni, Rome, 1995

Rome 2007
Dürer e l'Italia, Kristina Hermann Fiore (ed.), exh. cat., Scuderie del Quirinale, Rome, 2007

Rome 2008
Sebastiano del Piombo 1485 + 1547, exh. cat., Palazzo di Venezia, Rome; Gemäldegalerie, Berlin, 2008

Rome 2013
Tiziano, Giovanni Carlo Federico Villa (ed), exh. cat., Scuderie del Quirinale, Rome, 2013

Rosand 1978
David Rosand, *Titian*, New York, 1978

Rosand 1983
David Rosand, *Tiziano*, Milan, 1983

Rosini 1843
Giovanni Rosini, *Storia della pittura italiana esposta coi monumenti*, vol. 4, Pisa, 1843

Rossi 1983
Francesco Rossi, 'Catalogo generale delle opere', in Pallucchini and Rossi 1983, pp. 99–372

Roy and Goldenberg 1996
Alain Roy and Paula Goldenberg, *Les peintures italiennes du Musée des Beaux-Arts. XVI*[e]*, XVII*[e] *et XVIII*[e] *siècles*, Strasbourg, 1996

Rusconi 1936
Antonio Rusconi, 'Per l'identificazione degli Acquerelli Tridentini di Alberto Durero', *Die Graphischen Künste*, 1, 1936, pp. 121–37

Rylands 1988
Philip Rylands, *Palma il Vecchio. L'opera completa*, Milan, 1988

Saffrey 1990
Henry D. Saffrey, 'Albrecht Dürer, Jean Cuno, O.P., et la confrerie du Rosaire à Venise', in *Philophronema. Festschrift für Martin Sicherl zum 75. Geburtstag*, Paderborn, 1990, pp. 263–91

Salvini 1961
Roberto Salvini, 'Giorgione: un ritratto e molti problemi', *Pantheon*, XIX, 1961, pp. 226–39

San Francisco 2011
Masters of Venice: Renaissance Painters of Passion and Power from the Kunsthistorisches Museum, Vienna, Sylvia Ferino-Pagden and Lynn Federle Orr (eds), exh. cat., De Young Museum, San Francisco, 2011

Sangiorgi 1976
Fert Sangiorgi, *Documenti urbinati. Inventari del Palazzo Ducale* (1582–1631), Urbino, 1976

Sansovino 1604
Francesco Sansovino, *Venetia città nobilissima et singolare descritta in XIIII libri hora con molta diligenza corretta, emendata, e più d'un terzo di cose nuove ampliata dal M. R. D. Giovanni Stringa*, Venice, 1604

Santos 1657
Francisco de los Santos, *Descripción breve del Monasterio de El Escorial*, Madrid, 1657

Saxl 1935
Fritz Saxl, 'Titian and Pietro Aretino' (1935), in *Lectures*, 2 vols, London, 1957

Schulz 2014
Anne Markham Schulz, *The Sculpture of Tullio Lombardo*, London, 2014

Schupbach 1978
William Schupbach, 'Doctor Parma's Medicinal Macaronic: Poem by Bartolotti, Pictures by Giorgione and Titian', *Journal of the Warburg and Courtauld Institutes*, XLI, 1978, pp. 147–91

Schmidt 1900
Wilhelm Schmidt, 'Die Bilder von Correggio in der München Pinakothek', *Repertorium für Kunstwissenschaft*, XXIII, 1900, pp. 395–97

Schmidt 1904
Wilhelm Schmidt, 'Zu Giorgione', *Repertorium für Kuntwissenschaft*, XXVII, 1904, p. 160

Segre 2011
Renata Segre, 'A Rare Document on Giorgione', *The Burlington Magazine*, CLIII, 2011, pp. 383–86

Segre 2012–13
Renata Segre, 'Una rilettura della vita di Giorgione. Nuovi documenti d'archivio', *Atti dell'Istituto Veneto di Scienze, Lettere ed Arti*, CLXXI, 2012–13, pp. 71–114

Seilern 1959
Antoine Seilern, *Italian Paintings and Drawings at 56 Princess Gate, London SW7*, 3 vols, London, 1959

Sgarbi 1981
Vittorio Sgarbi, 'Aggiunte al catalogo di Lorenzo Lotto', in *Lorenzo Lotto: Atti del convegno internazionale di studi per il V centenario della nascita (Asolo, 18–21 settembre 1980)*, Pietro Zampetti and Vittorio Sgarbi (eds), Venice, 1981, pp. 225–35

Shakeshaft 1986
Paul Shakeshaft, '"To Much Bewiched with Thoes Intysing Things". The Letters of James, Third Marquess of Hamilton and Basil, Viscount Fielding, Concerning Collecting in Venice, 1635–1639', *The Burlington Magazine*, CXXVIII, 1986, pp. 114–34

Shapley 1979
Fern Rusk Shapley, *National Gallery of Art. Washington: Catalogue of the Italian Paintings. Text*, vol. 1, Washington DC, 1979

Shearman 1967
John Shearman, *Mannerism*, Harmondsworth, 1967

Shearman 1983
John Shearman, *The Early Italian Paintings in the Collection of Her Majesty The Queen*, Cambridge, 1983

Silvestri 1755
Girolamo Silvestri, *Compendio dell'Istoria ma breve della terra di Lendinara co' gli avvenimenti accaduti in essa per lo spatio d'anni trenta scritta da Francesco Malmignato cittadino della medesima terra* (1755), MS. Silvestriana, 34, n. 17, Biblioteca dell'Accademia dei Concordi, Rovigo

Sman 2003
Gert Jan van der Sman, *Le Siècle de Titien. Gravures vénitiennes de la Renaissance*, Zwolle, 2003

Somov 1899
Andrei Somov, *Ermitage impérial. Catalogue de la galerie des tableaux. Première partie, les écoles d'Italie et d'Espagne*, St Petersburg, 1899

Sorce 2003
Francesco Sorce, 'Di ninfe, astrologi e pastori. Studi di iconologia sulle incisioni di Giulio Campagnola', *Venezia Cinquecento*, XIII, 26, 2003, pp. 47–110

Sorce 2007
Francesco Sorce, 'Domenico, Mancini', in *Dizionario Biografico degli Italiani*, vol. 68, Catanzaro, 2007, pp. 474–76

Suida 1930
Wilhelm Suida, 'Die Austellung italienischer Kunst in London', *Belvedere*, XVI, 1930, pp. 35–45

Suida 1931
Wilhelm Suida, 'Zum Werke des Palma Vecchio', *Belvedere*, XVI, 1931, pp. 135–42

Suida 1933
Wilhelm Suida, *Tizian*, Leipzig and Zurich, 1933

Suida 1935
Wilhelm Suida, 'Giorgione. Nouvelles attributions', *Gazette des Beaux-Arts*, XIV, 1935, pp. 75–94

Suida 1955
William Suida, *The Samuel H. Kress Collection: M. H. De Young Memorial Museum*, San Francisco 1955

Tallard 1756
Catalogue raisonné des tableaux, sculptures, tant de marbre que de bronze, desseins et estampes des plus grands maîtres, porcelains anciennes, meubles precieux, bijoux, et autres effets qui composent le Cabinet de seu Monsieur le Duc de Tallard, Paris, 1756

Tempestini 1992
Anchise Tempestini, *Giovanni Bellini. Catalogo completo dei dipinti*, Florence, 1992

Tempestini 2010
Anchise Tempestini, 'Domenico Mancini: un pittore enigmatico nella Venezia di primo Cinquecento', in *Der Mensch als Muster der Welt. Untersuchungen zur italienischen Malerei von Venedig bis Rom*, Nina Schleif (ed.), Berlin, 2010, pp. 93–108

Tempestini 2012
Anchise Tempestini, 'Il mito di Adone nella pittura di Sebastiano del Piombo: le due tavolette Lia ed il dipinto degli Uffizi', *Konsthistorisk tidskrift*, LXXXI, 2012, pp. 225–30

Testa 1994
Laura Testa, 'Un collezionista del Seicento: il cardinale Carlo Emanuele Pio', in *Quadri rinomatissimi: il collezionismo dei Pio di Savoia*, Jadranka Bentini (ed.), Modena, 1994, pp. 93–100

Thausing 1884
Moritz Thausing, *Wiener Kunstbriefe*, Leipzig, 1884

Theatrum Pictorium 1660
Theatrum Pictorium in quo exhibentur ipsius manu delineatae ejusque cura in aes incisae picturae archetipae italicae quas ipse ser. arch. in Pinacothecam suam Bruxellis collegit, Antwerp, 1660

Thode 1898
Henry Thode, *Correggio*, Leipzig, 1898

Thompson de Grummond 1975
Nancy Thompson de Grummond, 'VV and Related inscriptions in Giorgione, Titian and Dürer', *The Art Bulletin*, 57, 1975, pp. 346–56

Tietze and Tietze-Conrat 1939
Hans Tietze and Erica Tietze-Conrat, 'Domenico Campagnola's Graphic Art', *The Print Collector's Quarterly*, XXIX, 1942, pp. 311–33, 445–65

Tietze and Tietze-Conrat 1944
Hans Tietze and Erica Tietze-Conrat, *The Drawings of the Venetian Painters in the Fifteenth and Sixteenth Centuries*, New York, 1944

Tokyo 1993
Masterpieces from the National Galleries of Scotland, exh. cat., Isetan Museum of Art, Tokyo, 1994

Trent 2006
Romanino. Un pittore in rivolta nel Rinascimento italiano, Lia Camerlengo, Ezio Chini, Francesco Frangi and Francesca de Gramatica (eds), exh. cat., Castello del Buonconsiglio, Trent, 2006

Trent 2014
Dosso Dossi. Rinascimenti eccentrici al Castello del Buonconsiglio, Vincenzo Farinella (ed), with Lia Camerlengo and Francesca de Gramatica, exh. cat., Castello del Buonconsiglio, Trent, 2014

Troche 1934
Ernst Günter Troche, 'Giovanni Cariani', *Jarbuch der Preuszischen Kunstsammlungen*, 55, 1934, pp. 97–125

Valentiner 1922
Wilhelm Reinhold Valentiner, *The Henry Goldman Collection*, New York, 1922

Vasari 1550 and 1568
Giorgio Vasari, *Le Vite de' più eccellenti pittori, scultori e architetti, nelle redazioni del 1550 e 1568*, Paola Barocchi and Rosanna Bettarini (eds), 6 vols, Florence, 1966–87

Velasco and Santos 1746
Palomino Velasco and Francisco de los Santos, *Las Ciudades, Iglesias y Conventos en España*, London, 1746

Venice 1955
Giorgione e i giorgioneschi, Pietro Zampetti (ed.), exh. cat., Palazzo Ducale, Venice, 1955

Venice 1976
Disegni di Tiziano e della sua cerchia, Konrad Oberhuber (ed.), exh. cat., Fondazione Giorgio Cini, Venice, 1976

Venice 1978
Giorgione a Venezia, exh. cat., Gallerie dell'Accademia, Venice, 1978

Venice 1990
Tiziano, exh. cat., Palazzo Ducale, Venice, 1990

Venice 1992
Leonardo e Venezia, exh. cat., Palazzo Grassi, Venice, 1992

Venice 1999
Il Rinascimento a Venezia e la pittura del Nord ai tempi di Bellini, Dürer, Tiziano, Bernard Aikema, Beverly Louise Brown and Giovanna Nepi Scirè (eds.), exh. cat., Palazzo Grassi, Venice,1999

Venice 2003
Giorgione. 'Le maraviglie dell'arte', Giovanna Nepi Scirè and Sandra Rossi (eds), exh. cat., Gallerie dell'Accademia, Venice, 2003

Venice 2012
Tiziano. La Fuga in Egitto e la pittura di paesaggio, Irina Artemieva and Giuseppe Pavanello (eds), exh. cat., Gallerie dell'Accademia, Venice, 2012

Venturi 1885
Adolfo Venturi, 'Zur Geschichte der Kunstsammlungen Kaiser Rudolf II', in *Repertorium für Kunstwissenschaft*, VIII, 1885, pp. 1–23

Venturi 1899
Adolfo Venturi, 'Bibliografia artistica', *L'Arte*, II, 1899, p. 471

Venturi 1900
Adolfo Venturi, 'I quadri di scuola italiana nella Galleria Nazionale di Budapest', *L'Arte*, III, 5–8, 1900, pp. 185–240

Venturi 1912
Lionello Venturi, 'Saggio sulle opere d'arte italiana a Pietroburgo', *L'Arte*, XV, 1912, pp. 121–40

Venturi 1913
Lionello Venturi, *Giorgione e il giorgionismo*, Milan, 1913

Venturi 1926
Adolfo Venturi, *Correggio*, Rome, 1926

Venturi 1928
Adolfo Venturi, *Storia dell'arte italiana. La pittura del Cinquecento*, vol. IX, 3, Milan, 1928

Venturi 1954
Lionello Venturi, *Giorgione*, Rome, 1954

Viana 1933
Dirce Viana, *Francesco Torbido*, Verona, 1933

Vienna 2004
Giorgione: Myth and Enigma, Sylvia Ferino-Pagden and Giovanna Nepi Scirè (eds), exh. cat., Kunsthistorisches Museum, Vienna, 2004

Vivian 1971
Frances Vivian, *Il Console Smith: mercante e collezionista*, Vicenza, 1971

Volpe 1963
Carlo Volpe, *Giorgione*, Milan, 1963

Volpe 1975
Carlo Volpe, 'Il Cristo portacroce di Vienna al Pordenone', *Paragone*, XXVI, 309, 1975, pp. 100–03

Volpe 1981A
Carlo Volpe, 'Lotto a Roma e Raffaello', in *Lorenzo Lotto: Atti del convegno internazionale di studi per il V centenario della nascita (Asolo, 18–21 settembre 1980)*, Pietro Zampetti and Vittorio Sgarbi (eds), Venice, 1981, pp. 127–45

Volpe 1981B
Carlo Volpe, 'La "maniera moderna" e il Naturalismo nel Cinquecento da Giorgione a Caravaggio', in *Giorgione e l'umanesimo veneziano, Atti del corso d'alta cultura (Venise, 26 agosto – 16 settembre 1978)*, Rodolfo Pallucchini (ed.), vol. 1, Florence, 1981, pp. 399–424

Votta 2001
Maria Votta, *Il bestiario figurato. Animali rappresentati tra scienza e arte*, La Spezia, 2001

Waagen 1857
Gustav Friedrich Waagen, *Galleries and Cabinets of Art in Great Britain*, London, 1857

Waagen 1864
Gustav Friedrich Waagen, *Die Gemäldesammlung in der Kaiserlichen Eremitage zu St. Petersburg nebst Bemerkungen über andere dortige Kunstsammlungen*, Munich, 1864

Washington DC 1997
Lorenzo Lotto: Rediscovered Master of the Renaissance, David Alan Brown, Peter Humfrey and Mauro Lucco (eds), exh. cat., National Gallery of Art, Washington DC, 1997

Washington DC 2006
Bellini, Giorgione, Titian and the Renaissance of Venetian Painting, David Alan Brown and Sylvia Ferino-Pagden (eds), exh. cat., National Gallery of Art, Washington DC, and Kunsthistorisches Museum, Vienna, 2006

Washington DC 2009
Tullio Lombardo and Venetian High Renaissance Sculpture, Alison Luchs (ed), exh. cat., National Gallery of Art, Washington DC, 2009

Waterhouse 1952
Ellis K. Waterhouse, 'Paintings from Venice for Seventeenth-century England: Some Records of a Forgotten Transaction', *Italian Studies*, VII, 1952, pp. 1–23

Waterhouse 1974
Ellis K. Waterhouse, *Giorgione*, Glasgow, 1974

Wickhoff 1909
Franz Wickhoff, 'Ludwig Justi, Giorgione', *Kunstgeschichte Anzeigen*, 1909, pp. 34–40

Wilde 1933
Johannes Wilde, 'Die Probleme um Domenico Mancini', *Jahrbuch der Kunsthistorischen Sammlungen in Wien*, VII, 1933, pp. 97–136

Wilde 1950
Johannes Wilde, 'The Date of Lotto's "St Jerome" in the Louvre', *The Burlington Magazine*, XCII, 1950, pp. 350–51

Wittkower 1927
Rudolf Wittkower, 'Studien zur Geschichte der Malerei in verona. III. Die Schüler des Domenico Morone', *Jahrbuch dür Kunstwissenschaft*, 1927, pp. 185–222

Wittkower 1938–39
Rudolph Wittkower, 'Transformations of Minerva in Renaissance Imagery', *Journal of the Warburg Institute*, II, 1938–39, pp. 194–205

Zampetti 1955
Pietro Zampetti, 'Postille alla mostra di Giorgione', *Arte Veneta*, IX, 1955, pp. 54–70

Zampetti 1968
Pietro Zampetti, *L'opera completa di Giorgione*, Milan, 1968

Zeri and De Marchi 1997
Federico Zeri and Andrea G. De Marchi, *La Spezia. Museo Civico Amedeo Lia. Dipinti*, Cinisello Balsamo, 1997

Zucker 1984
Mark J. Zucker, *The Illustrated Bartsch: Early Italian Masters: 25, Commentary*, New York, 1984

LENDERS TO THE EXHIBITION

Antwerp
Koninklijk Museum voor Schone Kunsten

Bergamo
Accademia Carrara

Berlin
Gemäldegalerie, Staatliche Museen zu Berlin
Kupferstichkabinett, Staatliche Museen zu Berlin

Birmingham
Birmingham Museum and Art Gallery

Budapest
Szépművészeti Múzeum

Edinburgh
Scottish National Gallery

Florence
Galleria degli Uffizi
Galleria degli Uffizi, Gabinetto Disegni e Stampe
Galleria Palatina, Palazzo Pitti

Genoa
Palazzo Rosso, Musei di Strada Nuova

Glasgow
Glasgow Museums

La Spezia
Museo Civico Amedeo Lia

Lendinara
Duomo di Santa Sofia

London
The British Museum
The Courtauld Gallery
The National Gallery
The Royal Collection

Madrid
Museo Nacional del Prado

Mattioli Collection

Munich
Alte Pinakothek, Bayerische Staatsgemäldesammlungen

Oxford
The Ashmolean Museum

Paris
Musée du Louvre

Rome
Galleria Borghese
Museo Nazionale del Palazzo di Venezia

St Petersburg
The State Hermitage Museum

San Diego
The San Diego Museum of Art

San Francisco
Legion of Honour, Fine Arts Museums of San Francisco

Strasbourg
Musée des Beaux-Arts

Francesca and Massimo Valsecchi

Vienna
Kunsthistorisches Museum, Gemäldegalerie
Kunsthistorisches Museum, Kunstkammer

Venice
Gallerie dell'Accademia

Washington DC
National Gallery of Art

and others who wish to remain anonymous

PHOTOGRAPHIC ACKNOWLEDGEMENTS

All works of art are reproduced by kind permission of the owners. Every attempt has been made to trace the photographers of works reproduced. Specific acknowledgements are as follows:

Antwerp, © Royal Museum of Fine Arts / www.lukasweb.be – Art in Flanders vzw. Photography: Hugo Maertens: cat. 31

© Archivio fotografico del Polo Museale del Veneto. Photography: Quartana, su concessione del Ministero dei beni e delle attività culturali e del turismo: figs 2, 3, 8; cats 30, 39

© Archivio fotografico dell'Ufficio Beni Culturali della Diocesi di Adria-Rovigo. Photography: Alberto Bonatti: cat. 35

Bergamo, © Comune di Bergamo, Accademia Carrara: cat. 33

Berlin, © bpk: cats 17 (Kupferstichkabinett, SMB. Photography: Jörg P. Anders), 23 (Bayerische Staatsgemäldesammlungen)

Berlin, © Gemäldegalerie, Staatliche Museen zu Berlin, Preussischer Kulturbesitz. With kind permission of the Gemäldegalerie, Berlin. © Photography: Jörg P. Anders: cat. 1

Birmingham, © Birmingham Museums Trust: cat. 29

Brunswick, © Herzog Anton Ulrich-Museum, Kunstmuseum des Landes Niedersachsen Fotonachweis: Museumsfotograf: fig. 22

Budapest, © Museum of Fine Arts: cats 10, 44

Edinburgh, © Scottish National Gallery: cats 7, 46

Florence, Scala © 2016: fig. 20; cats 2, 9, 38 (courtesy of the Ministero Beni e Att. Culturali); figs 4, 17, 18 (Cameraphoto); fig. 14 (Photo Fine Art Images / Heritage Images); fig. 6 (Bildagentur für Kunst, Kultur und Geschichte, Berlin, photography: Hans-Peter Klut)

© Alex Fox at Roy Fox Fine Art: cat.45

© Gabinetto Fotografico del Polo Museale Regionale della Toscana: cats 12, 16, 41

Genoa, © Genova, Musei di Strada Nuova – Palazzo Rosso: cat. 4

Glasgow, © CSG CIC Glasgow Museum Collections: cat. 34

La Spezia, © Museo Civico 'Amedeo Lia': cats 20, 21

London, Bridgeman Images © Devonshire Collection, Chatsworth / Reproduced by permission of Chatsworth Settlement Trustees: fig. 13

London, © National Gallery/Victoria and Albert Museum: fig. 23

London, © The National Gallery: fig. 12; cat. 19

London, © The Samuel Courtauld Trust, The Courtauld Institute: cat. 11

London, © The Trustees of the British Museum: figs 11, 21; cats 24–26

Madrid, © Museo Nacional del Prado: cat. 32

© Collezione Mattioli, Italia: cat. 40

© Ministero per i Beni e le Attività Culturali e del Turismo o MiBACT – Galleria Borghese: fig. 10; cat. 37

Oxford, © Ashmolean Museum, University of Oxford: cat. 28

Paris, © RMN-Grand Palais (musée du Louvre): fig. 15 (Photography: Hervé Lewandowski); cats 18 (Photography: Gérard Blot), 22 (Photography: Thierry Le Mage)

© Private collection: figs 16, 19; cat. 36

Royal Collection Trust / © Her Majesty Queen Elizabeth II 2016: cats 3, 6, 43

St Petersburg, Photograph © The State Hermitage Museum / Vladimir Terebeni: cat. 27

San Diego, © The San Diego Museum of Art, www.sdmart.org: cat. 5

San Francisco, © Fine Arts Museums of San Francisco: cat. 14

Strasbourg, © Photo Musées de Strasbourg, M. Bertola: cat. 15

Vienna, © KHM-Museumsverband: figs 1, 5, 7, 9; cats 8, 42, 47

Washington DC, © Courtesy National Gallery of Art: fig. 24; cat. 13

INDEX

All references are to page numbers; those in **bold** type indicate catalogue plates, and those in *italic* type indicate essay illustrations

SUPPORTERS OF THE ROYAL ACADEMY

Major Benefactors

The President and the Trustees of the Royal Academy Trust would like to thank all those who have been exceedingly generous over a number of years in support of the galleries, the exhibitions, the conservation of the Collections, the Library, the Royal Academy Schools, the education programme and capital redevelopments projects:

HM The Queen
Her Majesty's Government
The 29th May 1961 Charitable Trust
Aldama Foundation
Lord and Lady Aldington
The Band Trust
Barclays Bank
B A T Industries plc
Sir David and Lady Bell
Big Lottery Fund (formerly New Opportunities Fund)
John Frye Bourne
William Brake Charitable Trust
British Telecom
Consuelo and Anthony Brooke
Sir Francis and Lady Brooke
Mr and Mrs John Burns
Mr Raymond M Burton CBE
The Cadogan Charity
Jeanne and William Callanan
Carew Pole Charitable Trust
The CHEAR Foundation
Sir Trevor Chinn CVO and Lady Chinn
The John S Cohen Foundation
Mr Jeremy Coller
John and Gail Coombe
The Lord Davies of Abersoch CBE
The Roger De Haan Charitable Trust
Sir Harry and Lady Djanogly
Clore Duffield Foundation
The Dulverton Trust
The John Ellerman Foundation
Mr Richard Elman
The Eranda Foundation
EY
John and Fausta Eskenazi
The Fidelity UK Foundation
The Foyle Foundation
Friends of the Royal Academy
Jacqueline and Michael Gee
J Paul Getty Jnr Charitable Trust
Mr Mark Getty
Mr Thomas Gibson
GlaxoSmithKline plc
Sir Ronald Grierson
Sir Nicholas Grimshaw CBE PPRA
Mr and Mrs Jim Grover
Diane and Guilford Glazer
The Golden Bottle Trust
Mr and Mrs Jack Goldhill
Maurice and Laurence Goldman
Horace W Goldsmith Foundation
Nicholas and Judith Goodison
HRH Princess Marie-Chantal of Greece
Mr and Mrs Charles Hale
Harold Hyam Wingate Foundation
Mr and Mrs Jocelin Harris
The Philip and Pauline Harris Charitable Trust
The Charles Hayward Foundation
Heritage Lottery Fund
Hermes GB
Mr Julian Heslop
Hiscox
Mr Damien Hirst
Holbeck Charitable Trust
Mr and Mrs Jeremy Hosking
The Idlewild Trust
Lord and Lady Jacobs
The J P Jacobs CharitableTrust
Mrs Gabrielle Jungels-Winkler
P Kahn
The Lillian Jean Kaplan Foundation
Daniel Katz Gallery
The Kirby Laing Foundation
The Kresge Foundation
The Kress Foundation
Jon and Barbara Landau
The Lankelly Foundation
The David Lean Foundation
The Lennox and Wyfold Foundation
The Leverhulme Trust
Lord Leverhulme's Charitable Trust
Christian Levett and Mougins Museum of Classical Art
Lex Service plc
The Linbury Trust
Sir Sydney Lipworth QC and Lady Lipworth
Miss Rosemary Lomax Simpson
Mr William Loschert
Mr and Mrs Mark Loveday
John Lyons Charity
Ronald and Rita McAulay
McKinsey and Company Inc
Mr and Mrs Donald Main
Sir John Madejski OBE DL
Her Majesty's Government
The Manifold Trust
Mr Javad and Mrs Narmina Marandi
Marks and Spencer
Philip and Val Marsden
The Paul Mellon Estate
The Mercers' Company
The Monument Trust
The Henry Moore Foundation
The Moorgate Trust Fund
Mr and Mrs Robert Miller
The late Mr Minoru Mori HON KBE and Mrs Mori
Robin Heller Moss
Simon and Midge Palley
The Peacock Trust
P F Charitable Trust
Olive Pettit
Mr and Mrs Maurice Pinto
The Edith and Ferdinand Porjes Charitable Trust
John Porter Charitable Trust
The Porter Foundation
Mrs Tineke Pugh
Rio Tinto plc
Mr John A Roberts FRIBA
Sir Simon and Lady Robertson
The Ronson Foundation
Rothmans International plc
The Rothschild Foundation
Mr Jonathan Ruffer
Dame Jillian Sackler DBE
Mr Wafic Rida Saïd
Mrs Jean Sainsbury
The Saison Foundation
The Basil Samuel Charitable Trust
Mrs Coral Samuel CBE
The Schroder Foundation
Mr Sean Scully RA
Mrs Louisa Service OBE JP
Mr and Mrs Jake Shafran
Mr Richard S Sharp
Mrs Stella Shawzin
Miss Dasha Shenkman
William and Maureen Shenkman
The Archie Sherman Charitable Trust
The late Pauline Sitwell
Mr James C Slaughter
Mr Brian Smith
Sir Paul and Lady Smith
Oliver Stanley Charitable Trust
The Swire Charitable Trust
Sir Hugh Sykes DL
The late Sir Anthony Tennant and Lady Tennant
Baron Lorne Thyssen-Bornemisza
Tomasso Brothers Fine Art
Ware and Edythe Travelstead
Mr and Mrs Julian Treger
The Trusthouse Charitable Foundation
The Douglas Turner Trust
Unilever plc
Sir Siegmund Warburg's Voluntary Settlement
The Weldon UK Charitable Trust
The Welton Foundation
Sian and Matthew Westerman
The Weston family
Mr W. Galen Weston and the Hon Mrs Hilary M. Weston
The Garfield Weston Foundation
Mr Chris Wilkinson OBE RA
Manuela and Ivan Wirth
The Maurice Wohl Charitable Foundation
The Wolfson Foundation

and those who wish to remain anonymous

Trustees

Lord Davies of Abersoch CBE (Chairman)
President of the Royal Academy (*ex officio*)
Treasurer of the Royal Academy (*ex officio*)
Secretary and Chief Executive – Charles Saumarez Smith
Petr Aven
Brooke Brown Barzun
Sir David Cannadine FBA
Sir Richard Carew-Pole Bt OBE DL
Richard Chang
Adrian Cheng
Lloyd Dorfman CBE
Stephen Fry
HRH Princess Marie-Chantal of Greece
Mrs Henry J Heinz HON DBE
Lady Suzanne Heywood
Mrs Anya Hindmarch MBE
Alistair Johnston CMG
Declan Kelly
Philip Marsden (Deputy Chairman)
Sir Keith Mills GBE DL
Mrs Minoru Mori
Christina Ong
Mrs Frances Osborne
Lord Rose of Monewden
Dame Jillian Sackler DBE
Robert Suss
Sir David Tang KBE
Sian Westerman
Peter Williams
Iwan Wirth

Honorary President
HRH The Prince of Wales

Emeritus Trustees
Lord Aldington
Susan Burns
Sir James Butler CBE DL
The Rt Hon the Lord Carrington KG GCMC CH MC
Sir Trevor Chinn CVO
John Coombe
Ambassador Edward E Elson
John Entwistle OBE
Michael Gee
The Rt Hon the Earl of Gowrie
Reverend C. Hugh Hildesley
Susan Ho
Lady Judge CBE
Gabrielle Jungels-Winkler
Lady Lever
Sir Sydney Lipworth QC
The Rt Hon Lord Luce GCVO DL
Lady Myners
Eddy Pirard
John Raisman CBE
John Roberts FRIBA
Sir Simon Robertson
Sir Evelyn de Rothschild
Mrs Maryam Sachs
Richard Sharp

Patrons

The Royal Academy is extremely grateful to all its Patrons, who generously support every aspect of its work.

Chair
Robert Suss

Platinum
Celia and Edward Atkin CBE
Mr and Mrs Christopher Bake
Mr Stephen Gosztony
Mr Jim Grover
Mr Maurice Pinto
Mr and Mrs Jake Shafran
David and Sophie Shalit

Gold
Mr and Mrs Thomas Berger
Molly Lowell Borthwick
Sir Francis Brooke Bt
Christopher and Alex Courage
The Licensing Company, London
Mrs Robin Hambro
Ted Hirst
Mrs Elizabeth Hosking
Mr Michael Jacobson
Miss Joanna Kaye
William and Lavina Lim
Sir Sydney Lipworth QC and Lady Lipworth CBE
Mr Nicholas Maclean
Sir Keith and Lady Mills
Lady Rayne Lacey
Jean and Geoffrey Redman-Brown
The Lady Renwick of Clifton
Richard Sharp
Jane Spack
David Stileman
Mr Robert John Yerbury

Silver
Ms Susanna Abu Zalaf
Lady Agnew
Mrs Anna Albertini
Miss H J C Anstruther
Mrs Jane Barker
Catherine Baxendale
The Duke of Beaufort
Mrs J K M Bentley, Liveinart
Eleanor E Brass
Mr and Mrs Richard Briggs OBE
Mrs Marcia Brocklebank
Jeremy Brown
Mrs Rosamond Brown
Mr and Mrs Zak Brown
Lord Browne of Madingley
Mr F. A. A. Carnwath CBE
Sir Roger and Lady Carr
Mrs Ann Chapman-Daniel
Sir Trevor and Lady Chinn
Mr and Mrs George Coelho
Denise Cohen Charitable Trust
Sir Ronald and Lady Cohen
Ms Linda Cooper
Mr and Mrs Ken Costa
Mrs Caroline Cullinan
Julian Darley and Helga Sands
Gwendoline, Countess of Dartmouth
Mr Daniel Davies
Peter and Andrea De Haan
The de Laszlo Foundation
Dr Anne Dornhorst
Mr and Mrs Jim Downing
Thomas A Doyle
Ms Noreen Doyle
Mrs Janet Dwek
Lord and Lady Egremont
Bryan Ferry
Benita and Gerald Fogel
Mr Sam Fogg
Mrs Jocelyn Fox
Arnold Fulton
Mrs Jill Garcia
The Robert Gavron Charitable Trust
Mrs Mina Gerowin Herrmann
Caroline and Alan Gillespie
Lady Gosling
Piers Gough RA
HRH Princess Marie-Chantal of Greece
Mrs Margaret Guitar
Mrs Jennifer Hall
Mr James Hambro
Sir John Hegarty and Miss Philippa Crane
Sir Michael and Lady Heller
Mrs Katrin Henkel
Ms Margarita Hernandez
Lady Heseltine
Mary Hobart
Anne Holmes-Drewry
Mr Philip Hudson
Mr and Mrs Jon Hunt
S Isern-Feliu
Mrs Caroline Jackson
Sir Martin and Lady Jacomb
Mrs Raymonde Jay
Alistair Johnston and Christina Nijman
Fiona Johnstone
Mrs Ghislaine Kane
Dr Elisabeth Kehoe
Princess Jeet Khemka
Mr D H Killick
Mrs Aboudi Kosta
Mr and Mrs Herbert Kretzmer
Joan H Lavender
Mr George Lengvari and Mrs Inez Lengvari
Lady Lever of Manchester
Miss R Lomax-Simpson
Mrs Caroline Lord
The Hon Mrs Virginia Lovell
Mr and Mrs Henry Lumley
Gillian McIntosh
Madeline and Donald Main
Scott and Laura Malkin
Mr and Mrs Richard C Martin
Andrew and Judith McKinna
Zvi & Ofra Meitar Family Fund
Professor Anthony Mellows OBE TD and Mrs Anthony Mellows
Mr Daniel Mitchell
Mrs Susan Moehlmann
Ms Bona Montagu
Dr Ann Naylor
Mr Richard Orders
Mr Michael Palin
John Pattisson
Nicholas B Paumgarten
Mr and Mrs D J Peacock
David Pike
Mr and Mrs Anthony Pitt-Rivers
Mr Basil Postan
Mrs Becky Quintavalle
Mr Pinto Rai Dhir
John and Anne Raisman
Serena Reeve
Mrs Bianca Roden
Rothschild Foundation
Miss Elaine Rowley
Mrs Janice Sacher
Mr Adrian Sassoon
Christina Countess of Shaftesbury
Mr Robert N Shapiro
Mr Richard Simmons CBE
Alan and Marianna Simpson
Roberta Downs Stewart Sandeman
The Lady Henrietta St George
Anne Elizabeth Tasca
Mr Tom Tempest-Radford
Lady Tennant
Anthony Thornton
Mr Anthony J Todd
Mrs Carolyn Townsend
Miss M L Ulfane
John and Carol Wates
Edna and Willard Weiss
The Duke and Duchess of Wellington
Anthony and Rachel Williams
Mrs Adriana Winters
David Zwirner

Patron Donors
Stephen Barry Charitable Settlement
Jean Cass MBE and Eric Cass MBE
Peter and Elizabeth Goulds, L.A. Louver
William Brake Charitable Trust
Jacqueline and Marc Leland
Mrs Josephine Lumley
The Michael H Sacher Charitable Trust
H M Sassoon Charitable Trust
Mrs Patricia Yunghanns

and those who wish to remain anonymous

Architecture Patrons

Platinum
David Giampaolo
Charles and Kaaren Hale

Gold
Mr Bruce Roe
Mr Peter Williams

Silver
Jacqueline and Jonathan Gestetner
Lifschutz Davidson Sandilands
Mr and Mrs Robin Lough
Stephen Musgrave
Mrs Noreen L Poulson
Christopher J Viney

and those who wish to remain anonymous

Benjamin West Group Patrons

Chair
Lady Judge CBE

Gold
Mr Steve Cardell
Mr Christian Levett
Ms Alessandra Morra
Afsaneh Moshiri
Mrs Deborah Scott

Silver
Lady J Lloyd Adamson
Mr and Mrs Amir Adnani
Mr Dimitry Afanasiev
Poppy Allonby
Mrs Spindrift Al Swaidi
Ms Ruth Anderson
Ms Sol Anitua
Mr Andy Ash
Marco and Francesca Assetto
Mrs Leslie Bacon
Mr Sam Bagot
Mr and Mrs Benjelloun
Mr Mark Bergman
Naomi and Ted Berk
Jean and John Botts
Ms Pauline Cacucciolo
Mrs Sophie Cahu
Brian and Melinda Carroll
Mrs Caroline Cartellieri Karlsen
Andrew and Stefanie Clarke
Mr and Mrs Paul Collins
Vanessa Colomar de Enserro
Ms Ruth Crabbe
Christophe de Taurines
Cathy Dishner
Mr and Mrs Jeff Eldredge
Mrs Stroma Finston
Cyril and Christine Freedman
Ronald and Helen Freeman
Ms Nicola Green
Mr and Mrs Jan Hagemeier
Katie Jackson
Suzanne and Michael Johnson
Syrie Johnson
Miss Rebecca Kemsley
Suzy Leguel
Lord and Lady Leitch
Mrs Stephanie Léouzon
Ms Ida Levine
Mr Guido Lombardo
Mrs Victoria Mills
Mrs Tessa Nicholson
Neil Osborn and Holly Smith
Luciana and Alessandra Price
Lady Purves
Ms Elena Shchukina
Mr Stuart Southall
Sir Hugh and Lady Sykes
Mr Ian Taylor
Miss Lori Tedesco
Frederick and Kathryn Uhde
Debra Valentine
Mrs Neena Vaswani
Mr Craig D Weaver
Professor Peter Whiteman QC
Mr and Mrs John Winter

and those who wish to remain anonymous

Contemporary Circle Patrons

Platinum
Robert and Simone Suss

Gold
Joan and Robin Alvarez
Ms Ilaria Bulgari
Mr Jeremy Coller
Ms Miel de Botton
Mr and Mrs Eric Dusansky
Shareen Khattar
Mrs Monika McLennan
Mr and Mrs Scott Mead
Simon and Sabi North
Francoise Sarre
Mr Kevin Sneader and Ms Amy Muntner
Manuela and Iwan Wirth

Silver
Mrs Susie Allen-Huxley
Mrs Charlotte Artus
Mr Timothy Attias
Mrs Niloufar Bakhtiar-Bakhtiari
Mr David Baty
Charles Dib and Aurore Belkin
Viscountess Bridgeman
Ms Debra Burt
Mr Steven Chambers
Nadia Crandall
Mrs Georgina David
Helen and Colin David
Patrick and Benedicte de Nonneville
Mollie Dent-Brocklehurst
Mr Paul Doyle
Mrs Jennifer Duke
Susan Elliott
Mr Timothy Ellis
Mr David Fawkes
Maria Almudena Garcia Cano
Mr Stephen Garrett
Simon Gillespie
Kate Gordon
Stephen and Margarita Grant
Jed and Allison Hart
Mrs Susan Hayden
Tristan and Michele Hillgarth
Mr and Mrs Urs Hodler
Zane Jackson, Director of Three Point Enterprises
Nozha Khader
Mr Gerald Kidd
Mr Matthew Langton
Mrs Julie Lee
Mr Jeff Lowe
Dr Carolina Minio Paluello
Mrs Sophie Mirman
Victoria Miro
Mrs Joanna Nicholls
Mr and Mrs Jeremy Nicholson
Roderick and Maria Peacock
Mr Malcolm Poynton
Mr Paul Price
Mrs Tineke Pugh
Mrs Catherine Rees
Mrs Yosmarvi Rivas Rangel
Miss Harriet Ruffer
Edwina Sassoon
Ms Elke Seebauer
Mr Eric Shen
Mrs Veronica Simmons
Karen Smith
Jeffery C Sugarman and Alan D H Newham
Mrs Arabella Tullo
Anna Watkins
Cathy Wills
Mrs Debora Wingate
Mr and Mrs Maurice Wolridge

and those who wish to remain anonymous

International Patrons

Mr Howard Bilton
Mrs Sophie Diedrichs-Cox
Jacques and Valentina Drouin
Mr and Mrs Stephen Fitzgerald
Mr Alexis Habib
Joanna Kalmer
Nelson Leong
Mrs Fatima Maleki
Mr Hideyuki Osawa
Frances Reynolds
Mr Thaddaeus Ropac
Mrs Sabine Sarikhani
Mr and Mrs Julian Treger
Mr Bruno Wang
Sian and Matthew Westerman
Mr and Mrs Basil Zirinis

Patron Donors
Mr Richard Chang

and those who wish to remain anonymous

RA Schools Patrons

Chair
Mr Keir McGuinness

Platinum
Mr Mark Hix
Lance and Lisa West

Gold
Sam and Rosie Berwick
Mrs Sarah Chenevix-Trench
Ms Cynthia Corbett
Christopher Kneale
Mr William Loschert
Carol Sellars

Silver
Lord and Lady Aldington
Mrs Elizabeth Alston
Sarah Barker and Daniel Freeman
Mr and Mrs Jonathan and Sarah Bayliss
Ms Sara Berman
Joanna Bird
Alex Haidas and Thalia Chryssikou
Rosalind Clayton
Mr Richard Clothier
Mark and Cathy Corbett
Marian Cramer
Ms Davina Dickson
Mrs Dominic Dowley
Nigel and Christine Evans
Miss Roxanna Farboud
Mrs Catherine Farquharson
Mrs Michael Green
Mr and Mrs G Halamish
Mr Lindsay Hamilton
Mrs Lesley Haynes
Mr Philip Hodgkinson
Professor and Mrs Ken Howard RA
Mark and Fiona Hutchinson
Mr Charles Irving
Mrs Marcelle Joseph
Mr and Mrs S Kahan
Mr Paul Kempe
Nicolette Kwok
Mrs Anna Lee
Mr and Mrs Mark Loveday
Philip and Val Marsden
The Lord and Lady Myners
Mr William Ramsay
Ms Mouna Rebeiz
Peter Rice Esq
Anthony and Sally Salz
Brian D Smith
Miss Sarah Straight
Mr Ray Treen
Marek and Penny Wojciechowski
Mrs Diana Wilkinson

and those who wish to remain anonymous

Young Patrons

Chair
May Calil

Gold
Mr Alexander Green

Silver
Ms Ingrid Anid
Ms Katharine Arnold
Miss Henrietta Ash
Sophie Ashby
Ms Vanessa Aubry
Mr Gergely Battha-Pajor
Ms Elif Bayoglu
Lucinda Bellm
Mr Alexander Bradford
Mr Alessandro Conti
Mr Alexander Flint

Ms Emily Fraser
Mr Rollo Gabb
Flora Goodwin
Ms Dalya Islam
Mrs Fernanda Jess
Mrs Huma Kabakci
Alexandra Ames Kornman
Mrs Alkistis Koukouliou
Benjamin Lockwood
Wei-Lyn Loh
Tessa Lord
gnacio Marinho
sabella Marinho
Florence Mather
Itxaso Mediavilla-Murray
Ziba Sarikhani
Ms Jane Singer
Mr Mandeep Singh
Emily Skeppner
Joanna Steingold
Sydney Townsend
Miss Navann Ty
Ms Zeynep Uzuner
Alexandra Warder
Mark Whitcroft
Miss Burcu Yuksel

and those who wish to remain anonymous

Library and Collections Supporters

Jonny Yarker

and those who wish to remain anonymous

Trusts, Foundations and Charitable Giving

Artists Collecting Society
The Atlas Fund
The Albert Van den Bergh Charitable Trust
The Bomonty Charitable Trust
The Charlotte Bonham-Carter Charitable Trust
William Brake Charitable Trust
R M Burton 1998 Charitable Trust
P H G Cadbury Charitable Trust
The Carew Pole Charitable Trust
C H K Charities Limited
The Clore Duffield Foundation
John S Cohen Foundation
The Evan Cornish Foundation
The Sidney and Elizabeth Corob Charitable Trust
The Dovehouse Trust
The Gilbert and Eileen Edgar Foundation
The John Ellerman Foundation
Lucy Mary Ewing Charitable Trust
M Finn and Co.
The Margery Fish Charity
The Flow Foundation
The Garfield Weston Foundation
Gatsby Charitable Foundation
The Golden Bottle Trust
Sue Hammerson Charitable Trust
The Charles Hayward Foundation
Heritage Lottery Fund
Hiscox plc
Holbeck Charitable Trust
The Harold Hyam Wingate Foundation
Intrinsic Value Investors
The Ironmongers' Company
The Emmanuel Kaye Foundation
The Kindersley Foundation
The de Laszlo Foundation
The Leche Trust
The Maccabaeans
The McCorquodale Charitable Trust
The Machin Foundation
The Paul Mellon Centre
The Paul Mellon Estate
The Mercers' Company
Margaret and Richard Merrell Foundation
The Millichope Foundation
The Mondriaan Foundation
The Monument Trust
The Henry Moore Foundation
The Mulberry Trust
The J Y Nelson Charitable Trust
The Old Broad Street Charity Trust
The Peacock Charitable Trust
The Pennycress Trust
PF Charitable Trust
The Stanley Picker Charitable Trust
The Pidem Fund
The Edith and Ferdinand Porjes Charitable Trust
Mr and Mrs J A Pye's Charitable Settlement
Rayne Foundation
The Reed Foundation
T Rippon & Sons (Holdings) Ltd
Rootstein Hopkins Foundation
The Rose Foundation
Schroder Charity Trust
The Sellars Charitable Trust
The Archie Sherman Charitable Trust
The Alfred Teddy Smith and Zsuzsi Roboz Art Fund
Paul Smith and Pauline Denyer-Smith
The South Square Trust
Spencer Charitable Trust
Oliver Stanley Charitable Trust
Peter Storrs Trust
Strand Parishes Trust
The Joseph Strong Frazer Trust
The Swan Trust
Taylor Family Foundation
Thaw Charitable Trust
Sir Jules Thorn Charitable Trust
The Bruce Wake Charity
Celia Walker Art Foundation
Warburg Pincus International LLC
Weinstock Fund
Wilkinson Eyre Architects
The Spencer Wills Trust
The Maurice Wohl Charitable Foundation
The Wolfson Foundation

Royal Academy America

Honorary Patron
HRH Princess Alexandra, The Hon Lady Ogilvy KG GCVO

Board Members
Professor Sir David Cannadine FBA
Jim Clerkin
The Hon Anne Collins
Elizabeth Crain
C Hugh Hildesley
David Hockney OM CH RA
Brian Kelley
Declan Kelly, Chairman
Mr Kenneth Jay Lane
Marc Lasry
Andrew Liveris
Monika McLennan
Sir David Manning GCMG CVO
Richard J Miller, Jr, Esq
Mr David Remfry MBE RA
Dame Jillian Sackler DBE
Ms Joan N Stern, Esq
Raymond Svider
Frederick B Whittemore

Chairmen Emeriti
James Benson
Ambassador Philip Lader
President Emerita
Kathrine (Kitty) Ockenden OBE

Honorary Trustees
Christopher Le Brun PRA
Sir Nicholas Grimshaw CBE PPRA
Professor Phillip King CBE PPRA

Royal Academy America Supporters
Mr and Mrs Charles N Atkins
Mr and Mrs Steven and Anne Marie Ausnit
John Berggruen
Mr Donald Best
Mrs CeCe Black
Mr Constantin R Boden
Mrs Deborah Loeb Brice
Mr and Mrs Calvin Cafritz
Ms Patrice Clareman
Ms Alyce Faye Cleese
The Hon Anne Collins
Zita Davisson
Edward Field and Jennifer Kyner
Katherine Findlay
Mr Lawrence S Friedland
Mr and Mrs Ellis Goodman
Mrs Helen Groves
Ms Harriet Heyman and Mr Michael Moritz
C Hugh Hildesley
David Hockney OM CH RA
Ms Jo Hannah Hoehn
Dr Bruce C Horten and Mr Aaron Lieber
Ellen E. Howe
Mr and Mrs Philip Keevil
Mrs Jeanne K Lawrence
The Hon General Samuel K Lessey, Jr
Leon Levy Foundation
Arthur L Loeb
Mr Henry S Lynn, Jr
The Hon and Mrs Earle Mack
Ms Clare E McKeon
Ms Christine Mainwaring-Samwell
J Maxwell Moran
Mr and Mrs Wilson Nolen
Mrs Charles W Olson III
Cynthia Hazen Polsky and Leon B Polsky
Mrs Eileen Powers
Mr Paul K Rooney
Mr and Mrs Elihu Rose
Dame Jillian Sackler DBE
Mrs Louisa Stude Sarofim
Mrs Sylvia Scheuer
Mr and Mrs Stanley De Forest Scott
Mrs Georgia Shreve
Sylvia Slifka
Mr and Mrs Morton I Sosland
Mrs Frederick M Stafford
Mr and Mrs Robert K Steel
Joan N Stern, Esq
Martin J Sullivan OBE
Mr Peter Trippi
Christopher Tsai
Frederick B Whittemore
Ms Margaret Williamson

Corporate and Foundation Support
Henry C Beck Jr Charitable Trust
British Airways plc
Crankstart Foundation
Sunny and Frederick Dupree Children's Trust
The Charles and Carmen de Mora Hale Foundation
Leon Levy Foundation
Andrew W Mellon Foundation
Morris and McVeigh LLP
Siezen Foundation
Smart Family Foundation
Starr Foundation

Corporate Members of the Royal Academy

Launched in 1988, the Royal Academy's Corporate Membership Scheme has proved highly successful. Corporate membership offers benefits for staff, clients and community partners and access to the Academy's facilities and resources. The outstanding support we receive from companies via the scheme is vital to the continuing success of the Academy and we thank all members for their valuable support and continued enthusiasm.

Premier Level Members
American Express®
The Arts Club
Bird & Bird LLP
BNY Mellon
Cazenove Capital Management
Chestertons
Christie's
Deutsche Bank AG London
FTI Consulting
HS1
Insight Investment Management
JLL
JM Finn & Co.
JTI
KPMG LLP
Linklaters
Newton Investment Management
Sanlam
Smith & Williamson
Sotheby's
Turkish Ceramics
XL Catlin

Corporate Members
Bloomberg LP
BMO Global Asset Management
The Boston Consulting Group UK LLP
Capital Group
Clifford Chance
Dechert
GAM London Ltd
Generation Investment Management LLP
GlaxoSmithKline plc
Hansteen Holdings
John Lewis Partnership
Lindsell Train
Marie Curie Cancer Care
Moelis & Company
Morgan Stanley
Native Land
Quilter Cheviot
Rathbones
Ridgeway Partners
The Royal Society of Chemistry
Slaughter and May
Trowers & Hamlins LLP
UBS Wealth Managment
Vitol SA
Weil, Gotshal & Manges

Associate Members
Bank of America Merrill Lynch
BNP Paribas
Bonhams 1793 Ltd
British American Tobacco
The Cultivist
EY
Heidrick & Struggles
Imperial College Healthcare Charity
Jones Day
Lazard
Lubbock Fine
Momart
Pentland Group plc

Supporters of Past Exhibitions

The President and Council of the Royal Academy would like to thank the following supporters for their generous contributions towards major exhibitions in the last ten years:

2015

Painting the Modern Garden: Monet to Matisse
BNY Mellon, Partner of the Royal Academy of Arts

Jean-Etienne Liotard
2009–2016 Season supported by JTI
The Pictet Group
Cockayne Grants for the Arts, a donor advised fund of London Community Foundation
Mr and Mrs Bart T. Tiernan
The Jean-Etienne Liotard Supporters' Group

Joseph Cornell: Wanderlust
2009–2016 Season supported by JTI
The Terra Foundation for American Art
The Cornell Leadership Circle

Premiums, RA Schools Annual Dinner and Auction and RA Schools Show 2015
Newton Investment Management

247th Summer Exhibition
Insight Investment

Richard Diebenkorn
2009–2016 Season supported by JTI
The Terra Foundation for American Art

Rubens and His Legacy
BNY Mellon, Partner of the Royal Academy of Arts

2015 Architecture Programme
Lead supporter Turkishceramics

2014

Allen Jones RA
Lead Series Supporter JTI

Giovanni Battista Moroni
2009–2016 Season supported by JTI
UBI Banca

Anselm Kiefer
BNP Paribas
White Cube

Radical Geometry: Modern Art of South America from the Patricia Phelps de Cisneros Collection
2009–2016 Season supported by JTI
Christie's

Dennis Hopper: The Lost Album
Lead Series Supporter JTI
Nikon UK

Premiums, RA Schools Annual Dinner and Auction and RA Schools Show 2014
Newton Investment Management

246th Summer Exhibition
Insight Investment

Dream, Draw, Work: Architectural Drawings by Norman Shaw RA
Lowell Libson Ltd
Collections and Library Supporters Circle

Renaissance Impressions: Chiaroscuro Woodcuts from the Collections of Georg Baselitz and the Albertina, Vienna
JTI
Edwards Wildman

Sensing Spaces: Architecture Reimagined
Scott and Laura Malkin
AKT II
Arauco

2013

Bill Woodrow RA
Lead Series Supporter JTI
The Henry Moore Foundation

Daumier
2009–2016 Season supported by JTI

Australia
National Gallery of Australia
Qantas Airways
The Woolmark Company

Richard Rogers RA: Inside Out
Ferrovial Agroman
Heathrow Airport
Laing O'Rourke

Mexico: A Revolution in Art, 1910–1940
2009–2016 Season supported by JTI
Art Mentor Foundation Lucerne
Conaculta
James and Clare Kirkman
Mexican Agency for International Development Cooperation
Catherine and Franck Petitgas
Sectur
Visit Mexico
Mercedes Zobel

245th Summer Exhibition
Insight Investment

George Bellows
2009–2016 Season supported by JTI
Edwards Wildman

Premiums, RA Schools Annual Dinner and Auction and RA Schools Show 2013
Newton Investment Management

Manet: Portraying Life
BNY Mellon, Partner of the Royal Academy of Arts

2012

Mariko Mori
JTI

RA Now
JTI

Bronze
Christian Levett and Mougins Museum of Classical Art
Daniel Katz Gallery
Baron Lorne Thyssen-Bornemisza
John and Fausta Eskenazi
The Ruddock Foundation for the Arts
Tomasso Brothers Fine Art
Jon and Barbara Landau
Janine and J. Tomilson Hill
Embassy of the Kingdom of the Netherlands
Eskenazi Limited
Lisson Gallery
Alexis Gregory
Alan and Mary Hobart
Richard de Unger and Adeela Qureshi
Rossi & Rossi Ltd
Embassy of Israel

244th Summer Exhibition
Insight Investment

From Paris: A Taste for Impressionism – Paintings from the Clark
2009–2016 Season supported by JTI
Edwards Wildman
The Annenberg Foundation

Premiums, RA Schools Annual Dinner and Auction and RA Schools Show 2012
Newton Investment Management

Johan Zoffany RA: Society Observed
2009–2016 Season supported by JTI
Cox & Kings

Building the Revolution: Soviet Art and Architecture 1915–1935
2009–2016 Season supported by JTI
The Ove Arup Foundation
The Norman Foster Foundation
Richard and Ruth Rogers

David Hockney RA: A Bigger Picture
BNP Paribas
Welcome to Yorkshire: Tourism Partner
Visit Hull & East Yorkshire: Supporting Tourism Partner
NEC

2011

Degas and the Ballet: Picturing Movement
BNY Mellon, Partner of the Royal Academy of Arts
Region Holdings
Blavatnik Family Foundation

Eyewitness: Hungarian Photography in the Twentieth Century. Brassaï, Capa, Kertész, Moholy-Nagy, Munkácsi
2009–2016 Season supported by JTI
Hungarofest
OTP Bank

243rd Summer Exhibition
Insight Investment

Premiums, RA Schools Annual Dinner and Auction and RA Schools Show 2011
Newton Investment Management

Watteau: The Drawings
2009–2016 Season supported by JTI
Region Holdings

Modern British Sculpture
American Express Foundation
The Henry Moore Foundation
Hauser & Wirth
Art Mentor Foundation Lucerne
Sotheby's
Blain Southern
Welcome to Yorkshire: Tourism Partner

2010

GSK Contemporary – Aware: Art Fashion Identity
GlaxoSmithKline

Pioneering Painters: The Glasgow Boys 1880–1900
2009–2016 Season supported by JTI
Glasgow Museums

Treasures from Budapest: European Masterpieces from Leonardo to Schiele
OTP Bank
Villa Budapest
Daniel Katz Gallery, London
Cox & Kings: Travel Partner

Sargent and the Sea
2009–2016 Season supported by JTI

242nd Summer Exhibition
Insight Investment

Paul Sandby RA: Picturing Britain, A Bicentenary Exhibition
2009–2016 Season supported by JTI

The Real Van Gogh: The Artist and His Letters
BNY Mellon, Partner of the Royal Academy of Arts
Hiscox plc
Heath Lambert
Cox & Kings: Travel Partner

RA Outreach Programme
Deutsche Bank AG

2009

GSK Contemporary
GlaxoSmithKline

Wild Thing: Epstein, Gaudier-Brzeska, Gill
2009–2016 Season supported by JTI
BNP Paribas
The Henry Moore Foundation

Anish Kapoor
JTI
Richard Chang
Richard and Victoria Sharp
Louis Vuitton
The Henry Moore Foundation

J W Waterhouse: The Modern Pre-Raphaelite
2009–2016 Season supported by JTI
Champagne Perrier-Jouët
GasTerra
Gasunie

241st Summer Exhibition
Insight Investment

Kuniyoshi. From the Arthur R. Miller Collection
2009–2016 Season supported by JTI
Canon
Cox & Kings: Travel Partner

Premiums and RA Schools Show
Mizuho International plc

RA Outreach Programme
Deutsche Bank AG

2008

GSK Contemporary
GlaxoSmithKline

Byzantium 330–1453
J F Costopoulos Foundation
A G Leventis Foundation
Stavros Niarchos Foundation
Cox & Kings: Travel Partner

Miró, Calder, Giacometti, Braque: Aimé Maeght and His Artists
BNP Paribas

Vilhelm Hammershøi: The Poetry of Silence
OAK Foundation Denmark
Novo Nordisk

240th Summer Exhibition
Insight Investment

Premiums and RA Schools Show
Mizuho International plc

RA Outreach Programme
Deutsche Bank AG

From Russia: French and Russian Master Paintings 1870–1925 from Moscow and St Petersburg
E.ON
2008 Season supported by Sotheby's

2007

Paul Mellon's Legacy: A Passion for British Art
The Bank of New York Mellon
Georg Baselitz
Eurohypo AG

239th Summer Exhibition
Insight Investment

Impressionists by the Sea
Farrow & Ball

Premiums and RA Schools Show
Mizuho International plc

RA Outreach Programme
Deutsche Bank AG

The Unknown Monet
Bank of America